THEOLOGY AND THE DIALECTICS OF OTHERNESS

On Reading Bonhoeffer and Adorno

Wayne Whitson Floyd, Jr.

UNIVERSITY
PRESS OF
AMERICA

Lanham • New York • London

Copyright © 1988 by

University Press of America,® Inc.

4720 Boston Way
Lanham, MD 20706

3 Henrietta Street
London WC2E 8LU England

Printed in the United States of America

British Cataloging in Publication Information Available

Library of Congress Cataloging-in-Publication Data

Floyd, Wayne W.
Theology and the dialectics of otherness : on reading Bonhoeffer
and Adorno / Wayne Whitson Floyd, Jr.
p. cm. Bibliography : p. Includes index.
1. Difference (Philosophy)—History—20th century. 2. Bonhoeffer,
Dietrich, 1906–1945—Contributions in philosophy of otherness.
3. Adorno, Theodor W., 1903–1969—Contributions in philosophy of
otherness. I. Title.
B809.9.F56   1988
.230'.01—dc 19   88–5428 CIP
ISBN 0–8191–6974–9 (alk. paper)
ISBN 0–8191–6975–7 (pbk. : alk. paper)

All University Press of America books are produced on acid-free
paper which exceeds the minimum standards set by the National
Historical Publications and Records Commission.

for Mara Elizabeth
sine qua non

ACKNOWLEDGMENTS

However much these actual pages remain my responsibility alone, their potential was nurtured by the inspirations and provocations of many teachers. Especially I would acknowledge Bill Mallard, who first suggested to me that whether or not 'God' is dead, Bonhoeffer's theology is not. And Walter Lowe, as mentor of my own style of thought, deserves much of the credit for whatever success I finally have had in making of this enterprise an intelligible whole.

I also thank the International Bonhoeffer Society, which provided several occasions to present sections of this project in the form of papers at its annual meetings. In particular, I have valued my conversations with Clifford Green, as well as his scotch, both of which repeatedly have helped to revive my lagging spirits.

A part of the cost of the revision of this manuscript was borne by a University Research Grant from the University of the South and by a Faculty Development Grant of The School of Theology thereof. Ray and Lynda Gotko assisted in preparing the manuscript for publication, including assembling the index.

My deepest, heartfelt gratitude goes to my parents and family, for their support of a project I am sure they never quite understood needing to be written at all. Most of all, I thank Mara Donaldson, who has suffered with me through many a dark night and, throughout it all, ever put this endeavor in the perspective it deserves.

In addition I wish to acknowledge the use of the following previously published material:

T. W. Adorno, "The Actuality of Philosophy," copyright c 1977, permission to reprint from Telos Press, Ltd.; Against Epistemology: A Metacritique. Studies in Husserl and Phenomenological Antinomies, translated by Willis Domingo, copyright c 1982, permission to reprint from The MIT Press and Basil Blackwell; Negative Dialectics, translated by E. B. Ashton, copyright c 1973, permission to reprint from Harper & Row Publishers, Inc.; Prisms, translated by Samuel and Shierry Weber, copyright c 1982, permission to reprint from The MIT Press.
Dietrich Bonhoeffer, Act and Being, translated by Bernard Noble, copyright c 1961, permission to reprint from Harper & Row Publishers, Inc.; "Man in Con-

TABLE OF CONTENTS

PREFACE

By reading the early work of the Protestant theologian, Dietrich Bonhoeffer, and that of the Jewish philosopher, Theodor Wiesengrund Adorno, this study inquires into nineteenth century liberalism's legacy to twentieth century **theology** of a certain problem with the **dialectics of otherness.** I wish to encourage a renewed deliberation upon theology's complicity in idealism's revisionist treatment of Kantian transcendental philosophy's **epistemological paradigm** of subject and object. In particular, contemporary theology has lost an understanding of the effect of idealism on our ways of thinking about the **sociality** of reality, and the **ethics** involved in the view of otherness which post-Hegelian thought has encouraged.

By approaching Bonhoeffer and Adorno as **occasions for** rather than the **point of** such reflection, the study attempts to contribute to contemporary philosophical-theological dialogue by means of a meditation 'in' rather than merely 'upon' their method and style. An 'epistemological' emphasis upon the non-identity of thought and being is ingredient to their thinking not only about the manner in which we **know** the world, but also about the way in which we **are** a social-world, and about the fashion in which we do or do not **value** our sociality.

Thinking guided by non-identity demands a particular form of **dialectics**--a **fragmentary** thinking which does not give up the utopian ethical vision of **coherent-diversity-without-domination.** In both Bonhoeffer's theological commitment to a Barthian 'revelational' model of otherness and Adorno's confrontation of the outcome of identity-philosophy in the ultimate obliteration of Otherness in Auschwitz, they argue that non-identity is the driving force within any form of conceptuality which refrains from the systematic domination of the Other.

The dialectics of non-identity provides a model for an anti-systematic or polyphonic theological conceptuality. Such a form of thought is necessary in order for theology to be adequate to the impenetrable mystery of those moments of particularity, or materiality, which are inherent to thought's responsible thinking of its recalcitrant, yet graciously indispensible, Other.

INTRODUCTION

No clearer indication exists of the troubled relationship between the transcendental philosophical tradition and modern theology than the eagerness of much contemporary theology to be rid of its traditional conceptual ally. The legacy of continental philosophy has become for us a deep shadow, rather than the illuminating light of generations past. We no longer argue about **which** interpretation of this tradition is germane to theological investigation. The conflict now is over **whether** the Enlightenment tradition, and the dialectical philosophical heritage it spawned, have or have not had their day. The challenge **of** the tradition of Enlightenment criticism is for us not nearly so pressing a concern as the growing challenge **to** that tradition--a challenge which calls into question theology's very capacity for critical reflection.

Yet other voices continue to warn that such a disengagement from the hegemony of the transcendental tradition may itself require a more radically critical form of theory than possibly can be mustered simply by turning one's back on philosophy--particularly its 'idealist' metaphysical legacy of subjectivity--as if theology's proper 'objectivity' will thereby automatically reassert itself. Such cautionary sentiments echo those of Jacques Derrida, who wrote that

> the step 'outside philosophy' is much more difficult to conceive than is generally imagined by those who think they made it long ago with cavalier ease, and who in general are swallowed up in metaphysics in the entire body of discourse which they claim to have disengaged from it. ... What I want to emphasize is simply that the passage beyond philosophy does not consist in turning the page of philosophy (which usually amounts to philosophizing badly), but in continuing to read philosophers **in a certain way.**[1]

As Martin Heidegger had similarly warned a generation earlier, "metaphysics cannot simply be discarded like an opinion. One can by no means leave it behind as a no longer cherished or defended doctrine."[2]

In its growing disquiet about the transcendental tradition, twentieth century theology risks merely re-enacting the nineteenth century post-Kantian drama. Such theology opts to turn its back on the unresolved transcendental epistemological antinomies--either for an 'ethicist', anti-metaphysical praxis, or a 'romanticist', experientially-broadened subjectivity-rather than engaging Kant directly. This study joins other contemporary archaeological inquiries into the state of the western metaphysical tradition by exploring the significance of modern theology's ambivalent investment in transcendental philosophy. We cannot avoid asking, at least, whether that tradition of thinking is indeed the cure, through criticism, of theology's contemporary malaise, or whether it is indeed the symptom of the disease against which theology would inoculate. Current theology must resist all reactionary efforts to sidestep the crisis in philosophy and the concomitant crisis in theological method. Rather, we need clarity concerning what is at stake in silencing the transcendental partner in the contemporary dialogue, however troubling and problematic the dialogue itself has become.

Our discussion proposes to read the early work of the Protestant theologian, Dietrich Bonhoeffer, and that of the Jewish philosopher, Theodor Adorno, **in a certain way**: as means by which to inquire into twentieth century post-Barthian theology's relationship to nineteenth century liberalism's legacy of the dialectics of otherness. We wish to renew deliberation on the **epistemological paradigm** of subject and object--particularly, its role in stating the conditions for theology's conceptuality about the **sociality** or relationality of reality, and the **ethics** involved in the view of otherness it encourages.

For despite the half century that has passed since Bonhoeffer, contemporary theology still finds itself ensnared in this same nexus of unresolved concerns. If current methodological deliberations in theology are to advance, the present study proposes, we must decide if this epistemological paradigm--our inheritance from the nineteenth century--itself should be, or indeed can be, discarded along with the metaphysical pretensions of transcendental philosophy. If not, the task of philosophy and theology in the late twentieth century must be to state the wisdom in retaining it.

The present study will interpret Bonhoeffer's <u>Act and Being</u> and Adorno's <u>Negative Dialectics</u> as occasions for, rather than the point of, an inquiry into the paradigmatic role of epistemology in establishing the parameters for reflection upon sociality and ethics. It intends to contribute towards the future constructive, as well as the comparative historical, theological task.

xiv

This work proposes **neither** a synoptic reading of the complete corpus of either thinker **nor** a comprehensive review of the secondary literature that has grown up around them, but rather a modest contribution to the contemporary debate concerning whether a dialectical theology of otherness is any longer possible.

We would place **Bonhoeffer** within the broader context of that intellectual tradition with which Act and Being was itself preoccupied--transcendental philosophy and ontology in systematic theology. We would ask whether Bonhoeffer's own proposals do or do not fulfill the threefold critical desiderata of the transcendental tradition mentioned above--epistemological, social, and ethical. On this basis we would then ask to what extent Bonhoeffer is or is not of assistance in furthering the current debate in theological methodology, given our continued disquiet concerning the transcendental tradition in the four decades since Bonhoeffer's death.

But the work of both Bonhoeffer and **Adorno** reflects what the latter called a style of "substantive thought--a thought of whose movement the thinker becomes aware only as he performs it."[3] The patience required in order to reap the benefit of such thinking, however, is particularly difficult in a time such as our own, in which as Adorno wrote, "no theory today escapes the marketplace," in which "each one is offered as a possibility among competing options, ... all are put up for choice; all are swallowed."[4] The result has been a decided impatience with **both** the early theology of Bonhoeffer **and** the philosophical writings of Adorno.

When this style is combined with the fact that both Act and Being and Negative Dialectics are written in a decidedly **polemical,** if not contentious, tone, it is little wonder that few, especially in theological circles, have paid close attention to the methodological significance of the manner in which they each, as Adorno had written of Kierkegaard, "opposed philosophy for philosophy's own sake"[5]--for the sake of that very dialectical subjectivity which appears increasingly prone either to uncritical acceptance or benign neglect. On a methodological level, therefore, the contribution which Bonhoeffer and Adorno may make to current discussion comes from the fact that they each continued to value and develop the Kantian-Hegelian, epistemological-ontological matrix of **questions,** at the same time that they each refused merely to acquiesce to the **answers** their predecessors had proposed. Together, they help us to renew a form of critical questioning of the relationship between theology and the dialectics of otherness.

A. Continuing to read ...

Theology approaching the twenty-first century is in danger of forgetting those very texts of the twentieth century on whose shoulders we still stand. The present study argues for the fruitfulness of **continuing to read** two of those exemplary texts which are already at risk of slipping from our scholarly memory: Dietrich Bonhoeffer's Akt und Sein, significantly subtitled Transzendentalphilosophie und Ontologie in der systematischen Theologie,[6] and Theodor W. Adorno's Negative Dialektik.[7]

Bonhoeffer's Habilitationsschrift, written in the summer and winter of 1929 and published in 1931, was a twenty-three year old theologian's ambitious attempt to fathom for the theology of his day the significance of its investment in the transcendental tradition's framework of subjectivity and objectivity, of **Act** and **Being.** The choice of **epistemology** as the terminus a quo of this book, Bonhoeffer's second, was an attempt to deepen and sharpen his criticism of the transcendental tradition's understanding of **sociality,** which he had begun in his first published writing, his dissertation, Sanctorum Communio, written in 1926-27, but first published only in 1930. Bonhoeffer began a search in Act and Being for a 'method' and conceptual 'style' which could honor both theology's category of revelation and the Enlightenment tradition of dialectics, "theology's legacy from Kant and idealism."[8] The profound **ethical** impact of transcendental philosophy on revelational theology's categories of epistemology and sociality provides the terminus ad quem of his investigation, under the headings of a theological methodology 'in Adam' and 'in Christ', which point forward to his posthumously published fragmentary drafts for a theological Ethics.[9]

The present study will focus even more specifically on 'Part One' of Act and Being, the usually cursorily treated methodological section--"Das Akt-Sein-Problem propaedeutisch dargestellt als Problem der Erkenntnistheorie am autonomen Daseinsverstaendnis in der Philosophie" ["The Act-Being-Problem Propadeutically Portrayed as the Problem of Epistemology in the Autonomous Understanding of Dasein in Philosophy"]. This section evidences just those concerns about the nature of a subject-object duality which we outlined above--its function as a paradigm for the heterogeneity of sociality and the ethics of otherness. It approaches these issues in the form of an appreciative critique of theology's own propensity **either** to allow its methodological duality to lapse into the risk of dualism--to allow its emphasis on the integrity of the other to lapse into an atomistic individualism which denies the 'concreteness' of community, to allow its affirmation of difference and transcendence to obscure the immediacy of immanent ethical dilemmas--**or,** in naively embracing 'concreteness' and 'immediacy', to risk lapsing into the a-sociality and ethics-of-domination of idealism. Therefore, Bonhoeffer's methodological reflections serve as a model for that theological method which would attempt to think with and beyond idealism, to fulfill rather than overcome the legitimate concerns of the transcendental tradition, to point theology in a direction which is true both to its own desiderata and those of the tradition of Kant's legacy to transcendental dialectics.

Adorno's Negative Dialectics, published in 1966, provides the present study with a way into a more sustained inquiry into the issues which had preoccupied Bonhoeffer almost four decades previously--transcendental philosophy's increasingly idealistic resolution of the problems of epistemology, and its contribution to our interpretation of sociality and ethics. Against any un-dialectical metaphysic, whether a metaphysic of subjectivity which overcomes the object or a metaphysic of objectivity which denies the subject, Adorno argues, as had Bonhoeffer, for the need to maintain **both** subjectivity and objectivity, related in a tensive force-field, or constellation.

The epistemological paradigm for the subsequent transcendental tradition, according to Adorno, demands a dialectics capable of not simply subverting the Kantian antinomies, but coming to terms with them. Against the positive ontological affirmation of 'subjectivity' in idealism, he calls his own project a **"Negative** Dialectics," which recognizes, but does not succumb to, the "ontological urge" towards totality. And against the 'objectivism' of the later positivistic traditions, which would overcome the role of the subject altogether, he stressed that what is required is still a "Negative **Dialectics,"** a tensive-dynamic retention of the poles of objectivity **and** subjectivity.

This last published work by Adorno before his death in 1969 points us, as well, to the connections between his critique of **epistemology,** his own earlier work on

sociality, and his own plans, at the time of his death, to write a thematic treatment of his long standing concern with **ethics,** or moral philosophy.[10] Epistemology itself, according to <u>Negative Dialectics</u>, both reflects and affects the sociality of human existence. And the manner in which we construe that sociality--whether we retain the epistemological legacy of difference or acquiesce to the idealist exigence towards totality--implies an unintentional ethical posture towards the 'other', the 'different', that which is alien-to-the-ego. There is a morality of thinking which undercuts all radical attempts to sever theory and practice, even, if not especially, the theory of epistemology and the ethical praxis of the sociality-of-otherness it demands.

B. ...In a Certain Way

This study proposes to read Bonhoeffer and Adorno **in a certain way.** The **specific** function of a conversation between them is to allow <u>Negative Dialectics</u> itself to function as an **intrinsic** criticism of <u>Act and Being</u>. Adorno's own particular 'method of criticism' is employed to amplify and correct Bonhoeffer's 'criticism of method' as reflected in the confluence of philosophical themes which preoccupied the latter's early 'theological' writing.

The broader, more **general** function of a dialogue between Bonhoeffer and Adorno is to allow Adorno to provide an **extrinsic** critique of a pervasive and misleading judgment that interpreters of Bonhoeffer continue to make concerning the latter's method and style. Bonhoeffer's **method** is interpreted by many commentators as arguing almost exclusively against epistemological models--if not against theoretical models altogether--for the sake of a 'concrete' sociality and ethics. And Bonhoeffer's **style** of thinking and writing continues to be neglected in even the most sustained and systematic expositions of his theology. A conversation with the method and style of Adorno will provide a heuristic model by which to make sense particularly of Bonhoeffer's early theology. Furthermore, in light of Adorno's investment in heterodox Marxian and Jewish mystical-theological perspectives, and Bonhoeffer's bourgeois-Christian neglect of the left-Hegelian and Jewish-mystical traditions almost altogether, a dialogue between Bonhoeffer and Adorno suggests the manner in which contemporary constructive theology might benefit when both these perspectives are placed into conversation.

This study will argue that it is precisely by means of an appreciative critique of epistemology that Bonhoeffer's method moves to a more adequate theory of the conceptual foundations of sociality and ethics. His early work is misunderstood when interpreted as a denial of the enduring significance of the epistemological problematic, as an endeavor to **substitute** social and ethical concerns for theoretical ones. Bonhoeffer will be shown to be no less 'theological' for all his 'philosophical' concerns--and no less 'Christian' for having been a 'critical' theologian. The question of the extent to which the early theoretical foundations continued to shape his later writings, as well, will have to await some further study. Yet, the dialogue with Adorno may allow the Bonhoeffer interpreter a way in which to approach the inherently 'fragmentary', un-systematic, and in-coherent nature of Bonhoeffer's thinking and writing. Perhaps his manner of expression was not merely the result of biographical circumstance, but was the result of his particular style and method of reflection as well.

The heavy reliance upon Adorno in clarifying issues of method and style should not suggest to the reader that Adorno is, despite any protestations to the contrary, really the **point of** and Bonhoeffer merely the **occasion for** this inquiry. For in the end the point that I wish to make is an eminently **theological** one, which means that it is the philosophers who will most likely feel betrayed. And it is clearly not theology in general, but the theology of **Bonhoeffer,** which has opened the way for the specific theological dialogue with Adorno which this study undertakes. Only taken together, we will argue, do we gain the richness and coherence of a possible contemporary 'dialectical theology of otherness'. Such a position seeks to be neither 'Bonhoefferian' nor 'Adornonian'. But it will be better if it has learned from them, and better still if it moves beyond them, whether or not thinking will ever really surmount either of their achievements.

C. Sources and Resources

To the extent possible, I have used the first edition of the standard English translation of Bonhoeffer's <u>Akt und Sein</u> [Act and Being], made by Bernard Noble in 1961.[11] When questions of accuracy or interpretation have made use of the original text necessary, I have used the second edition of <u>Akt und Sein</u> from which the English translation was made. All additional translations are my own and are noted as such.

Despite my intention to center the discussion of Bonhoeffer on Act and Being, several other primary sources are drawn into the argument, chiefly as they clarify or amplify points already made in the former text. These all come from the period between Bonhoeffer's first dissertation and his final Berlin University seminar in the summer of 1933 entitled, "Religionsphilosophie bei Hegel."[12] In particular I have had recourse to Bonhoeffer's first dissertation, Sanctorum Communio: Eine dogmatische Untersuchung zur Soziologie der Kirche [The Communion of Saints. A Dogmatic Inquiry into the Sociology of the Church],[13] written during 1926-1927, and first published in 1930. As with Act and Being, the present study focuses in particular on Chapters One and Two, where Bonhoeffer lays out much of the conceptual framework for his entire discussion of sociality. Again I have used the English translation whenever possible, referring for the most part only on matters of technical terminology to the Fourth German edition of 1969.

In addition, three essays provide significant insights into Bonhoeffer's thinking during this period up to the appearance of Act and Being in 1931. The first of these is his inaugural lecture at the University of Berlin on July 31st, 1930, "Die Frage nach dem Menschen in der gegenwaertigen Philosophie und Theologie" ["Man in Contemporary Philosophy and Theology"].[14] The second was a lecture prepared in English and delivered to fellow students while studying at Union Theological Seminary in New York in 1931, "The Theology of Crisis and its Attitude Toward Philosophy and Science."[15] And the third was an article written in English in 1931 and published in The Journal of Religion in 1932, "Concerning the Christian Idea of God."[16]

Finally, two other texts figure significantly into the thematic of this study, and demark the latter end of the time frame with which we are concerned. These are Bonhoeffer's Berlin lectures, "Schoepfung und Suende," delivered in the winter of 1932-33, and "Christologie," delivered just prior to his final lectures on Hegel in the summer of 1933. The former was published in 1933 as Schoepfung und Fall [Creation and Fall], while the latter was reconstructed from student notes and published posthumously in Gesammelte Schriften, III [Christ the Center].[17]

My discussion of Adorno is based for the most part on his Negative Dialektik [Negative Dialectics], as found in the Gesammelte Schriften, Volume Six.[18] I have quoted from the English translation,[19] unless noted otherwise. In addition, as with Bonhoeffer, several additional texts--both books and individual essays--have been brought into the discussion at appropriate points. These include, but are not restricted to the following: Adorno's inaugural lecture at Frankfurt on May 7, 1931, "Die Aktualitaet der Philosophie" ["The Actuality of Philosophy"], which was not published until Volume One of the Gesammelte Schriften;[20] Zur Metakritik der Erkenntnistheorie. Studien ueber Husserl und die phaenomenologischen Antinomien [Against Epistemology: A Metacritique. Studies in Husserl and the Phenomenological Antinomies],[21] of which the first, second, and fourth chapters were written during his stay in London during 1934-1937, and the "Introduction" and third chapter, with which we are chiefly concerned, were subsequently written in 1955-56, for the book's publication in 1956; "Husserl and the Problem of Idealism," published in English in The Journal of Philosophy in 1940;[22] Dialektik der Aufklaerung. Philosophische Fragmente [Dialectic of Enlightenment],[23] co-authored with Max Horkheimer in 1947; Minima Moralia. Reflexionen aus dem Beschaedigten Leben [Minima Moralia. Reflections from Damaged Life],[24] published in 1951; Prismen. Kulturkritik und Gesellschaft [Prisms],[25] published in 1955; and "Subjekt und Objekt" ["Subject and Object"], published in Stichworte. Kritische Modelle 2[26] in 1969, the year of Adorno's death.

D. Outline of the Project

Chapter One will, first, state the relationship between dialectics and theological method, both in general and then with specific relationship to Bonhoeffer. Second, it will examine the philosophical presuppositions underlying Bonhoeffer's and Adorno's conceptions of the epistemological paradigm and dialectics. Third, it will go on to examine the historical, social, and biographical context within which the legacy of transcendental philosophy was inherited by Adorno and Bonhoeffer. The chapter pays particular regard both to the way in which the subject-object conceptuality was influenced by this context within which they wrote, and to the influence of epistemology, in turn, upon the method of immanent criticism which they each employed.

Chapter Two then turns to Bonhoeffer's Act and Being in order to detail the threefold constellation of epistemology, sociality and ethics in his early writings. The study argues that, despite the misleading subtitle of the book--"transcendental philosophy and ontology in

systematic theology"--Bonhoeffer's execution of the project makes obvious that the conceptual tension which
concerns him is actually that between a genuine transcendental philosophy, represented by Kant's <u>Critique of
Pure Reason</u>[27] and transcendental philosophy's evolution
into the idealism of Hegel's <u>Phenomenology of Spirit</u> and
<u>The Christian Religion</u>.[28] Twentieth century phenomeno-
logy and ontology, particularly the work of Husserl and
Heidegger, are understood by Bonhoeffer as responses to
this tension within the transcendental tradition, interpreted as a struggle over the nature of dialectical method and the ontological conclusions to be drawn from its
epistemological foundations.

The chapter then turns to the theme of sociality,
the question of intersubjectivity, the fate of genuine
'otherness' in the transcendental tradition. It summarizes Bonhoeffer's own nascent social ontology and his attempts to disengage it from what he understood to be
the lingering shadow of idealism, as seen in the oblivion
of the concrete 'other'. The second chapter then concludes with Bonhoeffer's discussion of the ethical implications of theology's investment in idealism. His attempt to resolve the dilemma through an engagement
with personalist philosophy, particularly that of Eberhard
Grisebach, is shown to have only sharpened, not
resolved, the methodological problem which Bonhoeffer
recognized, but could not adequately overcome.

Chapter Three turns to Adorno's <u>Negative Dialectics</u>
in pursuit of a refined understanding of the enduring
subject-object epistemological problematic and its effect
on philosophical reflection upon sociality and ethics.
The discussion traces the fate of the 'object' from Kant's
<u>Critique of Pure Reason</u>, to Hegel's attempted resolution
of the problem of 'otherness' through a dialectics of
mediation, to Husserl's renewed phenomenological endeavor to overcome the cunning of Hegel.[29]

It explores the task of social ontology in the twilight of a viable philosophy of otherness. Adorno's project is shown to be a double critique of idealist dialectics and the 'negativity' of otherness--the one by the
other. The unresolved transcendental problem of sociality is shown to result in the perpetual marginality of the
other, and thus to open up a particular moral problem
within social philosophy itself.

The chapter concludes with an exploration of Adorno's treatment of the idealistic concept of 'totality' as a
moral or ethical problem--what Nietzsche had described

as an ethics of the subjective domination of the object. The discussion of Adorno's <u>Negative Dialectics</u> ends with a reflection on what he came to call "the morality of thinking"[30] or--drawing upon his appropriation of the Marxian critique of ideology--the "ethical function of materialism,"[31] and its impact on philosophical method.

Chapter Four in conclusion turns from the previous two chapters' concern with the immanent criticism of the transcendental tradition to the aporia of retaining a concomitant transcendent criticism in the work of both Adorno and Bonhoeffer. The discussion begins by outlining the possibility of a transcendent form of criticism in Adorno. This would have to take account of both the Marxian-sociological and the Jewish-theological influences upon his form of criticism. Turning to Bonhoeffer, the conclusion examines the methodological priority of transcendent criticism in his theology, and its ironic relation to his immanent de-construction of idealism.

This final chapter argues that a theological understanding of revelation such as Bonhoeffer's can benefit from the conceptuality of the 'negative dialectical' stance of Adorno. The revelational theme of otherness, or non-identity, I argue, structures the relationship among several themes in Bonhoeffer's early work, particularly the constellation of the traditional dogmatic loci of Christology, creation, sin, and community (the Church). I argue that it is precisely the **juxtaposition** of these four theological loci, rather than the reduction of Bonhoeffer's position to the utter priority of one of them, which must define the agenda of post-Bonhoefferian theology.

The chapter concludes with the potential contributions of Adorno's heterodox-Marxian "Melancholy Science"[32] and Bonhoeffer's bourgeois-Christian "Melancholy Theology."[33] Both of their projects point towards the need for a sustained archaeology of the nature of theological method at the supposed end of idealist metaphysics, towards the continuing present fruitfulness of dialectical method, and towards the future realization of concrete theory.

NOTES

[1] Jacques Derrida, Writing and Difference, trans. Alan Bass (Chicago: University of Chicago Press, 1978), pp. 284, 288.

[2] Heidegger, The End of Philosophy, trans. Joan Stambaugh (New York: Harper & Row, 1973), p. 85; this translation by Fred R. Dallmayr, Twilight of Subjectivity. Contributions to a Post-Individualist Theory of Politics (Amherst: University of Massachusetts Press, 1981), p. 3.

[3] Theodor W. Adorno, Negative Dialektik, in Gesammelte Schriften, Band 6 (Frankfurt am Main: Suhrkamp Verlag, 1973) [Negative Dialectics, trans. E. B. Ashton (New York: The Seabury Press, 1973)], p. xix.

[4] Ibid., p. 4.

[5] Ibid., p. 123.

[6] Dietrich Bonhoeffer, Akt und Sein. Transzendentalphilosophie und Ontologie in der systematischen Theologie, 2nd ed. (Munich: Chr. Kaiser Verlag, 1956) [Act and Being, trans. Bernard Noble with an Introduction by Ernst Wolf (New York: Harper & Brothers, Publishers, London: William Collins Sons & Co. Ltd., 1961)]. All citations to Act and Being will come from the English translation, except where it has been altered, in which case the page in the German original will be given in square brackets, preceded by a "G". See Walter Lowe, "Christ and Salvation," in Christian Theology: An Introduction to Its Traditions and Tasks, ed. Peter C. Hodgson and Robert H. King (Philadelphia: Fortress Press, 1982), p. 216, who calls Act and Being "one of the finest discussions of theology and transcendental philosophy...."

[7] See note 3 above.

[8] Act and Being, p. 12.

[9] Dietrich Bonhoeffer, Ethik, sixth edition (Munich: Chr. Kaiser Verlag, 1963) [Ethics, trans. Neville Horton Smith and edited by Eberhard Bethge (New York: The Macmillan Company, 1955)].

[10] Gillian Rose, The Melancholy Science. An Introduction to the Thought of Theodor Adorno (New York: Columbia University Press, 1978), p. 148; also see the "Editorisches Nachwort" in Theodor Adorno, Gesammelte

Schriften, Band 7, Aesthetische Theorie (Frankfurt am Main: Suhrkamp Verlag, 1970), p. 537.

[11]See note 6 above.

[12]Little is known of the content of Bonhoeffer's lectures on Hegel, because the text of them was lost. One copy of student notes from that seminar reportedly exists in the possession of one of Bonhoeffer's former students, Franz [Ferenck] Lehel in Budapest, Hungary, although these are not at this time available. Eberhard Bethge gives a sketch of them in Dietrich Bonhoeffer. Theologe. Christ. Zeitgenosse (Munich: Chr. Kaiser Verlag, 1967), pp. 266-267, which was omitted from the English translation, [Dietrich Bonhoeffer. Man of Vision. Man of Courage, trans. Eric Mosbacher, Peter and Betty Ross, Frank Clarke, and William Glen-Doepel, under the editorship of Edwin Robertson (New York: Harper and Row, 1977)], leaving the impression that the Christologie lectures were actually his last classroom appearances.

[13]Dietrich Bonhoeffer, Sanctorum Communio, fourth edition (Munich: Chr. Kaiser, 1969) [Sanctorum Communio, trans. Ronald Gregor Smith from the third German edition (London: Collins, 1963); The Communion of Saints, same translation (New York: Harper & Row, Publishers, 1963)]. Since the present study was completed, the new critical German edition of Sanctorum Communio has become available, edited by Joachim von Soosten, as Band 1, Dietrich Bonhoeffer Werke (Munich: Christian Kaiser Verlag, 1986).

[14]Dietrich Bonhoeffer, "Die Frage nach dem Menschen in der gegenwaertigen Philosophie und Theologie," in Gesammelte Schriften, Band III, pp. 62-84 ["Man in Contemporary Philosophy and Theology," trans. Edwin H. Robertson in No Rusty Swords, (London: William Collins Sons & Co., Ltd., 1965; New York: Harper and Row, 1971), pp. 46-65.]

[15]Dietrich Bonhoeffer, "The Theology of Crisis and its Attitude Toward Philosophy Science," in Gesammelte Schriften, Band III, ed. Eberhard Bethge (Munich: Christian Kaiser Verlag, 1966).

[16]Dietrich Bonhoeffer, "Concerning the Christian Idea of God," in Gesammelte Schriften, Band III, ed. Eberhard Bethge (Munich: Christian Kaiser Verlag, 1966).

[17]Dietrich Bonhoeffer, Schoepfung und Fall (Munich: Chr. Kaiser Verlag, 1937) [Creation and Fall. Two Bib-

lical Studies, trans. John C. Fletcher (New York: Mac-millan, 1976), pp. 11-94; Christologie, in Gesammelte Schriften, III, ed. Eberhard Bethge (Munich: Chr. Kaiser Verlag, 1960), pp. 166-242 [Christ the Center, trans. Edwin H. Robertson (New York: Harper & Row, 1978).

18Theodor W. Adorno, Gesammelte Schriften, Band 6, ed. Rolf Tiedemann (Frankfurt am Main: Suhrkamp Verlag, 1977).

19See Gillian Rose, "Review of Negative Dialectics," American Political Science Review 70 (1976):598-599 for a discussion of the English translation.

20Theodor W. Adorno, "Die Aktualitaet der Philoso-phie," Gesammelte Schriften, Band 1 (Frankfurt am Main: Suhrkamp Verlag, 1973) ["The Actuality of Philosophy," Telos 31 (Spring, 1977):120-133.]

21Theodor W. Adorno, Zur Metakritik der Erkennt-nistheorie. Studien ueber Husserl und die phaenomeno-logischen Antinomien (Stuttgart: W. Kohlhammer, 1956); also found in Gesammelte Schriften, Band 5 (Frankfurt am Main: Suhrkamp Verlag, 1971) [Against Epistemology: A Metacritique. Studies in Husserl and the Phenomeno-logical Antinomies, trans. Willis Domingo (Cambridge, MA.: The MIT Press, 1983); the "Introduction" was previ-ously published under the title, "The Metacritique of Epistemology," trans. Michael B. Allen, Telos 38 (Winter 78-79): 77-103.]

22Theodor W. Adorno, "Husserl and the Problem of Idealism," The Journal of Philosophy 37/1 (January 4, 1940):5-18.

23Max Horkheimer and Theodor W. Adorno, Dialek-tik der Aufklaerung. Philosophische Fragmente (Amster-dam: Querido, 1947); also in Gesammelte Schriften, Band III (Frankfurt am Main: Suhrkamp Verlag, 1981) [Dialectic of Enlightenment, trans. John Cumming (New York: The Seabury Press, 1972.]

24Theodor W. Adorno, Minima Moralia. Reflexionen aus dem Beschaedigten Leben (Frankfurt am Main: Suhr-kamp, 1951), also in Gesammelte Schriften, Band IV (Frankfurt am Main: Suhrkamp Verlag, 1980) [Minima Moralia. Reflections from Damaged Life, trans. E. F. N. Jephcott (London: Verso Editions, 1984).]

25Theodor W. Adorno, Prismen. Kulturkritik und Gesellschaft (Berlin und Frankfurt am Main: Suhrkamp,

1955), also in <u>Gesammelte Schriften</u>, Band 10/1 (Frankfurt am Main: Suhrkamp, 1977) [<u>Prisms</u>, trans. Samuel and Shierry Weber (Cambridge, MA.: The MIT Press, 1981).]

26Theodor W. Adorno, "Subjekt und Objekt," in <u>Stichworte</u>. <u>Kritische Modelle 2</u> (Frankfurt am Main: Suhrkamp, 1969), also in <u>Gesammelte Schriften</u>, Band 10/2 (Frankfurt am Main: Suhrkamp, 1977) ["Subject and Object," in <u>The Essential Frankfurt School Reader</u>, ed. and with introductions by Andrew Arato and Eike Gebhardt (New York: Urizen Books, 1978), pp. 497-511.]

27All subsequent citations come from Immanuel Kant, <u>Critique of Pure Reason</u>, trans. Norman Kemp Smith (New York: St. Martin's Press, 1965). Citations follow the convention of stating the First (A) or Second (B) Edition, followed by the pagination from the German original, as given in the margins of the Smith translation.

28All subsequent citations come from G. W. F. Hegel, <u>Phenomenology of Spirit</u>, trans. A. V. Miller (Oxford: Oxford University Press, 1979) and <u>The Christian Religion</u>, ed. and trans. Peter C. Hodgson (Missoula, Montana: Scholars Press, 1979).

29In particular see Edmund Husserl, <u>Cartesian Meditations</u>. <u>An Introduction to Phenomenology</u>, trans. Dorion Cairns (The Hague: Martinus Nijhoff, 1977).

30<u>Minima Moralia</u>, pp. 73-75.

31Martin Jay, <u>Adorno</u> (Cambridge, MA.: Harvard University Press, 1984), p. 59.

32'Melancholy Science' was Adorno's ironic inversion of Nietzsche's 'gay' or 'joyful science'. He refers to his own philosophy by this term in the dedication to <u>Minima Moralia</u>, p. 15.

33Karl Barth posthumously ascribed to Bonhoeffer "the melancholy theology of the North German plain" in a letter to Landessuperintendent P. W. Herrenbrueck, written in 1952, and published in part in <u>World Come of Age</u>, p. 91.

CHAPTER ONE

DIALECTICS AND THE THEOLOGY OF OTHERNESS: PRESUPPOSITIONS, CONTEXT AND METHOD

There can be little argument that modern theology has been wedded for better or worse to the transcendental philosophical tradition of **epistemology,** in particular its **subject-object** paradigm. The rehearsal of theology's alliance with such a transcendental epistemology has become one of the commonplaces of modern discussion. The results had been twofold. (a) The entire metaphysical underpinnings of previous theology, one can hardly deny, were made problematic by the Kantian turn to the epistemological centrality of subjective constitution. (2) Thus, the coherence of reality could not any longer be based upon transcendent metaphysical foundations, but must at all times take critically into account the radically constitutive, perhaps even all-encompassing, activity of the knowing subject.

This study begins with the modest observation that what has **not** been so self-evident to post-Kantian theology is its indebtedness to the other moment of Kant's project. This is the 'critical', 'transcendental' function of the 'resistance to subjectivity <u>par excellence</u>'--Kant's infamous thing-in-itself. In particular we have lost an awareness of the manner in which it has continued to inform our conceptual options concerning **both** what this study calls **sociality**--a relational concern with 'otherness' or extra-subjectivity--**and** the manner of our **ethical** valuation of and response to that 'object'--the non-subjective, receptive moment of 'being' which persisted in even the Kantian epistemological paradigm. In particular, we have lost an appreciation for Kant's contribution to the maintenance--perhaps even the cultivation--of a certain non-metaphysical sense of the **mystery** of finite reality. We have lost a Kantian sense for the limits of theoretical speech, a sense of metaphysical reticence in the face of a radically 'other' reality, irreducible to univocal epistemological, much less ontological, terms.

Reflection subsequent to Kant has endeavored, more or less, to overcome rather than fulfill his form of epistemology. Post-Kantianism has been much less hesitant to draw metaphysical conclusions concerning **otherness** from the preponderance of **subjective activity** in its dialectic of thought and being. In such philosophy and theology as well, the 'triumph of subjectivity', whose exemplar was idealism, increasingly has obscured the

1

recalcitrance of the 'thing-in-itself'--and thereby the limits the latter implies regarding the ontologically constitutive power of finite subjectivity. The Kantian tactical **duality** has been denounced as **dualism.** The heterogeneity of the object has been vilified, often on apparently orthodox Kantian grounds, as mere heteronomy. The affirmation of the autonomy of the subject has tended in the main to argue for an abolition, in fact if not intention, of the critical function of any sort of priority placed on the 'other', the object. Kant's 'critical' philosophy has been taken as warrant for the **denial** that non-subjective otherness has any ultimate ontological status. The meaningfulness of any radical ontological **plurality,** or **sociality,** has been excoriated as pre-critical and thus a lapse back behind Kant's own Copernican turn. And with the loss of **otherness** has been lost the particular desideratum of a genuinely 'Kantian' form of critical, even nascently **dialectical,** reflection as well.

Once placed within this larger epistemological problematic of transcendental philosophy, the problem of otherness has been confronted by what might be called a kind of 'Nietzschean' challenge. For the Enlightenment affirmation of the **freedom** of the subject has always bordered on the legitimation of that subject's freedom for the **domination** of the object. The systematic attempt at a philosophy or a theology of the **unity** of reality has relentlessly been faced with its concomitant urge towards the abolition of otherness--the Nietzschean will to power of subjectivity. Domination has threatened to replace diversity, sameness to subvert plurality. The post-Kantian, particularly the idealist, tradition did struggle (with varied results) with the relational **sociality** of reality, with a view of 'knowledge' which would not only passively allow but also actively sustain the otherness of objectivity. But it less consistently faced, much less resolved, the **ethical** problem of the value of non-identity, or difference, between subject and object, thought and being.

Often it has been this issue of ethics that has encouraged transcendental philosophy--and theology as well--simply to break away from any continued constructive meditation on the epistemological model itself, particularly in the wake of idealism. Significant strands of theology, **on the one hand,** have tended to follow strategies like Ritschl's of severing their investment in the Kantian or Hegelian tradition of **theoretical** critique. They have limited theology proper to the tradition of the <u>Critique of Practical Reason</u>. Yet, ironically, this apparent turn towards a preoccupation with 'the ethical'

2

has meant a loss of our understanding precisely the enduring ethical challenge of the very epistemological categories which the entire transcendental project presupposes. And, **on the other hand**, when theology has tried to renew its reflection upon the subject-object model for thinking, it has tended to do so by following the romanticist lead in **subverting** the Kantian epistemological dichotomy (subject and object, transcendental apperception and <u>Ding an sich</u>), thereby losing sight of the crucial problem of the relation between subjectivity and the domination of objectivity. In neither case has theology perceived the subject-object paradigm to be, at the least, an enduring challenge to **all** theological methodology, if not also a promising heuristic model.

Yet, ironically, this study will argue, the attempt of idealism has proved superior to either the 'ethicist' or the 'romanticist' stances. This is because in its multiple attempts to think of reality 'concretely', as a 'social' complex of mediations, idealism had at least continued to pose the **ethical** question of the status of the object, precisely as a function of its questions concerning the very **sociality** of 'otherness'. When theology has attempted, through an engagement of the idealist strand of the transcendental tradition, to obtain a **coherent** sense of reality <u>vis a vis</u> the Kantian dualities, it has at least benefited from idealism's having heightened, rather than resolved, precisely the **ethical** problematic of thinking **sociality** epistemologically--the relationship of thought and the domination of otherness.

But at its worst, theology's confluence with idealism has fueled the fire in which objectivity and otherness are consumed. The difficulty in maintaining the **richness** of reality as heterogeneous sociality entails the dual challenge of resisting idealism's Promethean claim to totality, while averting a Manichean fall into metaphysical dualism. And theology has been for the most part so mesmerized with the latter danger that it has ignored the ethical challenges in accomplishing the former. <u>De facto</u>, at least, the Promethean fire and the darkness of Manes risk becoming one. In both cases the 'otherness' of the 'object' tends to be devalued, pushed into a 'moral' status of disenfranchised marginality. And were this the unavoidable consequence of engaging in dialogue with the transcendental tradition, particularly its idealist developments, then one can easily understand the righteous indignation with which most ethicist and romanticist theologies have tended to resist it altogether.

In addition to the broadly **idealist, romanticist** and **ethicist** strategies that dominated so much of the nineteenth century's reactions to Kant, there have been two remarkable exceptions in twentieth century theology to the prevalence of the eclipse of the object. Each in its own way represents a reassertion of a concern with the 'object'. Each proposes to cut through the proliferating questions of the transcendental tradition to robustly affirm, post-Kant, a renewed and radicalized **theology of otherness.**

Karl Barth's 'second Copernican revolution' in particular was an attempt to turn the tables and, under the influence of Kierkegaard's 'infinite qualitative distinction' to think theologically the paradoxicality of God-the-other, the <u>totaliter aliter</u>, who 'is' as the divine communication to humanity of the personal object of revelation. And Martin Buber's 'I-Thou' was an attempt to rethink the social dialectic in terms that made the 'other' more than an ethically eviscerated 'it', but rather a rich and ontologically relational 'Thou'.

Yet in each of these cases a certain ambivalence about the otherness of the object has remained. In the case of the theology of crisis, if God is thought as the Other-as-Subject, it is humanity-as-receptive-**object** of God's activity that tends to take on a problematic status, albeit for theological reasons. And in the case of personalist existentialism, the **immediacy** of the Thou to the I still resonates with the danger that dialogical familiarity may yet breed a real, if complexly and relationally sublimated, contempt of that which would genuinely resist 'relation'.

In both cases the possibility and nature of a critical **dialectical** conceptuality of subjects and objects--an authentic heterogeneousness, an autonomy which allows diversity, the **sociality** of reality--has been shown to require, at the least, further sustained attention. The **distinctiveness** of the subject vis-a-vis the object (and of the object vis-a-vis the subject) has been called into question. Thus, there has arisen the possibility that theology, in its need to clarify that form of **dialectics** which can assist it in formulating the parameters of its own proper concept of **otherness,** might well profit from a 'new' form of 'Kantian' reflection. Theology might best be conceived by means of a post-Hegelian Kantianism which can account for, and surmount, the idealist legacy of otherness--yet precisely within Kantian limits. Such, the present study will argue, is the horizon in which further work may be able to understand the contribution of Bonhoeffer and Adorno to an evaluation of the transcendental bequest to theology.[1]

The manner of Bonhoeffer's and Adorno's appropriation of the methodological debate between a 'Kantian' dialectic-of-difference and a 'Hegelian' dialectic-of-totality reflects not only their individual biographical particularities, but also the cultural and historical context in which their thinking originated. In the case of Adorno, these **historical** and **cultural** factors have dominated discussions of his intellectual developments and changes. And in the case of Bonhoeffer a **biographical** emphasis on the moral and religious turning points of his life has produced scholarship whose tone often has approached hagiography. In both cases the plethora of historical, cultural and biographical elements has usually contributed more to the **richness** than to the **coherence** of our interpretations of the development of their projects.

Bernard Lonergan has suggested a typology in his Method in Theology, according to which the significant changes, 'new beginnings' or 'conversions' in a person's life "may be [described as] **intellectual** or **moral** or **religious.**" (a) "Intellectual conversion is a radical clarification and, consequently, the elimination of an exceedingly stubborn and misleading myth concerning reality, objectivity, and human knowledge." (b) "Moral conversion changes the criterion of one's decisions and choices from satisfactions to values." (c) "Religious conversion is being grasped by ultimate concern."[2] To borrow from his schema, we can say that much has been written about the **intellectual**[3] conversions in Adorno's career, which themselves came about as a result of not only the historical exigencies of late-Weimar Germany, but also as a result of Adorno's shifting cultural circle of friends and mentors. Likewise, much has been said about the **moral** and **religious** conversions in Bonhoeffer's biography and their effect on his historically-and socially-contextual theological vocation.[4]

Chapters Two and Three, partly in response to these trends, will be concerned to redress the balance by speaking more directly than has heretofore been the rule about the centrality of the **intellectual** conversion that was being deliberated in Bonhoeffer's Act and Being and then the significance of the **moral** 'new beginnings' that began to be evident in Adorno's early work and personal associations, later coming to fruition in his Negative Dialectics. The concern of Chapter One, however, is to show how certain **presuppositions** concerning transcendental epistemology[5] were tempered by the historical-

5

cultural **context** of the inheritors, and how in turn an enduring concern with the unfulfilled desiderata of the problematic subject-object duality influenced the particular **method** of these two thinkers.

A. Bonhoeffer's Theological Presuppositions Concerning Epistemology and Dialectic

Coming as it did in the midst of the unresolved debate among four mutually exclusive options for theological method--the ethicist, the romanticist, the idealist and the dialectical/relational--it is little wonder that the provocative legacy of Dietrich Bonhoeffer should have functioned in actuality as a veritable Rorschach test for the self-understanding of almost an entire generation of contemporary Protestant theology.[6] The principle of selectivity from among the Bonhoeffer corpus has often said more, that is, about an epochal disquiet about the business and prospects of the theological task itself than it said about the enduring constructive contribution of Bonhoeffer.

From the earliest post-war discovery, public perception of Bonhoeffer's theology has tended to succumb to what Vincent Descombes has characterized in another context as a "clamorous approach," which from among the variegated themes of Bonhoeffer's work tended to "retain only what created a stir among the widest possible audience."[7] And subsequent scholarly Bonhoeffer-interpretation has allowed itself, all to easily, to "slide into a Bonhoeffer orthodoxy, an ultimately sterile imitation."[8] This has risked making Bonhoeffer's legacy into a historical curiosity rather than an enduring contribution to the constructive tasks of contemporary theology.

This is not, however, to suggest the emergence of any clear consensus from among the commentators regarding the systematic unity of even those 'clamorous' themes that have come to be considered "the legacy of Bonhoeffer." A reading of David H. Hopper's often neglected book, <u>A Dissent on Bonhoeffer</u>,[9] alone should dispel any illusion that a common **convergence** of themes among the canonical commentary tradition implies any common agreement on the manner of the **coherence** of Bonhoeffer's theology. As Andre Dumas concurs, in the face of the kaleidoscopic 'legacy of Bonhoeffer', even today "Barth's question is unavoidable: did this 'impulsive young thinker' really have a systematic point of view if his readers can organize his thought into so many contradictory systems?"[10]

Bonhoeffer's early proposals concerning theological method, this study argues, did have a coherent, although a deliberately un-systematic, point of view. Its dynamism came from his attempt to mediate the richness of both the transcendental tradition of **dialectics** and that of the revolutionary Barthian **theology of otherness.** For all his indebtedness to Kierkegaard and Barth, Bonhoeffer never envisioned that theology could dissociate itself from the tradition of western Enlightenment criticism, particularly as expressed in the **dialectical** conceptuality of that transcendental philosophy "which Kant and idealism handed down to theology."[11] "Sapere aude! 'Have courage to use your own reason!'," Kant had written in his essay, "What is Enlightenment?" "That is the motto of enlightenment," which declares the possibility of "man's release from his self-incurred tutelage."[12] A commitment to these Enlightenment ideals of rationality and freedom not only gave implicit structure to Bonhoeffer's early, methodological proposals in <u>Sanctorum Communio</u> and <u>Act and Being</u>. It also continued to provide increasingly explicit shape to his later ethical formulations, as seen in the second draft for the fragmentary <u>Ethics</u>.

> Intellectual honesty in all things, including questions of belief, was the great achievement of emancipated reason and it has ever since been one of the indispensable moral requirements of western man. Contempt for the age of rationalism is a suspicious sign of failure to feel the need for truthfulness. If intellectual honesty is not the last word that is to be said about things, and if intellectual clarity is often achieved at the expense of insight into reality, this can still never again exempt us from the inner obligation to make clean and honest use of reason.[13]

Bonhoeffer's affirmation of such critical 'liberality'[14] was consistently at the center of his entire theological enterprise.

And yet Bonhoeffer's early allegiances lay equally with that **theology of otherness,** of the non-identity of God and humanity, which Bonhoeffer had inherited from the Lutheran notion of the paradox of the hidden and revealed God--as filtered through Kierkegaard and deeply influenced by the revelational theology of Barth. In fact it was precisely the 'Barthian' issue of the need for a conceptuality adequate to the theological category of **revelation** which originally posed for Bonhoeffer the inescapability of confronting the problematic relationship between transcendental philosophy's and theology's treatments of 'otherness'.

Bonhoeffer stated the sharpest possible formulation of the problem in his essays, "Concerning the Christian Idea of God" and "The Theology of Crisis and its Attitude Toward Philosophy and Science,"[15] both of which were written in 1931 when Bonhoeffer was a student at Union Theological Seminary in New York. They both carry the tone of an apology for the at that time largely unknown position of Barth, in a climate which Bonhoeffer found overwhelmingly and uncritically theologically-liberal. Yet the points being made, however overstated for effect, reflect the cardinal concerns of Bonhoeffer throughout the entire period with which we are concerned in this study.

First, Bonhoeffer charges, the liberal legacy of idealism is a conception of thought as "in itself a closed circle," which "does violence to reality, pulling it into the circle of the ego," since "thinking always means system and system excludes reality."[16] In idealism,

> there are no limits for the ego; its power and its claim are boundless; it is its own standard. Here all transcendence is pulled into the circle of the creative ego... Man knows himself immediately by the act of the coming of the ego to itself....[17]

Second, according to Bonhoeffer, idealism's premises thereby reflect the theological understanding of the sinfulness of the human being after the fall. Fallen humanity "refers everything to himself, puts himself in the center of the world, does violence to reality, makes himself God, and God and the other man his creatures."[18] In the "essential boundlessness of thinking, in its claim to be a closed system, in its egocentricity," Bonhoeffer sees "a philosophical affirmation of the theological insight of the Reformers, which they expressed in terms of the cor curvum in se, corruptio mentis. Man in statu corruptionis is indeed alone, he is his own creator and lord, he is indeed the center of his world of sin."[19]

Third, such thinking is therefore incapable of conceiving that "the Christian messages comes: entirely from outside of the world of sin God Himself came in Jesus Christ."[20] The idealist tradition, Bonhoeffer argues in Kierkegaardian fashion, cannot conceive of "God as the absolutely free personality [who] is therefore absolutely

8

transcendent,"[21] and yet who "revealed himself in 'onceness' ... in a historical fact, in a historical personality"[22]--"God's real acting for mankind in history," in Jesus of Nazareth.[23] Since humanity cannot "get outside of the circle of sin" on our own, "revelation in Christ, justification, means breaking ... the circle of sin. ... Since only the revelation in Christ claims to constitute the real outside of man, it implies that it is the only criterion of any revelation."[24]

Fourth what is needed is "a genuine theological epistemology" which, "as thinking per se, ... is not excepted from the pretension and boundlessness of all thinking," but which "knows its own insufficiency and its limitations" and thereby can "leave room for the reality of God..." even in theological thought.[25] What is needed is a form of theological thinking which can affirm the **finitude** of God's "revelation in history,"[26]--"the foolishness of the Christian idea of God, which has been witnessed to by all genuine Christian thinking from Paul, Augustine, Luther, to Kierkegaard and Barth," that "God himself dies and reveals himself in the death of a man, who is condemned as a sinner."[27] And yet such thinking must be able to distinguish between God's finite, **historical** "revelation in hiddenness," and humanity's **sinful** desire for "revelation in openness,"[28] the ironic 'openness' of "the captivity of human thinking within itself"[29] which is the sign of human sinfulness.[30]

Thus for Bonhoeffer, if the idealist resolution of the epistemological tension between subject and object does not know "its own insufficiency and limitations,"[31] then "the idea of revelation must yield an epistemology of its own."[32] Revelation needs a form of thinking which attends both to the 'immediacy' of that historical particularity of revelation, which can "take seriously the ontological category in history."[33] And yet a form is needed which continues to distinguish itself, as thought, from the reality whose presence it mediates. For Bonhoeffer has inherited from Kierkegaard the suspicion that all immediacy <u>per se</u> is paganism. And yet he suspects in the theology of revelation of his mentor, Barth, that mediacy itself has been carried to such an extreme that God is only tangential to history, not ontologically **in** history in graspable, haveable particularity. What sort of thinking, then, can theology be if it would (1) avoid the pitfalls of idealism (2) take account of sin (3) affirm the particularity of revelation in history, and (4) still **be thought**, affirming that "in every theological statement we cannot but use certain general forms of thinking," which "theology has ... in common with philosophy"?

9

This is especially difficult to answer, Bonhoeffer realized, if it is true that even "in accepting a certain philosophical terminology theology becomes indissolubly connected with a whole philosophy."[34]

In formulating his own response to this question, Bonhoeffer takes his clue, clearly, from Barth's own 'Kantianism'. For

> although Barth knows that even [Kant's] philosophy remains in boundlessness, he sees here the attempt of philosophy to criticize itself basically and takes from here the terminology in order to express the eternal crisis of man, which is brought upon him by God in Christ and which is beyond all philosophical grasp.[35]

Bonhoeffer concludes that **for Barth** "there is no Christian philosophy nor philosophical terminology at all."[36] Then, "what according to Barth and his friends," Bonhoeffer asks, "ought to be the task of philosophy?"[37]

Bonhoeffer's response to his own rhetorical question, intentionally or not, is significant because. Coming after his dissertation <u>Act and Being</u>, it provides a revealing clue to his own divergence already from orthodox Barthianism, despite his defense of dialectical theology against its liberal detractors.

> Barth himself has not answered this question sufficiently, **but his friends have thought a great deal about the problem.** Philosophy remains profane science; there **is** no Christian philosophy. But philosophy has to be **critical** philosophy, not **systematic.** And yet since even critical philosophy is bound to be systematic (as we have seen before), philosophy must work in view of this fate. It must try to think truth with regard to the real existence of man and must see that it is itself an expression of the real existence of man and that by its own power it not only cannot save man, but it cannot even be the crisis of man. **By doing so it gives room, as far as it can, for God's revelation, which indeed makes room for itself by itself.**[38]

Our present study is an exploration of Bonhoeffer's attempt to push the transcendental tradition to 'give room, as far as it can, for God's revelation'. He never wavered in his confidence that revelation 'indeed makes room for itself by itself'. But neither did he waver in his sense of the urgency for theology to find for itself a form of conceptuality which is adequate to these twin demands. What was needed, Bonhoeffer will argue, is a form of thinking that takes seriously philosophy's own attempt to surmount its intrinsic tendencies towards system, towards totality. Theology requires a form of thinking capable of realizing transcendental philosophy's own attempts to be **critical** rather than **systematic**, its attempts to articulate a genuine dialectics of otherness.

Thus, despite the fact that Bonhoeffer was motivated predominantly by this nexus of concerns raised from within the tradition of the **theology of otherness**, the concerns of transcendental **dialectics** were not thereby simply obviated for him. Rather, theology itself raised the need for a critical evaluation of the extent to which the transcendental tradition could and could not assist the theological enterprise in its own proper work. For Bonhoeffer, a conceptuality adequate to theology's own investments in the problems of **sociality** and **ethics** would be possible only on the basis of a renewed dialogue with and critique of the transcendental tradition of **epistemology**.

If theology, Bonhoeffer felt, were to find a dialectical conception of otherness adequate to its own intrinsic criteria, it could do so only by engaging, not avoiding, idealism's claim to have resolved 'otherness' itself into a comprehensive **systematic totality**. Thus, a theology in the manner of Bonhoeffer must demonstrate its ability to articulate meaningfully its own claims for heterogeneity and otherness, all the while resisting falling back into the very dualistic metaphysics against which idealism and liberal theology had so courageously fought. It must be able to state the extent to which it can or cannot affirm transcendental epistemology as the paradigm for that theological thought which remembers the sociality of the other, the ethics of difference.

B. Philosophical Presuppositions
Concerning Epistemology and Dialectics

Bonhoeffer and Adorno each sought to understand the potential for a 'critical dialectical method'. They did so by means of an 'archaeological' inquiry into the dominance in theology and philosophy, at least since Kant's Critique of Pure Reason, of the epistemological, subject--object paradigm.[39] This second section of Chapter One rehearses the topology of the post-Kantian landscape, not

11

as an exercise in the history of ideas, but rather for the sake of recalling the specific conceptual arena in which the methodological proposals of Act and Being and Negative Dialectics are to be interpreted. For these two works each point towards a form of renewed 'Kantian critique' of the predominance of those particular dialectical methods which have developed since Hegel. And this latter tradition of 'dialectic' in turn can be understood only within the context of its appropriation of and argument against the subject-object paradigm of Kant's epistemology.

This section is organized by six presuppositions which, the present study will argue, Bonhoeffer and Adorno share concerning the 'modern' exemplary status of epistemology. The first three concern the origin and terms of the discussion; of these three the first two are now commonplaces. (1) The epistemological model came to dominate contemporary reflection by way of certain specific developments in the transcendental philosophical tradition which originated with Immanuel Kant. (2) Since the epistemology of Kant, there has developed a growing consensus that it is impossible to deny some manner of priority for the role of the subject in whatever can be known of 'reality'. The third presupposition is not only more controversial, but more central to both Bonhoeffer and Adorno. (3) As signaled by Kant's intractable retention of the notion of the thing-in-itself, there has remained a recalcitrant sense of the antinomy of reality, a problematic duality, which would retain not only the integrity of the subject but of the **object** as well.

The second set of common presuppositions concern the ambivalence among post-Kantians over the implications of this lingering, apparent dichotomy for methodology per se. Again, two of these are more familiar, and less debatable, observations than the final point. (4) Since Kant, subjectivity and objectivity have been interpreted increasingly in terms of the quality of that **relationship** in which they are mutually involved. (5) The future viability of the tradition of post-Kantian criticism increasingly came to be understood as a matter of the fate of the subject-object relationship understood precisely as **dialectic.** (6) Finally, in the matter of method both philosophy and theology have taken one or the other of two broad tactics, which we shall initially designate as the 'Hegelian' or the 'Kantian', by which to approach the future of dialectic--as incipient totality or as destined duality, as fundamentally a dialectic of **identity** or as dialectic of **difference.**

12

The significance of the similarities between the method and style of the theology of Bonhoeffer and those of the philosophy of Adorno--as exemplified in Act and Being and Negative Dialectics, respectively--cannot be understood outside the context of twentieth century theology's inheritance of just this six-fold legacy from transcendental epistemology. This is not to suggest that we can 'reduce' either the influences upon, nor the significance of, the work of Bonhoeffer and Adorno to their epistemological concerns. The present study argues to the contrary that an inquiry into the status of the epistemological paradigm in Act and Being and Negative Dialectics serves to enrich our ability to understand **not only** the context--intellectual, social and cultural--within which their thought was nourished and to which it was addressed, **but also** the method of thought and expression which they believed to be adequate both to the exigencies of their own times and to the tasks of thinking to come.

1. The Epistemological Paradigm as Transcendental Philosophy

The dialectic of subject and object is so integral to the very fabric of contemporary theology and philosophy that this epistemological paradigm obtrudes into even those re-visionings of methodology whose goal is either to overcome it or to deny it as a fundamental problem.[40] Yet because this so-called 'cartesian' legacy, however much maligned, is so ingrained in modern theology, its very everydayness breeds a neglect of the more precise nature of this distinctive hallmark of theology's 'modernity'.

Therefore, James Brown's perceptive reminder in his Croall Lectures at the University of Edinburgh at mid-century is still instructive for theology approaching century's end. Despite a long line of conceptual dualities stretching back to the pre-Socratics, Brown reminds us, substantively as well as "terminologically the current usage of Subject and Object is surprisingly modern, deriving from the technicalities of the Kantian critical philosophy."[41] As he explains,

> if the immanent philosophy of language has always implied this distinction and relation of Subject and Object; if the systems of ancient Greece and western Europe have all along worked with some consciousness of this fundamental structure of human thought; if it

appears as the substance of the problem which engaged reflection from Descartes' distinction of thinking and material substance down to Hume; still it was only in Kant that the modern formulation of the relation clearly emerged and that the terminology in which we still discuss the problems of the relationship was fixed.[42]

Bonhoeffer's and Adorno's work stands as an invitation to a **continued** reflection upon a tradition which tends to be merely accepted as a commonplace, rather than as an enduring challenge to theological and philosophical reflection.

Bonhoeffer, therefore, centered his methodological deliberations in Act and Being on "theology's legacy from Kant and idealism," understood precisely "als Problem der Erkenntnistheorie," as the problem of epistemology.[43] His very terms **Act** and **Being** are to be understood from the outset on the model of transcendental epistemology's **Subject** and **Object,** his study inquiring into the sufficiency or insufficiency for theology of this epistemological paradigm. Likewise, Adorno's Negative Dialectics provides a more extended commentary on the methodological implications of just this originally **Kantian** epistemological problematic, inquiring into the fate of the relation of subject and object in the century following Hegel. Taken together, the Kantian critical statement of the **duality** of subject and object and the idealist search for coherent **totality** define the tensive parameters of what we mean in this study by the 'transcendental tradition'.

2. The Priority of the Subject

Contrasted with the passive knower of Scholastic and post-Scholastic naive realisms, and the skeptical proposals from Descartes to Hume to limit knowledge to induction from particular sense impressions, Kant's own epistemological subject was 'critical', first off, as we now take for granted, precisely in its all-pervasive activity. He

formulates a central problem of modern philosophy by refusing to accept the world as something that has arisen independently of the knowing subject. For Kant, a radical divorce and independence of the subject that knows

14

from the object that is known entails an illusion.[44]

Kant had proposed that philosophy disenchant itself,
following "the lines of Copernicus' primary hypothesis,"
whereby the astronomer had "dared, in a manner contradictory of the senses, but yet true, to seek the observed movements [of the planets], not in the heavenly
bodies, but in the spectator." Philosophically this involved a "new method of thought, namely, that we can
know a priori of things only what we ourselves put into
them," versus the "merely random groping" of a skeptical
empiricism whose mind-as-the-mirror-of-nature was unable to inquire into the conditions of its own possibility.[45] To this extent, even from the time of Kant's
own Critique of Pure Reason, the notion of the constitutive subject proscribed any 'pre-critical', completely
'naive', or not subjectively mediated experience of reality. The perceived unity of reality is the fulfillment of
a 'subjective' exigency, for reality is only "apprehended
in a mediated fashion by means of a priori categories of
the mind."[46]

However, the Kantian subject is an activity-within-
limits. It is indeed constitutive of "the necessary conditions for making judgments about reality."[47] But the
'transcendental I', without whose synthetic function,
"there could be no self-consciousness (no 'memory of
experience') and thus no knowledge of an object as an
object," is opaque to its own gaze; it can never itself be
made an object of knowledge.

This is the point where Kant's transcendental
deduction must stop; all that can be known
about transcendental apperception is that it is
the fundamental logical condition of knowledge
and expresses the unity of consciousness.[48]

The subject's radical activity mediates even its own
ability to articulate definitively its constitutive function.
As Paul Ricoeur has noted, the subjective unity of reality
"...is wholly exhausted in the task of bringing about
objectivity; for itself the imaginative synthesis is
obscure."[49]

Theologians, as did most continental thinkers in the
post-Kantian era, pursued this paradigm of subjective
exigency-within-limits along three distinct lines, each of
which understood itself to be faithful to Kant. Yet
these three approaches had in common some form of an
attempt to transcend the Kantian sense of 'limits', the

15

constraints of the subject-object epistemological duality of speculative reason. And this led in turn to the need to clarify the significance of Kant's distinction between theoretical and practical reason itself, between "the epistemologically active subject (in the Critique of Pure Reason) and the ethically, practically active subject (in the Critique of Practical Reason)."[50]

First, what has been called a right-wing Kantianism, a broadly 'ethicist' approach, attempted to accept "both the Kantian critique of theoretical reason and the adoption of the moral [focus of the Critique of Practical Reason] as the basis for proceeding" in matters religious --a tactic "which was to be taken up most dramatically in the Ritschlian school."[51] In this effort, Kant's critique of pure speculative reason was seen to apply in matters of 'speculative' reason, but simply not to apply to the realm of religious experience, which was understood as altogether a matter of practical reason and thus to involve no metaphysical claims whatsoever. Thus the Kantian 'limits' and 'constraints' on the theoretical subject were 'overcome' by denying the theoretical subject any sway in matters religious, which were rather the concern of the **practically** active subject.

Second, a broadly 'romanticist' tactic attempted to overcome the anti-metaphysical intention of Kant's definition of the inherent duality of 'experience', by endeavoring "to enlarge the category of direct experience by turning to Gefuhl (Schleiermacher) or Ahnung (deWette), or by finding in a fuller 'reason' the possibility of knowing the spiritual order (Coleridge)."[52] Advocates of this option argued that "the 'subject' of the Critique of Pure Reason is merely the theoretic, knowing subject, not the concrete, whole subject in whom knowing and acting, thinking and existing, are dialectically united."[53] Thus the Critique of Pure Reason was itself criticized for its too restrictive definition of experience. The alternative was to attempt to invalidate Kant's very definition of experience by means of a broader definition of subjectivity itself. Thus in the romanticist tradition, as in the ethicist tradition, there eventuated, on the one hand, a chastened significance of the **epistemological** subject for theology, and on the other hand, a reorientation of theology in a different but equally subjective fashion--but with the emphasis on the **practical,** non-epistemological subject.

Third, in the **idealist** reactions against the Kantian philosophy, with which our study is primarily concerned, Kant's **epistemology itself** was radicalized by the emer-

16

gence of a concept of the total 'effective' priority of the subject in **all** possible reality--religious as well as epistemological. The limits of Kantian **understanding** [Verstand] were overcome by the idealists' Reason [Vernunft]. Despite the ensuing plethora of nuanced and mutually-exclusive interpretations of such 'subjectivity', from Fichte and Schelling onward, the watchword of post-Kantian reflection for more than a century is aptly suggested by Hegel's assertion in the Phenomenology, that "essentially the True is Subject."[54]

The idealist position radicalized Kant in **beginning** with the assumption of a single 'subjectivity', whose activity was constitutive of **all** possible realms of human experience. Hegel's vision of "the epistemological subject is [of] a dynamically unfolding phenomenological movement, which is consciousness traveling the road of experience,"[55] broad and complete. Hegel thereby united in the process of reflection the theoretical and practical moments in Kant's view of reason--a "knowing self of consciousness and an acting self of free will"--now thought of "as a simultaneously moral and knowing subject."[56] The ultimacy of the Kantian 'limits' and constraints on the finite subject were thus softened and finally eliminated, for finitude itself came to be interpreted as a movement in an infinitely unfolding subject.

The result for post-Kantian **theology,** as Claude Welch has argued, was that in one form or another from Schleiermacher forward it "now had to start from, to articulate, and to interpret a subjective view of the religious object."[57] Thus even the most polemical detractors of idealism, such as Kierkegaard, stated their self-consciously anti-idealist positions with ironically and inescapably 'idealist' language: "Subjectivity is the truth."[58]

3. The Recalcitrance of the Object

Despite this pervasive, though diverse, tendency to prioritize the subject, a concomitant objectivity--a recalcitrant sense of 'otherness' or non-subjectivity--had remained integral to the critical enterprise. All human experience for Kant was **a priori** in that the subject's categories were presupposed by any knowledge that comes about. It was **synthetic** in that experience does 'come about' by the subject's synthesizing the necessary orientation towards nonconceptual reality ('objectivity) and the necessary conditions or categories which that orientation presupposes in order to occur ('subjectivity').

The challenge lay in articulating this 'orientation towards reality' in a manner consistent with the Kantian subject's radical activity, that is to say, without simply lapsing back into a pre-Kantian notion of objectivity.

Yet to ignore the 'orientation towards reality', the subjective **receptivity** to extra-subjective 'otherness', according to Kant, is to engage uncritically in **metaphysics:** that unjustified enterprise "which soars far above the teachings of experience, and in which reason is indeed meant to be its own pupil." For "metaphysics rests on concepts alone."[59]   Kant was thus led into the position of maintaining **both** that reflection is never able to "transcend the limits of possible experience," so that "knowledge has to do only with appearances," **and** that, integral to the critical nature of the epistemological paradigm, we must continue to speak of "the thing in itself as indeed real per se, but as not known by us."[60]

The status and function of the thing-in-itself served as a watershed for the entire subsequent transcendental tradition's understanding of objectivity.   The manner in which the subsequent post-Kantian tradition dealt with Kant's caveats concerning **objectivity** proved to be as revolutionary as Kant's own treatment of the issue of **subjectivity.**   Indeed one's entire interpretation of the history of philosophy since Kant can be understood to hinge on whether and in what way one can continue to speak of any 'object' that retains an integrity that 'transcends' the activity of the post-Kantian subject.   The corollary to the increasing priority of the subject had been an increasing, apparent marginality of the Kantian sense of the **limits** of experience--his sense of the equiprimordiality of the **object.**   The Ding an sich was crucial because it forced philosophy to come clean, whether intentionally or unintentionally, with regards to the 'metaphysical' implications of its 'epistemological' presuppositions.   After Kant it was impossibly naive to **presuppose** positive metaphysical foundations for critical knowledge.   The crucial question, rather, was that of what ontological inferences, if any, concerning objectivity could be drawn from critical subjectivity itself.

There was clearly a certain necessary **'ontological** restraint' implied in Kant's own critical stance.   The thing-in-itself implies an unresolvable ontological urge, distinct from the function of the transcendental object-- which provided for the formal **unity** of the indeterminate object of knowledge--or from the function of the noumenon understood in a negative sense--which provided for the **epistemological limit** of sensibility and understanding only to phenomena. In Paul Tillich's terms, the thing-in-itself is a boundary concept of a different sort from that of the limits of knowledge. It implies a nascent sense of the **ontological** boundaries of experience, for "it limits the identity of subject and object, of unity and manifoldness. Not all that is objective has been brought into the internality of the subject. Not all of the manifold has been grasped in the unity of the synthesis."[61] Being 'transcends' thought, but that transcendence can never be completely comprehended by finite rationality, and is thus ineluctably negative.

Understood in terms of the function of the thing-in-itself, the Kantian notion of objectivity held unresolved, 'unknowable', and radically 'open' the finite encounter with otherness.[62] P. Christopher Smith concurs that "there is an ontological, not just logical negation here," for "that which is present [appearance] **is** fundamentally (gleichurspruenglich) with that which is not [things-in-themselves]."[63] The thing-in-itself is the 'known-object' precisely in its most radically 'critical' mode of recession into its opaque integrity--its presence precisely as absence. The thing-in-itself is 'impossible' to knowledge, but expresses the inescapable urge towards the 'possibility' of the ontological reality of the thing-in-itself--within the constraints of the finitude of knowledge.[64]

Indeed, it was precisely this critical function of the thing-in-itself against which Hegel reacted in the Phenomenology of Spirit. Kant and Hegel parted company most significantly not concerning their particular epistemologies, but concerning the ontological and metaphysical conclusions which can be drawn from the 'transcendental' or 'critical' enterprise itself, of which the distinction between the appearance and the thing-in-itself had become the crucial symptom.

This distinction between appearance and thing-in-itself was just what idealists such as Fichte and then Schelling argued must be overcome. Yet even so, Fichte, and then Hegel himself, made clear the distinction between their own emphasis on 'subjectivity' and any 'absolute' idealism, such as that of Schelling, which would resolve the object completely into the subject. As Hegel remarked against the latter,

> to pit this single insight, that in the Absolute everything is the same, against the full body of articulated cognition, ... to palm off its Absolute as the night in which, as the saying

goes, all cows are black--this is cognition naively reduced to vacuity.[65]

Particularly in the cases of Fichte and Hegel, there was no intention to obliterate objectivity. They intended only to argue for a particular reading of the dominance of 'subjectivity' for the constitution of 'objective' reality --a dominance by which the **obduracy** of the object would yield to the **familiarity** offered by subjective intelligibility, in which would become evident the significance of **identity** for **difference,** rather than, as for Kant, vice versa.

4. Subject and Object as Relation

Thus in the transcendental tradition itself, there was never a debate concerning the **terms** of the discussion itself, that is to say, **whether** or not both subject and object were to be retained at the heart of transcendental conceptuality. Rather, the debate concerned **how** they were understood to be related, and thus the nature of the **relationship** itself.

Kant himself had offered the architectonic of this emphasis upon **relationality** by means of his doubly-critical notion of objectivity. **On the one hand,** Kant asserted "that the 'object of thought' can be viewed as something creatively conditioned by categories of the understanding or consciousness," whereby "the object becomes a mediated construct of the subject."[66] But Kant had implied, **on the other hand,** through the retention of the function of the thing-in-itself, that 'constitutive subjectivity' can be viewed only as the condition of the possibility of knowledge of reality, **which the subject cannot totally (ontologically) comprehend.** Thus the possibility is opened to interpret Kant's subject as in a sense mediated by the object-serving-as-limit to the ontological pretensions of constitutive subjectivity. Subject and object are not by any means isolated terms, but rather state the boundaries of a relationship.

A common thread in the idealism after Kant was the attempt to determine the ontological significance of just this Kantian epistemological premise that subject and object exist "**in a unique kind of relation which is constituted by their togetherness, in which each implies the other.**"[67] The limits of the Kantian duality came to be questioned from the perspective of the 'relational' coherence, or identity, of the reality which they circumscribed. For in Gadamer's words,

> no one knew better than did German idealism that consciousness and its object are not two separated worlds. It even found a word for it by coining the term 'philosophy of identity'. It showed that consciousness and object are in fact only two sides that belong together and that any bifurcation into pure subject and pure objectivity is a dogmatism.[68]

Whereas Kant had criticized as 'metaphysical' any attempt to sidestep the **duality** of the epistemological paradigm, the subsequent 'idealist' approach criticized any philosophical attempt that could not inquire into the origin of its own epistemological premise that "Subject and Object are poles of a **relation,** and **either, taken by itself, is an abstraction.**"[69] Active subjectivity and objective reality, "thought and being[,] are together from the beginning."[70]

Thus as Paul Tillich has noted, virtually "the whole history of epistemology" **since** Kant has been "a cognitive attempt to bridge this [subject-object] split by showing the ultimate unity of subject and object, either by annihilating one side of the gap for the sake of the other or by establishing a uniting principle which contains both of them."[71] The tactical engagements with the Kantian tradition of epistemology thus have not tended to radicalize Kant's epistemological paradigm, or the concomitant notion of truth as the **correspondence** between subject and object. Rather they have evidenced an inclination to collapse the subject-object duality, if not a desire to abolish altogether a suspected 'metaphysical' "dualism of thought and being in its Kantian form." Post-Kantian approaches thereby have intended to "assert in some fashion an original and abiding togetherness of thought and being."[72] Thus they have attempted an explication of the nature of truth as the systematic, mutual **coherence** of subject and object.

The transcendental tradition after Kant thereby became preoccupied increasingly, that is to say, with just those 'metaphysical' implications of Kant's intentionally 'epistemological' assertion that all knowledge involves the appearance of an object to a subject. The idealist tradition cannot be understood merely as a reductionist, 'subjectivist' approach. Rather, it inquired into the possibility that reason, Vernunft, can penetrate the very process of the constitution of the epistemological duality

21

itself--object coming to be in relation to subject--thereby providing both the richest and most coherent, thus most concrete, possible 'objectivity'.

Increasingly, we can conclude, the **terms** of the relation--subject and object--have held less significance for philosophy than the **relationship** itself. The restriction of philosophy to a supposedly 'Kantian' inquiry into the correspondence of two separate entities, subject and object, came to be understood as the grossest philosophical error. Truth is rather the coherence of a dynamic relation. Idealism thus worked out concretely its presupposition that "the whole of reality is a totality that is mediated to itself by its relations with its parts, so that the 'whole' itself is a mediated relation."[73] In the words of Hegel's <u>Science of Logic</u>, the whole

> is the whole Relation and the independent totality; but for this very reason it is only a relative term, for that which makes it a totality is precisely its Other, the Parts; and it has its consistence not in itself but in its other.
>
> Thus the Parts are also the whole Relation .... Further, they have this Whole in themselves as their moment.[74]

Thus 'objectivity' came to be intelligible not as the Kantian radical limit, or <u>Grenze</u>, ontological as well as epistemological, but as one moment in the **coherent relation** of subject-and-object, itself open to the inquiry of reason.

For idealism "it is neither the [abstract] whole nor the parts which is ontologically fundamental, but the relations among them."[75] The 'concrete' is the relational. This means that a renewed and more radically 'critical' subjectivity is proposed, one which is understood to be more sufficient because it is more capable of inquiring not only into the metaphysical implications of constitutive subjectivity, but also into the ontological significance of the very coming about of objectivity, which Kant had seen as an intractable and impenetrable limit, impermeable to the subjectivity of pure speculative reason.

The nature of this **relationship itself** has thus been rendered more problematic, not less, by idealism's emphasis upon coherence. The enduring question has been what to make of the fact that even in attempting to overcome the insufficiencies of the Kantian legacy, reflection has remained enmeshed in the framework of the subject and object relationship. From the Hegelian phenomenology to the present we have been bequeathed ever more complex, because more critical, questions, all circumscribed by the language and conceptuality of the relation of subject to object.

5. Criticism and the Future of Dialectics

The transcendental tradition from Kant forward can be interpreted as the continued **search for** rather than the **application of** a new method by which to speak of the totality-of-reality--objectivity as well as subjectivity. The idealist legacy is therefore best understood as the attempt to apply a radicalized 'Kantian' criticism to the inheritance of Kant. **Dialectics** became the name for that critical enterprise after Kant which would question the **need for,** the **attempts toward,** and the **implications of** a method adequate to both subject and object, thought and being. Now both are consciously understood not as a presupposed separation but as a dynamic relationship.

In order to see the radicality and distinctiveness of the idealist position, it is important to remember that Kant, no less than the idealists who later renounced him, had been concerned to pose a criticism of the notion of the 'givenness' of objectivity to the knowing subject, the passive mirror of given reality. The Critique of Pure Reason was itself a refined polemic not just against rationalist metaphysics, but against the empiricist tradition. As Norman Kemp Smith has observed, "in eliminating a priori principles, and appealing exclusively to sense experience," empiricism had removed "all grounds of distinction between inductive inference and custom-bred expectation."[76] The Kantian understanding of 'objects of experience' was a rejection of the assumption that, as Herbert Marcuse has put it, "the unity of reason is but the unity of custom or habit, adhering to the facts but never governing them."[77]

And yet, if **on the one hand,** Kant had attempted to answer the skepticism Hume had tried to show was inherent in empiricism, **on the other hand** he had intended to curb the pretension of a Leibnizian rationalism to penetrate into the very heart of reality. According to the Kantian epistemological paradigm, the noumenal realm left open **in general** the possibility that finite human knowledge was not finally the only mode of knowledge. But the function of the thing-in-itself **in particular** was to focus understanding's attention on the fact that finite

23

knowledge is constrained by an ontological limit within whose bounds such knowledge occurs. Therefore understanding, as well as morality, culture, and history "is inevitably referred to an unknowable Ansich beyond itself,"[78] an inalienable, 'eschatological' limit to the pretensions of constitutive subjective activity.[79]

However, the idealist treatment of the epistemological paradigm of subject and object not only turned the discussion toward the manner of the coherence of their relationship. It also radicalized Kant's agnosticism concerning this coherence as a dynamic, teleological process. According to Hegel, there is no Kantian an sich beyond the movement of consciousness. Yet for Hegel, too, the originating **epistemological** concern was with the status of just such 'objectivity', and the need to understand it 'critically'. "Quite generally," said Hegel, "the familiar just because it is the familiar, is not cognitively understood."[80] As Marcuse paraphrases, "an **immediate** unity of reason and reality never exists,"[81] but is the goal of philosophy.

Thus, in Hegel's words, "of the Absolute it must be said that it is essentially a **result,** that only in the **end** is it what it truly is."[82] As Marcuse rightly concludes, "Hegel's concept of reason thus has a distinctly critical and polemic character. It is opposed to all ready acceptance of the given state of affairs."[83] The "'real' comes to mean not everything that actually exists ... but that which exists in a form concordant with the standards of reason."[84] Hegel attacked Kant's thing-in-itself because it stops thinking **short;** the Ding an sich limits not just error but, according to Hegel, the legitimate freedom of human knowledge to draw ontological conclusions about its own finitude.

Hegel's position was revolutionary because he wished to demonstrate that finitude itself, both as epistemological limit and as ontological constraint for culture and history, is but one moment of a 'final', infinite and absolute knowing. Philosophy, morality and history are not caught in the Kantian eschatological 'betweenness' of subject and object. They exhibit a concrete-methodological **apocalypse**--a 'showing forth' of the constitution of the very thing-in-itself, which 'showing-forth' for Kant was an 'impossibility'.

Kant had been left with an impenetrable finite 'givenness'--an **ontologically** opaque 'otherness' or 'objectivity' which was closed to rational penetration. Thus the only knowledge which appearances could mediate was a knowledge whose metaphysical foundation was thoroughly chastened by the limit-function of the thing-in-itself. Hegel sought to surmount just this Kantian limit-concept through a new method of dialectics. This required that Hegel "reinterpret the epistemological relation of subject and object," seeking an alternative to the Kantian "theory of knowledge which separates," or better, **differentiates,** "knowledge of phenomena from the thing-in-itself"[85] in its function of ontological limit.

Methodologically this meant that Hegel, particularly in the <u>Phenomenology</u>, treated "Kant's synthetic unity of apperception," and the thing-in-itself as well, "not as a given but as something to be demonstrated, and thus as a result rather than a precondition of experience."[86] Thus the issue of dialectic for Hegel addressed the problem of allowing Reason its own proper method, thereby allowing Reason its true Freedom to move toward its proper end, "the **progressive** unfolding of truth."[87] If, as Hegel believed, history had taken a decisive turn with the French Revolution--the turn by which "man came to rely on his mind and dared submit the given reality to the standards of reason"[88]--then the only proper philosophical method was one which could, in Hegel's words, "sink this freedom in the content, letting it move spontaneously of its own nature, by the self as its own self, and then ... contemplate this movement."[89] This took the form, for Hegel, of a <u>post hoc</u> teleological explication of the movement of consciousness, morality, and history. That is to say, as Robert Solomon puts it, "Hegel's divergence from Kant does not consist solely in the scope and primacy which he allotted to teleology, but also in Hegel's insistence that teleological explanation be **demonstrated,"[90]** not limited to a heuristic or regulative value.

To summarize, the Hegelian critical method, dialectics, was "led from epistemology as a categorization of a priori principles to epistemology as a philosophy of history," but now conceived 'apocalyptically' rather than 'eschatologically'.[91] Kant's and Hegel's attitudes toward history are analogous to their understandings of the relationship between epistemology and metaphysics. Kant had firmly believed, in Findlay's words, that "there are and must be aspects of things that we can indeed conceive negatively .... but of which we can never have knowledge."[92] Thus experience, and knowledge of it, was for Kant a duality of appearance/thing-in-itself--historically speaking, the age of enlightenment and the enlightened age. Because of this initial distinction, human knowing must concern itself--if it is to be truly philosophical, scientific--with the preliminary determination of its 'proper conditions'. It must ascertain the 'grounds for the possibility' of knowledge within the bounds of appearances, the bounds of the finitude of history. There resulted a certain Kantian methodological concern with **error,** particularly with regards to determining knowing's proper **limits,** which, however, he did not develop in terms of a positive philosophy of history.

However, in Hegel's opinion, the Kantian philosophy stagnated at the level of prolegomenon.[93]   What in Kant "calls itself fear of error reveals itself rather as fear of the truth."[94]   As Hegel later wrote in his Logic,

> [Kant] demanded a criticism of the faculty of cognition as preliminary to its exercise. ... Unfortunately there soon creeps in the misconception of already knowing before you know--the error of refusing to enter the water until you have learnt to swim. True, indeed, the forms of thought should be subjected to a scrutiny before they are used: yet what is this scrutiny but ipso fact a cognition?[95]

To the contrary, according to Hegel, philosophy must not be construed as the 'avoiding of error'--which is error itself--but rather as a 'working through error'.[96]

For Hegel, despite the appearance of a certain two-sidedness to knowledge, such distinctions as that between appearance and thing-in-itself, when they are drawn, must themselves be drawn within consciousness. Experience [Erfahrung] was to Hegel the **"dialectical** movement which consciousness exercises **on itself** and which affects **both** its knowledge and its object."[97]   Hegel's epochal conclusion, in contrast to the Kantian distinction between appearance and thing-in-itself, was that any an sich, in being known, "becomes something that is the **in-itself** only for consciousness. And this then is the True: the being-for-consciousness of this in-itself."[98] There can be no Ding an sich which is not related to consciousness. The Kantian duality of appearance and thing-in-itself, of speculative and practical-reason, for Hegel evidences an insufficiently conceived rationality.

6. Identity and Difference

In a sense, the debate between Kant and Hegel is over precisely the question of what constitutes error, and its corollaries: the manner in which a 'working through' of error is understood to occur, and the ontological inferences to be drawn from that occurrence. Thus Hegel's divergence from Kant extends beyond formal method. It is a debate rather between competing presuppositions about dialectic understood as radical demystification. And these presuppositions are intimately tied to competing understandings of the ontological significance of the finitude of reality--as either demanding **difference,** or duality, or as making possible, if not reflecting, totality, the **identity** of reality. It is a matter of the ontological presuppositions each assumed concerning the relationship of the method of thought to the whole of reality.

The "legacy of Kant and idealism" to modern theology has been the unresolved question of whether or not the **Kantian** emphasis on the irreducible duality of the epistemological paradigm has indeed been once and for all exposed as error and surpassed by the **idealist** relational proposals concerning the totality of the mutual coherence of subject and object. Hegel proposed, in sharp contrast to the intractable duality of Kant, that "consciousness will arrive at a point at which it **gets rid** of its semblance of being burdened with something alien, with what is only for it, and some sort of 'other', at a point where appearance becomes identical with essence..."99

For Hegel, the subjective constitution or mediation of the object is "a **becoming-other** that has to be taken back..."100 Rather than proving to be an impenetrable ontological limit designating the duality of thought and being, the limit-as-**negativity** of the thing-in-itself is shown by idealism to be thought's **own** limit. In encountering the negativity of the 'other', consciousness "is something that goes beyond itself, and since these limits are its own, it is something that goes beyond **itself.** ... Thus consciousness suffers this violence at its own hands: it spoils its limited satisfaction."101 Even the negative, 'eschatological' limit encountered by consciousness can be shown to be but a moment in a 'realized eschatology' or 'apocalypse', a showing-forth of being, morality, history.

According to Hegel, the defect, the error, in any subject-object relational duality such as Kant's is that the disparity [ungleichheit] "which exists in consciousness between the 'I' and the substance which is its object" has not been comprehended as "the disparity of the substance with itself." This is what Hegel has in mind when he continues to say that this substance has not shown

27

itself "to be essentially Subject."[102]   Until consciousness
comprehends this, Spirit has not yet made "its existence
identical with its essence"--it is not "absolutely mediated."[103]   It is in this sense that one can summarize
Hegel's conclusion by saying that "absolute knowledge is
only attained when subject and object become totally
identical and the opposition between knowing and all
objecthood is superseded."[104] "No longer is the object
par excellence (the Ding an sich) beyond the reach of
the knowing and experiencing subject. The principle
which unifies this relation is **thought,** which becomes for
Hegel both the function of the knowing subject and the
governing nucleus of the reality of the object."[105]

The process of this "education of consciousness
itself to the standpoint of Science" is what Hegel calls
Bildung,[106] In Findley's words, for philosophy the result
is that "the teleological view of objectivity ... will
prove, on a sufficiently deep examination, to be so wholly appeasing and satisfying that no shadow of the hidden
or inexplicable will remain to haunt us."[107]   The Hegelian 'education' of the subject is radical vis a vis Kant in
that it insists "on demonstrating the formative process of
reflection leading up to the confrontation of consciousness with the object," even the Ding an sich, "while
Kant takes this confrontation as his starting point."[108]

For Kant the thing-in-itself served to preserve the
'otherness' and 'difference' necessary for the freedom of
a relation-between-terms to exist. For Hegel the thing-
in-itself only serves to preserve a conformism to the
'givenness of otherness' which is itself intolerable to the
Hegelian rational ideal of freedom. "Thus Hegel's recovery of 'totality' not only expands the limits of knowledge
but offers a view of reality where the 'concrete' is the
mediated whole of relations and the 'abstract' is the
immediate specificity of separated parts of the whole."[109]

And yet, ironically, the Hegelian totality is most
problematic in Kantian eyes precisely at the point that
freedom becomes an issue. For Hegel the paramount
virtue of rationality is its freedom to bring about the
comprehension of its own sufficiency to all of reality.
Thus the Kantian thing-in-itself had to be de-constructed, shown to be a moment in the larger process of rea-
son-coming-to-itself. Yet once the limit-quality of the
thing-in-itself has become comprehended within the negativity of the dialectic of reason itself, method and knowledge take on for Hegel a curiously 'positivist' posture as
"contemplative and passive, or phenomenological in the
sense of the reflective reconstruction of experience."

They are deceptive precisely in the apparent 'movement' of the dialectical process and the immense detail which that process brings to light.[110]   Warren's concluding remarks on Hegel are worth quoting in full

> Here Hegel seems to retreat behind Kant in terms of a concrete dialectic of subject and object, for the Hegelian human subject never gives order to the formless or in any way 'deforms' Being in the process of knowing. Knowledge is a becoming self-conscious and manifestation of the movement of Logos already resident in the world. Rationality is never really put in the world by the knowing subject.   Spirit as absolute subject-substance is dialectical, but at the level of human inquiry and exposition the dialectic deflates.   The dialectic becomes description of the dialectical structure of Being and the self-realization of spirit.   ...   In this sense, the human mind for Hegel becomes less powerful and creative than it was for Kant, albeit for Kant it operated in a much more limited realm.[111]

The Kantian suspects that there 'is' no longer any radical contingency, finitude--no 'otherness' to challenge the fundamental identity of thought and being, understood as the totality of their adequacy to each other.

In its 'freedom from' the apparent heteronomy of the object, thought of not only as appearance but as thing-in-itself, Hegel's phenomenology of totality risks being finally 'freedom for' nothing but itself and its own movement.

> The True is the whole.   But the whole is nothing other than the essence consummating itself through its development.   Of the Absolute it must be said that it is essentially a **result,** that only in the **end** is it what it truly is; and that precisely in this consists its nature, viz. to be actual, subject, the spontaneous becoming of itself.[112]

The Kantian thing-in-itself had sought to preserve just that **double** freedom which Hegel challenges--**from** heteronomy, but **for** the contingency of radical encounter with otherness.   The richness and coherence of absolute knowledge--concrete reality--are for Kantian criticism the errant, illusory result of the loss of an adequate engagement with finite, contingent reality.   Kant's object is always 'other' than thinking. It is never, as Hegel would later argue, heteronomously 'free from' reason, but, in a manner that fundamentally challenges idealism, is 'free for' that being to which thought is ever related, but which thought cannot comprehend--that which is genuinely ambiguous and plural. Dialectic beyond the pale of Kant risks therefore becoming no longer a **critical method** but an affirmative **metaphysic** which predetermines all inquiry.

Heidegger was to echo the Kantian concern when he asked

> What is the significance of the struggle initiated in German idealism against the 'thing in itself' except a growing forgetfulness of what Kant had won, namely, the knowledge that the intrinsic possibility and necessity of metaphysics, i.e. its essence, are, at bottom, sustained and maintained by the original development and searching study of the problem of finitude?[113]

But clearly for the Hegelian Identitaetsphilosophie, understood as the history, the Bildung, of thought and being, "the standpoint of consciousness which knows objects in their antithesis to itself, and itself in antithesis to them, is for Science the antithesis of its own standpoint."[114] As Warren summarizes the Kantian anxiety, "any epistemological dialectic is resolved into ontological dialectic, to which knowledge surrenders, and which it can only describe."[115]

Thus, at least with regard to the enduring methodological significance of the epistemological paradigm following idealism, the present study proposes to construe the options for reflection as following either a broadly 'Kantian' or a broadly 'Hegelian' tactic. Either thought exhibits an ineluctable urge or desire towards an 'otherness' which it presupposes but cannot comprehend within itself. Or thought is the totality of subject and object, which comprehends all possible experience and which all possible dualities presuppose. Either subject and object, thought and being, are conceived as duality--as difference--or as totality--as identity. Either methodology exacerbates the duality for the sake of a relationship between authentically plural terms, or methodology heals the bifurcation for the sake of a therapeutic wholeness.

The question is not **whether** a 'critical mediation' of subject and object is superior to either empiricist or

rationalist immediacy or presence. The question is **which**
understanding of the nature of dialectical mediation is
more sufficient to reality. Is it the Kantian sense for
epistemological 'tragedy'--the retained concealment and
absence of the thing-in-itself, and thus the inability to
overcome a constitutive duality? Or is it the Hegelian
sense for a sort of phenomenological 'sorcery'--the ultimate revealment and bringing-to-presence of a 'coherent' and 'concrete' totality? As Derrida has commented,

> [For Hegel] the ... **relevance** of man is his
> <u>telos</u> ... The unity of these two **ends** of man,
> the unity of his death, his completion, his
> accomplishment, is enveloped in the Greek
> thinking of <u>telos</u>... Such a discourse, in Hegel
> as in the entirety of metaphysics, indissociably
> coordinates teleology with an eschatology, a
> theology, and an ontology. **The thinking of
> the end of man, therefore, is always already
> prescribed in metaphysics, in the thinking of
> the truth of man.** What is difficult to think
> today is an end of man which would not be
> organized by a dialectics of truth and negativ-
> ity, an end of man which would not be a
> teleology in the first person plural.[116]

Kant criticized the immediacy of identity for the sake of
articulating the mutually-mediated antinomies at the
heart of finitude. Hegel criticized the "apparent opposition of subject and object at our lower, more immediate
forms of experience"[117] for the sake of the totality at
the end of a concretely mediated reality. Kant argued
for the critical function of 'difference', against the
metaphysical pretensions to totality. Hegel argued for
the critical function of 'identity', against given-dualities
which disallow thought the freedom to understand itself
as "profoundly ontological as well as epistemological."[118]
The choice has become one between the critical search
for an **open** or for a **closed** dialectic. Do we facilitate a
sustained, if not exacerbated difference--with the risk
that, as Hegel charged, fear of error turns into fear of
the truth? Or do we encourage the total reconciliation
of thought and being, a constitutional, even if teleological, identity--with the risk that the fear of un-ra-
tionalized reality turns into a suspicion, if not elimination, of all genuine otherness?

31

C. Context: Historical, Cultural, Biographical

1. The Historical Fate of Dialectic after Hegel

Historically speaking, after the peak of Hegelian philosophy, the choice of one's conceptual mentors was indeed between **either of these forms of dialectic** and some form of **non-dialectical** vision of reality.[119] The argument, more often than not, was between (a) those who retained any significant role whatsoever for Kant's critical, theoretical distinctions in reality--the fate of which, epistemology had forced philosophy to decide--and (b) those who saw the unresolved antinomies of the subject-object paradigm of epistemology as but an abstract denial or avoidance of the pressing concrete realities of the age.

Thus, **on the one hand,** a critical-dialectical approach momentarily prevailed along a wide spectrum of thinkers. This included theologians such as P. K. Marheineke and A. E. Biedermann who attempted varieties of 'conservative', or Right-wing appropriations of Hegel, which yet retained the dialectic for distinctly theological purposes.[120] Also there were increasingly those philosophers like Rudolf Hermann Lotze (a central influence, later, on the liberal theologian, Albrecht Ritschl) who, after flirtations with both idealist and materialist positions, argued "against both Hegelianism and materialism," on the basis of "an epistemological skepticism of Kantian provenance."[121] In addition, the radical or so called Left-wing Hegelians, from Feuerbach to Marx and Engels, began to transform idealism towards a materialism, which was yet **dialectical**-materialism in that it did not renounce the subject, but rather began to put the subject at the service of the object, rather than vice versa.[122] In each of these cases, the critical tradition from Kant to Hegel was modified, sometimes in dramatic fashion. Yet an affirmation of the critical agenda and some form of dialectical method remained normative to the philosophical task.

On the other hand, as early as the 1850's, for many scholars in diverse fields, this broad legacy of "idealism, the strongest of German traditions, seemed in full retreat," gradually bringing into question the very foundation of the critical dialectics, "the rationality of the real"--"faith in the progress of reason."[123] Prominent and respected scientists such as Hermann von Helmholtz (1821-1894) "vigorously rejected metaphysics but extolled philosophy as an ancilla to science."[124] **Non**-dialectical forms of materialism, such as can be seen, for example, in Ernst Haeckel's <u>God-Nature, Studies in Monistic Religion</u>, began during the same time to move more dramatically and self-consciously against the epistemological premises of the Kantian dualities and the Hegelian dialectics, offering a non-relational or monistic resolution that lacked the subtlety or richness of either the Kantian antinomies or the Hegelian relational approach.[125] Likewise 'phenomenalism' such as that of Ernst Mach's <u>Knowledge and Error</u> attempted to get behind and subvert the subject-object epistemological tension, which was itself seen as the root of the error of metaphysics. From Auguste Comte's <u>Course of Positive Philosophy</u> at mid-nineteenth century--through Hans Vaihinger's <u>The Philosophy of As-If</u> and Alois Riehl's rejection not only of metaphysics but of values, and moving towards the positivism of the Vienna Circle--significant antecedents of twentieth century philosophy increasingly prepared the way for an ironic 'dialectic of diminished subjectivity'--if not an outright anti-dialectical and non-subjective monism.[126]

Ironically, therefore, the post-Hegelian 'Kantian' critique of idealism, as well as of materialism, often found its staunchest allies in "the revival of idealism," as we shall see below in the cases of the teachers of Bonhoeffer and Adorno, "in the neo-Kantian current of that revival." The neo-Kantians had emerged as an identifiable movement in the late 1850's and early 1860's,[127] signaled by Otto Liebmann's 1865 book, <u>Kant und die Epigonen</u>, which originally "raised the cry of 'Back to Kant!'"[128] As Lewis White Beck has noted,[129] the fact that they were called not only neo-Kantians, but neo-Hegelians, or neo-Fichteans, emphasizes the fact that neo-Kantianism was a hybrid response to materialism, on the one hand, and, on the other hand, to the post-Hegelian inflation of idealism to an absolute ontology. "In other words," according to various factions of neo-Kantianism, "both the idealists and the materialists [had] justified by their fruits the limitations which Kant had set to man's theoretical knowledge."[130] Thus neo-Kantians in general not only resisted any facile idealistic return to metaphysics. But also "their restatement of the Kantian criticism helped to check unsophisticated exploitations of the common-sense fallacy at a decisive moment in the history of German thought. While an untutored empiricism and 'scientism' threatened to dominate the intellectual scene, they managed to show that the problems of cognitions continued to demand logical and philosophical analysis." "In that sense," according to Ringer, the Marburg school of neo-Kantianism in particular, "helped to reverse the incipient trend toward positivism and materialism in nineteenth-century thought."[131]

In order to begin to understand this state of affairs we only need recall that the methods of Hegel and Kant had agreed, despite the grave differences between them which we have sketched, that humanity is "not at the mercy of the facts that surround" us. Rather, and crucially, we are "capable of submitting them to a higher standard, that of reason."[132]. The result for the post--Kantian transcendental tradition had been that the 'real' came "to mean not everything that actually exists," but rather that which is "opposed to all ready acceptance of the given state of affairs."[133] Thus the transcendental, nascently phenomenological, attempt was at the least an anti-**empiricist** enterprise, opposed in principle to Hume's statement that "'tis not ... reason, which is the guide of life, but custom."[134] The tradition of philosophical **criticism** with its principle of the mediation of reason, served to resist humanity's being reduced, as Hegel himself polemicized, to the immediacy of "bestial and goggle-eyed contemplation of the world around us."[135] In the transcendental view, to deny reason any power to organize reality implied "not only skepticism but conformism."[136] Thus, even if one wishes ultimately to argue against the consequences of the **Hegelian** form of dialectic, it is crucial at the outset that care be taken to recall that Hegel's position originally was "based upon a destructive conception of the given," in which all existing forms of 'reality' "are seized by the dissolving moment of reason which cancels and alters them until they are adequate to their notion"--until they become 'true'. In this sense Marx was **continuing** a crucial transcendental argument when he wrote that "the philosophers have only interpreted the world in various ways. The point is to change it."[137]

In summary, we can say that in the century between the death of Hegel and the rise of Nazism, there arose the aporia of a dialectic, which **not only** risked becoming **object-less** and thus conducive to the totalizing, 'subjectivist' tendencies in forms of idealism such as Schelling's towards an absolute identity-philosophy. **But also**, and with growing urgency, dialectic risked succumbing to increasingly popular forms of **subject-less** materialism or naturalism, which tended merely to retreat into forms of pseudo-pre-Kantian 'objectivism' which in effect denied the revolution of critical, constitutive subjectivity in the Kantian and the Hegelian traditions.

Yet as we have argued in the section on "Identity and Difference," Hegel's own dialectical orientation towards coherent totality, towards "all-embracing system," biased his position finally towards a form of monism. In this way his system risked serving "as a theodicy justifying the status quo," because of its denial of authentic freedom for any ultimate otherness which escapes the identity of absolute spirit.[138] The legacy of Hegelianism therefore came to be two-fold, best described not as left-or right-wing, but as depending upon which of these two sides of Hegel, the critical or the affirmative, were emphasized.

First, the 'de-constructive' dialectical method, which was indebted to the critical tradition of Kant and Fichte, gave expression to Hegel's "conviction that the given facts that appear to common sense as the positive index of truth are in reality the negation of truth, so that truth can only be established by their destruction."[139] Second, the 'constructive' ontological judgment, that a rational totality can be a historical, even if teleological, achievement, raised the possibility that philosophy be understood as the systematic explication of an already given, posited or 'positive' ontological structure of reality.[140]

During the nineteenth century, the fruitfulness of the former, the tradition of **criticism**--the "confidence in the general tenets of liberalism bequeathed to modern civilization by the Enlightenment"[141]--was increasingly eroded not only by philosophical positivism, but also by the promulgation of romantic and voelkisch themes in the popular culture at large. In this situation, what we have called post-idealism's dialectic of diminished subjectivity reinforced a widespread non-rational, and in many cases "strikingly conformist skepticism,"[142] abetted by nothing less than Hegel's affirmative dialectic.

Whereas the methodologically-oriented Hegelians understood idealism to imply a dynamic, dialectical approach to society, the conformist Hegelian tradition understood idealism to imply a static, systematic explication of given (even if being-given) forms, thereby reflecting wittingly or unwittingly the romantic conservatism of post-Bismarckian Germany.[143] As Martin Jay has pointed out, it was this second line of 'Hegelianism', if we can really call it that any longer, which ultimately was to nourish "the voelkish ideology of the national Gemeinschaft transcending social contradictions," and transcending, too, reason's ability or function to penetrate them.[144] Marcuse agrees: "this demotion of reason

35

made it possible to exalt certain particularities (such as race or the folk) to the rank of the highest value," thereby threatening not just the particular **transcendental critical** tradition, but the value of rationality, of theory, at large.[145]

2. The Evolving Cultural Crisis

As a result, "by the early 1920's," according to Fritz Ringer, German academics "were deeply convinced that they were living through a profound crisis, a 'crisis of culture', of 'learning', of 'values', or of the 'spirit'." But, he continues,

> it would be wrong to trace the intellectual concerns they shared solely to the theoretical or philosophical antecedents which they had in common. No matter how many German intellectuals of the Weimar period read Kant or Hegel, their manner of thought was not just the product of an inherited logic. It was a certain constellation of attitudes and emotions which united them, infecting even their language and their methods of argument. We must seek to account for the mood which gripped them, not just for their scholarship...[146]

Thus a more nuanced sense of the interrelationships among three broad currents in inter-bellum German culture will help us to understand the position in which Bonhoeffer and Adorno found themselves in the 1920's and 1930's: (1) the academic tradition of 'positive philosophy' that emerged in reaction to the 'de-constructive' reading of Hegel after his death in 1831; (2) the popular 'voelkisch' mentality which was to be exploited so extensively by National Socialism; and (3) the broadly 'neo-Kantian', or neo-Idealist, attempts in cultural undertakings, including but extending beyond the university setting, to renew a concern with critical and dialectical rationality. This latter neo-Kantian movement, as we shall see below, offers us insight into the starting point from which Bonhoeffer and Adorno were to attempt to critique the positivist and voelkisch traditions, which were to play such a crucial role in mobilizing German culture behind the National Socialist banner.

Herbert Marcuse has argued that "in the decade following Hegel's death, European thought," as we indicated above, can be interpreted as having "entered an

36

era of 'positivism'," from which emerged Comte's <u>Cours de philosophie positive</u>, F. J. Stahl's "positive philosophy of the state," and Schelling's "Berlin lectures on the <u>positive Philosophie</u>."[147] Thus, as Marcuse continues, although it cannot be gainsaid that "in its fundamental aspects, Schellings's positive philosophy is certainly greatly different from Comte's, ... nevertheless ... there is a common tendency in both philosophies to counter the sway of [transcendental philosophy's] apriorism and to restore the authority of experience," particularly **empirical** experience.[148]

Such 'positive philosophy' was not just anti-Hegelian, but **anti-Enlightenment,** "a conscious reaction against the critical and destructive tendencies of French and German rationalism, a reaction that was particularly bitter in Germany."[149] The critical, transcendental philosophical tradition, particularly as it had climaxed in Hegel's genetic phenomenology, was understood, pejoratively, by German positivism as 'negative philosophy'. In its repudiation of any "irrational and unreasonable reality," the 'negative' Enlightenment tradition was charged with having denied "to the given the dignity of the real." As F. J. Stahl charged, transcendental philosophy, contained "the principle of revolution,"[150] a dangerous, anti-establishment 'negativity'. To the contrary, the 'positive philosophy', Russell Jacoby summarizes, represented

> an explicitly conservative orientation toward preserving and defending the existing reality; with Saint-Simon and Comte it was directed against the 'negativity' of the French Revolution. [With German positivism] the positive was identified with the organic, with that which grew naturally out of existing reality, ... local customs and laws.[151]

Negative, or dialectical, philosophy was for positive philosophy a social, not merely a conceptual, danger in that it refused to "stay clear and clean of antagonisms and contradictions"[152]--cultural and political as well as rational. Thus, as Willey notes, the methodologically 'deconstructive' Hegelianism "was assailed from conservative quarters." For example, "the obscurantist regime of Frederick William IV brought Schelling and Friedrich Julius Stahl to Berlin to 'trample the dangerous dragon's seeds' planted by Hegel's philosophy, which the Prussian conservatives believed was inherently revolutionary."[153]

37

This tradition of 'positive philosophy' was to be exploited by National Socialism as a philosophical justification for its concomitant preemption of the broader, popular trend from the nineteenth century known as the voelkisch movement. This voelkisch tradition itself drew upon and vulgarized at least four broader historical antecedents: (i) nature mysticism,[154] (ii) Protestant pietism,[155] (iii) nationalism, and (iv) the peculiarly German romantic reaction to the French Revolution and Enlightenment. For our purposes here, the paramount connection is that between German nationalism and the voelkisch reaction against 'rationalism'.

Following the defeat of Napoleon, as Koppel Pinson has documented, came a period in which the heirs of the Enlightenment and rationalism fought a losing battle against the swelling tide of romanticism.[156] Moreover, the peculiarly German type of romanticism was influenced by the history of Germany's political relationship with France. While other western European forms of romanticism joined with the French revolutionary spirit which had developed out of the Enlightenment, "because of the French occupation of Germany..., German romanticism became an ideological weapon ... against French rationalism, and against the revolutionary spirit."[157] Therefore, while in France and England the romantic spirit produced an emphasis upon **individual** freedom, in Germany this political situation increasingly focused romantic expression into decidedly **holistic** and nationalistic themes.[158]

Therefore it is no accident that one is tempted to subsume the entire voelkisch phenomenon beneath the umbrella of German nationalistic concern.[159] But to do so is to miss the connection between the voelkisch mentality and anti- or ir-rationalism, towards which Nietzsche pointed when he wrote that in the nineteenth century

the whole tendency of the Germans ran counter to the Enlightenment, and to the revolution of society which, by a crude misunderstanding, was considered its result: piety toward everything still in existence sought to transform itself into piety toward everything that had ever existed, only to make heart and spirit full once again and to leave no room for future goals and innovations. The cult of feeling was erected in place of the cult of reason.[160]

38

The voelkisch movement in the nineteenth century combined this line of romantic reaction with the baser tendencies of a vulgarized Protestant pietism and German mystical theology, thereby reinforcing a strain of popular German "irrationalism, anti-intellectualism and emotional mysticism."[161]

One result, as Pinson has noted[162] was that the originally pietistic religious conception of individual conversion was transformed gradually into an idea of a national regeneration, no longer in league with the idealist, rational pedagogy. The voelkisch tradition came to be characterized by the subordination of the need for Bildung, understood as the rational formation or education of individual **self**-identity to the non-rationally oriented need to belong to the larger **cosmos,** a hope to reconstruct the 'whole' of social reality as a Volk.[163] "The voelkisch movement and accompanying 'politics of cultural despair', ... often voiced demands for a new totality. In fact, German bourgeois culture in general during much of the nineteenth century tended to favor holistic modes of thought."[164] Thus, according to Jay, at first "whenever liberalism was identified solely with its laissez-faire, utilitarian, individualistic traditions, holism was an anti-liberal phenomenon."[165] But later this 'conservative' reaction to Enlightenment 'individuality' came to be wholly defined in pseudo-Romantic and agrarian terms of chthonic and social-belonging, which could be achieved not by critical, rational means, but by the cultivation of the natural identity of the nation. The Volk, rather than critical Enlightenment rationality, came to be seen as the key to 'reality', particularly the social whole.

An illuminating and disturbing indication of the penetration of such voelkisch ideas into the German establishment between the World Wars can be found, of all places, in Bonhoeffer's biography itself. Bonhoeffer had grown up during what his biographer, Eberhard Bethge, has described as "the time of the German youth Movement (Jugendbewegung), with its anti-rationalist philosophy of life;" he had "read all of Nietzsche very carefully."[166] He had belonged to the Igel, the student association at Tuebingen, between which "and other nationalist fraternities" that he had seen elsewhere, according to Bethge, his brother Karl-Friedrich "had been able to discover no difference."[167] Thus, although we perhaps should be prepared, it still comes as something of a shock to see that the same Bonhoeffer, who only two days after Hitler's accession to power in 1933 would deliver a radio broadcast denouncing the voelkisch conflation of "the religious attitude of the group towards its Leader in the youth movement with the pietistic ideal of community," could still write, as late as 1929, rhetoric which claimed that

> every Volk has a call of God in itself to make history, to enter into the contest of the life of Voelker. ... God calls the Volk to manliness, to battle [Kampf], and to victory. ... Should not a Volk which has experienced the call of God to its own life, to its own youth and its own strength, should not such a Volk follow this call, even if this means treating as unimportant the life of other Voelker? God is the Lord of history. If a Volk humbly bows before this holy will which guided history, then in its youth and strength it can, with God, overcome the weak and the cowardly; for God will be with it.[168]

The early writings of Bonhoeffer and Adorno, as we shall see below, can be understood only against the background of an increasingly urgent need for conceptual tools with which to counter the implications of this positivist-voelkisch strand within post-Hegelian German culture. For them this was clearly not a matter simply of academic dispute, but of coming to terms with the debilitating effects of cultural antecedents which, by the time of Weimar Germany, had become the plausibility structures for the precedence of an emerging ir-rationalist public consensus.

Fritz Stern has argued that at least with regard to these legacies of 'positive philosophy' and the 'voelkisch tradition', emerging Nazi ideology, within whose increasingly public context Bonhoeffer and Adorno found themselves working, was "not so much coerced from above as volunteered from below; earlier traditions could readily be bent to Nazi requirements."[169] In significant respects, by the time of the rise of National Socialism, George Mosse is right to conclude: "Hitler only promised to **fulfill** a concept of life which had permeated much of the nation before he ever entered the scene."[170] And two of the basic elements of this concept of life were clearly these legacies of philosophical positivism, nurtured by the conservative and conformist reading of the Hegelian ontology, and the popular voelkisch emphasis on the non-rational nature of the unity of a people.

By the early 1930's the defenders of National Socialism, now deeply dependent for ideological purposes upon such academic positivism and this popular voelkisch mentality, realized that they must reject outright the social effects of the critical, dialectical tradition from Kant to Hegel, precisely on the grounds of the revolutionary thrust of what Marcuse calls that tradition's "rational humanitarianism."[171] Nazism understood, Marcuse argues, that "Hegel's philosophy," that is to say his 'de-constructive', dialectical-method, not his ultimately monistic ontology, "was an integral part of the culture which authoritarianism had to overcome."[172] For it threatened Nazi ideology's conception of the Volk as "a natural reality bound together by 'blood and soil' and subject to no rational norms or values."[173] If, "in Hegel's view, the decisive turn that history took with the French Revolution was that man came to rely on his mind and to submit the given reality to the standards of reason,"[174] then it was just this 'submission to reason' which Nazi ideology conspired to repudiate, under the guise of 'positive philosophy' and the voelkisch tradition. Thus it should come as no surprise that Carl Schmitt, whom Marcuse calls "the one serious political theorist of National Socialism," victoriously proclaimed on the day of Hitler's ascent to power in 1933: "Hegel, so to speak, died."[175]

Yet, as Thomas Willey has convincingly argued, there was another distinct and prominent antecedent to the intellectual and cultural ethos of the German 1920's, a tradition which to a significant degree, as we shall see momentarily, nurtured the early mentors of Bonhoeffer and Adorno.

> Nothing more quickly dispels the notion that the Second Reich was an era exclusively of voelkisch neo-romanticism, ambivalent social democracy, and state-worshiping liberalism than a study of neo-Kantianism, for here is revealed the complexity, the richness, and--unhappily--the unrealized possibilities of German intellectual life before World War I.[176]

The critical function of the Kantian dualities and antinomies was seen by its later inheritors as proposing a philosophical paradigm "wholly incompatible with Nazism's monistic integration of blood and spirit in the racial myth."[177] Thus neo-Kantianism should be understood as perhaps the most significant attempt to "retrieve consciousness and reason from irrationalism and determinism, which by the latter part of the [nineteenth] century had formed an alliance with positivism" to dethrone the centrality of a critical, rational paradigm not only for philosophy, but for German culture at large.[178]

The label 'neo-Kantian' is, however, misleading. It has been used to designate **not only** the competing Marburg and Heidelberg (or Baden or Southwestern) approaches, **but also** to speak of such diverse thinkers as Rudolf Otto, Max Weber, Eduard Spranger, Karl Mannheim, Georg Simmel and Wilhelm Dilthey.[179] Yet, the Marburg and Baden varieties of neo-Kantianism may be taken as representative of a basic tension, not only within the movement as a whole, but also within German academia more generally. And these two polar approaches can be seen to have several assumptions in common which help to specify the particular significance of this movement for understanding the work of Bonhoeffer and Adorno.

The Marburg School, including Hermann Cohen, Paul Natorp, Nicolai Hartmann, (in dialogue with whose positions several crucial sections of Bonhoeffer's Act and Being were to be written) and later, Ernst Cassirer, "can be said to have concentrated principally on logical, epistemological and methodological themes," particularly relating to the natural sciences.[180] The Baden School, including Wilhelm Windelband and Heinrich Rickert, alternatively "emphasized the philosophy of values and reflection on the cultural sciences."[181] Yet, as Thomas Willey has shown in his excellent study, Back to Kant, there were at least five assumptions shared by both schools of thought:[182] (1) the use of a 'transcendental method' to ascertain the conditions of the possibility of knowledge, value and action; (2) the 'critical' rejection of "knowledge of contents or essence" beyond experience, resulting in a shared metaphysical agnosticism; (3) the continued inquiry into the broad tradition of idealist epistemology; (4) the rejection of Kant's thing-in-itself; and (5) the assertion of the primacy of practical reason.[183] As we shall see below, Bonhoeffer's and Adorno's positions can be defined to a significant extent according to which of these neo-Kantian premises they accepted and rejected.

Against the general "tendency in the twenties for the revolt against academic sterility ... to take the form of an affirmation of the irrational,"[184] particularly as seen in some popularized forms of Lebensphilosophie, or the 'philosophy of life', the neo-Kantian movement's methodological emphases upon "the imperative need to criticize and examine the foundations of knowledge itself, and the superior claim of practical over theoretical reason,"[185] appeared as radical alternatives. Thus, as Martin Jay has noted, "in German philosophy, the movement most closely identified with liberalism, and thus the frequent target of holists' abuse, was neo-Kantianism."[186] In point of fact, however, the neo-Kantians were often seen as part of this very academic sterility. "German philosophers of the 1920's," according to Fritz Ringer, were, for example, "almost unanimous in treating the Marburg tradition itself as a part of the general decline of philosophy during the decades before 1900."[187]

Therefore it is not surprising that Bonhoeffer himself in Act and Being treated his neo-Kantian forebears as risking merely continuing an unproductive idealism. And in his inaugural lecture at Frankfurt in 1931, Adorno wrote that "the Neo-Kantianism of the Marburg School, which labored most strenuously to gain the content of reality from logical categories, has indeed preserved its self-contained form as a system, but has thereby renounced every right over reality and withdrawn into a formal region in which every determination of content is condemned to virtually the farthest point of an unending process."[188] Even within neo-Kantianism itself, such a leading figure as Paul Natorp had been

> deeply affected by the [First World] war and spent the last years of his life in an atmosphere of spiritual crisis. To Natorp and many other German intellectuals, epistemology was an arid, useless occupation in the midst of moral chaos and political instability. The dulling of the critical edge in German philosophy after 1914 was largely the result of disorder and disillusionment in German life and the attendant desire for something more conducive to one's spiritual security than cold logic.[189]

And many in Weimar Germany would have agreed with Susan Buck-Morss's recent judgment that "whereas Kant's critique of metaphysics had been radical in its social implications, these new Kantians turned critical reason into an ideology of resignation that was really the passive acceptance of the world in its given form."[190] Even Willey is forced to conclude that

> the apogee of Marburg neo-Kantianism unfortunately coincided with Wilhelmine Weltpolitik, the Pan-German movement, the rise of giant industry, the spread of fashionable irrationalism, and the erratic diplomacy of Bismarck's successors. The social liberalism, humanism,

and moral rationalism of Marburg philosophy were overwhelmed by the political rhetoric and clanking machinery of empire. Eventually, the Marburg group itself was shattered by the frequently conflicting loyalties of humanism and patriotism.[191]

Between 1920 and 1933, responses to this crisis eventuated in what "could be described as a neo-Romantic and neo-Hegelian revival."[192] As Buck-Morss has described the situation,

> a shift was occurring in intellectual alliances: the advocates of reason, since the Enlightenment identified with progressive social and political forces, had abandoned the impulses of revolution and passively accepted the 'given' state of things. Rationality had become synonymous with compromise and resignation, manifested in political life by the <u>Vernunftrepublikaner</u> who, with a claim to being 'reasonable', accepted without enthusiasm the given reality of the Weimar Republic, which was in many respects very unrepublican and undemocratic. On the other hand, revolt which grounded itself in irrationalism slipped easily into a formula for fascism.[193]

The calls for 'wholeness', "one of the central categories of Romantic philosophy," and 'synthesis', "a popularization of the Hegelian dialectic," came from academic podium and popular newspaper alike.[194] They renounced the 'abstraction' of 'rationality' and urged the 'concreteness' of a renewed 'philosophy of life', if not also of <u>Volk</u> and nation.

Yet however misguided its irrationalist denouement, this movement appears in retrospect to have been the expression of a fundamental philosophic and social question within German culture: Could the tradition of Western Enlightenment rationalism cope with the historical realities of the modern age? In this setting, the effect of the resources available for theology and philosophy with which to resist the onslaught of the cries for <u>voelkisch</u> wholeness and the attacks on rationality ranged from the ironic to the demonic. **On the one hand,** the neo-Kantian philosophy and the protestant liberalism it had inspired through Hermann Lotze to Albrecht Ritschl and Adolf von Harnack (Bonhoeffer's teacher at Berlin), had reinvigorated the Kantian transcendental approach. But it had waged its consistent battle for metaphysical agnosticism and the primacy of practical reason only at the price of losing the critical, de-ontologizing, de-totalizing function of Kant's retention of the thing-in-itself, which, as we have seen, was itself engendered only by retaining the methodological priority of the epistemological critique of pure speculative reason. **On the other hand,** the Schleiermachian-romanticist and the Hegelian-monistic strategies, which had originally arisen, we should remember, as superior alternatives to the 'abstractness' of Kantian 'criticism', were both all too easily co-opted by the "antirepublican, chauvinist, Pan-German, and volkish sentiments"[195] of totality, wholeness, identity. Thus, as Karl Barth reflected, looking back on the Nazi rise to power a quarter century later: from a theological perspective, anyone "who in 1933 may still have been spellbound by the theology of the 19th century was hopelessly condemned, save for a special intervention of grace, to bet on the wrong horse in regard to national socialism and during the clash between the Confessing Church and the German Christians who supported the new regime (Kirchenkampf)."[196]

Culturally, not just academically, the time begged for some renewed assertion of the transcendental epistemological "principle that the matters of fact of experience have to be justified before the court of reason." It was a point at which "the interpretation of these 'data'," of reason and culture demanded "a comprehensive **critique of the given itself**"[197] --a reawakening of the Kantian and Hegelian critical insight "that there is an antagonism and strain between truth and fact, between thought or mind and reality."[198] Willey reasonably concludes, however, that "the forces that were threatening reason and freedom in Germany could not have been defeated by Kant's doctrines alone, for far more was required than a philosophical conversion."[199]

Yet Bonhoeffer, implicitly, and Adorno, more explicitly, appear in their early work to be wagering that the moral, religious, and cultural conversion that was needed at the least involved a **philosophical metanoia**--a turning away from those traditions which at best had been unable to resist the rising tide of irrationalism and at worst had provided ideological support for the rise of Nazism. For the sake of the potential of such an intellectual conversion, they each undertook a critical reappraisal of the Kantian-Hegelian tradition. Each inquired particularly into the discarded Kantian Ding an sich, as clue to reopening just that enduring epistemologically-inspired 'revolutionary humanism' which romanticism, Hegelian ontologism, neo-Kantianism and theological liberalism had failed, often despite their intentions to the contrary, to embody in the midst of the cultural crisis of the 1920's.

3. Intellectual Biography

Despite the fact that the academic theological and philosophical writings of Bonhoeffer and Adorno arose from this same historical and social setting, their biographies ordained that they encounter this crisis from dramatically different perspectives. Bonhoeffer was a product of a professional, liberal, protestant family. His father was a professor of psychiatry and neurology at Berlin; his maternal grandfather and great-grandfathers had been Christian theologians.[200] Adorno was a child from an upper-bourgeois marriage between an assimilated Jewish father, Oskar Wiesengrund, a wine merchant, and a catholic mother, Maria Calvelli-Adorno.[201] One result of these differences was that, despite the strikingly parallel courses taken by their early careers, Bonhoeffer and Adorno moved in entirely different circles of friends and acquaintances, personal and professional. Yet this shaped the externals of their responses to the 'culture crisis' of the 1920's in ways that belie their deeper and intriguing affinities of thought.

Adorno was born Sept. 11, 1903 in Frankfurt am Main. Bonhoeffer was born Feb. 4, 1906 in Breslau. While Adorno was finishing his third and final year at Frankfurt, Bonhoeffer spent 1923-1924 studying theology at the University of Tuebingen. In June, 1924, Bonhoeffer began his own three year program at the University of Berlin, at the same time Adorno was finishing his dissertation at Frankfurt in July under Hans Cornelius, "Die Transzendenz des Dinglichen und Noematischen in Husserls Phaenomenologie." The remaining time that Bonhoeffer was at Berlin, Adorno spent as a student of musical composition of Alban Berg in Vienna.

Then in 1927, the year Bonhoeffer's dissertation, Sanctorum Communio, was accepted at Berlin, Adorno's first attempt at a Habilitationsschrift at Frankfurt, "Der Begriff des Unbewussten in der transzendentalen Seelenlehre," on Kant and Freud, was rejected by Cornelius. In February, 1928, Bonhoeffer left Berlin to take an assistant-pastorate at a German-speaking congregation in Barcelona. At that time Paul Tillich replaced Hans Cornelius in the chair of philosophy at Frankfurt. And in 1929-1930, while Bonhoeffer was back in Berlin, working as assistant to Wilhelm Luetgert, Adorno was writing his

46

new Habilitationsschrift, under the direction of Tillich, Kierkegaard: Konstruktion des Aesthetischen. Bonhoeffer's Habilitationsschrift, Act and Being, was accepted in 1930; and in July of that year Bonhoeffer presented his inaugural lecture at Berlin, "Man in Contemporary Philosophy and Theology." Bonhoeffer then spent the academic year of 1930-31 at Union Theological Seminary in New York, during which time Adorno's Frankfurt Habilitationsschrift was accepted and he presented his inaugural lecture at Frankfurt, "The Actuality of Philosophy."

Thus, despite beginning their graduate education three years apart, the actual academic careers of Bonhoeffer at Berlin and Adorno at Frankfurt were virtually identical--mid-1931 to the summer of 1933. In the summer of 1933 Bonhoeffer presented his final lectures at Berlin on Christology and the Philosophy of Religion of Hegel; and in September of 1933 Adorno's right to teach at Frankfurt was rescinded, whereupon he moved to Berlin. In October of that year Bonhoeffer took a German speaking parish in London, where he remained until mid-1935; Adorno himself moved to London in the Spring of 1934. In June, 1937, Adorno visited New York for the first time, during which time Bonhoeffer's underground seminary at Finkenwalde was closed. In January, 1938, Bonhoeffer was refused further entry to Berlin; in February, Adorno left Germany for New York. In 1941, Adorno moved to California, during the same year that Bonhoeffer was being forbidden to print or publish further. On April 5, 1943, Bonhoeffer was arrested and imprisoned for his participation in one of the plot's against Hitler's life; on April 9, 1945, he was executed. Adorno returned to the University of Frankfurt in 1949, where he remained the two decades until his death.

a. Bonhoeffer

The profound similarities between Bonhoeffer and Adorno are made further prone to neglect by common characterizations of Bonhoeffer's having been motivated primarily by reactions **against** neo-Kantian philosophy and theology and Adorno's having leaned heavily **toward** heterodox-marxian social analyses. This is misleading precisely because it overlooks the extent to which Bonhoeffer himself can best be understood only if we include, as we will argue shortly, the enduring questions raised by the neo-Kantian ethos of his early education. Such a reading misdirects us, too, because it assumes a marxian **starting point** for Adorno's project, whereas the

47

overtly marxian thematic in Adorno's work was actually, as we shall see below, quite some time in developing.

Indeed, in the case of Bonhoeffer, it is not so much that the philosophical influences on his early work have been **mis**-represented as that they have not yet been reconstructed in anything approaching a comprehensive manner. And yet there are hints throughout the existing biographical material that philosophy, particularly the problematic relationship between the Kant of the First Critique and Hegelian idealism, was an early and consistent influence on Bonhoeffer's academic theology. Bethge himself notes that even in secondary school, "his [Bonhoeffer's] brother Karl-Friedrich's skepticism, against which he had to defend himself, spurred him into grappling with epistemology at an early age, and he worked hard at philosophy during his last years at [secondary] school."202 When he went to Tuebingen to study theology, in addition to Karl Heim's "Dogmatic Theology" lectures on Schleiermacher and Ritschl,203 Bonhoeffer made numerous "excursions into epistemology."204 He attended Karl Groos's lectures on "logic" and on the "history of modern philosophy" and joined Groos's seminar on Kant's Critique of Pure Reason, for which Bonhoeffer wrote a paper.205

Bonhoeffer's philosophical training at Tuebingen and during his first year at Berlin was evidently sufficiently thorough so that, as Bethge recounts, "in 1925, when Reinhold Seeberg, after a first encounter with Dietrich, met his colleague Karl Bonhoeffer [Dietrich's father] at a meeting of the Senate of Berlin University, he expressed his surprise and admiration at the solidity of the young man's philosophical preparation and his wide knowledge of contemporary philosophy."206 Thus it is unfortunate that Bethge, in tracing the influences on Bonhoeffer's academic development as a graduate student, omits any mention of Bonhoeffer's continued philosophical training at Berlin.207 For, despite the fact that numerically, Bonhoeffer took far more historical- and systematic-theological courses than philosophical courses at Berlin, his philosophical training provides a crucial clue to Bonhoeffer's persistent grappling with topics philosophical in his dissertation and Habilitationsschrift.

He attended lectures by Heinrich Maier in the summer of 1924 on epistemology;208 lectures by Privatdozent Rieffert in the winter of 1925 on the "History of Logic;" lectures again by Maier in 1925 on "Freedom and Necessity;" and those by Eduard Spranger, who was "a leading figure of the German Neo-Hegelian revival of the

48

1920's,"[209] in 1927 on the "Philosophy of Culture." Thus we would not disagree when Bethge tells us that Bonhoeffer "familiarized himself with Seeberg's great models--Schleiermacher, Hegel and Albrecht Ritschl--and that he also acquired from Seeberg the difficult technical jargon of his student years, which is saturated with Seeberg's Hegelian concepts" and "Ritschl's aversion to metaphysics."[210] But we should resist letting this suggest that Bonhoeffer's knowledge of and opinions about philosophy had come only at second hand, always and only filtered through the theological concerns of his mentors. Thus Bethge's further downplaying of the influence on Bonhoeffer of Wilhelm Luetgert, whom Bethge himself calls "a specialist on German idealism,"[211] and for whom Bonhoeffer worked as an assistant for over a year while writing <u>Act and Being</u>,[212] should at the least make us more vigilant in asking to what extent the existing canonical biographical interpretation of Bonhoeffer's antagonism towards philosophy is not more Bethge's than Bonhoeffer's.[213]

b. Adorno

When we turn to Adorno, the matter of early philosophical influences and inclinations is somewhat clearer, in large measure because the commentator tradition has not been as averse, as has been the case in Bonhoeffer scholarship, especially until recently, to taking his early work as providing clues to the philosophical anchorage of his project as a whole. Like Bonhoeffer, Adorno was a philosophically precocious adolescent. During his secondary schooling, at age fifteen, he "for over a year ... regularly spent Saturday afternoons with [Siegfried] Kracauer studying Kant's <u>Critique of Pure Reason</u>, lessons he would recall as far more valuable than those he received in his formal university education."[214] And in 1921, when "Adorno graduated from the Kaiser Wilhelm Gymnasium in Frankfurt and enrolled in the city's newly founded and in many ways progressive Johann Wolfgang Goethe University," he was to emerge "with a doctorate in philosophy only three years later in 1924 at the age of twenty-one."[215]

Surprisingly it is not a Marxist, but a definite neo-Kantian, thread that we find winding through the beginnings of Adorno's intellectual development, particularly embodied in his teacher at Frankfurt, Hans Cornelius.

Against irrationalists, Cornelius firmly defended the Enlightenment tradition, but not in its

49

present, quasi-scholastic form. Cornelius was an Aufklaerer of the old sort, a radical, philosophically speaking, more of a Kantian than Kant himself in his commitment to [criticism] ... His rejection of the Kantian doctrine of the thing-in-itself, which he claimed was a metaphysical residue, was in effect slipping behind Kant to earlier British and French empiricism. It was also in accord with the neo-Kantianism of his Viennese contemporaries Avenaius and Mach. Yet if there was a positivist bent to Cornelius's interpretation of Kant, he lacked the positivists' uncritical acceptance of the 'given' world and their passive notion of the subject.[216]

It was under Cornelius's direction that Adorno submitted his first dissertation at Frankfurt, "The Transcendent Status of the Thing and Noema in Husserl's Phenomenology." According to Dallmayr, the dissertation's "arguments reflected faithfully the teachings of Cornelius--including the latter's contention that mind was completely able to engulf or absorb reality..."[217] This issue of transcendental idealism, "inspired by Kant but actually fashioned by Cornelius, ... continued to dominate Adorno's thinking for several more years, although reality (especially social reality) began to impinge increasingly on transcendental formulas."[218]

Adorno's stay in Vienna, which followed upon the thesis under Cornelius, only served to reinforce the neo-Kantian context in which Adorno's thinking took shape. Buck-Morss has noted that, significantly, in Vienna during Adorno's time there in 1925-26, "the philosophical climate was neo-Kantian, which meant that metaphysics was discredited and problems of truth were equated with problems of logic and language..."[219] Indeed it has been claimed that "in Wittgenstein's Vienna, everyone in the educated world discussed philosophy and regarded the central issues in post-Kantian thought as bearing directly on his own interests, whether artistic or scientific, legal or political."[220]

Thus although "Cornelius's philosophy had been out of the academic mainstream in the early twenties," when Adorno had written his first dissertation under him, and despite the fact that "it was even more so by the time Adorno returned from Vienna in 1926," it should not be surprising that it was to the neo-Kantian method of his former advisor that Adorno returned in his first attempt at a Habilitationsschrift in 1927.[221] For it was a time in Germany when

> antirationalist tendencies were increasingly evident in philosophy and art, as well as the rapidly expanding realm of popular culture... Such antirationalism was what Adorno chose to attack in his Habilitationsschrift..., and his method followed closely the neo-Kantianism of his mentor Hans Cornelius,[222]

for it allied him with a viable and ready-to-hand 'critical' modus operandi for such an attack. For "matters were relatively simple in the treatise of 1927. At that time what was at issue was the ...confrontation between idealism and naturalism, between reason and unreason."[223]

> This thesis of 1927, "The Concept of the Unconscious in Transcendental Psychology,"

> in denouncing vitalistic and organismic ontologies and their attempt to convert depth psychology into a weapon against 'rationalism' ... meant to challenge broad currents of the Zeitgeist which played a 'clearly specified and dangerous role' in the social situation of the time. Briefly put, this role was to provide an alibi and ideological camouflage for prevailing social and economic practices.[224]

Some interpreters have pointed out that the concluding pages of the thesis, which bring Marx into Adorno's formal writing for the first time, "attempted to find compatibilities not only between his teacher's heterodox neo-Kantianism and Marxism, but also between them and ... the psychoanalysis of Sigmund Freud."[225] But more striking, given the usual assumptions about the centrality of Marx in the work of Adorno, is the fact that the thesis attempts its central "simultaneous rejection of idealism and objectivism,"[226] largely still on the basis of neo-Kantian, not Marxian, presuppositions.

This is by no means to suggest that it is possible or desirable to attempt a revisionist, non-Marxian, reading of even the early Adorno. For as Martin Jay's study of Adorno makes clear, upon Adorno's return to Frankfurt from Vienna, indeed "his circle of friends widened to include a group of heterodox Marxists, then in Berlin, which comprised Ernst Bloch, Bertolt Brecht, Kurt Weill and, most important of all, Walter Benjamin. Adorno's

51

writings during these years began to show evidence of
his newly acquired Marxist sympathies, which in fact had
been initially stimulated earlier in the decade when he
read Bloch's Spirit of Utopia and Georg Lukacs's History
and Class Consciousness."227   But it should alert us to
the fact that from the beginning of Adorno's career, the
Kantian problematic was central, as it remained even to
the end of his career, and, as we shall see, his Negative
Dialectics.

   Bonhoeffer and Adorno are to be understood as
having faced the same dilemma: how to determine what
sort of thinking was still possible, given the failure of
the neo-Kantianism, or neo-Idealism, of their forebears
to provide the conceptual tools for an adequate response
to the 'culture crisis' in Germany between the World
Wars.   As a prelude to examining their attempts to resolve this issue, we have detailed some of the vast com-
plexities and confusions of the 1920's.   We have done so
out of the same motivation as Adorno, who, of the retrospective opening paragraphs of his inaugural lecture,
said

> I have discussed the most recent history of
> philosophy, not for a general intellectual his-
> tory orientation, but because only out of the
> historical entanglement of questions and an-
> swers does the question ... emerge precisely, ...
> whether, after the failure of the last great
> efforts, there exists an adequacy between the
> philosophic questions and the possibility of
> their being answered at all...228

This problematic 'adequacy between philosophic questions
and the possibility of their being answered at all' led
Bonhoeffer as well as Adorno on the search for a more
adequate methodological paradigm, as seen in Act and
Being and Negative Dialectics.

D. Method: Immanent Criticism

   With this as our provisional chart of the conceptual,
cultural and biographical terrain within which to locate
the early work of Bonhoeffer and Adorno, let us turn
now to the issue of their early methodologies.   In particular we will be concerned with the manner in which
this fate of the epistemological paradigm in philosophy
and theology shaped Bonhoeffer's and Adorno's sense of
priorities regarding which questions most needed to be
asked and their ways of asking them.   As guides we will

take Bonhoeffer's inaugural lecture at Berlin in 1930, "The Question of Man in Contemporary Philosophy and Theology," and Adorno's inaugural lecture at Frankfurt the following year, "The Actuality of Philosophy." For these two lectures provide valuable insight into Bonhoeffer's just completed Act and Being and the philosophical program which will culminate, at the end of Adorno's career, in his Negative Dialectics.

Each of these works was a critique of the philosophic tradition of idealism. And each attempted to avoid lapsing into the malaise which had paralyzed the powers of response to the 'culture crisis' of the previous neo-Idealist, or neo-Kantian, movement. Both lectures proposed to undertake what Adorno later was to call an intrinsic or **immanent criticism** of idealism, as an initial 'archaeological' moment in the attempt to articulate a new methodological paradigm--to describe the heuristic horizon within which theology and philosophy can be understood meaningfully to occur. Theirs is an 'immanent' approach, since it started **within** the presuppositions of idealism, with "its own standards and ideals and confronts it with its own consequences,"229 "adhering strictly to the elements under scrutiny."230 The immanent procedure, according to Adorno, therefore approaches idealism by pursuing

> the logic of its aporias, the insolubility of the task itself. A successful work, according to immanent criticism, is not one which resolves objective contradictions in a spurious harmony, but one which expresses the idea of harmony negatively by embodying the contradictions, pure and uncompromised, in its innermost structure.231

Theirs is a 'critical' approach insofar as it endeavors to **expose the contradictions** within the assumptions of idealism itself, until idealism collapses from the weight of its own unresolved aporias. Thus in Buck-Morss's words, an immanent critique starts by accepting the presuppositions of the idealists and then presses "the antinomies of their theories to the point where the **dialectical negation** of idealism might be achieved,"232 where it collapses of its own inner impossibility. In Adorno's words, "the immanent procedure ... seeks to grasp, through the analysis of [idealism's] form and meaning," the contradiction between idealism's own idea of itself and "its pretension to correspond to reality."233 Immanent criticism is thus a method of protest against the transcen-

dental tradition; such criticism would explode its idealist
pretensions from within.

1. Bonhoeffer and Immanent Criticism

What, Bonhoeffer begins by asking his theological
audience, is the "firm point of unity" [Einheitspunkt]
from which humanity can call into question and try to
understand the continuity of its existence?234 He proceeds to propose two options, which correspond to the
two types of dialectic we have been exploring; both are
based on alternative readings of the epistemological paradigm. First, the 'I' can understand itself as an 'I' which
"cannot seize hold of itself,"235 and thus can understand itself "only from the perspective of its limit
[Grenze]"236--its "act of referring to transcendence
[Aktbezug auf Transzendenz]." The 'I' knows itself only
in relation to "a limit which is no longer surmount-
able,"237 with reference to that which is different from
itself, and beyond its "longing for that which cannot be
lost [unverlierbar Gegebenen]"238 to its reflexive grasp.
This is the 'I' of what we have called the Kantian dialectic of difference.

Second, "the other possibility is ... to take possession of one's own I, to see the central occurrence of all
intellectual happening in the coming-to-itself of the
I."239 The 'I' understands itself only when it denies any
radical act of transcendence by the subject, any open-
ended act of reference towards genuine otherness, towards the not-I, and beyond the transparency of reality
effected by the knowing subject. As Bonhoeffer continues, in this 'I' of what we have called the Hegelian
dialectic of identity,

> the thinking of one's own I, as thinking from
> unity [Einheit], here becomes the primal posi-
> tion of all philosophy. ... Philosophy [for
> idealism] is the work of man par excellence.
> Man understands himself from his own work.
> ... He is a world which rests on itself, he
> needs no Other [keines anderen] than himself
> to come at his nature. ... [This is] the man
> of the inexhaustible, inalienable fullness of
> possibilities...240

These two conceptions of the nature of humanity, growing out of differing ontological presuppositions about the
implications of the subject-object paradigm, Bonhoeffer
summarizes, arise "according to whether the question of

man is made the limiting point [Grenzpunkt] or the systematic starting point [systematischen Ausgangspunkt]" of philosophy and theology. The question whether the knowing 'I' "submitted at this limit," and the dialectic of difference, or "whether the I snatched at transcendence and drew it into itself," into what we have called the dialectic of identity--this is for philosophy and theology "the decisive question."241

On the one hand, therefore, Bonhoeffer tests this thesis on those contemporary philosophers whom he interprets to fall into this latter idealist category, particularly Max Scheler (who had just died in 1928) and Martin Heidegger (whose Being and Time had just been published in 1927).242 In Bonhoeffer's interpretation, Scheler, particularly in the early period of what Bonhoeffer calls his "phenomenological epistemology," clearly fell heir to the method of a dialectic of identity. For Scheler,

> man is able to see God, not in the intellectual process, but in the feeling of value [Wertfuehlen], whose purest form is love. ... In love man soars to the vision of the eternal and highest value of the holy, God. He embraces the all in himself, he is able to embrace God himself in passionate gazing. That is the 'totality of life' ['Totalitaet des Lebens'] which the totality of values discloses and comprehends in itself. ... Man is understood from his possibilities. He bears within himself the possibility of drawing the transcendent into himself in a vision. And that is his nature.243

For Bonhoeffer, Martin Heidegger's position in Being and Time is superior to Scheler's, insofar as Heidegger understands the human being as existing "in time and in the world," and as such as "a person who must on every occasion question himself."244 Scheler, to the contrary, viewed humanity as able to grasp itself "in the deepest undisclosed strata of [its] being, which, untouched by all alteration, remain in eternal rest and order...."245 Yet in Heidegger's concept of death, according to Bonhoeffer,

> totality [Ganzheit] of Dasein ... signifies for itself the being of Dasein. Dasein carries its unity [Einheit] in itself. That is the necessary consequence of the understanding of Dasein as simply being-possible. The possibilities of

Dasein also comprise the possibility of coming to unity,[246]

the unity of authentic being-unto-death. Here, in Bonhoeffer's words, "we notice that we are thrown back firmly on Hegel...."[247] For in Heidegger's notion of authenticity, the human being surmounts the limits even of its finitude: "he does not come to the end [zum Ende], but to the fulfillment [zur Vollendung], the totality [Ganzheit] of Dasein."[248] The critical **questioning** of Kant's Critique of Pure Reason, "becomes the **answer**,"according to Heidegger, for "man in fact has knowledge of himself," which is adequate to his being as Dasein; thus "the question has no ultimate seriousness."[249] It signifies no real limit to knowledge, only an unrealized possibility.

On the other hand, with the philosophies of Paul Tillich and Eberhard Grisebach,[250] Bonhoeffer thought, "the whole picture seems to have altered completely."[251] For Tillich, "it is the essence of man that he must question himself, and that he still remains questionable to himself,"[252] caught ever within the limits of finitude. Humanity, as Bonhoeffer interprets Tillich, understands itself from "the limit-situation [Grenzesituation]" itself. And this understanding of humanity stands in "fundamental contrast to the man who understands himself from his possibilities: the man who fulfills himself in himself confronts the man who at the limit protests against any human self-imposition or assurance."[253]

Grisebach significantly extends this interpretation of humanity at its limits, Bonhoeffer proposes,

> to a point where he will no longer fix even the limits of man by thought, but declares the concrete 'Thou' [das konkrete Du] as the limit of man. Existence is in reality only in encounter with a Thou. Here is a real limit, no longer an imagined one, and therefore one which is no longer involved in reflection, here is the 'present' [Gegenwart]. Human existence is only in the present, where it sustains the claim of the other, does not do violence to the other, but enters with him into a dialegesthai. ... Here the recognition that man can understand himself only from his limits, i.e. in reference to transcendence [in Bezug auf Transzendenz], in contrast to any self-understanding of man from his immanent possibili-

ties, seems to be given extremely pointed expression.[254]

Thus Grisebach offers the advantage, Bonhoeffer concludes, of having conceived the epistemological limit in more 'concrete' terms.

But despite his obvious appreciation of Tillich's emphasis on limit-situations, and the significant extension of this by Grisebach to the point of not being able to "think of man without the concrete other man [ohne den konkreten anderen Menschen]"[255] as that limit, Bonhoeffer argues that there is a clearly 'Hegelian' problem in such attempts, analogous to Hegel's argument against the Kantian Ding an sich. With the Tillichian Grenzesituation, "the limitation through which man limits himself remains a limitation drawn by himself. But that means it is a limitation which man has always already gone beyond in principle, beyond which he must first have stood in order to be able to draw it."[256] Even in the more radical attempt of Grisebach, in which "the I makes the other person absolute, recognizes him as its concrete absolute limit, ... I myself make the claim of the Thou absolute...." And since "I could in fact also make it relative, so with my possibilities I remain lord of the other person, too."[257]

Thus, if this is the case, Bonhoeffer concludes, even though "Grisebach's intentions certainly deserve serious consideration, ... he is unable to carry them through with his own means."[258] Both Tillich's and Grisebach's

> attempts to understand man from his limitations in their own turn take their place among those against which they were directed, the attempts to understand man from his possibilities. Man has essentially no limits in himself, in himself he is infinite.[259]

"In this, idealism is right," Bonhoeffer writes. "the only question is, how this fact is to be interpreted."[260]

2. Adorno and Immanent Criticism

Adorno, in his inaugural lecture, likewise began with the enduring pretensions of idealism as the justification for his own statement of the need for 'immanent criticism'. Bonhoeffer had argued in his lecture that his contemporaries either **submitted to** or **snatched at** the act of reference towards transcendence, towards

57

the 'otherness' of being vis a vis thought. Adorno similarly argued that the options were clearly between those
who held that "only polemically does reason present itself
to the knower as total reality," and those who retained
the illusion that "the power of thought is sufficient to
grasp the totality of the real."261 The question to be
answered was what sort of reason could "rediscover itself
in a reality whose order and form suppresses every claim
to reason," a reality only in whose "traces and ruins is
[reason] prepared to hope that it will ever come across
correct and just reality."

> The crisis of idealism comes at the same time
> as a crisis in philosophy's pretensions to to-
> tality. The autonome ratio [autonomous rea-
> son]--this was the thesis of every idealistic
> system--was supposed to be capable of deve-
> loping the concept of reality, and in fact all
> reality, from out of itself. This thesis has
> disintegrated.262

Yet, as Bonhoeffer had done, Adorno notes the same two
well known examples of those who still held, in their
own fashion, the sufficiency of thought to grasp the
totality of the real: Scheler and Heidegger.

Bonhoeffer had emphasized the early work of Scheler, in which philosophical thought "embraces the all,"
the "'totality of life' ['Totalitaet des Lebens']."263 Adorno looks at Scheler's later phase, his own attempt at a
more concrete, 'material phenomenology', "the transition
of phenomenology from the formal-idealist to the material and objective region."264 As Adorno laments...,

> the images of transhistorical truth, which at
> one time [Scheler's] philosophy projected so
> seductively onto the background of closed,
> Catholic theory, became confused and disin-
> tegrated as soon as they were sought for in
> just that reality, the comprehension of which
> was in fact precisely what constituted the
> program of 'material phenomenology'.265

Scheler, in Adorno's estimation, is to be applauded for
having recognized "the gap between the eternal ideas [of
his early period] and reality, the overcoming of which
led phenomenology to enter the material sphere" rather
than staying with its earlier, purer idealism.266 But in
making this transition, as Bonhoeffer had already noted,

it is staggering to see how Scheler's system is shattered under the overwhelming impact of the demonic world of human desires. In its rigidity, Scheler's thought-construction shows itself to be too brittle to withstand this reality which all at once breaks in upon it. It collapses without a trace [Es bricht restlos zusammen].267

Scheler's work began with the idealists' confidence in the adequacy of thought to the being of humanity. It ended--precisely in its attempt to take account of social reality--by abandoning that "reality to a blind impulse [Drang]." It embraced a "metaphysics of the impulse" toward a nonrational totality, or identity, which retains the Hegelian affirmative ontology only at the expense of the critical, rational method of penetration of social reality.268 As Bonhoeffer also had argued, Scheler's original notion of humanity as "a creature who 'is' in the form of a timeless entity," in the end had no way critically to respond to the experience of humanity at the limits of its existence. It could not account for humanity confronting "the powers of society [von den Maechten der Gesellschaft], which ran diametrically opposed to that being which was assumed to be his original one."269

And like Bonhoeffer, Adorno also censures Heidegger's Being and Time for having assumed, rather than having demonstrated, that "being itself is appropriate to thought and available to it."270 Thus in his own fashion Heidegger had averred to the premise of totality, "fundamental to the idealist systems."271 "With Heidegger's metaphysics of death," Adorno concludes (in agreement with Bonhoeffer), "phenomenology seals a development which Scheler already inaugurated with the theory of impulse. It cannot be concealed, Adorno warns, that in Scheler and the early Heidegger, "phenomenology is on the verge of ending in precisely that vitalism against which it originally declared battle..."272 In Heidegger's notion of **thrownness** [Geworfenheit], "which is set forth," according to Adorno, "as the ultimate condition of man's being," Heidegger's attempt at the idealist goal of totality is both completed and shattered. "...The claim to totality made by thought is thrown back upon thought itself; ... life by itself becomes as blind and meaningless as only it was in Lebensphilosophie..."273 Ontology has thereby foreclosed the option for radical criticism of the totality of the real.

Adorno claims that, like Simmel's Lebensphilosophie, which resisted the perceived sterile formalism of the

59

Marburg neo-Kantians, the work of the later Scheler and Heidegger "has admittedly maintained contact with the reality with which it deals. But in so doing each has lost all claim to make sense out of the empirical world which presses in upon it," and each has thereby in their own way submitted to the positivist tradition's irrationalist tendencies merely to accept idealism's ontology, without retaining its dialectical rational method.[274] Ironically this parallels the results, Adorno points out, of "scientistic philosophies" as well--which "give up from the beginning the basic idealist question regarding the constitution of reality," and thus also give up even **raising** questions about the autonomy of the ratio. The sciences risk having forgotten the critical foundations of their very disciplines, and in that conspire in the assumption of the immediate adequacy of thought to being.[275] Even those more sophisticated scientific disciplines which "have long since rid themselves of the naturalistic conceptual apparatus that, in the 19th century, made them inferior to idealist theories of knowledge,"[276] Adorno argues, have done so only by having "totally annexed the contents of cognitive criticism."[277] The result is that

> the Kantian question as to the constitution of
> a priori synthetic judgments would be utterly
> meaningless, because there is absolutely no
> such thing as this kind of judgment; every
> move beyond that which is verifiable by the
> power of experience is prevented; philosophy
> becomes solely an occasion for ordering and
> controlling the separate sciences, without being
> allowed to append anything essential from
> itself to their findings.[278]

Yet, two nagging problems remain with any such attempt to dissolve philosophical questioning "into that of the separate sciences": [1] the transcendental question of the constitution of the subject and the object: "the problem of the meaning of the 'given' itself, the fundamental category of all empiricism, which maintains the question of the accompanying subject..."; and [2] "the problem of the unknown consciousness, the alien ego, [which] can be made accessible for empirio-criticism only through analogy, composed subsequently on the basis of one's own experience, whereas in fact the empirio-critical method already necessarily assumes unknown consciousness in the language it has at its disposal." Thus "solely by posing these problems," a positivist approach like "the theory of the Vienna School is drawn into precisely that philosophic continuity from which it wanted to distance itself."279   Thus, unintentionally, even positivism retains the potential for the reawakening of immanent criticism.

Where Bonhoeffer had pointed to Tillich and Grisebach as stepping into this opening, however finally insufficient, for an immanent argument against idealism on the basis of a more adequate notion of reason's Grenz- punkt, Adorno inquired into the similar role of phenomenology.   For the retention of both the 'givenness' of objectivity and the 'criticism' of subjectivity had been the central contribution of Husserl's philosophy: "the effort, following the disintegration of the idealist systems and with the instrument of idealism, the autonome ratio, to gain a trans-subjective, binding order of being."

> It was the authentically productive and fruitful discovery of Husserl...that he recognized in the meaning of the concept of the non-deducible given (unableitbaren Gegebenheit), as developed by the positivist schools, the fundamental problem of the relationship between reason and reality.280

Husserl, according to Adorno, "has renounced the [idealist] claim of the productive power of mind, ... and resigns himself, as only Kant himself had done, to take possession of the sphere of that which is adequately within his reach."281   Adorno's assessment of Husserl parallels Bonhoeffer's conclusions about Tillich's and Grisebach's attempts to find adequate limits to the pretensions of subjectivity.   He argues that insofar as "the 'jurisdiction of reason' (Rechtsrechnung der Vernunft) remains the court of final appeal for the relation between reason and reality," Husserl had "purified idealism from every excess of speculation and brought it up to the standard of the highest reality within its reach, ... but he didn't burst it open."282

3. Immanent Critique as Dual Protest

Thus taken together, the inaugural lectures of Bonhoeffer and Adorno mounted a method of protest against these developments of the transcendental tradition. Theirs was a dual critique not only of the loss of the recalcitrant **objectivity** by idealism, despite the attempts of phenomenology and 'personalist' philosophies such as that of Grisebach to do just the opposite.   But also they criticized the loss of critical transcendental **subjectivity** in naturalism, positivism, and non-dialectical materialism. The present study will argue that the form of **immanent**

61

criticism which Bonhoeffer and Adorno both undertook in their inaugural lectures led them towards what can thus best be described as a method of critical, or to use Adorno's later terminology, **negative dialectics.**[283] The immanent critique was twofold: it argued not only that **thought** was inadequate to reality. But also it argued that in a certain sense **reality** was itself 'fractured' and thus was 'inadequate' to totalizing thought, incomplete and thus incomprehensible, as is seen in particular in their sense that **social reality** was the rock upon which Scheler's thought broke.

Thus their inaugural lectures reveal a common concern to oppose the illusion of idealism's autonome ratio. Compared to Hegel's ontologically affirmative dialectic, theirs is, therefore, a negative, or agnostic dialectic. As Rudiger Bubner has noted, Adorno's "Negative Dialectics, even in its title, takes the protest to the door of Hegel, who has robbed the dialectic of its critical salt by misusing it to give a positive legitimacy to an evil reality."[284] Yet their projects evidence a renewed meditation on the Kantian antinomy of an autonomous subject, as well, free precisely in its working within the limits of its ability fully to grasp either itself or the 'objectivity' of the otherness of reality. And thus theirs is a **critical dialectical** approach, whether to the problem of the reality of God or to that of the world. Adorno himself put it this way:

> While the mind extricated itself from a theological-feudal tutelage, it has fallen increasingly under the anonymous sway of the status quo. This regimentation, the result of the progressive societalization of all human relations, did not simply confront the mind from without; it immigrated into its immanent consistency.[285]

The extrication of thought from the sway of the status quo required, therefore, both a new, critical rationality, and a new priority of the object which was capable of resisting the totalizing exigency of idealist reason. Each was undergoing, we are arguing, what, borrowing Lonergan's terminology, we have called an "intellectual conversion." That is to say, each engaged in "a radical clarification and, consequently, the elimination of an exceedingly stubborn and misleading myth concerning reality, objectivity, and human knowledge."[286] For Bonhoeffer and Adorno, the **point of attack**--but not simply the **point of the attack**-on such an 'exceedingly stubborn and misleading myth' was idealism, and its affirmative dialectics of totality. They each were moving away from such a dialectics of totality, towards a new paradigm which they each described in variants of the language of the tradition of Kant's epistemology, and what we have called its critical dialectics of difference.

Philosophy and theology required a methodology which both criticized and retained not only the subject, but the object--not only thought, but being as well. For Bonhoeffer as well as Adorno, "subject and object are constituted by one another but are irreducible to each other--neither can be wholly subsumed by the other. They are internally related, interdependent structures..."287 The challenge was in doing so without merely lapsing back into **either** the assumption that thought is adequate to the articulation of the totality of reality **or** the assumption of the non-dialectical primacy of the object, as in naturalism, scientism and some forms of materialism. Thus Adorno's method of dialectics, to which Bonhoeffer's early method is analogous, resisted both (1) skepticism, "as manifested, for example in the empiricist tradition," which "serves to block the critical assessment of social existence," and (2) subjectivism, for example, "in bourgeois idealism" and its identity thinking, which "aims at the subsumption of all particular objects under general definitions and/or a unitary system of concepts."288

Adorno's strategy then is twofold: (a) it begins with the priority of the object--the positive contribution of empiricism and materialism;289 but (b) it respects equally the object's constitution by the subject, its **theoretical** aspect, the insight of idealism. Yet (b') the subject is disallowed its systematic pretensions towards totality, and (a') the object is disallowed its constitutional independence from criticism. The role of the subject is not to accomplish totality but to maintain difference, to disallow its own pretensions to identity with the object, the commensurability of thought and reality. The role of the object is not to maintain a dualism, but to impinge upon the solipsistic subject and demand a recognition both of the subject's incompleteness, its inability to conceptualize reality completely, and the object's incompleteness, its brokenness and fragmentation in a finite and socially distorted reality.290 Thus the renewed primacy of the object itself depends upon a renewed inquiry into the priority of that theoretical, immanently critical subjectivity which neo-Kantianism's turn to the primacy of the practical subject had encouraged philosophy and theology to neglect.

It is this latter importance of the theoretical subject which is most easily lost in interpretations of Bonhoeffer's early work, and the restoration of which to our picture of Bonhoeffer is one of the central contributions of a comparison between his method and that of Adorno. Indeed Bonhoeffer is usually assumed to the contrary to have allied himself with a sort of neo-Kantianism, as mediated by the theology of Albrecht Ritschl, in a thoroughly anti-metaphysical campaign (including a rejection of the thing-in-itself and an affirmation of the primacy of practical reason). Thus it is understandable that his early investment in a continued inquiry into the significance for theology of Kant's transcendental method and Hegel's idealist development of the epistemological paradigm (as well as his fascination with the critical, negative-ontological thing-in-itself and the theoretical reason of the Critique of Pure Reason)--have gone all but unnoticed. The extent of the loss of an appreciation of the theoretical, **epistemologically** 'subjective', moment in Bonhoeffer's own methodology is indicated by such remarks as that by Bethge that Bonhoeffer, "coping with the term 'reality', struggling with its dangers of sheer positivism or even more of idealism," indeed "would rather fall into positivism than into idealism..."291 The encounter between Bonhoeffer and Adorno is intended, at the very least, to call such a standard assumption fundamentally into question.

The sort of critique proposed by both Bonhoeffer and Adorno--responsive to the challenges from the two sides of positivism and idealism--could be accomplished only if it retained a close relationship between the 'constructive' task and a 'de-construction' of the historical memory of previous failed attempts. This is the methodological significance of the strong archaeological, or historical, component in both Bonhoeffer's and Adorno's early work. Placed into such 'historical' perspective, their methods clearly did not take their particular forms solely from either extrinsic **theological** concerns or from external **Marxist** allegiances. Rather their early work shows both striking resonances and stringent arguments with a long line of conceptual forebears.

In particular, the tradition of neo-Kantianism sheds important light on the early work of Bonhoeffer and Adorno. For they affirmed, in agreement with their neo-Idealist forebears, (1) the employment of a form of Kantian 'transcendental' method, versus the loss of the function of critical subjectivity in materialism, scientism and positivism; and (2) a Kantian argument against metaphysics, versus the total rationalizing of all objectivity in absolute idealism. Yet (3) whereas the neo-Kantians had increasingly employed an idealist epistemology which collapsed the 'difference' at the heart of the subject-object duality, Bonhoeffer and Adorno continued to struggle with the implications of the antinomies of the Kantian subject and object, the critical distance between thinking and being which the epistemological paradigm encouraged thought to examine. Likewise, they each broke significantly with the two other key neo-Kantian traits which we have discussed above, arguing against (4) its rejection of Kant's thing-in-itself;[292] and (5) its presupposition of the primacy of practical reason. For the Ding an sich, we have argued above, had been crucial to the ontological dimension of the Kantian dialectic of difference. And the primacy of the critical function of theoretical reason had been the fundamental condition of the possibility of all knowledge itself for Kant.[293] Given this background, the immanent critiques with which Bonhoeffer and Adorno began their inaugural lectures, can be understood as caveats against their contemporaries for having merely re-enacted, rather than surmounted, the shortcomings of the course of transcendental philosophy since Kant.

NOTES

[1] As an excellent example of the direction some such work is taking, see Steven G. Smith, The Argument to the Other. Reason Beyond Reason in the Thought of Karl Barth and Emmanuel Levinas (Chico, CA.: Scholars Press, 1983).

[2] Bernard Lonergan, Method in Theology (N.Y.: Seabury Press, 1972), pp. 238, 240.

[3] For example, see Susan Buck-Morss, The Origin of Negative Dialectics, (N.Y.: The Free Press, 1977), Chapter 1, "Intellectual Beginnings: A Biographical Essay." Also see Martin Jay, The Dialectical Imagination. A History of the Frankfurt School and the Institute for Social Research, 1923-1950 (London: Heinemann, 1973), pp. 21--24.

[4] The standard for almost two decades now has been Eberhard Bethge, Dietrich Bonhoeffer. Also see Clifford J. Green, Bonhoeffer: The Sociality of Christ and Humanity; and Thomas I. Day, Dietrich Bonhoeffer on Christian Community and Common Sense, Toronto Studies in Theology, vol. 11; Bonhoeffer series, no. 2 (N.Y. and Toronto: The Edwin Mellen Press, 1982), pp. vii-xiv, 1-9.

[5] As Thomas E. Willey remarked in his Back to Kant. The Revival of Kantianism in German Social and Historical Thought, 1860-1914 (Detroit: Wayne State University Press, 1978), p. 38: "It would be stretching the point to say that nineteenth-century philosophy in Germany was a series of footnotes on Kant, but there is no gainsaying that all subsequent German philosophers, in addressing themselves to the central questions of truth and value, were compelled to accept, reject, or modify Kantian principles."

[6] Harvey Cox, "Using and Misusing Bonhoeffer," Christianity and Crisis 24 (1964):199-201.

[7] Vincent Descombes, Modern French Philosophy, trans. L. Scott-Fox and J. M. Harding. (Cambridge: Cambridge Univ. Press, 1980), p. 2.

[8] Hanfried Mueller, "Concerning the Reception and Interpretation of Dietrich Bonhoeffer," in World Come of Age, ed. Ronald Gregor Smith (Philadelphia: Fortress Press, 1967), p. 183.

[9]David H. Hopper, A Dissent on Bonhoeffer (Philadelphia: The Westminster Press, 1975).

[10]Andre Dumas, Dietrich Bonhoeffer: Theologian of Reality, trans. Robert McAfee Brown (New York: The Macmillan Company, 1971), p. 276, referring to Karl Barth, "From a Letter to Superintendent Herrenbrueck," in World Come of Age, ed. Ronald Gregor Smith (Philadelphia: Fortress Press, 1967), pp. 89-92.

[11]Bonhoeffer, Act and Being, p. 12 [G 9], translation mine.

[12]Immanuel Kant, "What is Enlightenment?," trans. Lewis White Beck, in On History, ed. Lewis White Beck (Indianapolis/New York: Bobbs Merrill, 1963), p. 3.

[13]Dietrich Bonhoeffer, Ethics, p. 97.

[14]See Alec R. Vidler, "Christianity, Liberalism, and Liberality," in Essays in Liberality (London: SCM Press, 1957), pp. 9-28.

[15]Bonhoeffer, "Concerning the Christian Idea of God," in Gesammelte Schriften, Band III, ed. Eberhard Bethge (Munich: Christian Kaiser Verlag, 1966), pp. 100-109; "The Theology of Crisis and its Attitude Toward Philosophy and Science," in GS III, pp. 110-126.

[16]Ibid., p. 101; cf. Bonhoeffer, "The Theology of Crisis and its Attitude Toward Philosophy Science," p. 120: "At the basis of all thinking lies the necessity of a system. Thinking is essentially systematic thinking, because it rests upon itself, it is the last ground and criterion of itself. System means the interpretation of the whole through the one which is its ground and its center, the thinking ego. Idealism saw and affirmed this as the proof of the autonomy and the freedom of man."

[17]"The Theology of Crisis and its Attitude Toward Philosophy and Science," p. 120.

[18]"Concerning the Christian Idea of God," p. 101.

[19]"The Theology of Crisis and its Attitude Toward Philosophy and Science," p. 122.

[20]Ibid., p. 123.

[21]"Concerning the Christian Idea of God," p. 103.

22Ibid., p. 105.

23"The Theology of Crisis and its Attitude Toward Philosophy and Science," p. 112.

24Ibid., pp. 115-116.

25"Concerning the Christian Idea of God," p. 102.

26Ibid., p. 105.

27Ibid., p. 108; cf. "The Theology of Crisis and its Attitude Toward Philosophy Science," p. 113 on "the awkwardness and foolishness of God's revelation."

28"Concerning the Christian Idea of God," p. 105.

29Ibid., p. 101.

30See "The Theology of Crisis and its Attitude Toward Philosophy and Science," p. 113-114: "It is revelation because it is **not** compatible with our own deepest essence, but entirely beyond our whole existence, for would it otherwise have had to be revealed, if it had been potentially in us before? ... All that means that God's revelation in Christ is revelation in concealment, secrecy. All other so-called revelation is revelation in openness."

31"Concerning the Christian Idea of God," p. 102.

32Act and Being, p. 15.

33"Concerning the Christian Idea of God," p. 106.

34"The Theology of Crisis and its Attitude Toward Philosophy and Science," p. 118.

35Ibid., p. 123-124.

36Ibid., p. 124.

37Ibid.

38Ibid.; emphases added.

39The epistemological issue has recently been the subject of renewed debate particularly in political and social theory. For example, see Scott Warren, The Emergence of Dialectical Theory. Philosophy and Political Inquiry (Chicago: The University of Chicago Press,

1984); Michael Theunissen, The Other. Studies in the Social Ontology of Husserl, Heidegger, Sartre, and Buber, trans. Christopher Macann (Cambridge, Mass.: The MIT Press, 1984); and Fred R. Dallmayr, Twilight of Subjectivity, pp. ix-37.

40The virtual ubiquity of the subject-object problematic in modern theology can be seen, for example, in Karl Barth, Church Dogmatics, II/1, paragraph 25, ed. G. W. Bromiley and T. F. Torrance (Edinburgh: T & T Clark, 1957); Paul Tillich, Systematic Theology, I (Chicago: University of Chicago Press, 1951), pp. 18ff.; Martin Buber, I and Thou, trans. Walter Kaufmann (New York: Charles Scribner's Sons, 1970), pp. 58-59; Karl Rahner, Hearers of the Word, Chapter 3 (New York: Seabury Press, 1969); Juergen Moltmann, Theology of Hope. On the Ground and the Implications of a Christian Eschatology (New York: Harper and Row, 1967), pp. 45-50; Bernard Lonergan, Method in Theology, pp. 13-25. Also see Nancy Carolyn Ring, "Doctrine Within the Dialectic of Subject and Object: A Critical Study of the Positions of Paul Tillich and Bernard Lonergan," Ph.D. dissertation, Marquette University, 1980.

41James Brown, Kierkegaard, Heidegger, Buber and Barth. A Study of Subjectivity and Objectivity in Existentialist Thought [Originally published as Subject and Object in Modern Theology] (New York: Collier Books, 1962), p. 28.

42Ibid., p. 18.

43Bonhoeffer, Act and Being, p. 12.

44Warren, The Emergence of Dialectical Theory, p. 28; cf. Brown, Kierkegaard, Heidegger, Buber and Barth, p. 160.

45Immanuel Kant, Critique of Pure Reason, B xxi; xviii; vii.

46Warren, The Emergence of Dialectical Theory, p. 29.

47Ibid., p. 29.

48Ibid., p. 30.

49Paul Ricoeur, "The Antinomy of Human Reality and the Problem of Philosophical Anthropology," in Readings in Existential Phenomenology, ed. Nathaniel Lawrence and Daniel O'Connor (Englewood Cliffs: Prentice Hall, 1967), p. 395.

[50]Warren, The Emergence of Dialectical Theory, p. 33.

[51]Claude Welch, Protestant Thought in the Nineteenth Century. Volume I, 1799-1870 (New Haven: Yale University Press, 1972), p. 48.

[52]Ibid.

[53]Warren, The Emergence of Dialectical Theory, p. 33.

[54]G. W. F. Hegel, Phenomenology of Spirit, p. 40.

[55]Warren, The Emergence of Dialectical Theory, p. 35.

[56]Ibid., p. 45. Cf. Willey, Back to Kant, p. 33, who insists that Kant himself "in the Foundations of the Metaphysics of Morals...insists on the essential unity of reason."

[57]Welch, Protestant Thought, pp. 59-60.

[58]Soren Kierkegaard, Concluding Unscientific Postscript, trans. David F. Swenson and Walter Lowrie (Princeton: Princeton University Press, 1968), p. 187.

[59]Kant, Critique of Pure Reason, B xiv; B 307.

[60]Ibid., B xix; xx. Perhaps the best introduction to the issue of metaphysics and the limits of reason is Kant's own exposition of the First Critique in the 1783 Prolegomena to any Future Metaphysics (Indianapolis: Bobbs-Merrill, 1977), pp. 99-113, "On the Determination of the Bounds of Pure Reason."

[61]Paul Tillich, Mysticism and Guilt-Consciousness in Schellings' Philosophical Development, trans. Victor Nuovo (Lewisburg: Bucknell University Press, 1974), p. 34. See P. Christopher Smith, "Heidegger, Hegel and the Problem of das Nichts," International Philosophical Quarterly 8 (1968), p. 383; and Richard F. Grabau, "Kant's Concept of the Thing in Itself: An Interpretation," Review of Metaphysics (1962-63), p. 774: "...Being is appearing and the thing in itself...serves as a guard against limiting things to the character they present in **our** intuition."

⁶²Cf. George Schrader, "The Philosophy of Existence," in The Philosophy of Kant and Our Modern World, ed. Charles W. Hendel (N.Y.: The Liberal Arts Press, 1957), p. 53.

⁶³P. Christopher Smith, "Heidegger's Critique of Absolute Knowledge," New Scholasticism, 45 (Winter 1971), p. 86.

⁶⁴Cf. P.C. Smith, "Heidegger, Hegel, and the Problem of das Nichts," p. 397.

⁶⁵Hegel, Phenomenology of Spirit, "Preface," p. 9.

⁶⁶Warren, The Emergence of Dialectical Theory, p. 32.

⁶⁷Brown, Kierkegaard, Heidegger, Buber and Barth, p. 20, emphasis mine. On idealism's indebtedness to Kant's Critique of Pure Reason, see Hans-Georg Gadamer, Hegel's Dialectic, trans. Christopher Smith (New Haven: Yale University Press, 1976); Quentin Lauer, Essays in Hegelian Dialectic (New York: Fordham University Press, 1977); Werner Marx, Hegel's Phenomenology of Spirit, trans. Peter Heath (New York: Harper and Row, 1975).

⁶⁸Gadamer, "The Philosophical Foundations of the Twentieth Century," in Philosophical Hermeneutics (Berkeley: University of California Press, 1977), p. 119; cf. Gadamer's Hegel's Dialectic, p. 9.

⁶⁹Brown, Kierkegaard, Heidegger, Buber and Barth, p. 22, emphasis mine.

⁷⁰Ibid., p. 154.

⁷¹Paul Tillich, Systematic Theology, III (Chicago: University of Chicago Press, 1963), p. 70.

⁷²Brown, Kierkegaard, Heidegger, Buber and Barth, p. 160.

⁷³Warren, The Emergence of Dialectical Theory. p. 45. On "the notion of the concrete," see G. W. F. Hegel, Vorlesungen ueber die Geschichte der Philosophie, Band I [Hegel's Lectures on the History of Philosophy, trans. E. S. Haldane (London: Routledge & Kegan Paul, Ltd, 1892)], in On Art, Religion, Philosophy, ed. J. Glenn Gray (New York: Harper Torchbooks, 1970), pp. 231-235.

[74]G. W. F. Hegel, _Science of Logic_, trans. W. H. Johnston and L. G. Struthers (London: George Allen and Unwin, 1929), 2:145.

[75]Warren, _The Emergence of Dialectical Theory_, p. 45.

[76]Smith, _The Argument to the Other_, p. xxvii.

[77]Herbert Marcuse, _Reason and Revolution. Hegel and the Rise of Social Theory_ (Boston: Beacon Press, 1960), p. 18.

[78]Smith, "Heidegger, Hegel and the Problem of _das Nichts_," p. 383.

[79]Immanuel Kant, _On History_, p. 8.

[80]Hegel, _Phenomenology of Spirit_, par. 31, p. 18.

[81]Marcuse, _Reason and Revolution_, p. 10.

[82]Hegel, _Phenomenology of Spirit_, par. 20, p. 11.

[83]Marcuse, _Reason and Revolution_, p. 11; cf. P.C. Smith, "Heidegger's Critique of Absolute Knowledge," p. 79.

[84]Marcuse, _Reason and Revolution_, p. 10.

[85]Warren, _The Emergence of Dialectical Theory_, p. 34.

[86]Ibid., p. 36.

[87]Hegel, _Phenomenology of Spirit_, par. 2, p. 2.

[88]Marcuse, _Reason and Revolution_, pp. 5-6.

[89]Hegel, _Phenomenology of Spirit_, par. 58, p. 36.

[90]Robert C. Solomon, _From Rationalism to Existentialism. The Existentialists and their Nineteenth-Century Backgrounds_ (N.Y.: Humanities Press, 1972), p. 47.

[91]Warren, _The Emergence of Dialectical Theory_, p. 37. See Ruediger Bubner, _Modern German Philosophy_, trans. Eric Matthews (Cambridge: Cambridge University Press, 1981), pp. 158-159 on the relationship between phenomenology and history, as seen in a comparison of Hegel's _Phenomenology of Spirit_ with the _Science of_

Logic. As Bubner rightly concludes, "the philosophy for which phenomenology prepares the way proves its superiority by the fact that it recognizes, rather than disavows, its **historically conditioned character,** and works its way through it rather than blindly leaping over it" (p. 160).

92J. N. Findlay, "Foreword" to Phenomenology of Spirit, p. xiii.

93Hegel, Phenomenology of Spirit, par. 73, p. 46.

94Ibid., par. 74, p. 47.

95G. W. F. Hegel, The Logic of Hegel, trans. William Wallace (Oxford: Clarendon Press, 1892), p. 84.

96Hegel, Phenomenology of Spirit, par. 76, p. 48; cf. Quentin Lauer, A Reading of Hegel's Phenomenology of Spirit (New York: Fordham University Press, 1976), pp. 24, 26; see Jean Hyppolite, Genesis and Structure of Hegel's Phenomenology of Spirit, trans. Samuel Cherniak and John Heckman (Evanston: Northwestern University Press, 1974),p. 6; Marcuse, Reason and Revolution, p. 27. Cf. Hegel's remarks on the method of dialectic in the final chapter of the Science of Logic.

97Hegel, Phenomenology of Spirit, par. 86, p. 55, emphases mine; see Hyppolite, Genesis and Structure, pp. 8, 10.

98Hegel, Phenomenology of Spirit, par. 86, p. 55.

99Ibid., par. 89, p. 59.

100Ibid., par. 20, p. 11.

101Ibid., par. 80, p. 51; see Lauer, A Reading of Hegel's Phenomenology of Spirit, pp. 35-38; Hyppolite, Genesis and Structure, p. 18.

102Hegel, Phenomenology of Spirit, par. 37, p. 21.

103Ibid., par. 37, p. 21.

104Warren, The Emergence of Dialectical Theory, p. 35.

105Ibid., p. 39.

106Hegel, Phenomenology of Spirit, par. 78, p. 50.

[107]Findlay, "Foreword," to _Phenomenology of Spirit,_ p. xiv; cf. Marcuse, _Reason and Revolution,_ p. 26.

[108]Warren, _The Emergence of Dialectical Theory,_ p. 35.

[109]Ibid., pp. 45-46.

[110]Ibid., p. 41.

[111]Ibid., p. 44.

[112]Hegel, _Phenomenology of Spirit,_ par. 20, p. 11.

[113]Martin Heidegger, _Kant and the Problem of Metaphysics_ (Bloomington: Indiana University Press, 1975), pp. 252-253.

[114]Hegel, _Phenomenology of Spirit,_ par. 26, p. 15.

[115]Warren, _The Emergence of Dialectical Theory,_ p. 42.

[116]Jacques Derrida, "The Ends of Man," trans. Alan Bass, in _Margins of Philosophy_ (Chicago: University of Chicago Press, 1982), p. 121.

[117]Warren, _The Emergence of Dialectical Theory,_ p. 39. See Bubner, _Modern German Philosophy,_ pp. 162-166 on recent attempts to propose a **semantic model** for understanding the Hegelian plurality-as-totality.

[118]Warren, _The Emergence of Dialectical Theory,_ p. 39.

[119]On the varieties of post-Hegelian philosophy, see Karl Loewith, _From Hegel to Nietzsche,_ trans. D. E. Green (Garden City: Anchor Doubleday, 1967) and William J. Brazill, _The Young Hegelians_ (New Haven: Yale University Press, 1970).

[120]See Barth, _Protestant theology in the Nineteenth Century,_ pp. 491-498 on Marheinecke; see James C. Livingston, _Modern Christian Thought From the Enlightenment to Vatican II_ (New York: Macmillan Publishing Co. Inc., 1971), pp. 157-168 on Biedermann.

[121]Willey, _Back to Kant,_ p. 40; Lotze was later to influence not only the 'personalist' movement but also the turn to ethics in the theology of Albrecht Ritschl.

See his discussion of Lotze on pp. 40-57, especially pp. 48-50. See B. M. G. Reardon, Religious Thought in the Nineteenth Century, Illustrated from Writers of the Period, (Cambridge: Cambridge University Press, 1966), pp. 125-137, who discusses and illustrates Lotze as precursor to 'personalism' and the turn towards 'values', and notes his influence on A. Ritschl, who in Reardon's opinion "chose to retain [from Lotze] the value-judgment whilst dispensing with the metaphysic" (p. 127).

[122]Ibid., p. 27: "Picking up the revolutionary implications of the dialectic, the left-wingers began to move along the entire range of radical politics, from socialism to anarchism. The right-wingers, or conservative Hegelians, stressed the identity of reality with reason and championed religious orthodoxy."

[123]Ibid., p. 24. Willey discusses the political events leading up to the situation that "through the 1830's and 1840's, the actual course of politics in Germany and Western Europe seemed increasingly to belie Hegelian confidence in the historical immanence of reason." (p. 28.) Thus "although the alleged correspondence between idea and reality was being challenged before the 1848 revolutions, it was the failure of reason to triumph in 1848 that brought final discredit to Hegel's rational logos" (p. 28.).

[124]Lewis White Beck, "Neo-Kantianism," in The Encyclopedia of Philosophy, ed. Paul Edwards (N.Y.: Macmillan Publishing Co., 1967), vol. 5, p. 469.

[125]As Willey remarks in Back to Kant, "Popular materialism and Haeckel's monism continued to grip the public mind long after scientist had rejected the gross simplifications" of the "crude materialism" of thinkers such as Jakob Moeschott, who "explained mental activity by using the physical analogy that the brain secretes thoughts just as the liver secretes bile" (p. 25).

[126]Frederick Copleston, A History of Philosophy, vol. 7/ii (N.Y.: Doubleday, 1965), p. 202: The Vienna Circle "was a question of the positivist mentality, which had become widespread in the nineteenth century, becoming reflectively conscious of itself and seeing its own presuppositions."

[127]Willey, Back to Kant, pp. 9, 21; see pp. 37f. on the general characteristics and variety of types of Neo-Kantianism.

128Copleston, A History of Philosophy, 7/ii, p. 134.

129Beck, "Neo-Kantianism," p. 468.

130Copleston, A History of Philosophy, 7/ii, p. 134.

131Fritz Ringer, The Decline of the German Mandarins. The German Academic Community 1890-1933 (Cambridge, Mass: Harvard University Press, 1969), p. 306.

132Marcuse, Reason and Revolution, p. 6.

133Ibid., p. 11.

134Quoted in Marcuse, Reason and Revolution, p. 19. Thus the anti-empiricist strain of the transcendental tradition itself already has a nascently **moral** dimension to its criticism.

135Quoted in Paul K. Feyerabend, "Against Method: Outline of an Anarchistic Theory of Knowledge," in M. Radnor & S. Winokur, eds., Minnesota Studies in the Philosophy of Science, vol. 4 (Minneapolis, 1970), p. 31.

136Marcuse, Reason and Revolution, p. 20.

137Ibid., p. 26; Karl Marx, "Theses on Feuerbach," No XI. in David McLellan, ed., Karl Marx: Selected Writings (Oxford: Oxford University Press, 1977), p. 158.

138Martin Jay, The Dialectical Imagination, p. 46.

139Marcuse, Reason and Revolution, p. 27.

140Willey, Back to Kant, p. 29: "No formulation of Hegel was more vehemently fought by the new generation of critics [in the 1850's] than his generally misunderstood statement in the Philosophy of Right that the rational is real and everything real is rational. This doctrine, more than any other, laid Hegel open to attack and make him sound like the voice of reaction, the soul of the status quo."

141Ibid., p. 9.

142Marcuse, Reason and Revolution, p. 256.

143Koppel S. Pinson, Modern Germany (N.Y.: The Macmillan Co., 1954), p. 51. It is the failure to make this distinction among Hegelians which leads to gross overgeneralizations such as Stackelberg's statement that "the effect of idealist attitudes was not to mobilize energies for social or institutional reform but instead to channel them into quiescent self-improvement;" see Roderick Stackelberg, Idealism Debased: From Voelkisch Ideology to National Socialism (Kent, OH: Kent State University Press, 1981), p. 3.

144Martin Jay, "Metapolitics of Utopianism," Dissent (July-August 1970): 347; cf. Marcuse, Reason and Revolution, pp. 399-400.

145Marcuse, Reason and Revolution, p. 267.

146Ringer, The Decline of the German Mandarins, p. 3.

147Marcuse, Reason and Revolution, p. 323; cf. E. M. Butler, The Saint-Simonian Religion in Germany: a Study of the young German Movement (Cambridge: Cambridge University Press, 1926) and Walter Simon, European Positivism in the Nineteenth Century (Ithaca: Cornell University Press, 1963); see Ringer, p. 257.

148Marcuse, Reason and Revolution, p. 324.

149Ibid., p. 325; for a critique of too loose an employment of the positivist-materialist labels, see Ringer, The Decline of the German Mandarins, pp. 295-304.

150Quoted in Marcuse, Reason and Revolution, p. 325.

151Russell Jacoby, Social Amnesia. A Critique of Conformist Psychology from Adler to Laing (Boston: Beacon Press, 1975), p. 60.

152Ibid., p. 61.

153Willey, Back to Kant, p. 28; cf. Marcuse, Reason and Revolution, p. 326.

154See George Mosse, The Crisis of German Ideology: Intellectual Origins of the Third Reich (New York: Universal Library, 1964).

155See Koppel S. Pinson, Pietism as a Factor in the

Rise of German Nationalism (New York: Octagon Books, Inc., 1968).

156Pinson, Modern Germany.

157Ibid., p. 39; compare Ringer's summary of the relationship between the French and German Enlightenments in The Decline of the German Mandarins, pp. 83-90.

158George Mosse, The Culture of Western Europe. The Nineteenth and Twentieth Centuries (Rand McNally & Company, 1961), p. 41.

159For a succinct statement of the relationship between volkism and nationalism, see Stackelberg, Idealism Debased, pp. 5-8.

160Quoted in Fritz Stern, The Politics of Cultural Despair (Berkeley: Univ. of California Press, 1961), p. 92.

161Pinson, Pietism, p. 34; Pinson, Modern Germany, pp. 39, 41. The result of such conflations was not without its intellectual ironies. As Stackelberg points out (p. 3): A "confidence in the ultimate beneficence of the world spirit enabled Hegel later in life to glorify the Prussian state. Nonetheless, voelkisch ideologues tended to be suspicious of the progressive implications of the Hegelian dialectic. The appealed instead to the more safely apolitical idealism of Goethe or Schiller. This, too, is not without irony, for classical self-cultivation (and the Romantic flight into dream and fantasy) also reflected frustration in the face of stultifying social reality."

162Pinson, Pietism, p. 48.

163Mosse, The Crisis of German Ideology, p. 14.

164Martin Jay, Marxism and Totality. The Adventures of a Concept from Lukacs to Habermas (Berkeley: University of California Press, 1984), p. 73.

165Ibid., p. 72.

166Eberhard Bethge, "The Challenge of Dietrich Bonhoeffer's Life and Theology," in World Come of Age (London: Collins, 1967), p. 27. See Ringer, The Decline of the German Mandarins, p. 308: "The Nietzsche revival which apparently took place on a popular level, in certain political and literary circles, and among young people, had no marked repercussions in the German academic world."

167Bethge, "Challenge," p. 31.

168Quoted in Green, Sociality, 161-162 from Gesammelte Schriften, V, pp. 156-180. No further such examples can be found after that date, for upon his return to Berlin from Barcelona, where this speech had been made, it became unequivocally clear that such language was not even rhetorically acceptable.

169Fritz Stern, The Failure of Illiberalism (New York: Alfred Knopf, 1972), p. xxxiii; see Roderick Stackelberg, Idealism Debased, p. 1: "National Socialism derived its strength in part because of the perception of many Germans that it was a movement of national regeneration, with roots deep in the German past. Regeneration in effect meant reversing the social consequences of the two major upheavals of modern times, the French Revolution and the Industrial Revolution."

170Mosse, Crisis, p. 301, emphasis mine.

171Marcuse, Reason and Revolution p. 390.

172Ibid., p. 411.

173Ibid., pp. 413-414.

174Ibid., pp. 5-6.

175Quoted in Marcuse, Reason and Revolution, p. 419. See pp. 409-419 for an excellent summary of National Socialism's antagonism towards Hegel.

176Willey, Back to Kant, p. 22.

177Ibid., p. 35.

178Ibid., p. 133.

179Beck, "Neo-Kantianism," pp. 472, 473.

180Copleston, A History of Philosophy, 7/ii, p. 135.

181Ibid., p. 137. See Theodor Adorno, "The Actuality of Philosophy," Telos 31 (Spring 1977), p. 121: "The southwest-German School of Rickert, ... purports that its 'values' represent more concrete and applicable philosophical criteria than the ideas of the Marburg School, and has developed a method which sets empirical reality in relation, however questionable, to those values." Cf. Ringer, The Decline of the German Mandarins, p. 311: "According to Rickert, the epistemologically real or objective is that which follows the norms of right thinking." "Knowledge is in the realm of theoretical reason; moral judgments are in the realm of practical reason; and in both spheres, there are norms of right thinking to guide us. The commitment to truth is itself a valuation...".

[182]See Willey, Back to Kant, p. 37; Cf. Beck, "Neo-Kantianism," p. 468 who remarks that the various schools of neo-Kantianism "had little in common beyond a strong reaction against irrationalism and speculative naturalism and a conviction that philosophy could be a 'science' only if it returned to the method and spirit of Kant."

[183]Jay, Marxism and Totality, pp. 76-77: "the neo-Kantians came increasingly to focus on Kant's moral teachings, his Critique of Practical Reason."

[184]Buck-Morss, The Origin of Negative Dialectics, p. 7.

[185]Willey, Back to Kant, p. 131.

[186]Jay, Marxism and Totality, p. 76.

[187]Ringer, The Decline of the German Mandarins, pp. 306-307.

[188]Adorno, "Actuality," p. 121. "Contemporary bourgeois philosophers felt ... compelled to opt for either (formal, absolute) reason or (historical, relative) reality as the foundation of theory. At one pole, the Marburg neo-Kantians held onto the idealist concept of reason as universal, but paid dearly for this by sacrificing (histori-cal and social) content. ... At the opposite pole, Leb-ensphilosophie, by accepting the historical relativity of truth, as well as the necessity of philosophy's dealing with empirical content (lived experience), 'has admittedly maintained contact with reality, but in so doing has lost every claim to make sense out of the empirical world which presses in upon it....';" from translation by Buck-Morss in The Origin of Negative Dialectics, p. 71.

[189]Willey, Back to Kant, p. 120.

190Origin of Negative Dialectics, p. 70. Contrast Willey, Back to Kant, p. 102: "Although much of the Marburg literature is abstruse epistemology, especially that part of it devoted to the logic of mathematics and science, a large portion deals mainly with ethical, political, and social questions of an eminently practical nature." And 102-103: "Hermann Cohen and Paul Natorp in their work give at least as much attention to social philosophy as to logic."

191Willey, Back to Kant, p. 104.

192Ringer, The Decline of the German Mandarins, p. 393.

193Buck-Morss, The Origin of Negative Dialectics, p. 7.

194Ringer, The Decline of the German Mandarins, p. 393.

195Ibid., p. 250.

196Karl Barth, "Evangelical Theology in the 19th Century," in The Humanity of God (Richmond, VA: John Knox Press, 1972), p. 28.

197Marcuse, Reason and Revolution, p. 327.

198Ibid., p. 405.

199Willey, Back to Kant, p. 181.

200See Bethge, Dietrich Bonhoeffer, pp. 3-28.

201Jay, Adorno, p. 25.

202Bethge, Dietrich Bonhoeffer, p. 27.

203Ibid., p. 35.

204Ibid., p. 43.

205Ibid., p. 36.

206Ibid., 36.

207It is also unfortunate that, apparently, none of Bonhoeffer's student-papers or notes in philosophy have survived.

[208]Bethge, <u>Dietrich Bonhoeffer</u>, p. 50 obliquely mentions that in the summer of 1924, when the only philosophy course that Bonhoeffer was taking was Maier's Erkenntnistheorie, Bonhoeffer was reading Husserl and Hegel.

[209]L. E. Loemker, "Spranger, (Franz Ernst) Eduard," in <u>The Encyclopedia of Philosophy</u> (N.Y.: Macmillan, 1967), vol. 8, p. 1.

[210]Bethge, <u>Dietrich Bonhoeffer</u>, p. 48.

[211]Ibid., p. 93.

[212]Bonhoeffer notes Luetgert's <u>Die Religion des Idealismus</u> in <u>Act and Being</u>, p. 20.

[213]On the question of the extent of Bonhoeffer's knowledge of Hegel, see Green, <u>Bonhoeffer: The Sociality of Christ and Humanity</u>, pp. 94-95, n. 49.

[214]Jay, <u>Adorno</u>, pp. 21, 25; cf. p. 22: Kracauer's "distrust of closed systems and his stress on the particular as opposed to the universal made a significant impression on his young friend." Also see Martin Jay, "Adorno and Kracauer: Notes on a Troubled Friendship," <u>Salmagundi</u>, 40 (Winter, 1978).

[215]Jay, <u>Adorno</u>, p.26. See Ringer, <u>The Decline of the German Mandarins</u>, p. 75: "The University of Frankfurt officially opened in 1914..." and took its peculiar character in part from its antecedent in Frankfurt, "an academy for social and commercial sciences".

[216]Buck-Morss, <u>The Origin of Negative Dialectics</u>, p. 7.

[217]Fred R. Dallmayr, "Phenomenology and Critical Theory: Adorno," <u>Cultural Hermeneutics</u> 3/4 (July 1976), p. 369. As Dallmayr continues, "despite the idealist recipe offered in its pages (a recipe he later vehemently disavowed), the focus of the study provided an avenue for probing important, unresolved issues in Husserl's thought. Briefly formulated, the dissertation tried to demonstrate that Husserl was insufficiently wedded to idealism--more precisely: that Husserl's attempt to trace all experience back to the 'primordial evidence' of consciousness was basically inconsistent, since it was flawed by a continued endorsement of the Cartesian mind-body dualism or of the Kantian bifurcation of mind and 'thing-in-itself'." See Theodor W. Adorno, <u>Philosophische</u>

Fruehschriften, Gesammelte Schriften, Vol. 1, ed. Rolf Tiedemann (Frankfurt am Main: Suhrkamp, 1973), p. 375.

[218]Dallmayr, "Phenomenology and Critical Theory: Adorno," p. 371. This had also been the case with Bonhoeffer, whose first dissertation was an inquiry into the relationship between the social-category in philosophy and theology and the prevailing idealist social philosophies of that time.

[219]Buck-Morss, The Origin of Negative Dialectics, p. 11; on the Vienna interlude in Adorno's career see Buck-Morss, pp. 11-17.

[220]See Allan Janik and Stephen Toulmin, Wittgenstein's Vienna (N.Y.: Simon and Schuster, 1973), p. 26.

[221]Buck-Morss, The Origin of Negative Dialectics, p. 17.

[222]Ibid., p. 17.

[223]Dallmayr, "Phenomenology and Critical Theory: Adorno," p. 372.

[224]Ibid., pp. 371-372.

[225]Jay, Adorno, p. 29.

[226]Dallmayr, "Phenomenology and Critical Theory: Adorno," p. 372.

[227]Jay, Adorno, p. 28. Cf. Buck-Morss, The Origin of Negative Dialectics, p. 20: "Beginning in 1927 Adorno spent much time in Berlin. He visited his future wife, Gretel Karplus, and their circle there included Walter Benjamin, Siegfried Kracauer, Ernst Bloch, Otto Klemperer, Moholy-Nagy, and, importantly, Bertolt Brecht and his friends..."; also see Buck-Morss, p. 206, n. 187: "He later estimated that by 1933 he had spent in sum almost four years there."

[228]"The Actuality of Philosophy," p. 124.

[229]Rose, The Melancholy Science, p. 151.

[230]See Buck-Morss, The Origin of Negative Dialectics, p. 100.

[231]Adorno, Prisms, p. 32.

[232]Buck-Morss, The Origin of Negative Dialectics, p. 66; emphasis added.

[233]Adorno, Prisms, p. 32.

[234]Bonhoeffer, "Man in Contemporary Philosophy and Theology," p. 46.

[235]Ibid., p. 46.

[236]Ibid., p. 46; trans. altered.

[237]Ibid., p. 47. Bonhoeffer's use of the term 'Transcendence' here should not be confused with Adorno's negative sense of 'transcendent criticism'. The emphasis clearly falls on the Aktbezug, the act-of-referring, which is an act of the subject **within** its process of finite knowledge.

[238]Ibid., p. 48; trans. altered.

[239]Ibid., p. 47.

[240]Ibid., p. 47; translation altered.

[241]Ibid., p. 48.

[242]Bonhoeffer's reading of Heidegger, based just on Being and Time was a common one, against which Heidegger himself responded in the years immediately following. See Steven William Esthimer, Max Scheler's Concept of the Person (Ann Arbor: University Microfilms, 1983), pp. 1-25 on the development of Scheler's thought and pp. 26-81 on Scheler's view of philosophy and phenomenology.

[243]Bonhoeffer, "Man in Contemporary Philosophy and Theology," p. 49.

[244]Ibid., p. 50.

[245]Ibid., p. 49; cf. pp. 52, 53.

[246]Ibid., p. 52.

[247]Ibid., p. 53.

[248]Ibid.

[249]Ibid.

250It is important to remember that Tillich was known at this time in Germany primarily as a philosopher, not a theologian, as was later the case in the United States.

251Bonhoeffer, "Man in Contemporary Philosophy and Theology," p. 53.

252Ibid.

253Ibid., p. 54.

254Ibid., p. 55.

255Ibid.

256Ibid.; see Bubner, Modern German Philosophy, pp. 180-181: "A comparison with Hegel's argument of the dialectic of the limit may be helpful in elucidating this point. Hegel cogently disproved Kant's thesis of the thing-in-itself in so far as he was able to show that to erect a formal limit already implies that one can stand on the other side of it. Limits which divide two domains can not be unilaterally established. The prohibition of knowledge of a thing-in-itself is ipso facto its conscious positing and thus already implies transgression of the limit which was supposed to be marked by the transcendence of that Something. Hegel inferred from his argument that the given limit of knowledge can ultimately be recognized by knowledge and thus relativized, or vice versa that nothing can limit knowledge as knowledge."

257Bonhoeffer, "Man in Contemporary Philosophy and Theology," p. 55.

258Ibid.

259Ibid., p. 56.

260Ibid.

261Adorno, "The Actuality of Philosophy," p. 120.

262Ibid.

263Bonhoeffer, "Man in Contemporary Philosophy and Theology," p. 49.

264Ibid., p. 122.

265Adorno, "The Actuality of Philosophy," p. 122.

266Ibid.

267Bonhoeffer, "Man in Contemporary Philosophy and Theology," p. 50.

268Adorno, "The Actuality of Philosophy," p. 122.

269Bonhoeffer, "Man in Contemporary Philosophy and Theology," p. 50.

270Adorno, "The Actuality of Philosophy," p. 120.

271Ibid., p. 120.

272Ibid., p. 123.

273Ibid., p. 124.

274Ibid., p. 121.

275Ibid.

276Ibid., p. 124.

277Ibid.

278Ibid., p. 125.

279Ibid.

280Ibid., p. 121; also see p. 122. Note that this reading of Husserl was dependent upon the work of Husserl prior to the introduction of the life-world into the discussion.

281Ibid., p. 122.

282Ibid.

283On the importance of "The Actuality of Philosophy," see Buck-Morss, The Origin of Negative Dialectics, p. 69: "Indeed, it is tempting to suggest that Adorno may have had this latter document before him when he was writing the introduction to Negative Dialektik, so great is the affinity of their philosophical intent. "Die Aktualitaet der Philosophie" is therefore a key document for introducing the concepts of Adorno's 'logic of disintegration' and the 'negative dialectics' into which it evolved."

[284]Bubner, Modern German Philosophy, p. 180.

[285]Adorno, Prisms, p. 21.

[286]See note 1 above.

[287]David Held, Introduction to Critical Theory. Horkheimer to Habermas (Berkeley: University of California Press, 1980), p. 202; compare the similarity in this position and that of several of the leading later neo-Kantians; e.g., see Beck, "Neo-Kantianism," p. 471, who notes that for Paul Natorp, "the objective and the subjective were not two realms, either opposed to each other or one including the other. Rather, they were two directions of knowledge, objectification and subjectification, each starting from the same phenomenon and each employing the transcendental method..." Thus "it is easy to see how Nicolai Hartmann, Natorp's pupil, could move over into the phenomenological camp."

[288]Held, Introduction to Critical Theory, p. 202.

[289]Cf. the later neo-Kantians, e.g. in Copleston, A History of Philosophy, 7/ii, pp. 211-212, who says that Nicolai Hartmann (1882-1950) "developed an impressive realist ontology" in his Principles of a Metaphysics of Knowledge (1921). "Hartmann's ontology, therefore, is an overcoming of Neo-Kantianism inasmuch as it involves a study of the objective categories of real being."

[290]See Franz Rosenzweig's Star of Redemption, trans. W. Hallo (New York, 1971).

[291]Eberhard Bethge, in World Come of Age, p. 42.

[292]See I.M. Bochenski, Contemporary European Philosophy (Berkeley: Univ. of California Press, 1956), pp. 88-93. See Beck, "Neo-Kantianism," p. 469, who says that Otto Liebmann's Kant und die Epigonen "argued that Kant made one great mistake: believing in the existence of the thing-in-itself. This belief, however, was not an essential part of Kant's doctrine, but only a dogmatic residue that could be removed without damage to the rest of the system." Beck continues (p. 470) that according to Hermann Cohen, "the thing-in-itself is not a thing at all. It does not exist, but is only a thought of a limit (Grenzbegriff) to our approach to a complete determination of things as they are; that is, as they would fully satisfy systematic thought." Compare Copleston's comment in A History of Philosophy, vol. 7/ii, pp.

136-137: "Both Cohen and Natorp endeavoured to overcome the dichotomy between thought and being which
seemed to be implied by the Kantian theory of the thing-
in-itself... But though Cohen and Natorp sought to unite
thought and being as related poles of one process, it
would not have been possible for them to eliminate ef-
fectively the thing-in-itself without deserting the Kantian
standpoint and making the transition to metaphysical
ideism."

[293]See section (B) (2) above.

CHAPTER TWO

BONHOEFFER'S ACT AND BEING:
THE PRIORITY OF THE OTHER AS CRITIQUE OF IDEALISM

Chapter One outlined the general manner in which the subject-object paradigm of transcendental epistemology provides the enduring parameters for a critical dialectical method, with particular regard to epistemology's implications for sociality and ethics. That discussion proposed two formal models of 'dialectics'. The Kantian model radicalizes, if not effects, the **difference** between subject and object. The Hegelian alternative is a dialectics which either presupposes or develops the **identity** of subject and object, the totality of rationality over against which there can be said to be no 'non-identical' or heterogeneous being. The chapter then detailed the specific historical, cultural and biographical context within which Bonhoeffer and Adorno formulated their markedly similar methods of appropriating the legacy of the debate surrounding the epistemological paradigm.

In Chapter Two we now turn directly to one of the two particular texts which was the original occasion for this study, Bonhoeffer's dissertation, Act and Being. This chapter centers specifically upon Bonhoeffer's proposals concerning the **method** of the immanent critique of idealism found in Section 'A' of this work. In addition, it draws significantly upon certain parallel concerns from his first thesis, Sanctorum Communio, regarding the **sociality** and **ethics** of epistemology. The chapter concludes that the central contribution of Act and Being to the immanent critique of idealism is Bonhoeffer's methodological typology by means of which to understand the stakes involved in his early general concern with the idealist fate of the Kantian epistemological paradigm.

The current chapter is divided into three main sections, which correspond to our overall concern with the **epistemological paradigm**, and the conceptions of **sociality** and of **ethics** implicit to it. The first outlines the centrality of epistemology in Bonhoeffer's immanent criticism of idealism as found in the first of the three main divisions of Act and Being.[1] The second and third sections of the chapter then look at the methodological connection between Act and Being and Sanctorum Communio. They inquire into the way in which Bonhoeffer's understanding of the tension between the Kantian epistemological paradigm and the idealist development of it provides a contribution to the basic formal problems of

91

sociality and ethics that are implied in the reactions against the subject-object paradigm, particularly in personalist, or dialogical, philosophy.

The text of Act and Being is itself divided into three main divisions. Besides the first section with which we are primarily concerned in this chapter, Part 'B' addresses "The Act-Being Problem in the Interpretation of Revelation and the Church as the Solution of this Problem," and Part C addresses "the Act-Being Problem in the Concrete Doctrine of Humanity 'In Adam' and 'In Christ'." The concerns of these three divisions of the text correspond roughly to the concerns of our tripartite typology of epistemology, sociality and ethics. Yet, we will argue, borrowing from Adorno's distinction, that Part 'A' is most profitably read as a form of 'immanent criticism' and that Parts 'B' and 'C' reflect the shift to a 'transcendent criticism' of the Act-Being Problem from a related, but extrinsic, Christian theological perspective. Bonhoeffer structured his own approach in Act and Being, and in Sanctorum Communio as well, for the most part both by the threefold concerns of our typology and by such an implicit distinction between the 'immanent' and the 'transcendent' methodologies. To the extent that he does not consistently do so, our study thus imposes a stricter set of distinctions than Bonhoeffer actually employed, but one which, we will argue, is legitimate to the extent that it helps us to make more intelligible Bonhoeffer's unique contribution to our study of the critical function of the epistemological paradigm. In claiming particularly the distinction between immanent and transcendent methodologies--for what are at first admittedly chiefly heuristic purposes--we obviously do not intend to beg the crucial question, which must still be addressed in our concluding chapter, of the manner of the relationship between these two approaches, the intrinsic and extrinsic forms of criticism.

Act and Being is central to our dialogue with Bonhoeffer because it explicates the precise nature of his gradual intellectual conversion towards a new paradigm for theology. This change will be most clear in relation to certain of Bonhoeffer's less rigorously formulated social-ontological concerns which had occupied his attention only a short time earlier in Sanctorum Communio. The themes of Act and Being, moreover, crystallize in a particular form the more universal and systematic claims of Chapter One.

The density and opaqueness of the methodological proposal of Act and Being indeed often have served

92

beneficially to turn the 'eminently quotable' Bonhoeffer of the Ethics and the Letters and Papers from Prison back into a genuinely questionable riddle. But this Bonhoeffer-who-provokes has all too easily proved to be Bonhoeffer-the-'misconstruable', due not only to his critics' lack of clarity concerning his method, but at points to Bonhoeffer's own. Our goal in this chapter is to turn the potentially misconstruable argument of the immanent critique of idealism, with which Bonhoeffer begins Act and Being, back into intelligible fragments and traces. These, along with the results of our conversation with Adorno, will then serve for us as the basis for our attempt, in the final chapter of our study, at a constructive contribution concerning those trial combinations and constellations of topics inherent to the enterprise properly called theo-logical.

A. Genuine Transcendental Epistemology: the Paradigm of the Suspended Dialectic

Bonhoeffer's Habilitationsschrift, as we interpret it, is based on the implicit premise that epistemology's concern with theoretical reason is still highly profitable for theology, even if it is not by itself sufficient to the entire theological task. Thus, we are proposing, Act and Being can be read as an attempt to spin conceptually what Adorno had metaphorically described as a "spider's web." It is a text enacting as well as describing a method of approach to the relation of theoretical reason and theology that takes the form of a dialectic, in which is 'caught', suspended, the non-identity of thought and reality, thinking and being, subject and object--even when the reality, being, or object of thought is, properly speaking, decidedly theo-logical. The approach that Bonhoeffer cultivated in Act and Being was deeply indebted to, but not uncritical of, the method of a dialectic of difference, a dialectic 'suspended' in motion, committed to non-identity, and thus unwilling to complete its own urge towards totality. It was a guide into the theological task which was sustained by the apparent incoherence of immanent and transcendent criticism, and which as often as not was expressed in the unavoidably evasive style of unintentional truth. By means of his engagement of this method of suspended dialectic, Bonhoeffer evidenced his own struggle to find a style of theology adequate both to the intellectual, and to the historical and cultural, context of the German academy and church between the World Wars.

He thereby attempted to say 'more' about the existential reality of contemporary humanity than had the perceived sterile 'abstraction' of many of his neo-Kantian forebears. This would lead him, as many of his generation, to feel the need to move from a purely **formal** conception of epistemology towards a **social** conception of the subject-object paradigm (the concern of the second section of this chapter), and its **ethical** implications (the concern of the final section of this chapter). But he refused simply to trade sterility of thought for any positivism, neo-romanticism or a-rationalism that gave up the critical function of theoretical reason. This meant that Bonhoeffer finally refused in Act and Being and the inaugural lecture, contrary to what his cursorily stated concern in Sanctorum Communio had at times suggested, to move from the perceived potential inadequacies of theoretical epistemology directly to an apparently 'more concrete' social or ethical approach. Rather, we will argue, he was searching for an enriched conception of human rationality, taking significant clues from epistemology, which would be adequate to the social and ethical theological vision which inspired him.

Unlike most of the neo-Kantians who had influenced him, Bonhoeffer continued in Act and Being to claim a priority for theoretical, as opposed to practical, reason. And he also argued against neo-Kantianism's attempt to do away with Kant's thing-in-itself--because this reductionist tactic had contributed, he would argue, to the neo-Kantians' increasingly idealistic collapse of the productive tension between the epistemological subject and object. Bonhoeffer, however, was motivated by a typically 'neo-Kantian' urge to **oppose** metaphysics. Yet he did so **for the sake of** the search for a transcendental method which could adequately state the conditions of the possibility not only of human theoretical knowledge, but also of the sociality and ethics implied by the paradigm of cognition. Thus Bonhoeffer's method was nuanced and complex, but for all that, as we will argue, eminently coherent as well.

1. The Inaugural Lecture vs.'Act and Being'

As we have seen in the preceding chapter, Bonhoeffer's inaugural lecture, which was to be his synopsis of the just finished Act and Being, would imply that because of the failures of any self-sufficient epistemology--even including the philosophy-of-**limits** of Tillich and the limit-as-**person** of Grisebach and Gogarten--the theologian was left with no recourse other than to turn to the quest for an adequate **extrinsic,** theological resolution of the problems of sociality and ethics which had been raised by epistemology. Yet Act and Being itself, upon which the inaugural lecture was to be based, actually had mounted a much more sophisticated and subtle argument than Bonhoeffer apparently credited himself in the latter with having accomplished.

His Habilitationsschrift, as opposed to his later interpretation of himself in the inaugural lecture, more subtly argued that a **particular** epistemology--that of idealism--raised issues concerning sociality and ethics which, despite their not yet having been resolved in the philosophical tradition, could not simply be **suppressed** without the gravest of consequences, even for theology itself. Most critiques of idealism, Bonhoeffer implied in Act and Being, threw out the baby with the bath-water. They assumed that an exposure of idealism's unsatisfactory resolution of the dualities of the Kantian epistemological paradigm, particularly an unmasking of idealism's ontologizing of the Kantian subject, simply **obviated** any further need to better understand the enduring significance of the paradigm of theoretical reason inherited from Kant. Bonhoeffer, as we understand him, saw the failure of idealism not as an excuse to get **out** of that tradition, but as an invitation back **into** the failure of idealism, in order to fathom the consequences of its shortcomings. He argued that without the continued cultivation of the challenge of epistemology's 'ontological difference' between thought and being--especially without a conception of the task of articulating limits to the pretensions of the thinking subject--idealism's affirmative ontology inevitably creeps back into the method of theology as well as philosophy. And sociality and ethics are thereby tragically left without the very critical faculty of epistemology's theoretical reason which they require in order to articulate, much less resist, the uncritical ontological urge. Thus idealism's own critical approach to reality must be extended to idealism's very ontological conclusions.

To the extent that Bonhoeffer was himself aware of this dynamic, we will see him in Act and Being appreciatively arguing for (a) a critical dialectical method, which (b) resists all forms of reductionism--whether of the object into the absolute subject of idealism, or the autonomous subject into the uncritical objectivism of systematic ontology--for the sake of an open-ended, suspended 'dialectic of difference'. However, to the extent that Bonhoeffer was himself **unaware** of the cunning of idealism and, finally, of the systematic pretensions of much ontology--as we will argue was still to a significant extent the case with regard to areas of his concern in Sanctorum Communio--we will see not only idealism's methodological approach to **epistemology,** but its affirmative **ontology** as well, continuing to reappear in the midst of Bonhoeffer's very attempts to overcome them. A sensitivity to his ambivalence towards idealism and its ontology of the subject--evidence of his continuing and incomplete intellectual conversion--thus will help us to define the constructive contributions of Bonhoeffer's project. And it will make us aware, as well, of the lingering problems with his understanding of the relation between the transcendental tradition and his concern with sociality and ethics.

An initial difficulty in understanding Act and Being arises from a disparity between the dissertation and its explication in the inaugural lecture. For example, the subtitle to Act and Being, which unfortunately was omitted from the English translation, is "Transcendental Philosophy and Ontology in Systematic Theology." The inaugural lecture's synopsis of Act and Being, to the contrary, hardly mentions ontology at all, and certainly not as a major typological category. Two points need to be made. **First,** Bonhoeffer's own introduction to Act and Being, "The Problem," does indeed speak of "choosing whether one is to use ontological categories ... or those of transcendental philosophy" as if this simply entailed deciding between alternatives.[2] Thus Ernst Wolf's introduction to the text of Act and Being, which begins the German publication as well as the English translation, states the usual reading of this work, one with warrants in Bonhoeffer's own introduction, according to which the Habilitationsschrift is to be understood as a study of the "confrontation between cardinal, mutually exclusive philosophical positions: Transcendentalism (Kant) and Ontology (Heidegger)."[3]

Yet, second, already in Bonhoeffer's introductory statement to Act and Being, there is some equivocation about the study's true purpose. For example, he speaks at one moment of "belief as act and revelation as being,"[4] as if, parallel to the concerns stated in the subtitle, the former was simply a 'transcendental' issue and the latter an 'ontological' issue. But at the next moment he speaks of revelation itself understood alternatively "in terms of the act [aktmaessig], and ... in terms of 'being' [seinsmaessig]."[5] One begins to suspect that there is something else going on here, that the fundamental problem is more subtle than theology's categorical choice between a transcendental emphasis upon 'act' and an ontological emphasis upon 'being'. And one suspects as well that some considerable care may need to be taken to distinguish what Bonhoeffer **said** he was going to do--perhaps even **intended** to do--in Act and Being, and what a careful reading of the text itself reveals.

Moreover, this confrontation, which takes place in Part One of Act and Being, with which we are concerned here, is labeled by Wolf a "philosophical introduction" [philosophischen Einleitung] to the dogmatic investigation [dogmatischen Pruefung][6] proper. But Bonhoeffer does not speak of this issue as a 'philosophical introduction' to his theology. Rather the first section of Act and Being is headed: "Das Akt-Sein-Problem propaedeutisch dargestellt als problem der erkenntnistheorie am autonomen Daseinsverstaendnis in der Philosophie."[7] The Act-Being problem is "**propadeutically** portrayed as the epistemological problem **in philosophy's autonomous understanding of Dasein.**" And as Bonhoeffer's reading of himself in the inaugural lecture later confirms, this 'autonomous understanding of Dasein' refers in particular to the epistemology of **idealism.**

An immanent criticism of the idealist-epistemology is, according to Bonhoeffer, not a **propadeutic** enterprise at all. It is not merely 'introductory' to a methodological turn to transcendent criticism. Rather, the immanent criticism of idealism wished to explore the potential for a more adequate **non**-idealistic, intrinsically philosophical resolution of the act-being problematic of epistemology--which resists the idealist presumptions of a totalizing subjective autonomy. And such immanent criticism is precisely for the sake of a more adequate conceptuality by which to articulate theological concerns which were themselves extrinsic to that very idealist framework. Thus, the epistemological paradigm here significantly takes precedence for Bonhoeffer over any facile move directly to sociality or ethics by means of a theological imperialism. To the contrary, "the problem of knowledge [Erkenntnisproblem]," Bonhoeffer clearly states, "offers the **first** context in which light is shed on the problem of act and being."[8] **And this is as true for subsequent 'theological' investigation as for the history of the apparently 'philosophical' problem at hand.**

The first section of Act and Being addressed Bonhoeffer's observation that, in his contemporaries' theology, there was evidence of a "widespread wrestling with the same problem, one which is theology's legacy from Kant and idealism."[9] As we will argue, this problem, **first off,** was whether or not a 'genuine transcendental

97

philosophy', one that embodied the original active-receptivity of the Kantian epistemological paradigm, was itself
possible.   Thus let us turn to Bonhoeffer's own interpretation of Kant's position as it had been stated in the
Critique of Pure Reason.

2. Bonhoeffer's Reading of Kant

Any adequately 'critical' method, according to Part
'A' of Act and Being, must be able to take simultaneously into account two prevailing inheritances from Kant's
theory of knowledge.   The first is Kant's insistence on
'transcendental apperception', on the pre-eminence of the
all-pervasive **activity** of the thinking subject--"the a
priori synthesis before the object, whose role it can
never assume."[10]   The second, and as traditionally interpreted more problematic, is "the resistance of transcendence to thought,"[11] which motivated Kant's maintenance
of the much maligned thing-in-itself.   'Subjectivity' for
Kant was a matter of the 'outwardly referential' **act** of
the thinking subject,[12] of "the 'I' [which] cannot seize
hold of itself."[13]   Yet 'objectivity' referred to the 'limit'
towards which the activity of thought refers,[14] indicating
not only a boundary to what we can know, but also a
more radical 'ontological restraint' to that subjective-
active-thinking, by which is expressed the fact that all
knowledge is intrinsically and unexpungibly indirect,[15]
'receptive to' or 'mediated' by the resistance of 'reality'
to absolute 'subjectivity'.

Not only is being mediated by thought; thought is
also mediated by being.   Bonhoeffer's summary of this
central contention is worth quoting in full:

> To the concept of genuine transcendentalism
> belongs the reference of thought to something
> transcendental, but not its having that some-
> thing at its disposal.   All thinking has a dou-
> ble reference to the transcendental: a **retro-
> spective,** inasmuch as it claims, qua thought, a
> meaning which it cannot give to itself, and
> inasmuch as meaning is connected with the
> logos of the transcendental, and also a **pro-
> spective** reference to objects within which,
> supposing they are truly **objective** ..., some-
> thing transcending thought stands over against
> it.   So long as the resistance of transcendence
> to thought is asserted, i.e. **so long as the
> thing-in-itself and transcendental apperception
> are understood as irreducible definitive con-**

cepts, neither of which is involved in the other, we may speak of genuine transcendentalism.[16]

To exist, to 'be' as finite humanity--as Da-sein--is to be "in tension between two poles. ... This 'being amid' transcendence is Dasein,"[17] as **genuine** transcendental philosophy interprets it.[18]

Such a genuine transcendental approach would be one in which, Bonhoeffer wrote, "the act, inasmuch as it is pure intentionality, must be wholly alien to being. ["Akt soll seinsfremd als die reine Intentionalitaet gedacht werden."]."[19] In such philosophy, the "outward reference, infinite extensity, restriction to the conscious, existentiality, and discontinuity"[20] comprised in the intentional act, would not presume totally to comprehend the "strict self-confinement, infinite **in**-tensity, transcendence of the conscious, and continuity"[21] of the being of that reality which is known. In such a genuine transcendental philosophy "the distinction between direct [consciousness] (actus directus) and consciousness of reflection [Bewusstsein der Reflexion] (actus reflexus)," would be strictly maintained. Such philosophy would effect the difference between thought that "is simply 'directed at' ['gerichtet auf']" its object--"act [understood] as restless 'in reference to', as simply intentionality," as 'direct' consciousness (actus directus)"[22]--and thought which "can become objectively conscious of itself in reflexion," which can totally grasp its object within its concept (actus reflexus)[23]

It is important to note here that the "legacy from Kant and idealism," of which Act and Being spoke, was precisely this problematic tension between the pure intentionality of Kant's suspended dialectic of thought-within-the-limits-of-finitude and the ontologically-affirmative-reflexive-thinking of the Identitaetsphilosophie of idealism.[24] To the extent that the only 'being' that idealism can finally claim to know is in its own 'act' of thinking, according to Bonhoeffer, idealism is prone to define all 'otherness', all non-activity, as potential-activity of the thinking I, as potential subjectivity. In Bonhoeffer's estimation, Kant's position was the richer and more subtle, to the extent that it distinguished between the epistemological and the ontological significance of the activity of the subject, between its significance for knowing and for being, respectively.

Thus the central distinction with which Part 'A' of Act and Being began is not that between transcendental philosophy and ontology, as the subtitle misleadingly implies. Rather it is the difference, in Bonhoeffer's words, "between genuine transcendental philosophy, the concept which Kant endeavoured to amplify from its long evolution reaching back farther than scholastic theology, and the concept of transcendentalist philosophy as understood by post-Kantian idealism."[25] The former understands epistemology to imply an approach to dialectics which sustains an ontological difference between thought and being. The latter understands epistemology to imply the possibility of acceding to the urge towards an all-embracing ontological identity of subject and object.

What is distinctive and significant about Bonhoeffer's approach is that he wished to **affirm** the fact that Kant, as Friedrich Heer described him,

> endured being a Tantalus. Those who came after him could not. They wanted to mix the fire from above with the waters from below; they wanted to be Prometheus, who stole the spirit of the Gods and Faust, who drew strength from the 'Mothers' to change the face of the earth.[26]

Kant's genius for Bonhoeffer was seen in his argument that although the subject's activity **pervades** all experience, it is actively-**receptive** as well, and thus does not **encompass** the whole of 'reality'.

> Only when existence, supposed in permanent orientation to transcendence, is said not to be able to understand itself (or only to understand that it does not understand itself) is the true sense of **the act** expressed: act as an ever-shifting 'with reference to', as utter intentionality, as ...--<u>actus directus</u>.[27]

Kant's position was, therefore, what Bonhoeffer called a "genuine transcendental philosophy,"[28] which, despite its placing **priority** on the subject's activity, affirmed inherent **limits** on the ontological interpretation of the comprehensiveness of that activity, thereby refusing any original or ultimate "conflation of act and being."[29]

The crux of the immanent critique of genuine transcendental philosophy clearly was for Bonhoeffer the question whether or not it could hold to its own intrinsic requirements. "The radical 'Critique of Reason' [of Kant]," according to Bonhoeffer, "is itself brought forth through human-self-understanding (Reason) being placed within such boundaries."30   But could thought maintain **both** its radical activity, without assuming the total transparency of a rational comprehension of the 'real', **and** its intractable receptivity, without bowing to the immediate, intuitive givenness of reality?   Could thought remain "utter intentionality"31--an _actus directus,_ in which "consciousness is simply 'directed at'"--without yielding to the urge to become _actus reflexus,_ in which thought is "objectively conscious of itself in reflexion," in which the subject understands itself to constitute its very receptivity?32   Could thought actually exercise the 'ontological restraint' to allow the difference between 'intentionality' and 'being'? Could thought refuse the metaphysical urge to **unite** transcendental apperception and the _Ding an sich_?   Here Bonhoeffer had put his finger on the pulse of much of the post-idealist phenomenological debate.

Bonhoeffer's judgment was that genuine transcendental philosophy, **at least historically speaking,** had repeatedly evolved into transcendental-ist, systematizing philosophies of identity. Even when thought made more of a 'skeptical' than a 'dogmatic' assessment of itself, as in that transcendental-ism after Kant which attempted to **exclude** affirmative answers to ontological "questions of Being"33 from epistemological activity, it could do so only by the submissive power of thought itself.   Reason had to submit to **it own limits.**34   Such transcendental-ism had developed "the transcendental thesis" of the dialectic of difference, first into a reluctant skepticism, but finally "into a system of reason."35   Thus, not just historically, but also methodologically speaking, "inasmuch as reason itself becomes the critic of reason" in all post-Kantian--even modern--transcendental-ism, "it is reinstated in its original rights; in other words, man understands himself in the last resort not from the transcendental but from himself, from reason or from the bounds which reason has prescribed to itself, be they ethical or rational in kind."36

Bonhoeffer, we would argue, was persuaded by the theoretical criteria of the genuinely transcendental starting point.   But he was also aware that philosophy had in fact been able to retain Kant's revolutionary theoretical stance.   This is the "inner contradiction," the "fault (_Bruch_) which lies deep in the heart of the matter" of every attempt at transcendental philosophy, and which, according to Bonhoeffer, must "be taken more seriously than any hastily ensuing attempts to restore an inner unity which proceed at the expense of the transcendental starting point altogether."37   Otherwise, into this gap flows the ineluctable idealist impulse, Bonhoeffer argued, to resolve "the concept of being ... into the concept of the act,"[38] for the act is finally assumed to be capable of totally and adequately mirroring the being of reality. Act is able to 'raise substance to subjectivity'.

In summary, Bonhoeffer's point was that Kant's 'genuine transcendental starting point' had argued that "being 'is' only 'with reference to' [in bezug auf] knowing."[39] This position "still leaves room for thought's essential reference back to the transcendental" object, yet for Kant the subject is "pure act" [reine Akt], "**without any possibility of attaining itself.**"[40] Moreover, Kant was confident that "thought can bow to this self-limitation," and be for that very reason, 'genuinely transcendental'.[41]

But whereas genuine transcendental philosophy "judges there is no knowledge capable of passing beyond the proposition that phenomena... 'refer to' the I and are therefore knowable only via the I," idealism--and here Bonhoeffer is speaking of Hegel--"feels impelled to add the finishing touch by replacing the transcendental reference with an ontological judgment entailing the creative power of the I..."[42] However, Bonhoeffer adds,

> the only thing which enabled idealism to a-chieve its resolution of ontological concepts was an unexpressed ontological judgment, and this produced a false position from the outset. The negative judgment of 'this "is" not' or 'this "is" only through me' remains in all circumstances an ontological judgment, and one, moreover, which does not lie within the confines of [genuine] transcendentalism but represents a frontier violation with the most fateful consequences.[43]

In so doing, Bonhoeffer concludes, "Hegel restored the ontology that Kant had dethroned; Kant's thing-in-itself was transformed into the concept of substance which Hegel found indispensable in defining mind."[44]

In idealism, 'with reference to' becomes 'through' or 'by' [durch],[45] which implies "the complete power of reason over transcendence,"[46] the subsumption of heterogeneous being to thought. The transformation of actus directus into a fully rationalized actus reflexus is more or less complete.[47] Thinking succumbs to its "great temptation," Bonhoeffer argues--using the language which, as we have seen, will frame the central distinction of the inaugural lecture--to make "the self-thinking I" the "point of departure" [Ausgangspunkt], rather than the "limit point" [Grenzpunkt] of philosophy.[48] "To be," Bonhoeffer concluded, "is to be **comprehended** by the I in the a priori synthesis."[49] Reflection (actus reflexus) "draws the transcendent into itself and unites act and being within itself."[50]

As the inaugural lecture would argue forcefully, 'being', the resistance to thought's act of transcendence--that ontologically radical, however unknowable, 'objectivity' which had been maintained by Kant's Ding an sich--is in idealism rationalized by the category of **possibility**.[51] The subjective act's 'outward reference towards...', its 'utter intentionality', is translated into the "realized and unrealized **potential**"[52] to complete the referential act's "constitutional incompleteness."[53] "Without I there is no being; I is creative, the sole efficient; I goes out from itself, and to itself returns."[54] Therefore, the Hegelian Bildung of the I, the subject's formation or "gradual development,"[55] is according to Bonhoeffer a "dialectically unreal movement."[56] For in fact thought is adequate to the object because the object is its own movement; "existence [Dasein] is 'contemplation', the homecoming of the eternal 'I' to itself..."[57] Thought embodies its own 'otherness', "overriding the subject-object bifurcation."[58] The Kantian epistemological paradigm yields to the all embracing totality of idealist epistemology. From Fichte to Hegel, to the neo-Kantians Cohen and Natorp,[59] idealism's program had been to avert all semblance of radical duality or difference.

B. Genuine Ontology: the Sociality of Epistemology

1. The Turn to the Object in 'Act and Being': Husserl, Scheler, and Heidegger

Following on the heels of Act and Being, the inaugural lecture would give "every indication," as Walter Lowe has observed, "that idealism and [genuine] transcendentalism suffice to delineate the dilemma of philosophy and that [the ontologists] Scheler, Heidegger, et al. amount to a series of (more or less unsuccessful) attempts to get beyond this dilemma," to set adequate limits to the pretensions of reason.[60] Yet Act and Being itself again provides a richer, more nuanced picture. When Bonhoeffer now extended his argument, as the subtitle had indicated, beyond 'transcendental philosophy' to a consideration of the then current renewal of inter-

103

est in 'ontology', he questioned too facile an assumption that our sole concern with both post-Kantian and post-Hegelian philosophy should be the matter of the **priority of the activity of the subject.** For, as Bonhoeffer said there,

> when we come to the concept of the object [Gegenstandsbegriff] it becomes an acute necessity to explain in terms of the act or of being; if we resolve the concept wholly in terms of the act-subject, this must produce intolerable consequences for any science insisting on the indispensability of objective ontological concepts--and vice versa.[61]

Thus as a corollary to Kant's 'genuine transcendental philosophy', in which the activity of the subject is understood as 'suspended dialectic', Bonhoeffer proposed that there is moreover a genuine, or **"true** [echten] ontology," which likewise sustains and is sustained by this 'dialectic of difference'. Only now, such genuine **ontology,** in contrast to Kant's genuine **transcendentalism,** began to shift the argument from the priority of the subject to the recalcitrance of the object itself. It had as its modest, "immediate aim ... no more than to say that there is 'a real being outside consciousness, outside the sphere of logos and the limits of ratio' [that] 'knowledge of objects refers to this being ... but it is not coincident with this being'."[62] Thus there is a dialectical emphasis on otherness in ontology which mirrors the sociality of the epistemological paradigm's concern with the status of objectivity.

In ontology in general, according to Bonhoeffer, "the claim of logos ... is disputed by the **on** which is in itself free."[63] **Genuine** ontology, according to Bonhoeffer's typology, does not insist that the **logos** of thought desist from its claim. But it does insist that thought--as-**spontaneity,** the 'utter intentionality' or **actus directus** of genuine transcendental philosophy, "must renounce the usurpation of creative power" which is the temptation of idealism. "... For the sake of the freedom of being, spontaneity must be transmuted into receptivity, i.e. in place of creative thinking must come showing [das Schauen], pure intuition [intueri=looking forth, having regard for]."[64]

Genuine ontology must leave 'being' "its full independence of thought."[65] And yet, for all its talk of a priority of 'intuition', it must "not even assume being as given,"[66] without its dialectical mediation by thought.[67]

104

For, in Bonhoeffer's appropriation of Hegel's language, "thought is at all times 'suspended' [Aufgehoben][68] in being, therefore **critically** involved in the process of cognition" of the object.[69] Genuine ontology would, however, reverse the priority of genuine transcendental philosophy, placing the emphasis on the fact that "at all times thought must be 'suspended' **in being,** "rather than vice versa.[70] Genuine ontology thus proposes a nuanced priority to extra-subjectivity, or sociality. Genuine ontology is by definition a critical social-ontology, understood as the affirmation of the ontological priority of the 'other', but a priority which is dialectically related to subjectivity.

Yet despite the apparent promise of a 'genuine ontology', Bonhoeffer laments, "it is but a step from this position"--which he associates most closely with the attempted fundamental ontologies of Martin Heidegger and, subsequently, Eberhard Grisebach--"to **systematic** ontology, which throws being itself open to the inspection of intuition, ... [which] supposes pure being to be intuitively beheld in its transcendence of consciousness,"[71] that is to say, no longer integrally related to a critical subjectivity. Thus Bonhoeffer distinguishes between a 'genuine ontology', which, from the perspective of a certain priority of 'being', retains reality's **difference** from thought (and, as a result, thought's distinctive, yet 'limited', role as well), and the subsequent 'systematic ontologies' which, as in transcendental-ism and idealism, collapse this difference, only now in the form of the emerging totality of being, rather than that of act.

Genuine ontology and **systematic ontology** are thus proposed as the typological obverse of actus directus and actus reflexus. In both cases the primary tension is between sustaining a methodological-ontological priority of **difference** (genuine ontology/actus directus) and, conversely, succumbing to some form of philosophy of **totality** (systematic ontology/actus reflexus). In Bonhoeffer's schema, 'genuine transcendental philosophy' and 'genuine ontology' represent philosophy's attempts, by means of the radical activity of the subject and, alternatively, the radical ontological integrity of the object, to **sustain** the limits, the **difference** between thought and reality. To the contrary, 'transcendental-ist/idealist'[72] and 'systematic ontological' approaches **collapse** this difference. On the one hand this occurs through a reductionist interpretation of the radical activity of the subject which subsumes all otherness, and on the other hand, through a reductionist understanding of 'objectivity' as a threat to

105

undercut critical thinking itself. Both are criticized for
having cut the Gordian knot of the dualities of the
Kantian epistemological paradigm for the sake of a renewed metaphysical identity or totality.

Bonhoeffer consistently argued that **either** genuine
transcendental philosophy **or** genuine ontology is superior
to transcendental-ism/idealism and systematic ontology.
This is based on the former two approaches' sustenance
of a critical dialectic of difference--versus the assumption of "the idea of unbroken harmony between reality
and reason...," whether archaeologically 'found' or teleologically 'anticipated', that defines the philosophies of
totality.[73]   Thus in a provisional sense, whether or not
the focus of such a dialectic of difference is weighted
towards the subjective act (genuine transcendental philosophy) or towards the being of the object (genuine ontology) is relatively inconsequential, so long as the paradigmatic duality, which Kant's epistemology had first
assured, is left intact.   The precariousness of such a
position is seen particularly clearly in Bonhoeffer's remarks on the work of Edmund Husserl, Max Scheler, and
Martin Heidegger, each of whom appears to have attempted a strategy for the sake of the object, and yet each
of whom finally also appears to have fallen victim to the
idealist/systematic-ontological urge.

According to Bonhoeffer, "two trains of thought
seem to cross paths," for example, "in Husserl."[74]   On
the one hand, "it is clear that the concept of essential
vision [Wesensschau] implies that there stands over a-
gainst the subject a being, independent of him and self--
contained, whose concept he forms from direct vision...
We may say that this train of thought accords with a
transcendental realism."[75]   Thus, Bonhoeffer concluded,
"a way is found at once through theory to the pre-theo-
retic givenness."[76]   On the other hand, "against this
must be set the contention that consciousness is the
constituent of all entities... Only the regularity which
consciousness projects **beyond** itself, so as to order reality within it, is transcendent of consciousness."[77]   Yet
despite the apparent subject-object duality of the structure of noesis referring to noema, Bonhoeffer charges
that Husserl's "'noeto-noematic parallel structure' remains
in the end **immanent in the consciousness.**"[78]   Adorno
likewise had charged that

> every one of the Husserlian analyses of the
> given rests on an implicit system of transcen-
> dental idealism, which Husserl ultimately for-
> mulated: that the 'jurisdiction of reason'

106

(Rechtsrechnung der Vernunft) remains the court of final appeal for the relation between reason and reality and that therefore all Husserlian descriptions belong to the domain of this reason. Husserl purified idealism from every excess of speculation and brought it up to the standard of the highest reality within its reach. But he didn't burst it open.[79]

The Other in Husserl is an alien- or alter-**ego**.[80] As Fred Dallmayr has commented, Husserl's "thesis regarding the derivative status of the alter ego and the final coincidence of the Other with 'my' ego," means that his notion of transcendental empathy "'does not presuppose the alter ego, but posits it first of all'."[81]

Therefore, in a significant fashion, Bonhoeffer writes of the Logical Investigations and the Ideas,[82] "the phenomenology of Husserl and his school, although it has an intense pre-occupation with ontological problems, is still within the pale of idealism."[83] Even as it frames itself in anti-idealist terms, at best it is but a 'systematic ontology'. Adorno had similarly remarked in his inaugural lecture, regarding Husserlian phenomenology, that

> it is the deepest paradox of all phenomenological intentions that, by means of the same categories produced by subjective, post-Cartesian thought, they strive to gain just that objectivity which these intentions originally opposed. It is thus no accident that phenomenology in Husserl took precisely its starting point from transcendental idealism, and the late products of phenomenology are all the less able to disavow this origin, the more they try to conceal it.[84]

Bonhoeffer concludes, in agreement with Adorno, that in Husserl finally "a **priority** belongs not on the side of the object but on the side of the consciousness. In this way Husserl joins hands with pure idealism in a manner that seems to me quite at variance with his original thesis ... Phenomenology poses no questions of **being,** only questions of essence."[85]

Thus Bonhoeffer looked to another of the then au courant ontologists, Max Scheler, who, particularly in his Der Formalismus in der Ethik und die materiale Wertethik, Bonhoeffer argued, had attempted to get beyond Husserlian phenomenology. "Where Husserl failed to prevent the emergence of a priority of logos over <u>on</u>, despite his intention to preserve being's independence, Scheler reverses the position with his lucid elaboration of being's priority over consciousness."[86] "Here ... is an obvious postulation of being transcending consciousness."[87]

Yet, as with Husserl, despite the fact that "a sphere transcending the logos--not to say a primacy--is reserved for being, i.e. for the 'essence',"

> nevertheless, according to Scheler himself, in the 'sense of values' the envisioning I is endowed with the capacity to take into itself the whole world, the fullness of life, the good and the very deity....[88]

Thus, despite Scheler's intention to retain a dialectical 'difference' between thought and being (precisely by affirming the extra-subjectivity of the object over against the **by means of** "the power of essential vision"), "the being which transcends the phenomenal entity, ... has been lost to sight, and the upshot is the system of pure immanence," the collapse of difference into identity.[89]

Just this "problem of being,"[90] in Bonhoeffer's interpretation, was the point of departure for the 'fundamental ontology' of Heidegger's then recently published <u>Being and Time</u>.[91] "For the placing of our question," Bonhoeffer writes, "what is essential" in Heidegger's project "is **the unconditional priority of the question about Being,** as opposed to the question about thinking."[92] Here, in contrast to his more petulant treatment of Heidegger in the inaugural lecture, Bonhoeffer accentuates the promise of <u>Being and Time</u> to articulate the genuine, critical ontology that would be analogous to Kant's genuine transcendental philosophy. As would Adorno in his inaugural lecture, Bonhoeffer turns to the notion of 'thrownness' [<u>Geworfenheit</u>] in Heidegger, the priority of being-in-the-world over theoretical thinking, the fact that "even thought does not produce its world for itself, but finds itself, as <u>Dasein</u>, in a world..."[93] Thus, according to Bonhoeffer, "from the standpoint of the problem of act and being it appears that here the two members of the dichotomy are established in a genuinely consistent relation ... Heidegger has succeeded in forcing act and being into partnership in the concept of <u>Dasein</u>..."[94] Yet even here, in Heidegger's "<u>Grundthesis</u>"[95] that "being, however, ... can only be understood within <u>Dasein</u>,"[96] and "that <u>Dasein</u> in temporality already possesses, at all times, understanding of being," Bonhoeffer concludes, "the **genuinely** ontological development of the suspension [Aufhebung] of thought in being is permeated by the **systematic** theme of man's having, qua Dasein, an understanding of being at his disposal."[97] In Bonhoeffer's judgment, the promise of a truly 'genuine ontology' again succumbs to the systematic impulse.[98]

Whatever one's misgivings about Bonhoeffer's polemical readings of Husserl, Scheler and Heidegger, what is most significant is that Bonhoeffer as a result does not conclude "that every ontological thesis is useless."[99] In fact "such outright rejection is no more applicable here," he responds, "than in the transcendental thesis" of Kant, which the post-Kantians could not maintain.[100] Rather, Bonhoeffer's criticism is that "**in so far as both--act as foundation of being, and being as foundation of act--- evolve into the I-enclosed system**,"[101] they lose their critical edge, their ability to hold autonomous act and heterogeneous being, subjectivity and objectivity **apart.** The issue for Bonhoeffer was the sort of critical thinking which could resist such an evolution into 'the system'.   The question was whether and to what extent "on one side[,] the genuinely transcendental thesis" could admit "a being transcendent of consciousness, a being 'with reference' to which existence was envisaged, but a being which itself remained non-objective;" and whether and to what extent "on the other side[,] genuine ontology" could consider "being the a priori of thought in such a way that thought is itself suspended in being," suspended in that which is Other-than-itself?[102]   Whatever our legitimate complaints concerning the way he arrived there, Bonhoeffer has again put his finger on a crucial enigma of the phenomenological/ontological endeavor.

As Lowe has perceptively noted, at this crucial juncture, Bonhoeffer's argument "turns on the issue of **mediation**,"[103] that central problematic of the very idealist tradition against which Bonhoeffer would define himself. For "where thought **or** intuition"--the totalizing act of idealism, or the immediacy of being of systematic ontology--claim to "have access to the object **without need of mediation**," Bonhoeffer explained, "there can be no genuine ontology, for [such critical ontology] insists that thought is at all times 'suspended' in being, and therefore **critically** involved in the process of cognition."[104] Only when thought and being, therefore, **mediate each other**--and precisely thereby sustain their **difference** from one another--is a genuine transcendental philosophy, or any genuine ontology possible.[105]   Other-

wise, Bonhoeffer summarizes, "it is an inescapable conclusion that in the first case the limits are prescribed by
reason itself, [and] that in the second case being somehow falls into the power of the thinking I, [and] consequently that in both cases the I understands itself from
itself within a closed system."106

To make explicit what is implicit in Bonhoeffer's
position, we will maintain that the lure of the systematizing impulse of both 'idealism' and 'systematic ontology'
is to make of dialectical mediation a metaphysical tactic
by means of which to bring about the total ontological
presence of the 'being of the object' and the 'activity of
the thinking subject', one to the other. 'Genuine ontology', to the contrary, is the name for a methodology
which sustains the dialectic of difference precisely to the
extent that **mediation** is understood as effecting the
resistance to such availability, the sustenance of **difference,** of plurality--by means of the methodological
retention **both** of the burden of the alien 'againstness' of
the limits of subjective activity, **and** of the impenetra-
bility of being.

Because idealism and systematic ontology assumed
mediation to be a tactic by which to gain identity or
totality, albeit by a deferred route, they inevitably en-
dorsed a method of affirmative consolation for the wound
to the subject's pretension of complete constitutiveness,
or to the presumption of the object's availability for
direct intuition. Systematic ontology becomes idealism
redivivus, a means towards the end of harmonizing reason and reality in a final apocalypsis, or showing forth,
of the totality. It is the expression of a new 'dogmatic
slumber', or, as Bonhoeffer says, "a flagrant retreat to
behind the transcendental and idealist skepsis,"107 a step
behind Kant's eschatological reserve, behind the primary
meaning of 'criticism'. And thereby, Bonhoeffer argued,
systematic ontology risks, ironically, terminating in the
very same monistic system as does idealism, although the
two philosophical approaches arrived from opposite directions, the latter by reducing being to act, the former by
reducing act to being.

To summarize, Bonhoeffer's notion of a genuine
ontology, therefore, is important for two reasons. First,
just as Kant's genuine transcendental philosophy had
maintained a 'dialectic of difference' between subject and
object, genuine ontology preserved this duality by demanding that the 'referential' activity of thought is
always itself mediated by being, and thus never can
'comprehend' being. Second, whereas genuine transcen-

110

dental philosophy had approached this issue from the priority of the subject, whose limits or boundaries then had to be set, the need for a genuine ontology shifted the locus of the argument towards an increasingly felt need for a way to affirm the priority of the limit, the 'object', itself, now understood not as an uncritically heteronomous 'being' but as, at the minimum, a heterogeneous 'other'. Genuine, or critical, ontology turned the argument towards the consideration of what we have called the second form of Kantian criticism--critique as guardian of plurality, of **sociality,** understood first off simply as the 'letting be' of the integrity of that which is alien to the subject, the dialectical affirmation of heterogeneous 'otherness'.

Thus, on the one hand, a 'critical ontology' raised again the question of the ontological assumptions of the epistemological paradigm, particularly the 'social onto-logical' implications regarding the status of the 'other', if and when the Kantian <u>Verstand</u> gives way to the Hegelian <u>Vernunft</u>. From <u>Sanctorum Communio</u>, through <u>Act and Being</u>, to the inaugural lecture, Bonhoeffer consistently criticized the claim of idealism that 'objectivity' is but a necessary fiction, or as Hegel put it in the <u>Phenomenology</u>, that

> in pressing forward to its true existence, consciousness will arrive at a point at which it gets rid of its semblance of being burdened with something alien, with what is only for it, and some sort of 'other'.[108]

The teleological orientation of idealism, in Bonhoeffer's view, encouraged a quasi-therapeutic, 'historical-genetic' approach. Through the rational reconciliation with the other, idealism 'repaired' the presumed fault of finitude: its being burdened by 'difference'. Thus, for idealism the role of 'mediation' was to demonstrate that any duality of subject and object was but **tolerated**--that the 'other' was but a <u>locum tenens,</u> temporarily designating a point at which subjectivity had not yet become present to itself. And systematic ontology was but the obverse. Yet it was more dangerous precisely because it benignly claimed to do the very opposite, to ground the negative moment of otherness.

As Thomas Day has stated the issue, "idealism has never come to grips with the problem of the real other, since its way to the 'other' is really the way to making the other an object of knowledge, i.e., to overcoming its otherness."[109] What is required is a 'genuine ontology'

111

understood as a **critical** 'social ontology', which can retain the 'eccentricity'[110] of the 'other' in a way that idealism's and systematic ontology's resolution of the Kantian, epistemological subject-object-conceptuality, in Bonhoeffer's estimation, had not.

Bonhoeffer's early work therefore was clearly concerned with the need for a more determinate concept of the 'object', a more 'concrete' sense for the limits to subjectivity. As we will discuss further below, he had originally been deeply influenced in this direction by various schools of 'personalism', particularly those like Grisebach's, which combined a concern for the sociality of the 'personal'-other with an ethical concern for the other-as-'moral'-demand.[111] And his first dissertation, Sanctorum Communio, had attempted to place this personalist position into the context of contemporary sociological discussion as well. But what was new in Act and Being was Bonhoeffer's increasing sensitivity to the fact that, at heart, every attempt to portray a more 'concrete' other, a more determinate limit, had to defend itself against the idealist/systematic-ontological presumption that any 'other' which is heterogeneous to the subject, and vice versa, is so marginal that finally it 'is' not at all.

The presumption of the possibility of such systematic totality, particularly in the case of idealism, belies its own melancholy a-sociality, for in it thought is 'with reference to' only itself. "From the original transcendental thesis has evolved a system," Bonhoeffer wrote, "characterized by thought's sheer self-transcendentalisation [Selbsttranszendentierung] or (which comes to the same thing) a monism unadulterated with reality."[112] Thereby, "the immensity of thought's claim" in idealism, to constitute even the 'otherness' of the object-par-excellence--seen in its ultimate claim that the Ding an sich no longer serves as any ontological limit to the power of thought--"is transformed into the opposite; thought languishes in itself, for where there is freedom from the transcendental, from reality, there is imprisonment in the self."[113]

Genuine ontology would counter this with a 'critical **sociality**', which admits to and cultivates the 'other' as perdurable demand. Genuine ontology understands mediation as the dialectical exacerbation of difference. It cultivates the enduring duality of subject **and object**--of object **and subject**--for which idealism and systematic ontology had proved methodologically insufficient. For genuine ontology, 'sociality' names the enabling of the

112

expression of the object as that to which the totalizing gaze of reason is not only epistemologically, but also ontologically, inadequate. The primary function of 'sociality', as we are using it here, is seen in Bonhoeffer's indictment--in agreement with genuine ontology--of the idealist assumption that the 'I' can understand itself solely from itself. To the contrary, understanding "can be said to occur only when this I is encountered and overwhelmed through an 'other' in its existence..." Otherwise, "the I believes itself to be free and is imprisoned; it stands in the fullness of power and has only itself as its vassal."[114] 'Sociality' names the critical 'otherness' by which the subject is kept from presuming its omnipotence'. 'Sociality' affirms the other-than-subject that idealism will not 'let be' as more than a 'moment' in an absolute process. Sociality avows the Grenze, the limit, which maintains its limit-quality even, and perhaps especially, when that limit is encountered by, or encounters the subject. Sociality is that limit which is not 'liminal', which is not on the threshold to something else, but which is 'itself' in its own integrity.

The impulse in idealist philosophy (as well as of systematic ontology), Bonhoeffer argues, is towards totality. In its attempt to "never get into the embarrassing position of 'being in reference to' the transcendental,"[115] it thereby forgets finitude. To the contrary,

> concrete man sees himself placed in a contingent here-or-there as one who has to find his whereabouts by asking, thinking and doing, one who has to relate to himself the position pre-given to him and at the same time define himself 'with reference to' it. And the imposition, the outrage, which man feels at 'being already' 'with reference to' some other thing which transcends him--is something essentially different from a certainty of bearing within himself the possibility of mastering the world.[116]

The systematizing, ontological urge towards totality, however, forgets as "Kierkegaard said, justly enough, ... that one exists."[117] For, in Kierkegaard's words, "existence itself ... keeps the two moments of thought and being apart..."[118] Thus Bonhoeffer summarizes, "in the very moment when the idealists pushed away the Ding an sich, Kant's critical philosophy was destroyed."[119] More polemically stated, Bonhoeffer concludes that "Hegel wrote a philosophy of angels, but not of human existence."[120]

Still, on the other hand, genuine ontology was clearly a meta-criticism of any position that, in criticizing Hegel, would thereby lapse back **behind** Kant's 'Copernican revolution' of constitutive subjectivity. Against any 'phenomenalism' or 'ontologism' which would attempt to gain the presence, the immediate intuition of the 'eccentric otherness' of objectivity without the mediation of theoretical subjectivity, Bonhoeffer would retain a '**critical** sociality'. There can be no non-or im-mediate relationship to the other, totally beyond the pale of subjectivity.

Thus, in contrast to any notion of the 'intuition' of the Other in systematic ontology, critical ontology did indeed conceive being as retaining a relationship to the activity of theoretical subjectivity, which **mediates** the other, but is incapable of **comprehending** it. This clearly had to be a relationship to subjectivity whose thrust it was to **maintain**, not **overcome**, its 'mediacy', its distinction from, as well as relationship to, being. Such a 'critical'-theoretical-subjectivity, Bonhoeffer argued, obviously could not be sustained by that notion of reason which, even given Hegel's resistance to an 'absolute' idealism, made a 'positive' ontological assessment of its capacities to comprehend reality, to penetrate the <u>an sich</u>. That is to say, theory's primary role in genuine ontology was to articulate and preserve the ontological integrity of extra-subjectivity, between which and the thinking subject a genuine 'social' relationship could be conceived to exist. Understood in this manner, 'mediation' <u>is</u> the task of allowing the moment of 'sociality'; mediation lets the Other 'be'.

2. The Other, Social Theory and Personalism in 'Sanctorum Communio'

In his first dissertation, <u>Sanctorum Communio</u>, Bonhoeffer had struggled with a dual problem. How can philosophy retain an emphasis on the integrity of the other, understood as the individual person, without lapsing into an atomistic individualism? And how can philosophy at the same time conceive the transcendental foundations of human community, the "metaphysic of sociality,"[121] without lapsing into the systematic totalities of idealism and systematic ontology? His concern with the first problem led to his engagement with the concerns of contemporary 'personalist' or 'dialogical' approaches to philosophy and theology, upon which for the most part we will concentrate our attention here. A

114

concern with the second problem led to his investments in the current social philosophy and sociology which was then being heatedly debated in German academia,[122] and on whose work Bonhoeffer drew in clarifying his conception of the sociology of empirical communities, particularly the community of the Christian church.[123]

These competing and often conflicting traditions and approaches, upon which Bonhoeffer drew in this work, make the task of any brief 'synthetic summary' of his own methodological position in <u>Sanctorum Communio</u> a highly problematic endeavor. Moreover, it would go beyond the limits of our current project to provide even the sorely needed historical account of Bonhoeffer's background in, and manner of appropriation of, these two broad areas of concern and discussion. It is rather our concern here briefly to locate Bonhoeffer in the twin debates over I-Thou personalism and over German social theory and empirical sociology in the 1920's. This will be done in order to clarify the precise contribution which <u>Act and Being's</u> category of genuine, or critical, ontology was intended to make. It is for this limited purpose that we inquire into the manner in which the divergent concerns of the two dissertations must be understood to be integrally related to each other.[124]

We take note of the latter, social-philosophical and sociological nexus of concerns at this point in our project chiefly in order to momentarily re-place Bonhoeffer's reflections on 'sociality' within the general intellectual context of his generation. Even a casual reading of <u>Sanctorum Communio</u> makes plain that the 'formal' category of 'genuine ontology' in <u>Act and Being</u>, understood as a negative-dialectic of the reciprocal mediation of subject and object, was the fruit of a line of inquiry which had preoccupied Bonhoeffer's thinking at least since the writing of the first dissertation. Given the social and cultural setting which we have described in the previous chapter, we should now be in a position, particularly with regard to the fields of social philosophy and sociology, to appreciate the fact that philosophic-'idealism' was not Bonhoeffer's only problematic interlocutor. For his was a cultural situation in which pseudo mysticism, voelkism, neo-romanticism, <u>Lebensphilosophie</u> and popular irrationalisms all called increasingly for 'immediacy', the conjuring of 'presence', 'wholeness' and 'concreteness'. As we shall discuss momentarily in the case of 'personalism', the epistemological paradigm for Bonhoeffer was increasingly conceived not as abstract, that is to say, not as merely formal. However it was difficult to find an adequate method and style of expressing epistemology's concrete 'sociality' without playing into the hands of one of two camps, **either** one of the varieties of post-Hegelian 'positivism' **or** the prevalent anti-critical, if not downright anti-rational, neo-Romantic ethos of Germany between the World Wars.

Bonhoeffer drew upon the terminology of Ernst Troeltsch to describe what he saw to be the two main approaches to sociology and social theory during this period. He called them the 'historical-philosophical-encyclopaedic' method and the 'analytical and formal' method.[125] Two observations about this distinction are germane to our study. First, it is significant that, as evidenced by its omission from this typology, Bonhoeffer seemed oblivious to any details of what Ringer has described as the Marxist, "'unmasking' type of criticism [which] was becoming more prevalent on the left wing of the academic community" in Germany during this period.[126] Thus he worked without the conceptual assistance which notable members of the left-Hegelian tradition, particularly from the Marxian wing, could have provided for his critique of idealism, particularly on matters of social theory.

Second, the discussions of social theory in Sanctorum Communio make plain that Bonhoeffer's sympathies were with the latter of the two groups which he **did** include in his typology, the 'analytical and formal', rather than with the former group of sociologists--those with a propensity, in Bonhoeffer's circumspect terms, to turn "sociology into a mere branch of history." By his examples of the sociologists involved, we can infer that the 'historical-philosophical-encyclopedic' designation was meant to cover right-wing sociologists with social Darwinist and Romantic, anti-modernist leanings. But it is not clear whether Bonhoeffer's avoidance of any substantive dialogue with such a position was a matter more of ignorance or of prudence.[127] In any case, de facto, at least, the 'analytical and formal' approaches to sociology provided Bonhoeffer with a moderate standpoint from which "modern social problems could be studied in their 'essence', that is, in isolation--or abstraction--from both Marxist and Romantic critiques of modern conditions."[128] For despite their diversity of positions, the 'analytical and formal' sociologists were united by their application of a broadly 'empirical' concern with particularity and individuality. This was undertaken in order to repudiate the sociological justification for an uncritical 'holism' espoused by the increasingly "militant neo-Romanticism"[129] of what Bonhoeffer referred to as the 'historical-philosophical-encyclopaedic' approach.

116

Thus Bonhoeffer's sympathy, however critically stated, with the work of Georg Simmel, Leopold von Wiese,[130] Alfred Vierkandt and Ferdinand Toennies[131]--with their emphasis upon an initial separateness of individuals and a secondary category of social-relation--implies, at least, more than being merely the occasion for an entry into an academic discussion.[132] He was indeed concerned that their emphasis upon the individual appeared to be based upon the unclarified presupposition of an 'atomistic' view of humanity.[133] And yet Bonhoeffer clearly wished to inquire, in conversation with these 'formal and analytical' sociologists, into the transcendental philosophical assumptions behind their approach to 'sociality'. This decision already implied, it thus could be argued, a 'political' as well as intellectual stance in the German 'cultural crisis' of the 1920's against any naive acceptance of the increasingly popular right-wing, neo-Romantic, organic, vision of social totality.[134]

The originality of Bonhoeffer's argument in Sanctorum Communio, however, did not come from a conversation with these social-philosophical and emerging empirical sociological traditions. Rather, it came in the form of Bonhoeffer's placing the broader concerns of this school of social philosophy into conversation with the then emerging 'personalist' or 'dialogical' approach to the understanding of the basic ontological structures that make 'sociality'--the relatedness of I to an eccentric Other--possible at all.[135] Bonhoeffer perhaps had first encountered a 'personalist' approach through his teacher Karl Heim during Bonhoeffer's year at Tuebingen, although Heim's chief work on the personalist-approach, Glaube und Denken (1931), was not to be published until after both Sanctorum Communio and Act and Being were written.[136] Bethge seems to be more on target when he states that Bonhoeffer's exposure to personalism came when he "apparently discovered Grisebach from his reading of Gogarten."[137] Yet, although Bonhoeffer had read Grisebach's Die Grenzen des Erziehers und seine Verantwortung in his research for Sanctorum Communio, he admits that he had not read Gogarten's seminal Ich glaube an den dreieinigen Gott prior to writing the crucial chapter in the first dissertation on personalism. And Grisebach's Gegenwart. Eine kritische Ethik, did not appear until 1928, after Sanctorum Communio was completed.

Moltmann[138] mentions the affinities between Bonhoeffer's 'personalist' interests and those of Martin Buber (Ich und Du, 1922) and Eugen Rosenstock-Huessy

117

(Angewandte Seelenkunde, 1924) as well. But there is no indication that Bonhoeffer was familiar with Buber's I and Thou. And Rosenstock-Huessy is mentioned only twice in Sanctorum Communio, both times only in relation to his Soziologie.[139] The general question of the relationship between the 'I' and the 'Other' or 'Thou' was being thematized during the 1920's in numerous other quarters--including Gabriel Marcel's Journal metaphysique (1927), Hans Ehrenberg's Disputation. Drei Buecher vom Deutschen Idealismus (I: Fichte, 1923, III: Hegel, 1925), Ferdinand Ebner's Das Wort und die geistigen Realitaeten. Pneumatologische Fragmente (1921),[140] and Franz Rosenzweig's Der Stern der Erloesung(1921). Yet with the exception of one brief mention of Ehrenberg, Bonhoeffer again appears to have been writing Sanctorum Communio with little or no knowledge of their similar work.[141] Thus, as Michael Theunissen has noted concerning the personalist movement in general,[142] Bonhoeffer was evidently quite typical in working out his position in relative independence of these others, at least in the early stages of his development of a version of the I-Thou model itself.[143]

This situation contributed to the fragmentary quality of Bonhoeffer's immanent criticism of 'personalism' in Sanctorum Communio. Yet despite the sketchiness of details, Bonhoeffer's at times ambivalent posture towards personalism is highly significant because its **concerns** prefigured the nuanced **method** for criticizing idealism which he proposed in Act and Being. Put another way, the personalist emphasis in Sanctorum Communio yields the original form of the **question** to which the category of genuine-or social-ontology was the **answer** in Act and Being.

Bonhoeffer's concern in his first thesis was to inquire into the basic social-ontological presuppositions of our understanding of the relationship between and among persons. Despite the fact that Bonhoeffer attempts to interpret these relationships in ever more 'concrete' fashion, the analysis itself begins on the level of 'social ontology,' not that of concrete social or sociological theory.[144] This becomes particularly clear in the typology which Bonhoeffer formulated in the second chapter of Sanctorum Communio by means of which to understand the ways in which social ontology's 'other' had been determined by various methodological approaches to sociality in the history of philosophy. Bonhoeffer proposed that the "basic social relations" [soziale Grundbeziehung, soziale Grundverhaeltnis]--the "basic ontic relations of social being as a whole"[145]--had been conceived in the history of western philosophy in four ways, corresponding to fours models by which the 'other' as 'person' had been conceived.[146]

First, there is the Aristotelian approach, according to which "man becomes a person only in so far as he partakes of reason," which is universal. For Aristotle, according to Bonhoeffer, "essential being lies beyond individual and personal being," and "the collective form, as more nearly approaching the genus, is therefore ranked higher than the individual person."[147] For Bonhoeffer this had remained the dominant model in all subsequent Western assumptions about 'the person': the genus supersedes the individual, the universal eclipses the particular.

Second, in the Stoic approach, the human being "becomes a person by submitting to a higher obligation" which is "universally valid, and by obedience [to which] persons form a realm of reason, in which each soul, submissive to the obligation, is at one with eternal reason and thus also with the soul of other persons."[148] Insofar as "for the Stoic the I is self-sufficient, and reaches the full height of reason without any other," it contrasts with the Aristotelian priority of the genus.[149] "But," as Bonhoeffer continues,

> here too, in spite of the emphasis upon the ethical and 'personal', that which really makes a person goes beyond the individual. It is the ethical and reasoning life of the person which is his essence, and it is so in abolishing him as an individual person.[150]

Thus, although for the Stoic "the concept of the genus offers nothing new in principle," and although "for the Stoic the person is something finished in itself, complete, and final" and thus "is regarded as somehow ultimate," still "the existence of a realm of reason ... indicates the existence of a realm of like beings." Thus, "the relation of moral person to moral person is always thought of as **a relation of like to like**, and this is the basic relation of social philosophy."[151]

Third, in the Epicurean approach, because "life in society serves only to heighten the pleasure of each individual,...each person confronts the other as alien and unlike." Thus "social life is purely [hedonistically] utilitarian, ... [since] each individual is completed by the individual pleasure which separates him from every other individual."[152] This approach, "with its starting-point in

119

Democritus's atomic theory"[153] reappears, Bonhoeffer argues, in the Enlightenment. There it takes on the guise of "sheerly utilitarian" relations among persons who "basically, ... [are] alien to every other."[154] The integrity of the individual is retained, but at the price of its being related to other individuals only by utilitarian concerns.

Fourth, Bonhoeffer sees in the Cartesian approach the "transformation of the metaphysical question into an epistemological one." This subsequently culminated in Kant's "fresh attempt in philosophy to master the problem of basic social relations" by making "the perceiving I the starting-point for all philosophy."[155] But, ironically, this led in idealism to making the epistemological question back into a metaphysical one. Bonhoeffer here in Sanctorum Communio shows no evidence of having yet made the crucial distinction between the 'genuine transcendental philosophy' of Kant and the 'systematizing' strategy of idealism, which, as we have seen, was to be central to the argument of Act and Being. Yet in his remarks about the Cartesian-epistemological position, it is clear that it is the **idealist** position which Bonhoeffer is criticizing here already in the first dissertation. In particular he is concerned with its re-metaphysicalizing of the originally epistemological revolution of Descartes and Kant.

However much we might argue with the particulars of this typology itself, it served Bonhoeffer to make the point that the **Aristotelian** and **Cartesian cum Idealist** types in particular had laid the foundations for modern conceptuality concerning "the metaphysic of sociality."[156] The result had been the widespread tendency for an 'idealist' social philosophy to "see the meaning of the subject to consist in its entering into the general forms of reason," in particular to see the individual as that which is "an object of knowledge."[157] Broadly speaking, "the metaphysical scheme" (which later will be more specifically identified with idealism) "involves a basic overcoming of the person by absorbing it into the universal,"[158] in this case, rationality. The result is that there comes to be "no distinction between the subject-object and the I-Thou relation," for "the latter is absorbed in the former."[159] That is to say, the **integrity** of the 'I' and the 'Thou' is subsumed in the **totality** of the idealist epistemological relation. Therefore, he concludes, "we are asking ... whether a person must necessarily be thought of **in relation to another person**, or whether a person is conceivable in an atomist fashion," by which he means solipsistically, or as he later put it in

Act and Being, according to the "autonomous self-under-standing of the I" as in idealism.[160]

Bonhoeffer's own imprecision with terminology, as the previous paragraph gives evidence however, threatens his argument at this crucial juncture. Let two remarks suffice, in place of a longer digression, to clarify a common misreading: (1) When Bonhoeffer continues, derogatorily, to say that "the epistemological subject-object relation does not advance beyond this, since the opposition is overcome in the unity of mind,"[161] he is clearly speaking not of the subject-object paradigm per se but of **idealist epistemology**, and particularly its problematic **sublation** of the subject-object duality which had maintained the original integrity of 'I' **and** eccentric 'Other'. (2) Thus when he continues, saying that in epistemology "there is no distinction between the subject-object and the I-Thou relation,"[162] the point being made is that the idealist **conflation** of the subject and object is not the same as the **distinction** between 'subjectivity' and 'objectivity' which the I-Thou paradigm is intended to sustain. Thus, although Bonhoeffer repeatedly, and imprecisely, uses the term 'epistemology' as a cipher for the particular totalizing-project of idealism, the context of such use makes clear that it is 'idealist-epistemology' which is meant, despite the fact that Bonhoeffer did not clarify this terminology until Act and Being's elaboration of the category of 'genuine transcendental philosophy'.

That this is not only the case--but also worth our brief detour--is borne out in the paragraphs in Sanctorum Communio which follow on the heels of those from which we have just quoted, where Bonhoeffer's examples are not from Kant, as might be expected (given his loose employment of the term 'epistemology'), but from Fichte and Hegel, concerning "the self-conscious I as arising from the Not-I."

> For his [Fichte's] Not-I is not I, but an object. Both are in the end resolved in the unity of the I. Hegel, too, sees the I as arising at the point where it is drawn into objective spirit, and reduced to absolute spirit. Thus here too the limit set by the individual person is in principle overcome. ... Such a concept is bound to lead to the consequences which idealism in fact drew.[163]

"The [idealist] subject-object scheme never leads to a sociological category,"[164] Bonhoeffer is arguing, because it never allows the plurality which is presupposed by sociality. For the Aristotelian-Cartesian-Idealist, rationality **levels** all persons into a generic 'likeness', thereby making the 'other' fungible, interchangeable with the 'I'. "One I is like another" for idealism, and "only on the basis of this likeness is a relation between persons conceivable at all."[165]

"But," Bonhoeffer argues, in idealism "this union of like beings--and this is the chief point--never leads to the concept of community, [to sociality], ... but only to that of sameness, of unity."[166] Bonhoeffer admits that of all the idealists, "Fichte considered the question of the 'synthesis of the world of spirits' more seriously than anyone else." Even more importantly,

> he was the only one to see that the presence of other living men 'in self-active freedom' was a philosophical problem, which threatened the whole system. ... [He was] the only idealist philosopher who felt the inadequacy of the idealist categories for mastering the problem of the 'other'.[167]

Yet, finally for Bonhoeffer, to the extent that even "Fichte says that 'the concept of the Thou arises by **union** of the "It" and the "I"'," he clearly is unable to maintain "any non-synthetic, original concept of Thou." For Fichte "the Thou is identical with the other I...," never the <u>Gegen</u>-stand of the Other-as-Thou.[168]

Bonhoeffer's own 'new thought' was the attempt, we would maintain, to retrieve **both** a quasi-Stoic emphasis on the integrity of the Other--that "the person is something finished in itself, complete, and final"--[169] **and** the Enlightenment's own retrieval of the Epicurean concern with "the other as alien and unlike," but now in Bonhoeffer shorn of its "sheerly utilitarian" presuppositions. Sociality, or community, requires a multiplicity, a plurality-in-unity. And social philosophy requires a new sort of 'rationality' by which to conceive this 'basic social relation'. Yet neither of these conditions could be met, according to <u>Sanctorum Communio</u>, by "the idealist philosophy of immanence."[170] For idealism cannot speak of the integrity of the 'Other' as any sort of fixed premise. 'Otherness' is rather for idealism a derived category emerging from its 'likeness to the I'.

Bracketing for the moment the possible specific, extrinsic theological presuppositions of this position, to which we will return below, let us take pause for a moment with the immanent-philosophical quandary with which Bonhoeffer was thereby presented. How can thought overcome the idealist concept of totality "by a concept which preserves the concrete individual concept of the person as ultimate...."[171] That is to say, how can we conceptually sustain the boundary [Grenze] of 'I' and 'Other', or in Dallmayr's phrase, "between the indigenous and the alien"?[172] If "from the purely transcendental category of the universal," rationality, "we can never reach the real existence of alien subjects, ... how then do we reach alien subjects," 'Thou's' whose integrity lies precisely in being 'not-I's'?[173]

His dominant approach to this issue reflects a form of personalism which thinks about the meeting of the 'I' and 'Thou' as a relation, or 'between' realm. It

> presupposes that the ones meeting each other exist upon a particular being level, and concede[s] to the between solely the power to transform the poles that impinge upon one another.[174]

In such a form of personalism, the integrity of the individual 'I' and 'Thou' in their difference from one another precedes, indeed occasions, the event of encounter in which they become 'persons' to each other.

Bonhoeffer's personalism is a significant development in his project because it first encouraged him to attempt to think of 'objectivity', encountered precisely as 'alien Other', vis a vis the pretensions to totality of the subject. Thus as Bonhoeffer says in Sanctorum Communio, "the individual exists only through the 'other'. The individual is not solitary. For the individual to exist, 'others' must also exist."[175] Moreover, the 'Thou' is not an 'other I'.[176] It is "independent in principle, over against the I," and thus essentially different from the idealist object, which ultimately is but the I-separated-from-itself. Initially what is important is the negative judgment by Bonhoeffer that "on the idealist path, from the idea of the universal we come at best to the possibility of the other," but on this "[idealist]-epistemological and metaphysical path one never reaches the reality of the other."[177] And 'social basic relations', Bonhoeffer is sure, must be conceived on the basis of the reality of the other person as Other. They must, Bonhoeffer states plainly, "be understood as built up interpersonally upon the uniqueness and separate-ness of persons. The person cannot be surpassed by an a-personal mind, or by any 'unity' which might abolish the multiplicity of persons."[178]

Such a social basic relation of the encounter with the Thou brings about, in Theunissen's words, "a kind of 'decentering' of the I," the "deperspectivalization of the initially subject-oriented world" of idealism. As had Grisebach, Bonhoeffer takes "the perspectivity of the world dominated by the subject for the basis upon which the I first arises in the meeting with the Thou. ... The dialogical present dislodges the I 'from its standardizing role', that is, 'from the midpoint' of the subjectively constituted world"[179] The encounter with the Other-as-Thou refutes the idealist premise of "the I as the midpoint of the world."[180] In Bonhoeffer's words, "the individual again and again becomes a person through the 'other'. Hence the individual belongs essentially and absolutely with the other, ... even though, or even because, each is completely separate from the other."[181] To be an 'I' is to be "the person summoned up or awakened by the Thou," by the "unknowable, impenetrable, alien other."[182] Personalism thus "belies the possibility of a subjective constitution of the originally encountered Other."[183] The radical alienness of the Other denies idealism's claim that ultimately the constitutive-I "is confronted with nothing of equal primordiality."[184]

Therefore, such personalism is itself confronted by the enduring challenge which its 'sociality' has in common with 'epistemology'. It must raise again the integrity, the 'reality' of the other-as-**person**, and the person-as-**other**, versus the other-as-idealist-object which seems unable to resist its own eclipse by the prevailing (Aristotelian-Cartesian-Idealist) rational subjectivity. To think about 'sociality' requires a mode of thought which can break the chain of **ontological** dependence of the 'Other' on the 'I'. Personalism needs a theory which resists the conception of 'otherness' as part of the pedagogy of the subject, a 'difference' which is resistant to being interpreted merely as the <u>Bildung</u>, the formative self-discovery by and of the 'I' in its encounter with otherness.[185]

To speak of the other-as-**person**, and the person-as-**other**, therefore, is not the **solution** to the continuing challenge raised by the transcendental tradition's paradigm of subject and object. Rather it is a more cutting form of confrontation, **on behalf of that tradition**, with idealism's resolution of the exigency of 'otherness' into subjectivity. When Bonhoeffer articulates his personalism in this style, which is his dominant tendency, it resembles Grisebach's argument against the circle of understanding as much as that of any other.[186] Bonhoeffer,

124

however, was one of the few in the personalist camp who realized that such a project retains a striking parallel to the anti-idealist intentions, however unfulfilled, of a significant strand of the transcendental tradition itself--that strand which Bonhoeffer himself would describe in <u>Act and Being</u> as 'genuine transcendental philosophy' and 'genuine ontology'.[187]

We therefore risk missing Bonhoeffer's contribution entirely if we suppose too facilely, as James Woelfel has stated the common interpretation, that "Bonhoeffer rejected the metaphysical," i.e. the 'epistemological', "completely for the social and ethical in his understanding of the I-Thou relation."[188] For Bonhoeffer, on a formal level the 'personalist' restatement of the problematic status of otherness entails no more--**but no less**--than to speak of the object-as-**limit** or 'barrier' to the subjective pretension of idealism. It is another way of stating the theme of the inaugural lecture, that "the question of transcendence will have to be put as the decisive question."[189] The sphere of 'sociality' can be entered, Bonhoeffer argues in <u>Sanctorum Communio</u>, "only when some barrier of principle appears at some point."[190] Far from implying a naive turn to personalist-'anthropology' as an alternative to the problematic aspects of idealism, Bonhoeffer is clear,

> it is the concept of **reality** which must be discussed, the concept which idealism has failed to think through exhaustively but has identified with self-knowing and self-active mind, involving truth and reality.[191]

Thus, **first off**, Bonhoeffer states clearly, "what matters is not the nature of this barrier, **but that it should really be experienced and acknowledged as a barrier.**"[192] He is even willing to go so far as to say that "this can happen in the intellectual sphere, ... that is, it can be experienced, for instance, in the conflict of perceptions." But this acknowledgement cannot occur in the **idealist** intellectual sphere, for "the idealist's object is not a barrier."[193] The idealist subject finally presumes itself to be adequate to comprehend even the resistance against subjectivity of objectivity itself.

Thus the question for Bonhoeffer already in <u>Sanctorum Communio</u> was that of "the philosophical status of 'Thou'," of how to speak **non-idealistically** of "this 'other',"[194] this "alien Thou,"[195] which must exist in order meaningfully to speak of "the individual [as] the concrete I," the 'I' in 'sociality'.[196] This emphasis was the nascent form of what would be developed in <u>Act and Being</u> as the question of a genuine ontology. The need for a conceptuality with which to think non-idealistically of the Thou-Other was the motivation behind the search for a social-ontology which **both** sustained a dialectic of difference--through the resistance to totality effected by the Thou-as-Other--**and** remained capable of being thought by means of a critical-subjectivity that remained actively-receptive, eschewing its systematic impulse.

Bonhoeffer clearly understood personalism as a call to mediation, but not the egological mediation of idealism. Personalist mediation for Bonhoeffer meant a Thou which transforms the ego-centric perspective of idealism by means of the Other's resistance to total availability to the subject. The Other mediates the subject because it is not the 'project of', but rather a 'demand upon', the I. Personalism **radicalizes** the immanent critique of idealism, the need for a genuine ontology; it does not obviate it.

C. Otherness and Ethics: The Thou as Moral Demand

Bonhoeffer's distinctive approach to the problem of maintaining the 'sociality' of Otherness entailed more, however, than merely a focus on the object-as-Other, on the Thou-as-demand.[197] As we have argued above, his contribution, **on the one hand,** was to relate this view of the Other to the immanent critique of idealism. Thus Bonhoeffer maintained that the transition from "radical epistemological idealism" to "the social sphere" occurs "only when some barrier of principle appears" to the subject's tendency to make itself the perspectival foundation of all reality.[198] The 'I' is therefore "the person summoned up or awakened by the Thou," who approaches the 'I' as "the unknowable, impenetrable, alien other."[199] Thus personalism shares with idealism the challenge to 'know' the 'unknowable', to be able to conceive that limit quality of Otherness which escapes the totalizing system of idealism. **On the other hand,** the new thought which Bonhoeffer began to formulate, encouraged significantly by his reading of Grisebach, was the proposal that this 'barrier', or 'limit' [<u>Grenze</u>], was adequate to its anti-systematic task precisely because it exercises a certain **priority,** a priority which, moreover, has the form of an "**ethical** transcendence."[200]

Thus we still must clarify the way in which these two sides of Bonhoeffer's personalism, the transcendental and the ethical, are related. We will begin with this notion of the **ethical transcendence** of the Other. This does not mean, Bonhoeffer is clear, that the Other-as-limit "must have **only** an ethical content," but that--and this is the crucial point--the acknowledgement of the limit, the 'real barrier' which epistemology had sought by an ever more determinate concept of the object, "is possible only in the ethical sphere."201 That is to say, **"the experience of the barrier as real is of a specifically ethical character."**202 Thus we must clarify what Bonhoeffer means by the 'specifically ethical character' of the Other-as-limit. And, second, we must further clarify the manner in which this is related to the search in <u>Act and Being</u> for an adequate way in which to **conceive** this limit, the search for a 'genuine ontology', whose concept of the Other--even when thought as **ethical**--does not deny the retention of a form of **actively**-receptive, genuinely **critical** subjectivity.203

1. Ethics and the Priority of the Other in Personalism

The introduction of an explicitly **ethical** dimension to the discussion deepens Bonhoeffer's concern with the Other, because it forced him to think the **priority** of the Other, not just its equality with the I. The moment of the 'between', the meeting of I and Thou, does not merely describe a naive **equiprimordiality** of subject and object, or even of person and Other. For

> not every self-conscious I knows of the moral barrier of the Thou. It knows of an alien Thou--<u>this may even be the necessary prerequisite for the moral experience of the Thou</u>--but it does not know this Thou as absolutely alien, making a claim, setting a barrier; that is, it does not experience it as real, but in the last resort it is irrelevant to its own I.204

Increasingly for Bonhoeffer, the encounter with the Thou cannot be adequately conceived ethically as originally a 'neutral' moment of mutuality. Rather the appearance of the Other-as-alien, as Thou--even if understood as the social-ontological "prerequisite for the moral experience of the Thou"--is to be conceived as a "value-related moment." It has a **priority** over the I precisely because the encounter is a moment of decision, of responsibility which is engendered by the Thou itself.205

The 'givenness' of the Other is not, <u>contra</u> Buber, 'immediate'. It is not a <u>fait accompli</u>, but a task. As Moltmann has interpreted Bonhoeffer, "this concrete situation of encounter does not mean just a casual meeting, but the event of the 'ethical barrier'."[206] Therefore Bonhoeffer straightforwardly concluded: "The Thou-form is to be defined as the other who places me before a moral decision."[207] Because the Thou **places** the I in 'the ethical situation', the 'ethical transcendence' of the Thou, first off, says something about its 'freedom from' the I, its "moral claim"[208] to 'be' at all. The 'freedom for' the Thou, which comes when the I "sustains the claim of the other, does not do violence to the other, but enters with him into a dialegesthai,"[209] comes only secondarily with a person's "intention to detach himself from the Thou as well as to enter into relations with it."[210] John A. Phillips has thus rightly interpreted Bonhoeffer, vis a vis the usual assumption, to mean that

> personality is created only in confrontation with others, which involves both 'being-for' and 'being-free-from' the other person. Transcendence would thus seem to signify that quality which a person possesses by virtue of the fact that he **is** person, of simultaneously being-for and being-free-from the other.[211]

'Relationship'--in both its 'negative' ('freedom from') and its 'positive' ('freedom for') moments--is thus an ethical **task**, a **moral** demand.

The ethical priority of the Thou, therefore, consists in the fact that in the encounter, the 'I' is **addressed** by the Thou. The 'I' is no longer in "command of his own ethical value," for the 'I' has not "entered by his own strength into the ethical sphere," but has been placed under the burden of responsibility by the integrity of the Other.[212] Thus, in Theunissen's words, "my being is a doing, ... previously enacted by the Other and ... ever anew enacted by him."[213] The result for the I is that "the more clearly the barrier is recognized, the more deeply the person enters into responsibility,"[214] that is to say, into the 'ethical sphere'. The priority of this moral responsibility in the face of the Other is thus decisive to the meaning of the 'I' itself, but only in a 'secondary' fashion. In Bonhoeffer's terms,

> it is in this sense that we think of the ethical concept of the individual as the basic concept of social relations; for the individual cannot be spoken of without the 'other' also being thought who has set the individual in the ethical sphere.[215]

128

Therefore Bonhoeffer concludes that only "when the concrete ethical barrier is acknowledged, or **when the person is compelled to acknowledge it,**" are we "within reach of grasping the basic social relations, both ontic and ethical, between persons."[216]

The factor which differentiates Bonhoeffer's personalist emphasis upon **the Thou** from epistemology's language about **the object** is, therefore, both more and less radical than many other exponents of personalism might suppose. It is more radical in that the Thou is understood to erect a sufficiently resistant "barrier to the subject," precisely to the extent that "it activates a will with which [an] other will comes into conflict..."[217] In this sense, to say that the encounter of the I and Thou "is a purely **moral** transcendence," is to emphasize that the ethical demand of the Thou is a demand for a responsive and responsible activity of will, and therefore "can only be grasped by one who is himself involved in responsibility."[218] Bonhoeffer clearly wishes to argue that the "I" does not necessarily reciprocally demand of the "Thou" the same responsibility that the Thou demands of the I. The Thou is thus not defined by its moral 'likeness' to the I, by the mutuality of the ethical relationship. In the moment of the encounter "I and Thou are not just interchangeable concepts,"[219] and thus the relationship between them is not that of 'like' to 'like'. For the **address** of the Thou and its being-suffered by the I 'is' an unlikeness. "This means that I can be shown limits by a Thou which is not an I in the sense of the I-Thou relation,"[220] by a Thou who may not have been grasped by the moment of responsibility to me.

This lack of mutuality paradoxically does not relieve the 'I' from its responsibility, but rather makes it all the more demanding. Responsibility occurs in the face of Otherness, of alienness, **not** as a moment in overcoming otherness, in effecting the likeness of the Thou to the I. The result, Bonhoeffer concludes, is that "the person cannot know but can only acknowledge the other person, 'believe' in him."[221] "'Thou' says nothing about its own being, but only about its demand." And "this demand is absolute."[222]

Therefore Bonhoeffer argues that just as in the domain of the sociality of the I-Thou relationship "self-consciousness arises together with the consciousness of being in community," in the domain of ethics we must conceive the will to be "by its very nature dependent on other wills."[223] The "will arises where there are 'oppositions'," of which the encounter with the Thou is the

129

paradigm. Bonhoeffer's position in <u>Sanctorum Communio</u> is 'personalist' because "strictly only another will can be an opposition of this kind," since "the will itself experiences opposition only in the will of a person who wills something different." And "such a struggle takes place in miniature wherever man lives in the community of the I-Thou relation."[224]

To this extent, Bonhoeffer can even claim that "the transcendence of the Thou has nothing to do with epistemological transcendence,"[225] especially the epistemology of idealism.[226] Yet to the extent that "where person meets person, will clashes with will, and each struggles to subdue the other,"[227] the conflict between integrity and totality, between difference and identity, is as operative in the personalist-ethical sphere as in the epistemological. Both require a way of conceiving the Other-as-**limit** which is adequate, first off, to the difference itself, and, secondly, to the **priority** of the Other-as-demand.

Thus, rather than being a moment of benign mutuality, as was the case with Buber, the **relation**, the encounter between distinct **wills**, is initially a moment not just of un-likeness but of **opposition**. And it is not just any opposition, but the opposition engendered by the priority of the Other in the world of an I which would rather establish its own egocentric perspective. This passage from <u>Sanctorum Communio</u>, striking in its divergence from the commonplace presumption of the idyllic tranquility of the I and Thou in the original moment of relatedness, bears quoting at length.

> The will arises where there are 'oppositions'. ... And strictly only another will can be an opposition of this kind, ... for the will itself experiences opposition only in the will of a person who wills something different. It is only in the struggle with other wills, in overcoming them and making them part of one's own will, or in being oneself overcome, that the strength and wealth of the will are deployed. Such a struggle takes place in miniature wherever man lives in the community of the I-Thou relation. For where person meets person, will clashes with will, and each struggles to subdue the other. Only in such encounters does the will reach its essential determination. As an isolated phenomenon the will is without meaning.[228]

130

'Difference' bears privilege of precedence over 'relation-ship', diversity over likeness, and both because of the priority of the Other in a perspectively I-oriented world.

It is this basic 'unlikeness' of I and Thou, as itself an ethical demand, which moves Bonhoeffer towards the position we have described above. His schema would combine the strengths of two of the 'social basic rela-tions' from his typology in Chapter II of <u>Sanctorum Communio</u>: (1) Stoicism's "concept of the ethical person," in which "a man becomes a person by submitting to a higher obligation,"[229] and (2) Epicureanism's concept that "every person confronts the other as alien and un-like,"[230] rather than in an immediate mutuality. Yet Bonhoeffer would deny the Stoic claim that the 'higher obligation' of the ethical person is any responsibility "of like to like."[231] For the 'like to like', as we have seen, risks the very denial of genuine 'otherness' which the encounter with the Thou demands. Thus, the 'higher obligation' is now to be thought of as 'I' to 'Thou'--the Thou who encounters the I in all its alienness--an alien-ness made all the more demanding when encountered as an alien will. And he would likewise deny Epicureanism's merely hedonistic utilitarian connections between I and Thou, which had recurred in the Enlightenment's denial of any "original, significant or essential relation" of I to Thou.[232] For the will arises not out of any impulse towards its own pleasure, but "is possible only in social-ity,"[233] the basic moment of which is the priority of the moral claim, the address, of the Thou to the I.

This is a significant development because it clearly shows that both **community**--even when conceived as "community of will"[234]--and the **respect** of the claim of the other are not 'givens', but moral tasks of finite individuals in relationship. True community **is** possible, Bonhoeffer argues--community understood not as "having something in common," but as "constituted by reciprocal will."[235] And the respect of the claim of the other to 'be' **can** occur to the extent that "the homo-geneity ... of persons" yields to a genuine ethical res-ponsibility to the alien-Thou.[236] But 'difference', the 'strife' between wills, not harmony, "is the basic socio-logical law."[237]

The second-level ethical issue is whether differences of will lead to a "**community** of will, built upon the separateness and the difference between persons," and enriched by the diversity of the "inner conflict of in-dividual wills," or to the contrary whether the differ-ences lead to relationships of **domination** and the abuse

131

of power. Likewise the issue is whether the heterogeneity of persons leads to a responsible respect for the claim of the Thou-as-Other, or whether the alien-Other is denied its integrity and its moral claim on the I and coerced into an ethics of like for like only.[238] Therefore, Bonhoeffer's concept of sociality is integrally related to the relationality of community, which, however, as a community of will, is

> built upon the separateness and the difference between persons, constituted by reciprocal acts of will, with its unity in what is willed, and counting among its basic laws the inner conflict of individual wills.[239]

This "concrete strife in the genuine sense,"[240] as we will explore in more detail below, must not be initially confused with sin or evil in which the will of the Other "is forced into one's own will and so overcome."[241] On the contrary, it is the social-ontological form of the genuine community, understood as the **sociality of the encounter of I and Thou,** the form of relationality of the ethically-responsive, finite human being.[242]

Yet if Bonhoeffer's personalism is more radical in the sense that it makes the Other into an ethical demand, it is less radical than many personalists might suppose to the extent that the turn to the category of the will does not **escape** the idealist dilemma any more than had the turn away from the egological pretension of the 'universal I' towards the sociality of otherness. To suppose too quickly that the turn to ethics gets us beyond the enduring pathos of transcendental philosophy's failure in idealism--that the problem of the 'will' actually surmounts the enduring problematic of the epistemological subject-object paradigm--is to risk losing sight of two profound ethical difficulties. The first is not being able to conceptualize 'other persons' in a manner which 'epistemologically' can allow the other to 'be' at all. The second is not being able to let the other be encountered receptively as 'ontologically' that-which-I-am-not-and--cannot-be. There is implied the deepest ontological-ethical--as well as epistemological--tragedy in Bonhoeffer's claim that in Hegel, "man's natural wonder at the other man's reality has been lost, or, as idealist philosophy imagines, 'overcome'."[243] If such wonder is not conceivable, if philosophy has no way of thinking or speaking of the ontological 'otherness' of the neighbor to begin with, then all additional 'ethical responsibility' beyond 'mere epistemology' is a moot point.

2. Personalism as Problem for Transcendental Philosophy

The turn from the personalist emphasis of Sanctorum Communio to the transcendental philosophical emphasis of Act and Being evidences Bonhoeffer's realization that from a methodological point of view, personalist sociality and transcendental epistemology struggle with the same ethical problematic. Or, put another way, the problem of ethics is no less of a problem in 'post-epistemological' personalist sociality than in epistemology per se.[244] Thus Bonhoeffer stated the ethical concern of Act and Being when he wrote that,

> whether thought demeans itself modestly, i.e. remains genuine transcendental thinking, or misappropriates the unconditional and becomes idealistic thinking, that is no longer a question of theoretical philosophy ... but a decision of practical reason. There is nothing to oblige thought, as free thinking, not to annex the unconditional or empower itself of its I. Yet it is no less an act of free thought if, in order to remain free, it contents itself with reference to transcendence and ... is only relative, referential...[245]

In the apparent conflict between personalism and transcendental philosophy we confront afresh Derrida's earlier warning, that however much we are sure of the insufficiency of the conceptual options of prior philosophy--in this case, of idealism--"the step 'outside philosophy' is much more difficult to conceive than is generally imagined."[246] Therefore, from this incipient **concern** in Sanctorum Communio with the ethics of difference, Bonhoeffer developed the **method** of genuine ontology in Act and Being, in order to explore the immanent transcendental problematic at the heart of those very personalist philosophies which had intended to surmount transcendentalism.

Yet, in addition, there sometimes appears in Bonhoeffer's early work a second, recessive form of the personalist argument which places the emphasis not upon the priority of the integrity of the 'Other'-as-person, but upon the basic **relationality** of I-and-Thou, the 'between' itself. From this perspective, as seen in its purest form, for example, in the dialogicalism of Martin Buber, the relationship, or 'between' itself, is the origin of both the I and the Thou. They both arise together in the moment of encounter, the 'between' claiming "an absolutely creative power,"247 prior to which there cannot be said to 'be' any I or Thou.

> Instead of the I and the Thou, as already finished beings, bringing the meeting into being, they must, according to [this second form of] the dialogical approach, themselves first spring out of the occurrence of the meeting.248

The emphasis in what we will call the **dialogical** approach is on the "immediacy and reciprocity of interpersonal relations and ... the simultaneous genesis of both partners through encounter (defined as an 'in between' realm)."249 Since Bonhoeffer himself at times appeared to tend towards such a position, particularly in Sanctorum Communio, we need to understand more precisely what is at stake in the decision between this second form of personalism and that personalism which places a decided priority, even when conceived as an **ethical** priority, upon the Thou.

A significant clue is provided in recalling that against which both schools of the personalist project had been waged: the transcendental philosophical tradition, in particular its idealist, and later, phenomenological, successors--the exponents of what we have called the dialectic of identity. Fred Dallmayr has stated the antithesis in the following manner:

> Dialogicalism's departure from the transcendentalist framework occurs in two basic, interrelated steps: namely, through the removal of the 'Thou' from the field of intentional objects, and through the segregation of 'I-Thou' contacts from the range of intentional-noetic acts.250

Basic to both forms of personalism, therefore, was the dual assumption that subjectivity per se entails the systematic circle of subjective constitution, and that this all-creative subjectivity is broken by the encounter with the Thou.

But, **on the one hand,** the apparently more 'radical' dialogical approach, which began with the 'between' itself--the **encounter** with the Thou--understood this starting point to remove the I-Thou encounter from the framework of transcendental philosophy altogether. It sought to overcome **all** dialectical thinking, as by definition an idealistic and 'subjectivist' tactic towards total-

ity. While, **on the other hand,** the more moderate personalist approach--which began with the priority of the
encounter by the **Thou**--left open the possibility, which
Bonhoeffer later exploited in Act and Being with the
category of 'genuine transcendental philosophy', that a
chastened theoretical subjectivity might remain, a dialectical active-receptivity shorn of its ontological pretensions. Given the fact that both approaches consider
themselves to be critiques of idealism, how does one
account for such divergent foundational assumptions?
Again, it is helpful to clarify more precisely the hidden
adversary in each case.

If the relationship itself bears a place of utter
privilege, there can be no **priority** given either to the
Other, to the Thou, or to the subject, to the I. That
which must be avoided at all costs, we can infer, is
precisely **priority.** And the legitimate concern behind
this bias against priority is the suspicion that, particularly as borne out in idealism, 'priority' implies a subjectively-perspectival hierarchy--and that all such hierarchies demean. That is to say, in Buber's language, any
priority describes an I-It relationship, in Theunissen's
words "a relationship of mastery and slavery, of **sub**-and
super-ordination."[251] Thus the opponent of such dialogical-personalism is the very 'autonomous self-understanding of existence' against which Bonhoeffer argued in the
first section of Act and Being. The antagonist is clearly
that notion of subjective-constitution which presumes to
be adequate to the definition of the Thou as Other. As
Theunissen says, "the I-It relationship is ... essentially a
relationship of dependence of the object on the
subject."[252] The adversary is therefore any concept of
mediation, since mediation is understood by dialogicalism
as the act of the subject, and the subject per se as
utterly free. Thus Bonhoeffer stated his own version of
the argument for such a tactic in Act and Being, saying
that even in "a free decision of practical reason" to
allow the reality of the Thou, "the outcome is nevertheless reason's **self-chosen** self-limitation, whereby it reinstates its own authority--as the reason which performed
this very limitation."[253]

Thus, as Michael Theunissen has argued, the 'radicality' of this second form of personalism is that it
would escape the dangers of the notion of subjective
constitution (mediation) by removing itself from the
idealist temptation altogether, for

...it is not possible to make out how the I
constitutes the Thou and, in conjunction

135

therewith, how the I is supposed to be constituted by it. In order to be able to constitute the Thou, it, for its part, would already have to be there. According to the theory of reciprocal constitution, however, it cannot be there without the Thou, which it has first to constitute. One escapes this vicious circle only when one understands the 'I-effecting-Thou and Thou-effecting-I' as the expression of a common interaction in the meeting. Then equiprimordiality discloses itself as what is genuinely intended in the thought about reciprocal constitution, an equiprimordiality that, admittedly, has nothing to do with the indifference with which things exist in isolation from one another.[254]

The equiprimordiality of 'I' and 'Thou' is taken to mean their immediacy and availability to one another in the moment of their genesis. The danger of subjectively-totalizing intentionality, or constitution, appears to be defended against only by the event of the im-mediate mutuality of like-for-like.[255]

The irony of such a position is that in taking what appears to be a more 'radical' form, in the language of Act and Being, dialogicalism begins the move from what Bonhoeffer will call a form of 'genuine ontology' into a form of 'systematic ontology', and in two ways. **First,** any heterogeneous 'otherness' that escapes the relation, which is not 'available' to the I, cannot be conceived to 'be' at all. 'I' and 'Thou' cannot be conceived as relata which precede the relatio. For to admit the "preexistence of the relata before the relatio" is for dialogicalism merely to state "the ontological condition of disconnectedness," 'the indifference with which things exist in isolation from one another'.[256] The Other as a burden or demand upon the I--an **alien**-other rather than a mutually-**like** relatedness--must be sublated in the relationship itself.[257] **Second,** if the I-Thou relation is immediate, "egologically not mediated," even by a genuine transcendental subjectivity--if it is totally impenetrable to the gaze of reason--then it can only be acknowledged, never critically examined. Dialogicalism ends up with a new form of dogma, of heteronomy, whose benevolence can only be assumed.

Bonhoeffer's personalism, to the extent that it sustains the radicality of the ethical priority of the Other, challenges philosophy, even what Theunissen has assumed to be the more 'radical' form of **personalist**

136

philosophy, to prove its capability to allow and sustain a radical receptiveness to--a 'letting be' of--heterogeneous otherness. The problem with a priority on the 'between', the relationship itself, is that its search for the point of **mutuality** between 'I' and 'Thou' contributes to the subversion of its own agenda of maintaining the very **difference** between 'I' and 'Thou' which makes relationship--sociality--possible at all. "Thought, if it is genuine thought, is bent on completeness," as <u>Act and Being</u> put it. And this is no less true, Bonhoeffer realized, with regard to the thought of the between, for such thought, continuing the quotation, "is even able to comprehend the claim of 'the other',"258 by means of its notion of the genesis of both 'I' and 'Thou' from the moment of relationship. Therefore the problem for personalism, no less than for idealism, is its inability to refrain from the urge towards system, to conceive of the 'difference' in the 'between' in a manner radical enough to preserve, rather than to heal, the lacuna between the systematizing-I and the resilient-Thou. In the context of a subjectively perspectival worldview, 'mutuality' merely consoles the imperial-Subject for the loss of its dominion; but it cannot sustain the absolute demand of the Other.

At times Bonhoeffer had shifted his own approach to personalism in a dialogical direction, as when he sought to move from a consideration of the concept of 'person'--and the social-ontological issues with which we have been concerned--to a relational understanding of 'community', for example, the community of the Church. Thus he argued that 'community' is itself made possible by the structural openness of personal being.

> There is no self-consciousness without community, or rather, self-consciousness arises together with the consciousness of being in community. ... The consciousness of the I and the consciousness of the Thou arise together, and in mutual dependence. ... The I and the Thou are fitted into one another in infinite nearness, in mutual penetration, for ever inseparable, resting on one another, in inmost mutual participation, feeling and experiencing together, and sustaining the general stream of spiritual interaction. Here the openness of personal being is evident.259

Yet in doing so, Bonhoeffer is aware, at least to a certain extent, that such an approach risks moving towards the neo-Romantic and idealist emphasis on the genesis of sociality from the social-whole, the unity of like for like.

That is to say, even in Sanctorum Communio he is concerned at times that his own 'dialogical' impulse risks
thereby undercutting the very **plurality** of heterogeneous
persons for which he has otherwise so consistently argued.

Already in Sanctorum Communio Bonhoeffer had
begun to realize that the dialogical approach was most
problematic, precisely at the point that he conceived
personalism and transcendentalism as warp and woof of
the same fabric, beset with the same difficulties. There
he asked the rhetorical question which we must take as
a serious challenge to his own lingering idealist propen-
sities: "is there any point in still speaking of I and Thou,
if," in speaking of a structural openness-towards-com-
munity "everything is now apparently one?"[260] Does not
"the idea of personal openness," the priority of 'relationality', threaten "to turn into that of an a-personal spirit," into systematic universality which subverts the integrity of the individual, particularly the individual
Other?[261]

Bonhoeffer clearly wished to avoid "the idealist
argument" of "the homogeneity and unity of persons,"[262]
and to affirm the structural separateness, the individuality that persists even in a **community** formed by a multiplicity of Thou's who encounter a multiplicity of I's.
There is no "overstepping the boundary of the I-Thou
relation;" there is no "mystical fusion."[263] Even in his
attempts to think through, with a 'phenomenological'
concern,[264] the sociality of the community, Bonhoeffer
wishes not to step back from the concern with individuality, the integrity of the person-as-Other. For "man
knows that his I is real only in the relation with the
Thou," an alien-other who confronts me with its very
otherness, not its immediate relatedness to the I. "So,"
Bonhoeffer admits, "the question whether there is an
individual being which is untouched by social links must
in a certain sense be answered affirmatively, if the idea
of the I-Thou relation is not to be abandoned."[265]
There is, at least in a certain form, a priority of Otherness which is integral to his very notion of 'relationship', of sociality.

And yet he was obviously concerned that "on the
other hand there is a danger that in trying to save the
idea of an a-social core of personal being we might be
thinking atomistically."[266] This was the dilemma which
Bonhoeffer felt was unavoidable, but which in Sanctorum
Communio led him no further than to state the antinomy:
"The individual personal spirit lives solely by virtue of

138

sociality, and the 'social spirit' becomes real only in individual embodiment. ... One cannot speak of the priority either of personal or of social being."[267] And his lack of conceptual clarity on this issue led Bonhoeffer in the first thesis into some of the most problematic proposals of his entire early corpus (a) that "the community can be understood as a collective person, with the same structure as the individual person,"[268] (b) that "the concept of person" can be used "to interpret the **corporate**, or collective, dimensions of social life,"[269] since (c) communities have an "objective spirit" that "leads an individual life over and above the individuals ..."[270] Peter Berger has thus noted with thinly veiled alarm that

> Bonhoeffer's concepts of social reality in Sanctorum Communio lead towards an extreme sociological realism that can with the greatest of ease become a full-blown social mythology. The reiterated use of the Hegelian concept of objective spirit shows this danger most clearly. In this way, human institutions, which exist only by virtue of human actions and human meanings, take on a strange character of independent being.[271]

Even Bonhoeffer appears unsure and defensive, as when he concludes the section in Sanctorum Communio on objective-spirit by saying:

> Those who have followed the course of the argument will certainly now raise the objection that idealism has after all carried the day. For the community of will which has been so emphasized, which is built upon the structural separateness and diversity of individuals, has now become the unity, with its own center of action. What are we to reply?[272]

And again Bonhoeffer later in Sanctorum Communio can do no more than re-state the conundrum: The unity-of-the-relationship-of-community is irreducible; but "this new unity does not annul the specific reciprocal movement of community," for "the individual persons remain entirely separate from one another."[273]

Thus, in his turn from the personalist orientation of Sanctorum Communio to the transcendental orientation of Act and Being, Bonhoeffer retained dialogicalism's sense of the real dangers of **subjective-constitutiveness.** Yet he increasingly turned his own engagement with per-

139

sonalism in the direction of formulating his response to a more cunning antagonist, that of the very **immediacy** and **totality** which were the hallmarks of dialogicalism, and which dialogicalism held in common with idealism. Rather than seeing in personalism the way **out** of the transcendental tradition altogether, Bonhoeffer's 'intellectual conversion' was to see it as a way back **into** the legacy of transcendental philosophy, but now with a more critical and cautious methodological approach. His decision in Act and Being to explore that transcendental tradition more fully resulted in the category of genuine ontology. Without it, Bonhoeffer began to realize, the promise of personalism merely comes full circle, again confronted by the same dilemma that had confronted the idealist position against which it had revolted: how to maintain the unity of the point of origin without lapsing back into a systematic totality, "where," as Bonhoeffer had put the matter, "thought or intuition have access to the object without mediation."[274]

We can conclude that personalism was an asset to Bonhoeffer to the extent that it helped him to develop the ethical dimension of his resistance to "the notions of an abstract-general consciousness and of the constitutive function of subjectivity," as these had come to dominate the idealist resolution of the transcendental legacy.[275] The introduction of an ethical dimension led them to the beginnings of his thinking about the **priority** of the other. But it was a liability to the extent that dialogicalism by definition had to remain a 'negative' social-ontology, in the sense that the I-Thou relation could be conceptually articulated only in terms of its being the 'negation' of the idealist subject-object schema--in terms that can only be stated, not examined by means of critical rationality.[276] Thus this more radical form of dialogical-personalism closed-off the new thought of the priority of the Other at the very moment of its inception.

In turning in Act and Being to the category of 'genuine ontology', Bonhoeffer therefore began to try to surmount the dilemma with which he left himself in the first dissertation, and which he shared with dialogicalists like Buber, for whom

> either the immediate meeting with the Thou is sought in its proper medium, that of the existential praxis of dialogical self-becoming, but not really analyzed, only conveyed--the theory then gives itself over to praxis and loses itself in edification--or the immediate encounter with

the Thou is brought out into the sphere of intentionality, and then analyzed, but with inadequate concepts and with reference to insufficient models.[277]

Bonhoeffer's strength, which led to the methodological deliberations of <u>Act and Being</u>, was that he was unwilling simply to cut the Gordian knot which entangled the concerns of personalism and the transcendental tradition. This allowed Bonhoeffer to address the fact that "in the eyes of the wider public," as Theunissen has remarked, "the philosophy of dialogue has become like a coin in circulation"--the fact that "one speaks of the Thou and thinks one understands what one means."[278] This he did by proposing that beyond the "inadequate concepts" of idealism, there was the form of critical thinking which he called 'genuine transcendental philosophy', which could both state the insufficiencies of the radical-personalist claims to immediacy and yet do so without reverting to the systematic pretensions of the idealist understanding of mediation as a tactic towards totality, if not monism.[279] And beyond the "insufficient models" of 'systematic ontology'--towards which tended the more radical form of personalism--the more moderate form of personalism suggested to Bonhoeffer the outlines of a 'genuine ontology' of sociality, by which to think the Otherness of the object-as-genuine-Thou.[280] Thus the same could be said of his engagement with personalism in <u>Sanctorum Communio</u> as Theunissen has concluded regarding dialogicalism:

> if philosophizing means risking failure by venturing upon the unthought, then the impotence of dialogical thought is in itself more philosophical than the power of transcendental philosophy, which arrives at less problematic results precisely because it is already less daring in its approach.[281]

In concluding this chapter, we can say that the enduring methodological contribution of <u>Sanctorum Communio</u> was its argument that the shortcoming of the idealist **epistemological** project was the result of a deeper ethical failure of nerve to admit the priority of the claim of the Other. This occurred "precisely because idealism has no understanding of the "moment in which the person is threatened by the absolute demand"[282]--the responsibility first off to let the Other 'be'. Idealism's dialectic of identity proved inadequate to the ethical demand of the Other for its 'difference', its integrity. It was insufficient for bearing the moral demand of the

Thou not only to be **alien** to the I, to be 'other' than an 'other-I', but also to have a certain **priority** over subjectivity which insures that the Thou is 'in-comprehensible' to the subject's pretensions to Absoluteness.

And, finally, the enduring methodological contribution of Act and Being was its refusal to separate the moment of ethical responsibility before the Thou, the unforseen "moment in which the person is threatened by the absolute demand," described by Sanctorum Communio, from the need to find a form of rationality adequate to it, which was its own project. Thus Bonhoeffer's category of 'genuine ontology' posed the need to think the priority of the Other, the moment of receptivity, in such a fashion that it **breaks through the idealist system** precisely because it is radically finite, particular, and thus "no longer subject to a compulsion of internal logic"[283] inherent to the totalizing system. Genuine ontology attempts to think the moment in which the 'I' is "confronted by a claim which overwhelms him" precisely because this claim of the Other is so thoroughly **non**-subjective, **un**-intentional.[284]

To think the Other of genuine ontology is to think the anti-system nonpareil. Such thinking, in Bonhoeffer's terms, would be a 'genuine transcendental philosophy', actively-**receptive**, and open to the Other. It would be a dialectical thinking in which subject and object mediate their diversity, their ontological plurality. A dialectic of difference, a resistance to totality, would be a social ontology countering the ontological pretensions of the subject. Thus the goal of our next chapter will be to compare these criteria, which were the fruit of Bonhoeffer's immanent critique of idealism, with those by which Adorno went about his own project, named, aptly enough, a Negative Dialectics.

NOTES

[1] Sections (A)(1) and (2) are indebted in particular to the argument of Walter Lowe, "The Critique of Philosophy in Bonhoeffer's 'Act and Being'," unpublished paper, 1966.

[2] Bonhoeffer, Act and Being, p. 12 [G 9]; page references to Act and Being will hereafter be given for the English translation, with the pagination in the original German edition following in brackets only if the existing translation has been altered.

[3] Ibid., p. 5.

[4] Ibid., p. 12.

[5] Ibid.

[6] Ibid., p. 6.

[7] Ibid., p. 7.

[8] Ibid., p. 14; emphasis added.

[9] Ibid., p. 12.

[10] Ibid., p. 23; see Kant, Critique of Pure Reason, A12.

[11] Ibid., p. 20; Bonhoeffer, unfortunately, is not very careful with his use of the terms Transcendence and Transcendent. On the one hand, the two terms are used synonymously as that 'with reference to which' thought occurs; this at times give Bonhoeffer's epistemology a more 'realistic' cast than he usually intends for it to have. On the other hand, Bonhoeffer uses Transcendence to refer to the act-of-reference itself, as when he contrasts transcendence (thought as referential) with reality (the transcendent 'with reference to which'.) And on some occasions it appears that he deliberately intends to imply both meanings at once. Thus in each usage of the term, we will make clear which sense is meant, if this is not evident from the context.

[12] Ibid.

[13] "Man in Contemporary Philosophy and Theology," p. 51.

[14]Bonhoeffer, Act and Being, p. 20.

[15]Ibid.

[16]Ibid.

[17]Ibid.

[18]The influence of Heidegger's just published Sein und Zeit is unmistakable here, as Bonhoeffer notes on Act and Being, p. 20. As we will see below, Heidegger's 'genuine ontology' was analogous for Bonhoeffer to Kant's 'genuine transcendental philosophy'. Cf. Eberhard Bethge's remark in Dietrich Bonhoeffer, p. 94 concerning a comment made by Wilhelm Luetgert, with whom Bonhoeffer was working as an assistant while writing Act and Being. According to Bethge, Luetgert was apparently under a strong impression that Bonhoeffer during this period was "a Heidegger man".

[19]Bonhoeffer, Act and Being, p. 12.

[20]Ibid., pp. 13-14.

[21]Ibid., p. 14.

[22]Ibid., p. 12; also see p. 29. At this stage in our argument, it is essential to be aware of the extent to which actus directus and actus reflexus refer merely to an immanently philosophical problem. Bonhoeffer has a transcendent-critical meaning for actus directus/actus reflexus as well. But the two usages of the terms should not tempt us to overlook their crucial role in Bonhoeffer's immanent critique of idealism.

[23]Ibid., p. 12 [G 9]; trans. altered. Thus there is a nascent, although undeveloped, phenomenological concern expressed in Bonhoeffer's reading of Kant, one which roughly approximates the understanding of 'intentionality' of Brentano and Husserl's application of the epoche to the noetic/noematic structure in his Ideas; see Richard M. Zaner, The Way of Phenomenology. Criticism as a Philosophical Discipline (Indianapolis: The Bobbs-Merrill Company, Inc., 1970), pp. 125-132.

[24]See Act and Being, pp. 13-14, 29. On Hegel's critique of Kant, see Quentin Lauer, Hegel's Concept of God (Albany: State University of New York Press, 1982), pp. 207-213.

[25]Bonhoeffer, Act and Being, p. 19.

26Friedrich Heer, <u>The Intellectual History of Europe</u>, trans. Jonathan Steinberg. (London: Weidenfeld and Nicolson, 1966), p. 436.

27Bonhoeffer, <u>Act and Being</u>, p. 28.

28Ibid., p. 20.

29Ibid., p. 28.

30<u>Akt und Sein</u>, [G 15]; trans. my own.

31Bonhoeffer, <u>Act and Being</u>, p. 28.

32Ibid., p. 13.

33Ibid., p. 22.

34Ibid., pp. 31, 32, 35, 36.

35Ibid., pp. 36-37.

36Ibid., p. 21.

37<u>Akt und Sein</u>, [G 15]; trans. my own.

38Bonhoeffer, <u>Act and Being</u>, p. 22.

39Ibid.

40Ibid., p. 23.

41Ibid., p. 24.

42Ibid., p. 29.

43Ibid., p. 42.

44Ibid., p. 49; Bonhoeffer has in mind here Hegel's <u>Enzyklopaedie</u>, par. 33.

45Bonhoeffer, <u>Act and Being</u>, p. 23.

46Ibid.

47Ibid., pp. 24-25.

48Ibid., p. 25 [G 17]; trans. altered.

49Ibid., p. 26; emphasis mine.

[50]Ibid., p. 36.

[51]Bonhoeffer, "Man in Contemporary Philosophy and Theology" pp. 64ff.; see Soren Kierkegaard, Concluding Unscientific Postscript, pp. 282-291; n.b. p. 288 on esse and posse; cf. Lowe, "Critique of Philosophy," p. 5.

[52]Lowe, "Critique of Philosophy," p. 6.

[53]Ibid.

[54]Bonhoeffer, Act and Being, p. 26.

[55]Ibid., p. 35.

[56]Ibid., p. 27.

[57]Akt und Sein, [G 19]; trans. mine.

[58]Bonhoeffer, Act and Being, p. 37.

[59]Ibid., pp. 34-35; Bonhoeffer refers here to Hermann Cohen, System der Philosophie I, "Logik der reinen Erkenntnis," 1902, and Paul Natorp, Praktische Philosophie, 1925, pp. 1-27. See Lauer, Hegel's Concept of God, pp. 77-80 on the relation of thought to reality. Cf. Louis Dupre, The Philosophical Foundations of Marxism (N.Y.: Harcourt, Brace & World, Inc., 1966), pp. 39-45, "From Liberalism to Prussianism: The Identity of Thought and Reality," and Werner Marx, Hegel's Phenomenology of Spirit. Its Point and Purpose--A Commentary on the Preface and Introduction, pp. 98-108 on "The Idea of the Phenomenology of Spirit and Its Significance for the Understanding of Post-Hegelian Philosophy," and Thomas E. Willey, Back to Kant, pp. 102-130 on Cohen and Natorp.

[60]Lowe, "Critique of Philosophy," p. 10.

[61]Bonhoeffer, Act and Being, p. 14.

[62]Ibid., p. 49; quoting N. Hartmann, Grundlagen einer Metaphysik der Erkenntnis, 1925, pp. 180ff.

[63]Bonhoeffer, Act and Being, p. 49.

[64]Ibid., pp. 50-51; emphases mine.

[65]Ibid., p. 51.

[66]Ibid., p. 50.

[67]See Lowe, "Critique of Philosophy," p. 11.

[68]Bonhoeffer adopts Hegel's term Aufhebung, not so much for its dual sense of retention and surpassing, but for its ability to convey 'lifting up' and 'preserving'--implying 'suspension' in a **spatial** sense. Thus to say that thinking is 'aufgehoben' in Being has the sense that thinking is 'raised up', 'preserved' for what it essentially is, when it is 'suspended' in the domain of being. The Hegelian meaning of Aufhebung has a much more temporally oriented connotation.

[69]Bonhoeffer, Act and Being, p. 51.

[70]Ibid., p. 50.

[71]Ibid., p. 51.

[72]Ibid., p. 36.

[73]Max Horkheimer, Critical Theory, trans. Matthew J. O'Connel and Others (New York: Herder and Herder, 1970) p. 12.

[74]Bonhoeffer, Act and Being, p. 53. Cf. Hans-Georg Gadamer, "The Phenomenological Movement," in Philosophical Hermeneutics, pp. 130-181; Pierre Thevenaz, "The Phenomenology of Husserl," in What is Phenomenology and Other Essays, trans. James M. Edie, Charles Courtney, and Paul Brockelman (Chicago: Quadrangle Books, 1962), pp. 40-53.

[75]Bonhoeffer, Act and Being, pp. 53-54.

[76]Ibid., p. 52; emphasis added.

[77]Ibid., p. 54.

[78]Ibid., p. 52.

[79]Adorno, "The Actuality of Philosophy," p. 122.

[80]Theunissen, The Other, p. 2.

[81]Fred Dallmayr, "Introduction," to Theunissen, The Other, p. xiv, quoting Theunissen.

[82]Bonhoeffer, Act and Being, pp. 52-54.

147

83Ibid., p. 52.

84Adorno, "The Actuality of Philosophy," p. 121.

85Bonhoeffer, Act and Being, p. 54.

86Ibid., p. 55.   Bonhoeffer refers in Sanctorum Communio to having read Scheler's Phaenomenologie und Theorie der Sympathiegefuehle and Formalismus in der Ethik und die materiale Wertethik, and in Act and Being to Scheler's On the Eternal in Man, trans. Bernard Noble (New York: Harper and Row, 1960).   See Alfred Schutz, "Max Scheler's Epistemology and Ethics," Review of Metaphysics 11 (1957):304-314 and 12 (1957):486-501; Manfred S. Frings, Max Scheler.   A Concise Introduction into the World of a Great Thinker (Pittsburg: Duquesne University Press, 1965); Ringer, The Decline of the German Mandarins, pp. 280-281, 372-373, 423-425.

87Bonhoeffer, Act and Being, p. 56.

88Ibid., p. 57.

89Ibid., p. 59.

90Ibid.

91Ibid., pp. 59-66.

92Akt und Sein, [G 47]; trans. mine, emphasis added. cf. Richard Schacht, "Husserlian and Heideggerian Phenomenology," in Hegel and After.   Studies in Continental Philosophy Between Kant and Sartre (Pittsburg: University of Pittsburg Press, 1975), pp. 207-227.

93Bonhoeffer, Act and Being, p. 62.

94Ibid., pp. 63, 64.   On Heidegger's interpretation of the duality of Kant, see W. B. Macomber, The Anatomy of Disillusion.   Martin Heidegger's Notion of Truth (Evanston: Northwestern University Press, 1967), pp. 154-168 and Thomas Langan, The Meaning of Heidegger (N.Y.: Columbia University Press, 1961), pp. 69-85.

95Akt und Sein, [G 50], trans. my own.

96Bonhoeffer, Act and Being, p. 63.

97Ibid., p. 65.

98See Theunissen, The Other, p. 264 on Eberhard Grisebach's similar argument in Gegenwart. Eine kritische Ethik (Halle: M. Niemeyer, 1928) that Heidegger's 'phenomenology' lies on the side of transcendentalism/idealism, despite its attempt to critique 'universal consciousness' by means of the 'thrownness' of Dasein. Theunissen quotes Grisebach, Gegenwart, p. 51: "The self stands at the midpoint of its world, which is related to it and formed in accordance with its essence." Bonhoeffer's argument against Heidegger parallels Grisebach's closely on this issue. For another interpretation of Heidegger's project with relation to Hegel, see Macomber, The Anatomy of Disillusion, pp. 168-189; Langan, The Meaning of Heidegger, pp. 176-182; Jacques Taminiaux, "Finitude and the Absolute: Remarks on Hegel and Heidegger," in Heidegger. The Man and the Thinker, ed. Thomas Sheehan (Chicago: Precedent Publishing, 1981), pp. 187-208.

99Bonhoeffer, Act and Being, p. 69.

100Ibid., pp. 69-70.

101Ibid., p. 70.

102Ibid.

103Lowe, "Critique of Philosophy," p. 11. See Andre Dumas, Dietrich Bonhoeffer, pp. 118-138 on the immediacy-mediation theme in Bonhoeffer.

104Bonhoeffer, Act and Being, p. 51.

105Note the similarity between Bonhoeffer's position here and that of some of the later neo-Kantians, e.g. Paul Natorp and his pupil Nicolai Hartmann. Also see Lauer, Hegel's Concept of God, pp. 96-113 on subject-object in Hegel.

106Bonhoeffer, Act and Being, p. 70; cf. Act and Being, p. 26: "A Being [Sein] that was not Being-understood [Verstandensein]--that was thought absolutely--would lead immediately to materialism. Idealism and materialism lie side by side, Hegel next to Marx."

107Ibid., p. 51.

108Hegel, Phenomenology of Spirit, par. 89, pp. 56-57.

109Day, <u>Dietrich Bonhoeffer on Christian Community and Common Sense</u>, p. 12.

110Ibid., pp. 13ff.

111This will be the center of our attention in the final section of this chapter.

112Bonhoeffer, <u>Act and Being</u>, p. 25.

113Ibid.

114Ibid., p. 32.

115Bonhoeffer, <u>Act and Being</u>, p. 27.

116Ibid., p. 28.

117Ibid., p. 25.

118Kierkegaard, <u>Concluding Unscientific Postscript</u>, Pt. 2, Ch. II, "The Subjective Truth, Inwardness; Truth is Subjectivity, n. 6, pp. 169-172; n.b. p. 171.

119Bonhoeffer, "The Theology of Crisis and its Attitude Toward Philosophy and Science," <u>Gesammelte Schriften</u>, III, p. 121.

120Bonhoeffer, <u>Act and Being</u>, p. 27.

121Bonhoeffer, <u>Sanctorum Communio</u>, p. 26. Edward Farley has described this early work of Bonhoeffer as reflecting a "phenomenological attitude," but having no "phenomenological method" [<u>Ecclesial Man. A Social Phenomenology of Faith and Reality</u> (Philadelphia: Fortress Press, 1975), p. 29]. Farley is one of the few who have made any connection between the early work of Bonhoeffer and phenomenology's concern with "the philosophical problem of the knowledge of other minds and the broader problem of intersubjectivity (the relation between selves)." (p. 241) Yet, as Farley rightly concludes, "Bonhoeffer's early attempt in <u>Sanctorum Communio</u> to formulate the constitutive corporate structures of a community of faith has not been pursued" in subsequent theology (p. 271).

122See Ringer, <u>The Decline of the German Mandarins</u>, pp. 227-241.

123See <u>Sanctorum Communio</u>, Chapters III and V.

124Although the method of 'immanent criticism' is
not nearly so clearly developed as it will be in Act and
Being, in Sanctorum Communio we do already see Bonhoeffer's determination to ferret out the social-**philosophical** underpinnings of the emerging empirical-socio-
logy of his generation, and its significance for theology.
There he speaks of the need for "a proper grasp of the
concept of the object in sociology," which "depends on
the most profound social and philosophical insights into
the nature of the person and of society..." (p. 19). Bonhoeffer characteristically begins by refusing too facile a
move to the level of extrinsic criticism. Therefore he
says of the theological agenda of Sanctorum Communio
that "in thus presenting basic social relations from the
standpoint of Christian dogmatics we do not mean that
they are religious; they are purely ontic, but seen from
the Christian perspective. ... We must look for the
scheme by which basic Christian relations are to be
understood. ... [But] we first ask whether the **philosophical** schemes are satisfactory" (p. 26; emphasis added).

125Bonhoeffer, Sanctorum Communio, p. 16. "His-
torical-philosophical-encyclopaedic" is a translation of
"Geschichtsphilosophisch-enzyklopaedisch;" see Sanctorum
Communio, manuscript p. 3.

126Ringer, The Decline of the German Mandarins, p.
241; this was corroborated in a private conversation
between the present author and Eberhard and Renate
Bethge.

127Bonhoeffer, Sanctorum Communio, p. 20. Bonhoeffer included among the historical-philosophical-encyclopaedic approach (1) August Schaeffle's application of
Darwinian evolutionary theory to sociology, (2) economist
and sociologist Othmar Spann's right-wing criticism of
'modernist sociology' (which, according to Ringer, p. 232:
"drawing on Romantic and corporative traditions, ... proposed to demonstrate the moral and logical priority of
the national and communal 'whole' over its members") (3)
Franz Oppenheimer, and (4) Franz Carl Mueller-Lyer.
Although Bonhoeffer never discusses Troeltsch's position
in Sanctorum Communio (which omission is striking due
to Troeltsch's former stature in the Berlin community),
he obviously agreed with Troeltsch on this issue, that
"history cannot be grasped by [an 'evolutionary-apologe-
tic'] principle, [for] it does not have a universal rational
structure (it is not 'panlogistic'). The evolutionary-apo-
logetic does violence to the particularity of history." [H.
Paul Santmire, "Ernst Troeltsch: Modern Historical
Thought and the Challenge to Individual Religions," in

Critical Issues in Modern Religion (Englewood Cliffs, New Jersey: Prentice-Hall, Inc., 1973), pp. 378-379. Troeltsch's indirect influence on Bonhoeffer also can be seen in their common attitudes towards Hegel. As Santmire continued, (p. 396) "Hegel sought to take the 'accidental' historical dimension of the religions of the world with full seriousness. For Hegel, the Absolute--which he identifies with ultimate Reason--works **through** the concrete forms of various religions, in all their diversity. At the same time, however, Hegel postulates a universal logic (interpretation) of history ... Troeltsch rejects the latter notion...." cf. John A. Phillips, Christ For Us in the Theology of Dietrich Bonhoeffer (New York: Harper and Row, 1967), pp. 35-39, 173-177 on Troeltsch.

[128]Ringer, The Decline of the German Mandarins, p. 163.

[129]Ibid., p. 230.

[130]Ibid., p. 229 which notes that Leopold von Wiese founded the Research Institute for Social Studies at Cologne, at which Vierkandt also worked.

[131]Bonhoeffer, Sanctorum Communio, p. 17. Given the neo-Romantic purposes for which Toennies' work was appropriated by many of his "orthodox popularizers," Ringer notes in The Decline of the German Mandarins (p. 167) that "it is all the more remarkable that Toennies himself was never attracted to any of the reactionary arguments which others derived from his theory." Thus Bonhoeffer himself placed Toennies in the 'analytical and formal' camp; see Sanctorum Communio, p. 208, n. 28: "It is true that Toennies deserves a special place in formal sociology; but still, his place is there."

[132]See Ringer, Decline of the German Mandarins, pp. 163-180.

[133]Bonhoeffer, Sanctorum Communio, pp. 17, 18: "... Basically they [Vierkandt and von Wiese] are agreed: we are presented with a multitude of isolated I-centres, which can enter into an outward connection with one another through some stimulus."

[134]See Ringer, The Decline of the German Mandarins, pp. 227-228: "German social scientists during the 1920's did their scholarly work in an atmosphere of extraordinary tension and instability. The academic community was politically more divided than ever before; ...

To write about government, economics, or society was necessarily to enter into the heated debate concerning contemporary political alternatives. The prevailing sense of crisis was so profound that even methods of analysis in the social sciences, not just the research results, acquired an immediate political relevance. It became increasingly easy to discover a man's party preferences in his methodological program for his discipline."

[135]Our discussion of personalism is deeply indebted to the detailed study by Michael Theunissen, The Other. We use the term 'personalism' in referring to Bonhoeffer, however, rather than Theunissen's adoption of Eugen Rosenstock-Huessy's term 'dialogicalism', because the former term is initially not only closer to Bonhoeffer's concern with 'the person' but also more neutral, less prone to the linguistic implications of the latter; see Theunissen, The Other, pp. 2; 385, n. 1, and Dallmayr's "Introduction," to The Other, p. xvii. Theunissen's own position led him, subsequent to The Other, to inquire into the similarities between the dialogical approach and the 'ideal speech' of Habermas; see Theunissen, Gesellschaft und Geschichte: Zur Kritik der kritischen Theorie (Berlin: Walter de Gruyter, 1970). As we shall see below, the philosophical premises of dialogicalism finally leave it in close proximity to the very idealism it intended to deny. On Bonhoeffer's relationship to the personalist school see Ernst Feil, Die Theologie Dietrich Bonhoeffers (Munich: Chr. Kaiser Verlag, 1971), p. 30, n. 7 and p. 33, n. 19; also see Tiemo Rainer Peters, Die Praesenz des Politischen in der Theologie Dietrich Bonhoeffers (Munich: Chr. Kaiser Verlag, 1976), pp. 119-127. For a contrasting interpretation of the influence of the personalist school on the later theology of Bonhoeffer, see Heinrich Ott, Reality and Faith. The Theological Legacy of Dietrich Bonhoeffer, pp. 74-95, who calls Bonhoeffer's approach an 'ontological personalism'.

[136]On the thesis that Heim was the chief influence on Bonhoeffer's personalism, see James W. Woelfel, Bonhoeffer's Theology. Classical and Revolutionary (Nashville: Abingdon Press, 1970), pp. 54-68. Although there is little direct evidence concerning the influence of Heim on Bonhoeffer, one cannot help but suspect that Heim's work on Husserl, his concern with existentialism and ontology, and his work on revelation were as well known to Bonhoeffer as Heim's position in the I-Thou personalist debate. Yet Bonhoeffer does not mention Heim in either of his dissertations. His published remarks on Heim are with regard to the first edition (1931) of Heim's Glaube und Denken, translated as God Tran-

scendent: Foundation for a Christian Metaphysic, trans. Edgar P. Dickie (New York: Charles Scribner's Sons, 1936) from the 3rd ed. of Glaube und Denken: Philosophische Grundlegung einer christlichen Lebensanschauung (Berlin, 1934). The tone of Bonhoeffer's review of the First Edition of Glaube und Denken in December, 1932 [Gesammelte Schriften III, pp. 138-159], particularly its trenchant criticism of Heim's ontology, indicates that, between the appearance of Act and Being and that time, Bonhoeffer's theological 'Barthianism' had grown much more pronounced, causing him increasingly to retreat, on extrinsic theological grounds, from some of the more original philosophical investigations of the two dissertations. Bonhoeffer had 'discovered Barth', according to Bethge, between the summer of 1924 and that of 1925, upon reading The Word of God and the Word of Man, trans. Douglas Horton (New York: Harper & Brothers, 1957). This followed right on the heels of the year's study with Heim at Tuebingen, and just preceded the beginning of work on Sanctorum Communio. The period of the two dissertations, up through the summer of 1933, can thus be seen as a time during which the influence of Barth waxed stronger, causing Bonhoeffer repeatedly to confront the issue of the extent to which his immanent philosophical concerns and the transcendent theology of revelation could learn from each other. By the third edition of God Transcendent, Heim had attempted to take into account some of the criticisms, such as those of Bonhoeffer, of his work. See Glaube und Denken, pp. 235-239.

137Bethge, Dietrich Bonhoeffer, p. 59. See Eberhard Grisebach, Gegenwart. Ein kritische Ethik. Cf. Michael Theunissen's illuminating remarks on Grisebach in Der Andere. Studien zur Sozialontologie der Gegenwart (Berlin: Walter de Gruyter, 1977), pp. 361-366, which were omitted from the English translation of The Other.

138Juergen Moltmann, "The Lordship of Christ and Human Society," in Two Studies in the Theology of Bonhoeffer, trans. Reginald H. Fuller and Ilse Fuller (N.Y.: Charles Scribner's Sons, 1967), p. 29. See Martin Buber, I and Thou. Cf. Heinrich Ott, Faith and Reality, pp. 257-270 on Bonhoeffer and Buber.

139Bonhoeffer, Sanctorum Communio, pp. 59, 236.

140Heinz Zahrnt, The Question of God. Protestant Theology in the Twentieth Century, trans. R.A. Wilson (N.Y.: Harcourt, Brace & World, Inc., 1969), p. 58: "He attacked German idealism in terms of linguistic philosophy; to the isolation of the self and the reserve of the non-self as conceived by idealism, Ebner opposes the I-Thou relationship as it occurs in speech, and which he sees as the deepest spiritual reality in human life. Man is a being who speaks, speech reveals him as a spiritual being. Thus Ebner regards all human existential life as conducted in a dialogue." Zahrnt sees Ebner as the chief influence on Gogarten, rather than Gogarten's colleague at Jena, Grisebach. On Ebner, also see Steven G. Smith, The Argument to the Other, pp. 229, 289.

141See G. Gloege, "Person, Personalismus," in Evangelisches Kirchenlexikon, Vol. III (Goettingen: Vandenhoeck und Ruprecht, 1959), cols. 129ff.

142Theunissen, The Other, pp. 266-269.

143cf. Tiemo Rainer Peters, Die Praesenz des Politischen in der Theologie Dietrich Bonhoeffer, pp. 122-127 on Bonhoeffer's personalism.

144See Theunissen, The Other, pp. 5-7 on his definition of 'social ontology', with which our study is in basic agreement. Given the significance of neo-Kantianism in the context in which Bonhoeffer was writing, it is not insignificant that Theunissen also notes (p. 259) that for most of the 'personalist' philosophers, neo-Kantianism was the purest form of a philosophy of subjectivity. Thus, again, the call for 'concreteness' came as a response to the perceived aridity and sterility of neo-Kantianism in Germany in the 1920's. Bonhoeffer's personalism could be construed, therefore as a kind of Kantianism-against-neo-Kantianism.

145Bonhoeffer, Sanctorum Communio, p. 22.

146Ibid., pp. 22-26; cf. the extended discussion in the original typescript of Sanctorum Communio, pp. 17-26, much of which was omitted from both the published German version and the English translation.

147Bonhoeffer, Sanctorum Communio, p. 23.

148Ibid.

149Ibid.

150Ibid.

151Ibid., p. 24.

152Ibid.

153Ibid.

154Ibid.; Bonhoeffer refers here in particular to Hobbes.

155Ibid.

156Ibid., p. 26. On the anti-idealist perspective of Sanctorum Communio see Rainer Mayer, Christuswirklich-keit. Grundlagen, Entwicklung und Konsequenzen der Theologie Dietrich Bonhoeffers (Stuttgart: Calwer Verlag, 1969), pp. 43-48 and Tiemo Rainer Peters, Die Praesenz des Politischen in der Theologie Dietrich Bonhoeffers, pp. 20-29 and 119-122.

157Bonhoeffer, Sanctorum Communio, p. 25.

158Ibid., p. 26.

159Ibid.

160Ibid.

161Ibid.

162Ibid.

163Ibid., p. 27; cf. note on Kant on Sanctorum Com-munio, p. 211, n. 5.

164Ibid.

165Ibid.

166Ibid. Cf. Lauer, Hegel's Concept of God, pp. 145-148 on "Only Spirit Knows Spirit".

167Ibid., p. 211, n. 8; Sanctorum Communio, p. 212, n. 12, which refers to Hirsch, Die idealistische Philoso-phie und das Christentum, 1926, 'Fichtes Gotteslehre,' pp. 140-290, esp. 260ff.

168Ibid., p. 212, n. 12, which refers to Fichte, Werke, ed. Medicus, III, 86, 1910, and Hirsch, op. cit. 236ff.

169Ibid., p. 24; Bonhoeffer identifies this with the Christian position on Sanctorum Communio, p. 25.

170Ibid., p. 28.

171Ibid.

172Dallmayr, "Introduction," to The Other, p. x.

173Bonhoeffer, Sanctorum Communio, p. 28.

174Theunissen, The Other, p. 366.

175Bonhoeffer, Sanctorum Communio, p. 32.

176Ibid.

177Ibid., p. 35; this issue of 'possibility', as we have seen, was further developed in the inaugural lecture.

178Ibid., p. 37.

179Theunissen, The Other, p. 368, quoting Eberhard Grisebach, Gegenwart, pp. 65, 586.

180Theunissen, The Other, p. 273.

181Bonhoeffer, Sanctorum Communio, p. 37.

182Ibid., p. 44.

183Theunissen, The Other, p. 370.

184Ibid., p. 260, referring to Ferdinand Ebner, Das Wort und die geistigen Realitaeten. Pheumatiologische Fragmente (Regensburg, 1921).

185See, for example, Dallmayr, "Introduction," to The Other, p. x.

186Thus, Theunissen's remarks on Grisebach might well have been written with regard to Bonhoeffer as well, e.g. The Other, pp. 260, 265 on Grisebach's Gegenwart, 7-8, 79, 137.

187See, for instance, Copleston's remarks on I. H. Fichte [A History of Philosophy, Vol. 7, Pt. II, p. 24]: He "laid emphasis on the individual human personality, and he was strongly opposed to what he regarded as Hegel's tendency to merge the individual in the universal." Fichte thus proposed a personalist idealism vis a vis "the Hegelian system in which ... finite personality was offered up in sacrifice to the all-devouring Absolute." Theunissen (The Other, p. 404, n. 22) also mentions the prior work of Georg Simmel, Die Religion [Sociology of Religion (New York: Philosophical Library, 1959)], of which Bonhoeffer also takes note in Sanctorum Communio (p. 210, n. 32) as a precursor to the Buberian I-Thou personalism, as well as the philosophy of Johann Georg Hamann and Wilhelm von Humboldt (Theunissen, The Other, p. 268). cf. Sanctorum Communio, p. 213.

188Woelfel, Bonhoeffer's Theology, p. 121; also see Clifford Green, Sociality, p. 57, who argues that "the epistemological subject-object relation is not a sociological category...."

189Bonhoeffer, "Man in Contemporary Philosophy and Theology," p. 48.

190Bonhoeffer, Sanctorum Communio, p. 29.

191Ibid. p. 29; emphasis added.

192Ibid.; emphasis added.

193Ibid.

194Ibid., p. 32. See Andre Dumas, Dietrich Bon-hoeffer. Theologian of Reality, pp. 77-96 on the philo-sophical background of Bonhoeffer's concept of com-munity.

195Bonhoeffer, Sanctorum Communio, p. 44.

196Ibid., p. 32.

197On this point the present study is in disagree-ment with the common interpretation stated by Molt-mann, Two Studies, p. 36: "...Sociality implies an equi-librium between personal and social being... There is no question of priority, but only of reciprocal relationship."

198Bonhoeffer, Sanctorum Communio, pp. 28, 29.

199Ibid., p. 44.

200Ibid., p. 29. The closest that the personalist tradition had come to such a conceptuality, according to Bonhoeffer, was the project of Eberhard Grisebach, par-ticularly in his work, Gegenwart. Eine kritische Ethik which, however, Bonhoeffer did not read until after Sanctorum Communio was written. As James Woelfel has noted in Bonhoeffer's Theology, p. 57: "Of all the I-Thou existentialist philosophers, Bonhoeffer found Eberhard

Grisebach the most congenial because of his two basic presuppositions: (1) man can understand his existence only from outside himself and contingently; and (2) this understanding is ethical, not theoretical." As Dallmayr (Twilight of Subjectivity, p. 309, n. 36) has commented, "in contrast to traditional metaphysics and the legacy of subjectivity, Grisebach advocated a radical reversal aiming at the replacement of constitutive human intervention by an attitude of patient **listening** and attentiveness (Hoerigkeit)...." For Grisebach, in Bonhoeffer's words (Act and Being, p. 86), idealist "theory is unable to form a concept of reality" adequate to a critical ethics, because it cannot conceptualize that "reality is 'experienced' in the contingent fact of the claim of 'others'." And only "in 'sustaining' the 'claim of my neighbor' [do] I exist in reality, [do] I act ethically." Thus Bonhoeffer affirms in "Man in Contemporary Philosophy and Theology," that "the really new thing in Grisebach is that he cannot think of man without the concrete other man"-- thereby Grisebach intends to overcome "any individualism, i.e. any imprisonment of the I in itself..." (p. 55).

201Bonhoeffer, Sanctorum Communio, p. 29. Contrast Woelfel, Bonhoeffer's Theology, p. 61: "Here, in Bonhoeffer's earliest writing, we find a clear rejection of any sort of epistemological (and, by obvious implication, metaphysical) understanding of transcendence in favor of a thoroughly ethical interpretation."

202Bonhoeffer, Sanctorum Communio, p. 29; emphasis added. cf. Day, Dietrich Bonhoeffer on Christian Community and Common Sense, pp. 26-33 on the ethics of Sanctorum Communio; also see pp. 33-42 on Bonhoeffer's Barcelona ethics and pp. 46-48 on the ethics of Act and Being. See Benjamin Reist, The Promise of Bonhoeffer (Philadelphia and New York: J.B. Lippincott Company, 1969), p. 53: "Bonhoeffer is a key figure in what could be called the ethicizing of theology. This is not to be confused with the **replacement** of theology by ethics. ... What is rather at stake is the **ethical intensification** of all theological concepts." It remains surprising that even recent work on Bonhoeffer's ethics pays little or no attention to Act and Being or even Sanctorum Communio. For example, neither Robin W. Lovin's Christian Faith and Public Choices. The Social Ethics of Barth, Brunner and Bonhoeffer (Philadelphia: Fortress Press, 1984) nor E. Clinton Gardner's Christocentrism in Christian Social Ethics. A Depth Study of Eight Modern Protestants (Washington, D.C.: University Press of America, 1983) mention Act and Being in their discussions of Bonhoeffer. The eleven essays in Ethical Responsibility: Bonhoeffer's

Legacy to the Churches, ed. John D. Godsey and Geffrey B. Kelly (N.Y. and Toronto: Edwin Mellen Press, 1981) make virtually no mention of either of Bonhoeffer's dissertations. And although both John W. de Gruchy's Bonhoeffer and South Africa. Theology in Dialogue (Grand Rapids: Wm. Eerdmans, 1984) and Thomas I Day's Dietrich Bonhoeffer on Christian Community and Common Sense mention the early work, neither seems to find any enduring methodological connection between the early and later ethical writings. James H. Burtness's Shaping the Future. The Ethics of Dietrich Bonhoeffer (Philadelphia: Fortress Press, 1985) is still forthcoming and therefore its treatment of Bonhoeffer's early work is unknown to this author.

[203] Although it goes beyond the scope of the present investigation, a fruitful further comparison could be drawn, as Michael Theunissen and Fred Dallmayr have done, with the work of Sartre, particularly his notion of the "direct impact of the Other on 'my' experience." See Dallmayr's "Introduction" to The Other, p. xvi, and Theunissen, The Other, pp. 199-254 on Sartre's relation to personalism.

[204] Bonhoeffer, Sanctorum Communio, p. 44-45; emphasis added.

[205] Ibid., p. 30.

[206] Moltmann, Two Studies, p. 31.

[207] Bonhoeffer, Sanctorum Communio, p. 33-34, which continues: "Whether the other is also an I in the sense of the I-Thou relation is something I can never discover."

[208] Ibid., p. 30.

[209] Bonhoeffer, "Man in Contemporary Philosophy and Theology," p. 55.

[210] Bonhoeffer, Sanctorum Communio, p. 214, n. 7.

[211] John A. Phillips, Christ For Us in the Theology of Dietrich Bonhoeffer, p. 78.

[212] Bonhoeffer, Sanctorum Communio, p. 29.

[213] Theunissen, The Other, p. 336.

214Bonhoeffer, Sanctorum Communio, p. 31. "Barrier" is a translation of "Schranke;" see Sanctorum Communio, manuscript, p. 39.

215Ibid., p. 32.

216Ibid.

217Ibid., p. 33.

218Ibid.

219Ibid.

220Ibid.

221Ibid., p. 35.

222Ibid., p. 36; where Bonhoeffer goes on to make clear that in saying that "the person-forming activity of the Thou is independent of its personal being," we must also affirm that "it is also independent of the will of the human Thou," for "no man can of himself make the other into an I, into a moral person conscious of responsibility." It is also significant that at this point Bonhoeffer distinguishes his position here from Kierkegaard's (Sanctorum Communio, p. 212, n. 12): "Our criticism of the idealist view of time and reality is close to his. But we differ where he speaks of the origin of the ethical person. For him to become a person is the act of the I establishing itself in a state of ethical decision. His ethical person exists only in the concrete situation, but it has no necessary connection with a concrete Thou. The I itself establishes the Thou; it is not established by it. Thus in the last resort Kierkegaard did not abandon the idealist position, and thus he founded an extreme individualism, which can only attribute a relative significance to the other." One is reminded of Kierkegaard's remarks on 'The Work of Love in Remembering One Dead,' in Works of Love, trans. Howard and Edna Hong (N.Y.: Harper Torchbooks, 1962), pp. 317-329. The other person here can be understood in two ways: (1) As usually understood, this position is attacked for its complete attention on the one-who-loves, with no con-cretely-embodied Other who is loved; it is thus individualistic and 'abstract'. (2) On the other hand, one can understand Kierkegaard to affirm here that the Other is loved, not on the basis of any possible likeness with the lover, but even in the most extreme limit case of its alienness--even in death.

[223]Bonhoeffer, Sanctorum Communio, p. 46.

[224]Ibid., p. 47; "oppositions" is a translation of "Widerstaende;" see Sanctorum Communio, manuscript, p. 74.

[225]Ibid., p. 33.

[226]See Act and Being, p. 31: "Even if it is to exercise a free decision of practical reason, the outcome is nevertheless reason's self-chosen self-limitation, whereby it reinstates its own authority--as the reason which performed this very limitation."

[227]Bonhoeffer, Sanctorum Communio, p. 47.

[228]Ibid.

[229]Ibid., p. 23.

[230]Ibid., p. 24.

[231]Ibid., p. 33.

[232]Ibid., p. 24.

[233]Ibid., p. 47.

[234]Ibid., p. 55.

[235]Ibid., p. 53.

[236]Ibid., p. 54.

[237]Ibid.; here Bonhoeffer notes his own indebtedness to Hobbes' bellum omnium contra omnes, Kant's position in Religion within the Limits of Reason Alone and his Ideen zu einer allgemeinen Geschichte in weltbuergerlich Absicht; see Sanctorum Communio, pp. 215-216, n. 19.

[238]See Sanctorum Communio, pp. 232-233: "...The Idealist conception of community ... is based upon the idea that persons are analogous and equal in value. These qualities are assured by the person's participation in universal reason (Kant and Fichte), or in the objective and absolute mind (Hegel). There are many I's, but there is no I-Thou relationship. Kant, who introduces the concept of the ethically responsible person in his concept of the kingdom of God (Religion within the Limits of Pure Reason III 1.4), or sees it, rather, as constituted by such persons, does not grasp the idea of

concrete community, since his concept of person is aper-
sonal. ... Hegel was open to concrete individual life, but
for him too it is merely a form of the universal spirit;
thus it is the fate of all individual life to be drawn up
into the spirit of the community. ... Everywhere we encounter the concept of unity...".

239Bonhoeffer, Sanctorum Communio, p. 55.

240Ibid.

241Ibid.

242Here we see the influence of Ferdinand Toennies's typology [Community and Society, trans. and ed.
Charles p. Loomis (East Lansing, Michigan: The Michigan
State University Press, 1957)]. As Ringer has explained
Toennies in his Decline of the German Mandarins (p.
164), "two contrary conceptions of law, two types of
association, and even two different styles of thought
arose from a fundamental dichotomy between two forms
of the will: Wesenwille [natural will] and Kuerwille [ra-
tional will]. ... In the case of natural will, thinking is
closely related to the whole personality and to its primary goals, whereas rational will proceeds upon more or
less 'impersonal', emotionally and morally neutral modes
of analysis. All human relationships and groupings, according to Toennies, may be classified with respect to
the quality of the will which creates them and holds
them together. The members of a community are united
in and through their natural will; the partners of a society come together to achieve some specific object of
rational will." Bonhoeffer draws on Toennies terminology
to describe 'communities of will' as determined either by
'will for a meaning' or by 'rational purposive will' (Sanctorum Communio, pp. 56ff.), and to distinguish between
'relations of power' and 'relations of authority' (Sanctorum Communio, pp. 58ff.). See Sanctorum Communio, p.
57: "The task of a sociological inquiry is not to disclose
the thousands of motives which give rise to a social
structure ... but to study the acts of will of which this
structure consists." Cf. Arthur Mitzman, Sociology and
Estrangement. Three Sociologists of Imperial Germany
(N.Y.: Alfred A. Knopf, 1973), pp. 39-131.

243Bonhoeffer, Sanctorum Communio, p. 232, n. 87.

244Cf. Dallmayr's comments on Theunissen's reser-
vations regarding Buber in his "Introduction" to The
Other p. xx.

245Bonhoeffer, Act and Being, p. 25.

246Derrida, Writing and Difference, 284.

247Theunissen, The Other, p. 366.

248Ibid., p. 280.

249Dallmayr, "Introduction," to The Other, p. xi.
As Dallmayr and Theunissen use the term, 'immediacy'
means "egologically not mediated" (Dallmayr, "Introduction," p. xvii). See Theunissen on Buber (The Other, pp.
274-275): "...The I-Thou relation is now above all characterized by 'immediacy'. ... The talk about immediacy is
the tenor of his [Buber's] entire work. ... 'Be immediate!'--that is the answer to the question posed by him in
1919: 'What should be done?'" "Buber has this universal
immediacy in view when, in I and Thou, he says, 'The
relation to the Thou is immediate. Between I and Thou
there is no conceptuality...'."

250Dallmayr, "Introduction," to The Other, p. xviii.

251Theunissen, The Other, p. 273, which continues:
"Cohen speaks of 'subordination,' 'submission', Grisebach
principally of 'mastery'." See H. Cohen, Religion der
Vernunft aus den Quellen des Judentums (Frankfurt am
Main, 1929), p. 148; Grisebach, Gegenwart, pp. 51, 94-95,
150, 552.

252Theunissen, The Other, p. 275.

253Bonhoeffer, Act and Being, p. 31.

254Theunissen, The Other, p. 286.

255See Michael Theunissen, "Bubers negative Ontologie des Zwischen," Philosophisches Jahrbuch 71 (1964):
319-330.

256Theunissen, The Other, pp. 281, 283.

257See Theunissen's remarks on Buber in The Other,
p. 275: "...As a community of equally primordial and e-
qually legitimate essences, of which no one disposes of
the other, the I-Thou relationship, to which alone Buber
ascribes the name 'relation', is a relationship of mutuality: 'Relation is mutuality.' Without the latter there is no
'dialogical' relationship." Cf. p. 278: "The I-It or subject-object relationship is ... a union of unequals, since
the activity of the one presupposes the passivity of the

other. _Ex negativo_, this circumstance throws light upon the I-Thou relation, that is, the community of partners of equal rank." And p. 279: "...Where action runs its 'for which' into passivity, it itself remains ensnared in its opposite. It first fulfills itself there where it responds to its equal. This, however, only happens in a dialogical manner when the acts of the partners make contact with one another **reciprocally**." Theunissen does note, however, that Buber attempts to balance this emphasis on **mutuality** with his concept of **grace**, e.g. pp. 279-280: "In the meeting, however, the alien deed encounters me, in the twofold meaning of the word, as a 'cooperation' of the Other and as an encounter in the sense of a reception of kindness and generosity. Buber speaks here of 'grace'. ... Grace is the gift of what is not at my disposal."

258Bonhoeffer, _Act and Being_, p. 88.

259Bonhoeffer, _Sanctorum Communio_, pp. 46-47.

260Bonhoeffer, _Act and Being_, p. 48.

261Bonhoeffer, _Sanctorum Communio_, p. 48.

262Ibid., p. 54.

263Ibid. Cf. Theunissen's remark which confirms the same care in the formulation of this position on the part of Buber, _The Other_, p. 277: "I and Thou are not imbedded in a totality and, so to speak, neutralized with respect to it. ... According to Buber, beginning with a unity consisting of me and the Other is no more appropriate than the point of departure from me as an isolated subject. ... The between really rules between the partners and so prevents their being taken up in each other."

264Bonhoeffer, _Sanctorum Communio_, p. 20; see p. 209, n. 31, which refers to Edith Stein, "Individuum und Gemeinschaft," Gerda Walther, "Zur Ontologie der sozialen Gemeinschaften," and Samuel Krakauer, _Soziologie als Wissenschaft_.

265Bonhoeffer, _Sanctorum Communio_, pp. 48-49.

266Ibid., p. 49.

267Ibid.

268Ibid., p. 50; cf. p. 52: "The structures of the individual and the collective unit are the same."

269Clifford Green, The Sociality of Christ and Humanity, pp. 61-62; cf. Sanctorum Communio, p. 51: "I-Thou relations are also possible between a collective person and an individual person."

270Bonhoeffer, Sanctorum Communio, p. 66; cf. pp. 67-68: "It is regarded as an achievement in sociology to have discarded such a metaphysical hypostatisation. It is the fear of Hegel which prompts this view. His idea of the 'spirit of a people' makes the individualist feel uneasy. But we cannot accept the criticism of his idea." Yet Bonhoeffer goes on to temper this position by arguing that (Sanctorum Communio, p. 68) "objective spirit lives its own life, but not in such a way that the life of the individual is absorbed into it, as Hegel suggests, when he says, 'It is mind that has reality, and individuals are its accidents.'" For Bonhoeffer's discussion of 'objective spirit' see Sanctorum Communio, pp. 65-70.

271Peter Berger in Martin Marty, ed. The Place of Bonhoeffer. Problems and Possibilities in His Thought (N.Y.: Association Press, 1962), p. 76.

272Bonhoeffer, Sanctorum Communio, p. 69.

273Ibid.

274Bonhoeffer, Act and Being, p. 51.

275Dallmayr, "Introduction," to The Other, p. xvii.

276See Theunissen, The Other, pp. 290, 363.

277Ibid., p. 373.

278Ibid., p. 361.

279Ibid., p. 376: "Existential praxis is ... resistant to logical resolution. But that does not mean that it is entirely inaccessible to thought. Only, one should not expect from a theory of existential praxis what can justifiably be demanded from a pure theory. It is not entirely capable of transforming darkness into light. It is, however, in a position to carry the light of understanding into the darkness. And that is a great deal."

280Cf. Theunissen's remarks on the desiderata of a critique of dialogicalism in The Other, pp. 362-363.

[281]Theunissen, The Other, p. 363; cf. pp. 363-364.

[282]Bonhoeffer, Sanctorum Communio, p. 31.

[283]Bonhoeffer, Act and Being, p. 26.

[284]Bonhoeffer, Sanctorum Communio, p. 31.

CHAPTER THREE

ADORNO'S <u>NEGATIVE DIALECTICS</u>: NON-IDENTITY SOCIAL ONTOLOGY, AND THE ETHICS OF OTHERNESS

The not insignificant, but largely underestimated, accomplishment of Bonhoeffer's immanent critique of the transcendental tradition in <u>Act and Being</u> had been his proposal of a novel heuristic typology of the relationship between thought and being. Its originality was twofold. First, it provided a formal distinction between those dialectical conceptual-strategies which assumed or undertook **identity**--idealism and systematic ontology--and those which assumed or undertook **difference**--genuine transcendental philosophy and genuine ontology. Second, it posed the problem, at least, of the relationship between the **theoretical epistemological** tension between identity and difference and the **social and ethical** tension between overcoming and maintaining the integrity of 'otherness'.

Now we turn to the other particular text which occasioned this study, Adorno's last major work before his death, <u>Negative Dialectics</u>. We will argue that Adorno's work can be interpreted as itself an attempt to further explicate just such a distinction. <u>Negative Dialectics</u> is significant for our study because it clarifies the methodological stakes involved in Bonhoeffer's concern with an immanent critique of "Transzendentalphilosophie und Ontologie"--particularly of **idealist** transcendental philosophy and **systematic** ontology, with their shared reductionist approach to the relation between thought and being. And Adorno's work makes its own constructive proposal in a fashion which follows the outline Bonhoeffer had sketched of the need for a 'genuine transcendental philosophy' and a 'genuine ontology'. It maintains the Kantian difference between 'subject' and 'object' precisely as the paradigm for a 'critical' post--Hegelian conception of the non-identity of thought and its 'other'.

Adorno's approach thus provides a more detailed case-study in Bonhoeffer's early attempt to state the manner in which the epistemological, subject-object duality was paradigmatic not only for the more formal level of transcendental analysis, but also for any critical reflection upon fundamental social and moral relations as well. The previous chapter has shown the way in which Bonhoeffer attempted to state the immanent critique of **epistemology** as an enduring paradigm for the critique of

169

sociality and **ethics.** For Bonhoeffer, we have argued, the immanent critique of epistemology graphically **deepened** the similarly intrinsic enigmas encountered in attempting to conceive of the non-identity or 'otherness' of basic social relationships and the ethical quandaries such 'duality' implied. The current chapter will argue that Adorno develops a more rigorous **methodological** proposal than had Bonhoeffer to deal with their common **concern** with the extent to which the immanent criticism of the transcendental tradition sheds light upon the aporias intrinsic not only to the more apparently 'formal' level of epistemology, but also to the levels of social and ethical conceptuality.

This chapter, therefore, shares the same three main divisions as the preceding chapter, reflecting our three-fold concern with (A) the epistemological paradigm, and the centrality of its conceptual duality, for (B) social ontology and (C) the ethics of otherness. Each main division is divided in turn into three sections, reflecting (1) Adorno's immanent critique of idealist dialectics, (2) his immanent critique of systematic ontology, and (3) finally, his own constructive proposals for surmounting them from within the context of their own presuppositions, after the fashion of Bonhoeffer's suggestions about a possible 'genuine transcendental philosophy' and a 'genuine ontology'. The chapter has as its goal to further disabuse theology, especially that in the tradition of Bonhoeffer himself, from ignoring the philosophical tradition's resolution of at least some of those conceptual enigmas which theology might otherwise assume only it can address from a 'transcendent', rather than an 'immanent' perspective. This will prepare us to ask in the next chapter about the possible **legitimate** function, in both philosophy and theology, of a turn to a perspective which **transcends** the limits of immanent criticism, but in full recognition of its accomplishments.

Adorno's philosophical career was bracketed by his inaugural lecture, "The Actuality of Philosophy," on the one hand, and by his Negative Dialectics, on the other hand. Given the polemical thrust of the former against the idealists' systematizing of the suspended-dialectic of the Kantian tradition of **transcendental philosophy**, it is fitting that the latter work in addition mounted an even more sharply stated argument against that very **ontology** which had waged perhaps the century's most cogent reaction against the modern inheritance of the legacy of idealism in favor of a renewed concentration on being's 'otherness' than thought.

Bonhoeffer's early work, as we have seen, remained weighted towards an immanent critique of idealism's egological pretensions, an orientation shared by Adorno's inaugural lecture. Thus while, on the one hand, Bonhoeffer readily affirmed a primary need for a 'genuine ontology', on the other hand, the possibility of a genuinely **critical** form of theoretical subjectivity, which could surmount the sheer non-conceptuality of systematic ontology, remained for Bonhoeffer an as yet unrealized possibility. Any 'genuine transcendental philosophy' required a more adequately conceived sense of the **limits** to thought, both social and ethical, which could place objectivity at the foundation of a chastened theoretical reason, as a requisite condition of its possibility.

Adorno's work, we will argue, in its productively ambivalent reaction against the philosophies of both Hegel and Heidegger, developed towards an increasingly weighted focus upon an immanent critique of ontology. Thus while, on the one hand, Adorno affirmed a primary need for a genuinely 'critical' form of non-idealist theory, on the other hand, the possibility of the genuine **priority of the object** remained, even in the age of the eclipse of the subject, an unaccomplished goal. For the priority of the object itself required an as yet unavailable form of dialectical thinking which escaped the totalizing pretensions of idealism, thereby putting theory at the service of non-identity, as the condition of its possibility.

Despite this difference between the weighted foci of Bonhoeffer's Act and Being and Adorno's Negative Dialectics, they shared a common concern to show the manner of the relationship between the immanent critiques (a) of idealism's 'subjective' resolution of transcendental 'objectivity' and (b) of systematic ontology's 'objective' resolution of transcendental 'subjectivity'. Idealism and ontology were, for Bonhoeffer and Adorno, warp and woof of the fabric of much of the legacy of transcendental epistemology. Whereas idealism had represented the **triumph** of totalizing thought and the **twilight** of trans-subjective being, ontology had attempted to turn the tables. Yet neither had surmounted the epistemological framework, which itself had been the origin of modern critical philosophical questioning.

Thus for **Bonhoeffer** (as well as Adorno in the inaugural lecture), the dominant target of immanent criticism was the subjectively-perspectival situation of Dasein, which must be conceived in a way that epistemology's egological perspective is not taken to be a

171

total definition of finite existence. In <u>Negative Dialectics,</u> to the contrary, it is clear that the by then dominant perspective against which immanent criticism must address itself is the 'opposite' tendency--to resist the totalizing pretensions of idealist subjectivity to the point that theoretical subjectivity is itself obliterated, rather than chastened, by being. This initial critique of what Adorno saw to be the destruction of theoretical subjectivity by the "jargon of authenticity" of Heidegger is, however, a methodological stratagem which is intimately linked to a 'second' moment of critique--against the very idealist subjectivity which would reassert itself as the only legitimate alternative to a heteronomous ontology. The two moments of critique are thus intertwined in their common desire to state a form of **critical theorizing** which resists in the name of non-identity either the ontologist's or the idealist's reductionist strategy, while at the same time asserting a certain sort of predominance for 'otherness', non-subjectivity, the non-conceptual itself.

A. Epistemology and the Dialectics of Non-Identity

1. The Immanent Critique of Idealism

The "Introduction" of <u>Negative Dialectics</u> states the anti-idealistic context within which Adorno's critique of systematic ontology is to be understood. Thus the anti-ontological starting point of the **body** of this work should not mislead us. From "The Actuality of Philosophy" to <u>Negative Dialectics,</u> Adorno waged a consistent argument against the epistemological subject's **systematizing**, identitarian pretensions, "the illusion ... that the power of thought is sufficient to grasp the totality of the real."[1] Indeed, as he wrote in <u>Against Epistemology</u>, the very "idea of philosophical critique ... has no other measure than the ruin of illusion,"[2] particularly that of totality.

Thus Adorno entitled his immanent approach "an anti-system,"[3] a dialectics of non-identity, or **negative** dialectics. It was preeminently negative <u>vis a vis</u> the fact that "as early as Plato, dialectics meant to achieve something positive by means of negation," to reconcile non-identity into an all-embracing totality. Adorno's approach would seek, to the contrary, "to free dialectics from such affirmative traits."[4] If "the claim [of identity] is a magic circle that stamps critique with the appearance of absolute knowledge," then "it is up to the self-reflection of [negative-dialectical] critique to extinguish

172

that claim, to extinguish it in the very negation of negation that will not become a positing."5 "The duality of
subject and object must be critically maintained against
the thought's inherent claim to be total."6

The task of the immanent critique therefore is to
de-center the claim to absoluteness of the subjective
perspective, to break out of the egological circle of the
concept, the reifying of the "appearance of identity ...
inherent in thought itself."7 Adorno's negative dialectics
is thus a renunciation of Hegel's argument that

> indeed, the grasp of an object consists in
> nothing else but that an I will make the ob-
> ject its own, will penetrate it, and will bring
> it into its own form. ... The object has this
> objectivity in the concept, and the concept is
> the unity of the self-consciousness in which it
> has been received; its objectivity, or the con-
> cept itself, is therefore nothing but the nature
> of this self-consciousness and has no other
> moments or definitions than the I itself.8

Thus immanent criticism, when Adorno emphasizes its
'negativity', is a critique of the idealist resolution of the
tension inherent to the epistemological paradigm in favor
of the subject, and to that extent is an "immanent critique of epistemology."9

Yet the immanent critique of idealism does not
thereby seek to escape the delusional context of the
"magic circle"10 of idealist epistemology, but rather to
enter more deeply into the dynamics of its problematic
claim to totality in order "to break out of the context
from within."11 Immanent criticism would challenge the
claim of the totally illuminating light of idealist subjectivity by means of a re-examination of the deep shadow
within its own provenance, the non-identity within totality, the enduring otherness of non-subjectivity which
epistemology had retained in its duality of subject **and
object.**

> Philosophical reflection makes sure of the
> nonconceptual in the concept. It would be
> empty otherwise, according to Kant's dictum;
> in the end, having ceased to be a concept of
> anything at all, it would be nothing. ... That
> the concept is a concept even when dealing
> with things in being does not change the fact
> that on its part it is entwined with a noncon-
> ceptual whole.12

173

The immanent critique of idealist-epistemology raises to philosophy's attention once again the **difference** between subject and object, their non-identity, as the negativity at the heart of the dialectical project, as, ironically, Hegel himself had done in the Phenomenology.[13]

In Hegel's idealist epistemology, however, the apparent duality of subject and object had proved to function as a sort of necessary fiction, a heuristic strategy employed to get the formal dialectic of thought into motion. The original, apparent heteronomy of the object was in idealist epistemology progressively attenuated in what Buck-Morss has described as "the movement of the concept toward its 'other', as merely a moment in a larger process toward systematic completion."[14] For Adorno, however, idealist epistemology's Enlightenment motivation to demystify the 'other', the object, leads merely to another mystification, that of philosophy's perennial illusion that thought is able to grasp reality as a whole. Hegel, according to Adorno, "sacrifices delimitation and plurality to the unity of reason, and thus slips into a mythical totality which he understands as the absolute idea of reconciliation."[15] Whether the totality, this reconciliation of subject and object, is conceived in Platonic-anamnestic or Hegelian-teleological terms, it presupposes that the duality of the epistemological paradigm serves a more fundamental identity. Totality is the primordial ideology, which "lies in the implicit identity of concept and thing...."[16]

It is this presupposition which immanent criticism questions: post-Kantian idealism's "equation of subjectively mediated truth with the subject-in-itself--as if the pure concept of the subject were the same as Being."[17] Immanent criticism is above all a penetrating study in difference, a renewed concern with the paradigm of that subject-object duality of 'pre-Hegelian', Kantian epistemology in which "reason and reality did not coincide."[18]

Idealism to be sure had not revitalized a naive form of 'Platonic' dialectics, an anamnestic totality fostering a vision of an "original state of happy identity between subject and object."[19] That which is undifferentiated, Adorno argues, as had Hegel, "is not ... one; even in Platonic dialectics, unity requires diverse items of which it is the unity."[20] In the case of the critical idealistic dialectics, the assertion of a teleological totality is more complex. For idealism, however finally circular its argument, does not naively **presuppose** the unity of thinking

174

and being. It would rather **comprehend** such unity dialectically, as the goal of that reason which has embraced
its negativity, its otherness, and made them precisely its
very own.

The immanent critique of such idealism begins,
therefore, by reopening the question of the adequacy of
such a dialectic's notion of the epistemological object.
Immanent criticism asks again the 'Kantian' question
whether the limit which 'objectivity' places on the potential for the reconciliation between thought and being
is not more radical than post-Kantian idealism had allowed. The immanent criticism of the idealist interpretation of the 'object' centers on the issue of whether or
not the opaqueness, the self-concealing nature of the
'other' as heterogeneously extra-subjective, has been
adequately accounted for by the idealist dialectic's notion
of the negativity of otherness.

Adorno's new dialectics is thus 'negative', but in a
fashion which challenges the previous Hegelian notion of
negativity. It returns to the long since presumably resolved issue of the moment of **receptivity** in the Kantian
epistemological paradigm. Negative dialectics inquires
again into the epistemological moment of 'intuition',
which the activity of the 'concept' wishes to inform.
Negative dialectics raises the question within the immanent context of idealistic dialectics concerning the
extent to which the epistemological object, precisely in
its 'otherness' to subjectivity, confronts the totalizing
urge of thought with its own intrinsic contradiction.

Adorno asks if there is not a certain predominance
to the epistemological object, which more radically 'sus-
pends' or interdicts any affirmatively-dialectical movement of thought than idealism had been able to allow.
He proposes that

> what transmits the facts is not so much the
> subjective mechanism of their pre-formation
> and comprehension as it is the objectivity
> heteronomous to the subject, the objectivity
> behind that which the subject can experi-
> ence.[21]

In this fashion Adorno's negative dialectics pursues the
possibility which Bonhoeffer had raised of a 'genuine
ontology', a form of dialectical thinking which thinks the
difference which the object claims over against the sub-
ject--being <u>vis a vis</u> thought--and thinks this appearance
of non-identity for its own sake, not as a 'moment'

175

which is ontologically inferior to a final rational totality. Negative dialectics resists the ontological conclusions to be drawn from the moment of subjective-constitutiveness in idealist dialectics, which in Adorno's view "repressively shapes its Other in its own image."[22]

Adorno's is a **negative** dialectics for the sake of a renewed meditation on the moment of receptivity which the epistemological paradigm had retained in its notion of the heterogeneous, extra-conceptual object. In Adorno's words, "disenchantment of the concept is the antidote of philosophy,"[23] particularly the philosophy of identity. Thus immanent criticism for Adorno, undertaken as a critique of idealism, leads inexorably from the priority of the 'subjective' act of thought towards the being of the 'object' to which thought refers--and therefore towards ontology.

2. The Immanent Critique of Ontology

But if Adorno's position is a **negative** dialectic vis a vis idealism's subjectively-affirmative resolution of the thought-being tension of epistemology, it is no less a negative **dialectic** which only 'critically' can entertain the ontological problematic broached by the retention of a concern with otherness.

> What must be eliminated is the illusion that ... the totality of consciousness, is the world, and not the self-contemplation of knowledge. The last thing the critique of epistemology--whose canon is the mediacy of the concept--is supposed to do is proclaim unmediated objectivism. ... Criticizing epistemology also means ... retaining it.[24]

Thus whereas Bonhoeffer's position wagered on the priority of a concern with the object--and only secondarily raised the question of the form of subjectivity adequate to such objectivity--Adorno's position emphasized the priority of a concern to maintain a **critical** subjectivity--and saw the question of an adequate form of objectivity as necessarily related to that of an adequately critical form of **theory.** The problem is not just an insufficient objectivity, but an insufficiently emancipated subjectivity, which has not been "confronted with its own claim to being absolute."[25] According to Adorno, "it is on this emancipation, not on the subject's insatiable repression, that objectivity depends today."[26] Thus Adorno firmly rooted himself in the Kantian tradition of transcendental philosophy, which he understood to provide, albeit largely unintentionally, its own critical parameters for resisting its historical outcome in idealism.

Bonhoeffer's Act and Being had begun with the immanent critique of idealism and went on to postulate the need for a genuine ontology, such as personalist philosophy and Heidegger had attempted--in Bonhoeffer's view, unsuccessfully. The body of the text of Adorno's Negative Dialectics, to the contrary, actually begins with a critique of the ontological tradition itself and then goes on to argue, in an ironic alliance with the methodology of idealism, for the need for a genuinely transcendental form of theoretical reason. Initially philosophy required not a direct critique of that 'theoretical need' of the subject which idealism had exploited in its "fetishism of knowledge."[27] It required a more indirect critique of what Adorno called the "ontological need"[28] upon which he felt that ontology, "Heidegger's in particular," had capitalized in is resistance to idealism.[29]

With classic polemical overstatement Adorno accused ontology, in its step back from the pretensions of idealist subjectivity, of a "readiness to sanction a heteronomous order that need not be consciously justified," a need to affirm Dasein's "home in Being,"[30] but at the price of blinding philosophy, destroying its theoretical vision altogether. Adorno had argued similarly in "The Actuality of Philosophy" that Lebensphilosophie, such as that of Simmel,

> has admittedly maintained contact with the reality with which it deals, but in so doing has lost all claim to make sense out of the empirical world which presses in upon it, and becomes resigned to 'the living' as a blind and unenlightened concept of nature ...[31]

Likewise ontology, according to Adorno, has reclaimed the question of the meaning of Being only by risking totally renouncing "the claim of the productive power of mind, the Kantian and Fichtean spontaneity ...."[32] As he continued in "The Actuality of Philosophy,"

> With the concept of 'thrownness' (Geworfenheit), which is set forth as the ultimate condition of man's being, life by itself becomes as blind and meaningless as only it was in Lebensphilosophie ... The claim to totality made by thought is thrown back upon thought itself, and it is finally shattered there too.[33]

177

There is in Heidegger, Adorno argues, "an undialectical negation (Negat) of subjective being," which places the phenomenological impulse with which Heidegger began "on the verge of ending in precisely that vitalism against which it originally declared battle...."[34]

Thus precisely here Adorno self-consciously affirmed the source of his immanent critique in none other than Hegel's own admonition that "genuine refutation must penetrate the power of the opponent and meet him on the ground of his own strength...."[35] Thus the ontological urge to turn from the primacy of the concept to that of the intuition of being, Adorno argued,

> would be unintelligible if it did not meet an emphatic need, a sign of something missed, a longing that Kant's verdict on a knowledge of the Absolute should not be the end of the matter.[36]

A critique of the ontological need required "an immanent critique of ontology itself"--not rejecting it "from outside," but instead, "taking it on in its own structure--turning its own force against it ... its validity traced, so to speak, in repetition."[37] Adorno therefore attempted a retrieval of the process by which ontology's reassertion of extra-subjectivity had resulted in the collapse of subjectivity itself, and an evaluation of ontology's warrants for having taken this course. A critical theory would thus affirm the ontological need, this longing, without capitulating to the ontological conclusion--once again, as previously in idealism--of the **identity** of subject and object. In Negative Dialectics "ontology is understood and immanently criticized out of the need for it."[38]

What had remained but an eschatological vision for Bonhoeffer--a genuinely transcendental form of philosophy which sustains the difference between thought and being--is for Adorno at the forefront of the philosophical enterprise. And it is this need for a genuinely **critical** theory which Adorno thinks has been fundamentally subverted by the manner of the affirmation of the predominance of Being in ontology--a predominance which is no less absolute, according to Adorno, than had been the absoluteness of the subject in idealism. The critique of ontology itself requires the reassertion of a form of subjectivity, a **dialectics**, which can sustain itself against the overwhelming weight of that longing for the Absolute, that "ontological pathos,"[39] which would reopen

178

the question of Being only by foreclosing on any prerogative of the subject. For "every concept of dialectic would be null without the moment of subjective reflection. What is not reflected in itself does not know contradiction."[40] Adorno endeavors in Negative Dialectics to develop the role of a 'critical' theoretical reason which places theory at the service of the apparent 'contradiction' of non-identity without thereby being any less 'dialectical'. For Adorno, "those who chide theory anachronistic obey the topos of dismissing, as obsolete, what remains painful as thwarted."[41]

Negative **dialectics** resists buying back the object at the price of the subject, that procedure which Bonhoeffer had himself denounced as 'systematic ontology'. Thus at the same time that Adorno affirms the resonances between the **negativity** of his procedure and the function of Kant's thing-in-itself, he also argues that

> if Kant meant to rescue that kosmos noetikos which the turn to the subject was attacking, and if, therefore, there is an ontological element in his work, it is still an element, and not the central one. His philosophy is an attempt to accomplish the rescue by means of that which menaces what he would save.[42]

Negative dialectics is foremost a critical **theory** which abjures both "the abdication of the concept and the despairing need for something absent"[43] which a systematic ontology encourages in its turn towards intuition.

Rather a critical theory proves itself by the very fact that it endeavors to use the epistemological 'concept' not to conjure the intuitive presence to thought of the absent being, but to maintain its absence, its 'otherness'-than, or difference-from, the concept itself. If a **negative** dialectics requires an immanent criticism of the absoluteness of those **concepts,** as negative **dialectics** it requires no less an immanent criticism of systematic ontology's presupposition of any subjectively non-mediated, or immediate, **intuition** of being. As Adorno had written in Against Epistemology, "nothing immediate or factical, in which the philosophical thought seeks to escape mediation through itself, is allotted to thinking reflection in any other way than through thoughts." Thus "the genuinely Eleatic doctrine of being as absolute" must be denied no less than the absoluteness of thought in idealism.[44] Adorno's negative **dialectics** denies ontology's desire "to be first philosophy, but innocent of the compulsion and the impossibility of deducing itself and what is from a first principle." It exposes the contradiction in the fact that ontologies "want the advantages of a system without paying the penalty."[45]

The result is a twofold criticism of both concept and intuition.

> Necessity compels philosophy to operate with concepts, but this necessity must not be turned into the virtue of their priority--no more than, conversely, criticism of that virtue can be turned into a summary verdict against philosophy,[46]

that is to say, against philosophy's investment in the concept. This brings Adorno into what we have called his ironic alliance with the 'Hegelian' tactic of immanent **critique.**

His project is an **alliance** with the critical "aversion to static, reified thought"[47] of Hegel's dialectics to the extent that it charges that the immediacy of **intuition** is as 'abstract' as the pure concept of pre-Kantian rationalism. Adorno refused to allow systematic ontology's hatred "of the rigid general concept," to lure philosophy into any alternative "cult of irrational immediacy."[48] He argued rather that even ontology's so-called 'immediacy' of being requires the mediation of the theoretical concept, "and needs it precisely at the moment of concretion"[49] with which systematic ontology intends to oppose idealism's absolutely-constitutive subjective activity. Adorno would embrace the "commandment to analyze" in the "Introduction" to Hegel's Phenomenology, which "bids us purely observe each concept until it starts moving, until it becomes non-identical with itself by virtue of its own meaning--in other words, of its identity."[50]

Thus Adorno affirms what he calls the "subjective side" of Hegel's dialectics, which "amounts to thinking so that the thought form will no longer turn its objects into immutable ones, into objects that remain the same."[51] As Adorno had claimed already in Against Epistemology,

> Hegel also asked no more than that the state-of-affairs should 'demand' a movement of consciousness. If heed were ever paid to that, then the traditional Cartesian idea of truth as fitting the concept to the thing would be shaken. As soon as the thing is thought, it ceases to be something to which one can fit

180

oneself. The realm of truth becomes reciprocal dependence, the mutual production of subject and object.[52]

Intuition, too, must again become a 'critical' notion, tied to that very subjectivity whose systematic pretensions to totality the non-identity of intuition refuses to admit.[53]

It is an **ironic** alliance because Adorno's form of criticism serves such non-identity, rather than the goal of totality, of absolute synthesis, of idealist rationality. Thus, as Gillian Rose has noted, Adorno's Hegelian methodology cannot be understood "unless it is realized that any 'Hegelian' terminology is reintroduced on the basis of a Nietzschean inversion."[54] "Objectively," according to Adorno, negative "dialectics means to break the compulsion to achieve identity, and to break it by means of the energy stored up in that compulsion...."[55] Thus Adorno can say that "even after breaking with idealism, philosophy cannot do without speculation, ... meaning speculation, of course, in a sense broader than the overly positive Hegelian one."[56] Thus even a negative **dialectics** serves the task of freeing dialectics from its Hegelian 'affirmative trait' of "the primacy of the subject, or--in the famous phrase from the Introduction to [Hegel's] Logic--the 'identity of identity and nonidentity'."[57] Adorno seeks a decidedly non-idealist dialectics which immanently critiques, rather than merely liquidates, "the system, the form of presenting a totality to which nothing remains extraneous...."[58]

Yet Adorno's dialectics resists the equally absolutizing tactic in ontology's distrust of the concept, if that distrust would blind philosophy to the fact that it is implicated in the concept even at the moment it supposes itself most exempt.

Though doubtful as ever, a confidence that philosophy can make it after all--that the concept can transcend the concept, ... and can thus reach the nonconceptual--is one of philosophy's inalienable features and part of the naivete that ails it. Otherwise it must capitulate, and the human mind with it.[59]

Thus, in full acknowledgement of the challenges and insufficiencies of the tradition, Adorno reopens to question the dynamic duality of the subject-object conceptual paradigm of epistemology. But the retrieval of the significance of epistemology is proposed as the route by means of which to immanently de-construe both the

181

conceptual fetish of "**synthesis** as a guiding and supreme idea" of idealist epistemology[60] and the fetish of intuitive **immediacy** which he understood to be the watchword of an equally reductionist ontology. There is "no way but to break immanently," Adorno writes, "through the appearance of total identity"[61] which plagues ontology no less than idealism. Such an immanent break is the work of a negative-dialectical epistemological conceptuality--a critical, but nonetheless undaunted, theory, which "corrects the naive self-confidence of the mind without obliging it to sacrifice its spontaneity...."[62]

Adorno's form of critical **theory**, his negative **dialectics**, sets out a strategy by which to fulfill what Bonhoeffer had called the need for a 'genuine transcendental philosophy'. As the previous chapter has argued was the case with Bonhoeffer's early work, in Adorno's Negative Dialectics the subject-object conceptuality inherited from epistemology is shown to be an enduring problematic **within** those very attempts to overcome it, notably existentialism, personalism and ontology.[63] The anti-systematic emphasis on the ontological integrity of the epistemological moment of **receptivity** itself requires a form of self-limiting subjective **activity** which sustains the non-identity of thought and being, as Bonhoeffer had argued was the case in the Kantian, critical form of the 'genuinely transcendental' subject-object paradigm.

3. Subject and Object as Dialectic of Non-Identity

Adorno's philosophy is above all an attempt to radicalize, rather than repress, meditation on the enduring significance **both** of that dialectic of non-identity which lay at the heart of the Kantian epistemological paradigm, **and** of the transmutation of non-identity into the moment of negativity in the idealist system. Thus Adorno noted of his own project that "a turn toward nonidentity is the hinge of negative dialectics."[64] Indeed, the same sense of the centrality of non-identity motivated, we have argued above, Bonhoeffer's call for a 'genuine transcendental philosophy' and a 'genuine ontology'. On the one hand, negative dialectics therefore takes this 'turn toward nonidentity' through an immanent critique of the evolution of **subjectivity** into the comprehensive reflection of idealism. It wishes to establish the 'genuinely transcendental' subject as that which takes us back into, rather than out of, a critical encounter with the extra-subjective, or 'objective' context of finite existence. And yet, on the other hand, negative dialectics undertakes a concomitant immanent critique of any resurgent emphasis on **objectivity** which can be bought only at the price of an undialectical conception of the very being towards which thought is directed. It wishes to articulate a 'genuine ontology' which sustains the otherness of the object as that which precisely invites, yet is irreducible to, a critical theoretical 'destruction' of its supposed immediacy. As he had written in "The Actuality of Philosophy,"

> only polemically does reason present itself to the knower as total reality; while only in traces and ruins is it prepared to hope that it will ever come across correct and just reality.[65]

Adorno's philosophy is therefore a meta-critique of Kant's epistemology which radicalizes **both** the moments of the subject **and** of the object of the traditional theoretical paradigm, and yet attempts to do so while avoiding the identitarian consequences of subsequent idealism and systematic ontology.

In its attentiveness to the epistemological moment of **receptivity** negative dialectics returns to reconsider the function in Kantian epistemology of the preeminent and most troubling case of 'otherness', that of the thing-in-itself. Adorno would have philosophy attend again to the very point at which subsequent idealism broke with Kant most decisively, the fact that Kant "refused to be talked out of the moment of objective preponderance," that "he stubbornly defended the transcendent thing-in-itself," refusing to "sacrifice the idea of otherness." Adorno's project is a vindication of the significance of the Kantian epistemological complaint that "without otherness, cognition would deteriorate into tautology" in which "what is known would be knowledge itself," no longer hindered by anything heterogeneous.[66] As Adorno concludes,

> what survives in Kant, in the alleged mistake of his apologia for the thing-in-itself [is] ... the memory of nonidentity. This is why Kant ... would rather convict himself of dogmatism than absolute identity (from whose meaning, as Hegel was quick to recognize, the reference to something nonidentical is inalienable). The construction of thing-in-itself and intelligible character is that of a nonidentity as the premise of possible identification; but it is also the construction of that which eludes identification.[67]

The thing-in-itself serves a meta-epistemological, even **ontological**, function for Kant. Therefore, **on the one hand,** Adorno argues that "the Copernican turn registered in conventional philosophical history does not exhaust him [Kant]," since "the objective interest retains primacy over the subjective interest in the mere occurrence of cognition, in a dismembering of consciousness in empiricist style." But, **on the other hand,** Adorno argues that "by no means ... can we equate this objective interest with a hidden ontology," at least not in any **affirmative sense.**[68] For Adorno the thing-in-itself has a **negative,** rather than a positive ontological function, to the extent that the thing-in-itself maintains the intractable **discontinuity** of thought and being, not their actual or potential rapprochement through the mediation of the subject. "Insight into the constitutive character of the nonconceptual in the concept would end the compulsive identification which the concept brings unless halted by such reflection."[69] A reappropriation of the function of the Kantian thing-in-itself provides the ultimate "disenchantment of the concept."[70] The immanent critique of idealism is thus a demonstration of the judgment that "the rebellion against the thing-in-itself, once critically enlightening, has turned into sabotage of cognition...."[71]

But, at the same time, the pervasive **activity** of the subject is precisely the means by which the non-identity, the 'otherness', of the object is to be maintained. "Reflection upon its own meaning is the way out of the concept's seeming being-in-itself as a unity of meaning."[72] Thus, a negative dialectics can return to the function of the thing-in-itself only in full recognition of the idealists' suspicion that, in so doing, philosophy risks merely regressing to a pre-critical attitude, which is not so much 'Kantian' as a pre-Kantian form of 'realism'.[73] The immanent criticism of the concept fetishism of idealism requires not only the **negativity** of the otherness of objectivity-par-excellence, but also its own, nonidealist form of **dialectical,** subjective mediation.

Adorno's meta-critique of epistemology was a **dialectics,** but of a different order than that of idealism. His was, rather, a non-idealist reading of the Kantian project, to which we have referred as a dialectics of difference, or non-identity, rather than of identity.

> By means of logic, dialectics grasps the coercive character of logic, hoping that it may yield--for that coercion itself is the mythical delusion, the compulsory identity. But the

184

> absolute, as it hovers before metaphysics,
> would be the nonidentical that refuses to
> emerge until the compulsion of identity has
> dissolved.[74]

Here the irony of immanent criticism comes to the fore, in that it "explodes Hegelian idealism"[75] by way of a tactic which uses idealism against itself, which turns idealism's critical method against its own ontological pretensions. That is to say, negative dialectics appropriates, as had--ironically--idealism, Kant's thesis of "the strength of the subject to break through the fallacy of constitutive subjectivity" of idealism itself.[76]

Thus in an age in which in many quarters the idealist, constitutive "thesis has disintegrated,"[77] particularly in the face of a resurgent ontology, Adorno warns that philosophy must neither allow itself to revert to a **nondialectical** affirmation of that which is 'other' than the concept, nor let its call for a critical **theory** be misunderstood as a naive re-affirmation of the identitarian subjectivity of **idealism.** Rather, the immanent critique of system proposes that--especially in the twilight of idealist claims to totality--philosophy must **both** resurrect idealism's own critical method--based as it itself was upon Kant's epistemological thesis of the all pervasiveness of subjective activity. **And** it must show how that method itself leads towards the immanent collapse of naive idealism's own intrinsic ontological pretensions-- based as they were on an insufficient conception of the function of Kant's thesis concerning receptivity.

> The idealistic magic circle can be transcended
> only in thoughts still circumscribed by its
> figure, in thoughts that follow its own deduc-
> tive procedure, call it by name, and demon-
> strate the disjointedness, the untruth, of to-
> tality by unfolding its epitome.[78]

"The immanent critic of idealism" thus paradoxically "defends idealism" in the very moment the criticism is itself waged. It does so "by showing how much [idealism] is defrauded of its own self--how much the first cause, which according to idealism is always the spirit, is in league with the blind predominance of merely existing things."[79] Idealism betrays itself when the illusion of totality inherent in its affirmative dialectics is allowed to deceive its own intrinsic critical method.[80] Thus Adorno's dialectics does not share idealism's logic of **integration**; "it does not tend to the identity in the difference between each object and its concept." Rather "its logic

185

is one of **disintegration**,"[81] an attentiveness to the originally epistemological problematic of the enduring difference, or non-identity which persists in any claim to
the identity between subject and object.

Yet Adorno is more circumspect in calling negative
dialectics a 'radical Kantianism' than had been Bonhoeffer in proposing Kant as an ideal--however historically
unrealized--for non-identitarian thinking. The "ascetic
reticence of Kant's theory"[82] to allow finite understanding to inflate into metaphysical reason was, for Adorno,
'true' to the extent that "it forestalled a mythology of
the concept."[83] Thus cognition's initial perception of
the dualism of subject and object is not, as idealism
proposed, revealed to be "a screen hiding ultimate
unity,"[84] which can be comprehended by Reason [Ver-
nunft]. Rather, the radical differentiation of subject and
object was necessary in order to obliterate "the spell of
the old undifferentiatedness ... the identity of a mind
that repressively shapes its Other in its own image."[85]
But the Kantian suspended-dialectic was 'false' to the
extent that it encouraged epistemology to accept the
'given' subject and object as representing "an ultimate
duality,"[86] of "positive, primary states of fact,"[87] as the
cognitively-modeled, static notion of Understanding [Ver-
stand] had presumed.

Kant had been right to emphasize the **difference**
between subject and object, to deny that the two are
"pieced out of any third that transcends them."[88] Yet
according to Adorno "the Kantian answer--withdrawing
the third, as infinite, from positive, finite cognition and
using its unattainability to spur cognition to untiring
effort--falls short,"[89] no less than had the idealist comprehension of the third itself in reason. For despite the
fact that the Kantian form of the subject-object paradigm remains lively for Adorno precisely because it "still
allowed dichotomies such as the ones of form and substance, of subject and object, without being put off by
the fact that the antithetical pairs transmit each
other...,"[90] Kant's epistemology in the Critique of Pure
Reason was insufficient to the task of a negative dialec-
tics--unable to sustain the very non-identity which it
intended--because it was unable finally to articulate the
way in which subject and object are both "resultant
categories of reflection, formulas for an irreconcilabil-
ity"[91] that cut across both subject and object. That is
to say, Kant's transcendentalism ironically "needs not
less subjectivity, but more"[92]--explicitly **dialectical**-sub-
jectivity which can **sustain** rather than merely **presuppose**
the problematic of the duality of subject and object.[93]

186

According to the immanent critique of epistemology, "the more consistent the procedures of epistemology, the less it expands. Thus it prepares the end of the fetishism of knowledge"[94] of idealism. That is to say, Kant's epistemological theory had not been too 'negative', but rather not 'dialectical' enough. It had been unable to demonstrate the manner in which subject and object, although they "appear to be an undialectical structure in which all dialectics takes place," actually "constitute one another as much as--by virtue of such constitution--they depart from each other."[95] Idealism had capitalized on just this feature of Kant's duality.

> If the dualism of subject and object were laid down as a basic principle, it would--like the identity principle, to which it refuses to conform--be another total monism. Absolute duality would be unity. Hegel used this for the purpose of taking the subject-object polarity into his thinking after all. ... As the structure of Being, he held, the dialectics of subject and object comes to be the subject.[96]

What is required is a form of **critical** thinking able to surmount the static duality with which Kant had been content, and yet able to remain, as had Kant, "open, in a grandiose ambiguity,"[97] which resists the idealist "passage to affirmation"[98]--its confidence that from the dynamic mediation of subject and object philosophy can infer their ultimate unity or identity. If Kantian transcendentalism had failed because it had an inadequately dialectical view of the subject, Hegelian idealism had failed because it had an inadequately dialectical view of the object as that which not only participates in the <u>Bildung</u> of the subject, but signifies the subject's perpetual inadequacy to its own subjective vocation.

B. Social Ontology in the Twilight of Otherness

1. Critique of Identity: the 'Otherness' of Dialectics

Bonhoeffer had forcefully argued **that** a profound parallelism existed between the epistemological subject-object problematic and the I-Thou relationality of philosophical personalism. Yet he had less successfully articulated **how** an intrinsic connection--immanent to the critique of transcendentalism itself--could be demonstrated between subject-object relationships in theories of knowledge and person-other relations in theories of so-

187

ciality and ethics. Adorno's original contribution is precisely his ability not just to state the relationship between epistemology and sociality, but to do so **dialectically**--without reducing either of the pairs of relationships to an un-dialectical genesis in the other. That is to say, Adorno provides the 'social ontology' by which to conceive of that sociality which Bonhoeffer had believed to be inherent to the epistemological paradigm itself.

The immanent critique of identity-philosophy, for Adorno, opens into a dialectical conception of sociality. In the twilight of otherness brought about by the bittersweet successes of idealism, the challenge to philosophy had become one of stating a genuinely **critical** social ontology of the non-identical other, the sociality of reality--as a deepening of the movement of immanent criticism itself. In the shadow of idealism, "having broken its pledge to be as one with reality or at the point of realization, philosophy is obliged ruthlessly to criticize itself."[99] The theoretical enterprise must become, as Adorno wrote in <u>Against Epistemology</u>, the demonstration of the manner in which "epistemology, the quest for the pure realization of the principle of **identity** through seamless reduction to subjective immanence, turns, despite itself, into the medium of **non**-identity."[100]

Adorno reiterated and developed this thesis of the **intrinsic** sociality of all philosophical categories in <u>Negative Dialectics</u>. "The only way to pass philosophically into **social** categories," he argued there, is not through an **extrinsic** importation of sociological concerns. Rather, it "is to decipher the truth content of **philosophical** categories" themselves.[101] Adorno's debt here to the section of Hegel's <u>Phenomenology of Spirit</u> on the master-slave relation is undeniable, in which Hegel's analysis "reveals the way in which all forms of consciousness develop and are inextricably intertwined with socio-life processes."[102] Yet Adorno's position is not to be taken for that reason as one-sidedly idealistic. Rather, he is arguing that **immanent criticism itself** is capable of becoming a form of **social** criticism which becomes able to see in the very eclipse of otherness in the idealist system "a **society** which actually does not tolerate anything qualitatively different."[103] Adorno stated this directly in his essay "Subject and Object," saying that "social critique is a critique of knowledge, **and vice versa.**"[104] Thus, for example, Adorno sees the historical development of the systems of Enlightenment philosophy as serving a compensatory social purpose in the face of the end of the preceding feudal order. "Out of itself, the bourgeois <u>ratio</u> undertook to produce the order it had negated outside itself" by its revolutionary expansion of rational freedom.[105]   If this so, then for Adorno

> anyone who desires to extricate himself from the system through thought, must translate it from idealist philosophy into the societal reality from which it was abstracted.[106]

Or as he wrote in <u>Negative Dialectics</u>, "the coercive state of reality, which idealism had projected into the region of the subject and the mind, must be retranslated from that region."[107]   Here Adorno's sympathies with the 'unmasking' tradition of the hermeneutics of suspicion which developed out of left-Hegelianism, Marxism, and the sociology of knowledge is clear.   "Beyond the magic circle of identitarian philosophy," he proposes, "the transcendental subject can be deciphered as a society unaware of itself."[108]

Such 'translation' or 'deciphering' of the hegemony of identity-philosophy requires, as we shall see below, a form of subjectivity, a **dialectics.**   Yet although deeply indebted to idealism's attempt to resolve the antinomies of the legacy of epistemology, Adorno's subjectivity needs to be capable of being stated in a thoroughly non-idealistic form which can affirm philosophy's ontological need, the longing for a content, without capitulating to a premature ontological conclusion concerning the identity of subject and object.   Theoretical subjectivity must be able to demystify idealism, to make it aware of the nature of the very sociality inherent to it.   Thus, in Adorno's mature work, dialectics from the start takes a distinctly **negative** stance.

> The name of dialectics says no more, to begin with, than that objects do no go into their concepts without leaving a remainder, that they come to contradict the traditional norm of adequacy.   Contradiction is not what Hegel's absolute idealism was bound to transfigure it into: it is not of the essence in a Heraclitean sense.   In indicates the untruth of identity, the fact that the concept does not exhaust the thing conceived.[109]

"Leaving a remainder" is the insistent reminder of what we have called the 'sociality' of the concept, whereas "the resolution of contradiction is the system <u>in nuce</u>."[110]   For Adorno the concept not only refers to an object, but an object which 'is' not only known, but also is ever a surplus to its rationality.   Even when it is

189

conceptualized, the object sustains an 'otherness-than' that concept of itself whose constitutional urge is towards the comprehension of all that the object can mean.

This was the enduring contribution of Kant's having given new respect to antinomical forms of thinking in the Critique of Pure Reason.

> The concept of the given, the last refuge of the irreducible in idealism, collides with the concept of spirit as complete reducibility, viz. with idealism itself. Antinomy explodes the system, whose only idea is the attained identity, which as anticipated identity, as finitude of the infinite, is not at one with itself.... By the retreat to formalism, for which first Hegel and then the phenomenologists reproached Kant, he did honour to the non-identical. He did not deign to involve it in the identity of the subject without residue.[111]

Thus 'dialectics' for Adorno names the antinomical form of thinking in which the subject and the object are "mutually mediated--the object by the subject, and even more, in different ways, the subject by the object,"[112] or what Negative Dialectics calls the "coherence of the nonidentical."[113] Adorno's non-affirmative understanding of dialectics means that not only does the concept mediate the object in dialectics, but also the 'residue' itself mediates the concept, which therefore cannot totally comprehend the object.

Therefore to speak again of dialectics means for Adorno to confront directly idealism's assumptions about identity, its model of the **knowledge** of objects as the **actualization** of potential-subjectivity. He concludes that

> if Hegel's dialectics constituted the unsuccessful attempt to use philosophical concepts for coping with all that is heterogeneous to those concepts, the relationship to dialectics is due for an accounting insofar as his attempt failed.[114]

Negative dialectics is therefore not a strategy, like that of idealism, by which to overcome this 'remainder', to establish the total rule of the telos of rational identification. Negative dialectics rather challenges idealism's claim of "inclusiveness and completeness,"[115] the "drive for system" which Nietzsche had taught it to mistrust.[116] As David Held has interpreted Adorno, the capacity of dialectics to transcend opposition is limited. Critique cannot escape the terms of reference of its object. The grounds for transcendence in history are strictly (and tragically) circumscribed--by particular historical conditions.[117]

In the notion of the 'remainder', Adorno argues, idealism "runs up against the impossibility of satisfying [such a claim]."[118]

Negative dialectics counters idealism's employment of mediation as a tactic to identity, its enactment of that compulsion towards system which makes of the duality of subject and object "an analytical judgment, a turning to and fro of the thought without citation of anything extraneous to it," in which "the new is the old and otherness is familiarity."[119] Hegel, to be sure, had transcended the **static** Kantian duality of subject and object-as-limit, arguing that Reason--if it is indeed free--must be capable of overcoming the perspective of epistemology's dualities,[120] of seeing them, as Marcuse has pointed out, from "the perspective of a rational totality."[121] In place of such a static duality he had affirmed the **dynamic** function of negativity--of otherness, of difference--in achieving a determinate, dialectical totality. If the 'otherness' of objectivity appears first off to be a violation of subjectivity, Reason is the dialectical process of becoming self-conscious of the fact that, as Hegel put it, "consciousness suffers this violence at its own hands."[122] Idealism thus never **encounters** limits, but **sets its own.** And mediation is for idealism the process by which the Other is discovered to be not the boundary of thought, but the means of its destiny. Or as Hegel put it, "in speculative [begreifenden] thinking ... the negative belongs to the content itself...."[123]

This means, obviously, that dialectical mediation could not be for Hegel finally **for the sake of** non-identity. Rather it was what Marcuse has called "the principle that will restore the missing unity and totality"[124] beyond the illusions of duality. Thus, ironically, according to Adorno, despite its polemical affirmation of dynamism, "the Hegelian system in itself was not a true becoming," since "implicitly each single definition in it was already preconceived,"[125] predetermined by the totalizing momentum of systematic thought. That is to say,

no matter how dynamically a system may be conceived, if it is in fact to be a closed sys-

191

tem, to tolerate nothing outside its domain, it will become a positive infinity--in other words, finite and static. The fact that it sustains itself in this manner, for which Hegel praised his own system, brings it to a standstill.[126]

A **negative** dialectics--a genuinely **critical**, rather than **affirmative** theory--would to the contrary be a radically **open** system. It would counter Hegel's dynamic **system** by means of a genuinely dynamic **non-identity**. By means of the sustained dynamism of a **negative** dialectic, Adorno would accomplish the unfulfilled desideratum of the 'negativity' of Hegel's dialectic, "that there always remains something outside,"[127] rather than join in idealism's "apologetic labor of Sisyphus: thinking away the negative side of the universal."[128] Idealist dynamics must be shown, by the consistent application of its own methodology, "to disavow its own product, the system."[129]

The 'anti-system' of negative dialectics is more dynamic, more open, than the Hegelian system, to the extent that it is better able to allow precisely the **static** epistemological 'elements' of subject and object to remain **non**-identical to each other. The idealist concept itself,

> no less than its irrationalist counterpart, intuition, ... as such has archaic features which cut across the rational ones--relics of static thinking and of a static cognitive ideal amidst a consciousness that has become dynamic.[130]

If dialectics does not mean "to achieve something positive by means of negation"[131]--to achieve identity by means of the non-identical or negative--this is because the dialectical 'remainder' signifies, above all, that "dialectics is the **consistent** sense of nonidentity,"[132] the sustained inquiry into just these apparently 'archaic features'. The 'adequacy' of thought to being consists not in "the actual cognition of things that resist cognition--of things which are, so to speak, atheoretical."[133] Rather, it consists in the recognition of the resistance of the **object** to the comprehension, the total 'definition', by the concept. What is needed is a genuinely 'critical' theory, whose concepts do not demand "an advance elimination of the counter-agent to those concepts, of that concrete element which idealistic dialectics boasts of harboring and unfolding."[134] However, Adorno adds,

> The more critically we see through the autonomy of subjectivity, ... and the clearer our awareness of its own mediated nature, the

192

more incumbent is it upon our thinking to take on what lends it the solidity it does not have in itself.[135]

Adorno's philosophy thus turned on what he called "identity's dependence on the nonidentical, as Hegel **almost** achieved it,"[136] rather than Hegel's actual system in which the nonidentical depends upon identity.[137]

Thus Adorno's difference from Hegel centers on this issue of the latter's exploitation of "the fact that the nonidentical on its part can be defined only as a concept."[138] For Hegel the **concept** of non-identity became "a vehicle for turning it into identity, into equality with itself."[139] Ironically, it had been through Hegel's anti-Kantian reproach against the static categories of epistemology--that "one becomes a smith only by smithing"[140]--that "philosophy had regained the right and the capacity to think substantively instead of being put off with the analysis of cognitive forms that were empty and, in an emphatic sense, null and void."[141] Whereas "to Kant, multiplicity and unity were already categories side by side ... Hegel, following the model of the late Platonic dialogues, recognized them as two moments of which neither is without the other."[142] And for this philosophy, even negative dialectics, is indebted to idealism.

But against the systematic unity of idealism--summarized in the Hegelian maxim that "the true is the whole"[143]--a negative dialectics returns its attention from the totality of the One to the non-identity of the multiplicity of the Many.[144] Adorno's position counters Hegel's assertion that while

truth also is positive, as knowledge coinciding with the object, ... it is this self-sameness only if knowledge has reacted negatively to the Other, if it has penetrated the object and has voided the negation which it is.[145]

Adorno argues that "even the Eleatic concept of the supposedly isolated One is comprehensible only in its relation to the Many that it negates," so that "without the Idea of the Many, that of the One could never be specified."[146]

Thus Adorno inverted Hegel's dictum, in order to claim that "the whole is the false."[147] By this, as Buck-Morss has pointed out, Adorno wished not only to expose "the untruth of identity (of the Hegelian claim that the

193

real was rational)," but also to claim "the converse as well: nonidentity was the locus of truth."[148] And for Adorno this entailed a nuanced, but emphatic reassertion of the problematic status of the 'other', versus "Hegel's consistent resolution of nonidentity into pure identity," in which "the concept comes to be the guarantor of the nonconceptual,"[149] a tactic which assumes not only the adequacy of thought to being, but the adequacy of being to 'be thought', rather than thinking's 'other'. "To use identity as a palliative for dialectical contradiction, for the expression of the insolubly nonidentical," Adorno counters Hegel, "is to ignore what the contradiction means."[150] In particular for Adorno, it is to ignore the Marxian admonition that the **present** whole is false, repressive because it denies the social bases of its fragmentariness by means the ideology of identity.

It is from idealism's own understanding of nonidentity that negative dialectics therefore must distinguish itself. The result is the heart of Adorno's argument--that

> the matters of true philosophical interest at this point in history are those in which Hegel, agreeing with tradition, expressed his disinterest. They are nonconceptuality, individuality, and particularity--things that ever since Plato used to be dismissed as transitory and insignificant, and which Hegel labeled 'lazy Existenz'.[151]

For a negative, rather than an idealistic-affirmative dialectics, "a matter of urgency to the concept would be what it fails to cover,"[152] precisely the non-identical in its own right, not as a moment in a closed, or closing, system. "It is an expression of its own negativity," Adorno argues, that the whole "remains unreconciled with the particular."[153] Thus a **negative** dialectics "must give up the great problems, the size of which once hoped to guarantee the totality, whereas today between the wide meshes of big questions," Adorno writes, "interpretation slips away."[154]

Dialectical critique, accordingly, seeks not a false reconciliation of universal and particular. Rather it seeks to express the negativity of the whole by seeking "to salvage or help to establish what does not obey totality...."[155] Thus the affirmation of "mediacy is not a positive assertion about being but rather a directive to cognition not to comfort itself with such positivity,"[156] not to trade intelligibility for a genuine encounter with the non-identical other. The non-conceptual must not be purged from dialectics by the ontologizing of the ontical,[157] despite idealist systems' propensity to disqualify their "heterogeneities--whether called 'sensation', 'not-I', or whatever--down to that 'chaos' whose name Kant used for heterogeneity at large."[158]

Therefore Adorno finds an important clue to the function of this nonconceptuality--which, "inalienable from the concept, disavows the concept's being-in-itself"[159]--in the epistemological function of sensation in Kant's Critique of Pure Reason. Adorno argues that if in the First Critique

> sensation were strictly required before the form, the transcendental subject, could function ... that subject would be quasi-ontologically tied ... to matter, the counter-pole of apperception. This would have to undermine the entire doctrine of subjective constitution, to which matter, according to Kant, cannot be traced back. With that, however, the idea of something immutable, something identical with itself, would collapse as well.[160]

Thus "epistemology," Adorno concludes, "obliges philosophy to be substantive,"[161] by which he means that even the "smallest ontical residue in the concepts" of transcendental philosophy "compels that philosophy to include existing things in its own reflection."[162] But this would be the end of the possibility of any systematic 'first philosophy', and the end of idealism.

> A basic philosophy, prote philosophia, necessarily carries with it the primacy of the concept. ... Since the basic character of every general concept dissolves in the face of distinct entity, a total philosophy is no longer to be hoped for.[163]

Thus philosophy's consistent attempt to fathom such antinomial pairs as that of Kant's transcendental and empirical subjects, Adorno maintains, is the beginning of the recognition of "the incompatibility of system and sheer encounterability."[164]

Non-identity, the negation of totality, Adorno argued, required not just a concept of 'negativity' but philosophy's investment in the 'negative' itself--not just 'particularity', but the 'particular' object which in each

case mediates the concept involved.   Hegel consistently
shrank, Adorno lamented,

> from the dialectics of the particular, which
> destroyed the primacy of identity and thus,
> consistently, idealism itself.   For the particular
> he substitutes the general concept of particu-
> larization pure and simple....[165]

To the contrary, "instead of making do with their mere
concepts and feeling sheltered there from what the concept means," negative dialectical "thinking crystallizes in
the particular, in that which is defined in space and
time."[166]   Whereas Hegel's "logic deals only with particularity, which is already conceptual," not "with the
particular as a particular at all," it is the **particular
itself** which concerns Adorno.[167]

This issue of the particular is therefore the hinge
for Adorno between idealist epistemology and a genuinely
determinate sociality.   "Hegel's transposition of the particular into particularity," Adorno argues, "follows the
practice of a society that tolerates the particular only as
a category, a form of the supremacy of the universal."[168]
The idealist transcendental subject must be able "to wipe
away telltale dregs of earth within prima philosophia, the
traces of the incompatible."[169]   Negative dialectics, to
the contrary, remains with the particular--meditates upon
the contradiction it introduces into the idealist system.
Adorno's project is thus a wager, as Buck-Morss has
described it, that "the antinomies of bourgeois thought
reflected a reality in itself contradictory," and thus "they
could not be reconciled in theory so long as social reality remained unchanged."   As Adorno himself said, "even
to imagine a transcendental subject without society,
without the individuals whom it integrates for good or
ill" is an impossibility.[170]

The particular, the individual--what we have referred to as the 'sociality' of the epistemological object--
thus "is what the concept of the transcendental subject
founders on."[171]   The particular challenges idealism's
"taboo against facticity,"[172] which had been the defensive result of Hegel's having been able to deal with "the
Kantian and Fichtean **dichotomy** of transcendental subject
and empirical individual"[173] only by ignoring the empirical with "the thesis of [its] identity" with the conceptual.[174]   Idealism was an impossibility "unless the essence of entity, and ultimately entity itself, was a mental
element reducible to subjectivity--unless concept and
thing were identical on the superior level of the

196

mind."[175] The particular challenges the hegemony of the constitutive subject by sustaining a moment of plurality which escapes that subject's identifying grasp--which demands a **negative** social ontology.

The particular is therefore key to understanding Adorno's otherwise idealist sounding position that mediacy "is really the demand to arbitrate dialectic concretely."[176] If "for Hegel the **system** was, according to the formulation of the <u>Encyclopedia</u>, a concrete totality,"[177] for Adorno the **anti-system** of negative dialectics must be a recognition of the **non-identity** of totality as the essence of concreteness, a 'difference' demanded by the refusal of the particular to "be measured by the unity of thought."[178] <u>Negative Dialectics</u> argues that

> totality is to be opposed by convicting it of nonidentity with itself--of the nonidentity it denies, according to its own concept. Negative dialectics is thus tied to the supreme categories of identitarian philosophy as its point of departure.[179]

And this transcendence of totalizing, subjective identification is encountered precisely in the object's individuality, the measure of its trans-conceptuality. It is the burden of **negative** dialectics, according to Adorno, to sustain such a 'sociality' of **object** and subject--of the being of the particular, not just the thought of its particularity.[180]

The 'sociality' of the plurality of subject **and object**--thought and being--places, therefore, a certain priority on thought's Other. "As thinking, dialectical logic respects that which is to be thought--the object--even where the object does not heed the rules of thinking."[181] Transcendental philosophy must, therefore, come to terms with the fact that

> what is decisive in the ego, its independence and autonomy, can be judged only in relation to its otherness, its non ego. Whether or not there is autonomy depends upon its adversary and antithesis, on the object which either grants or denies autonomy to the subject. Detached from the object, autonomy is fictitious.[182]

Thus, "carried through, the critique of identity is a groping for the preponderance of the object."[183]

In this case, according to Adorno, "it is up to dialectical cognition to pursue the inadequacy of thought and thing, to experience it in the thing."[184] Such inadequacy, as "an index of the object's preponderance," he argues, can be seen in

> the impotence of the mind--in all its judgments as well as, to this day, in the organization of reality. The negative fact that the mind, failing in identification, has also failed in reconcilement, that its supremacy has miscarried, becomes the motor of its disenchantment.[185]

And the result, he explains, is that

> if the thought really yielded to the object, if its attention were on the object, not on its category, the very objects would start talking under the lingering eye.[186]

If a truly negative-dialectical thinking accorded the object such a priority, it would begin to understand that "the aporetical concepts of philosophy are marks of what is objectively, not just cogitatively, unresolved."[187] Philosophy's antinomies are not just a matter of "incorrigible speculative obstinacy,"[188] but of its repressed awareness that

> it is not true that the object is a subject, as idealism has been drilling into us for thousands of years, but [that] it is true that the subject is an object. ... The practice of its rule makes it a part of what it thinks it is ruling; it succumbs like the Hegelian master. It reveals the extent to which in consuming the object it is beholden to the object. ... The subject's desperate self-exaltation is its reaction to the experience of its impotence, which prevents self-reflection. Absolute consciousness is unconscious.[189]

Therefore a resurgence of the object--and with it a certain form of negative ontology, the 'genuine ontology' for which Bonhoeffer had called--comes to serve dialectics itself as its **negative** moment. A 'negative ontology' of the preponderance of the object denies idealistic dialectics its own affirmative ontological conclusions concerning the identity of subject and object, of thought and being. "If ontology were possible at all," Adorno concludes, "it would be possible in an ironic sense, as the epitome of negativity."[190]

2. Critique of Ontology: the 'Dialectics' of Otherness

Yet the preponderance of the **object** is in a certain sense the result of taking the **subject** with utter seriousness. In the words of <u>Negative Dialectics</u>, "it is the mind's definition as an activity which immanently compels philosophy to pass from the mind to its otherness."[191] And this 'passage' means that subject and object are not to be retained in a static, paradoxical 'relationship', but rather must be caught in the moment of 'passing'--that is to say, dialectically. Thus Adorno's ontology, if we can be allowed to call it that, is indeed 'ironic': it maintains the preponderance of the **object,** yet precisely for the sake of the **subjectivity** of a "changed philosophy" which ceases "persuading others and itself that it has the infinite at its disposal."[192] He wishes, on the one hand, "to adhere as closely to the heterogeneous" as possible, even to the point of "total self-relinquishment."[193] Yet just as surely, on the other hand, Adorno intended thereby to resist precisely what he called the "authoritarian intentions" of much of "the new ontology,"[194] which would subsume theory beneath the overbearing weight of being. In Buck-Morss's words, for Adorno "truth resided in the object, but it did not lie ready at hand; the material object needed the rational subject in order to release the truth which it contained."[195] Thus, if idealist dialectics required a genuinely **negative** ontological moment to counter its metaphysical pretensions, this ontology itself required a **dialectical** conception of that otherness whose non-identity from the subject such a social ontology would sustain.

The immanent critique of idealism led, therefore, to the need for an immanent critique of ontology, and thus to Adorno's peculiar style of thinking in aporias. Adorno's **negative** dialectics demanded genuine otherness; but that otherness was to be available to **thought.** The **otherness** of dialectics required a concomitant **dialectics** of otherness. Thus if ontology served dialectics as its **negative** moment, dialectics serves the ontological urge as its **critical** moment. "An ontological moment is needed," Adorno is adamant, but only "in so far as ontology will critically strip the subject of its cogently constitutive role without substituting it through the object, in a kind of second immediacy. The object's preponderance is solely attainable for subjective reflection, and for reflection on the subject."[196]

The meditation on the being of the 'other', demanded by the particular, belongs squarely within the context of that dialectics which gives the individual its intelligibility. In the words of <u>Negative Dialectics,</u>

> in criticizing ontology we do not aim at another ontology, not even at one of being nonontological. If that were our purpose we would be merely positing another downright 'first'--not absolute identity, this time, not the concept, not Being, but nonidentity, facticity, entity. We would be hypostatizing the concept of nonconceptuality and thus acting counter to its meaning.[197]

The anti-idealist interruption of the ontological urge <u>via</u> the opaque object cannot be taken as a static, **immediate limit**--modeled after the spatial image of a fixed **barrier** --to thought. Rather dialectics must become that dynamic mode of a genuinely **negative** ontology which cannot even posit the particular, the individual--entity--as **immediately** given. The quasi-ontological emphasis on the intuition of otherness does not obviate dialectics, but calls for a **radicalized** dialectics--a **dialectics** of otherness, a sense of the subjectivity of the object itself.

Adorno's sustained meditation on the subject-object paradigm of epistemology results, therefore, in his caution that the particular itself is no more immediate, no more brutely **given**, than its concept. As he wrote of Bergson: "Intuitions succeed only desultorily...."[198] The critique of idealist mediation by means of Adorno's notion of the preponderance of the object

> does not mean that objectivity is something immediate, that we might forget our critique of naive realism. ... It means a moment in dialectics--not beyond dialectics, but articulated in dialectics.[199]

"Because entity is not immediate, because it is only through the concept," Adorno states in deliberate tension with his nascent negative-ontology, "we should begin with the concept, not with the mere datum."[200] As he later continues,

> the insight into the fact that thinking is mediated by objectivity does not negate thinking, nor does it negate the objective laws that make it thinking. The further fact that there

200

is no way to get out of thinking points to the
support found in nonidentity--to the very
support which thought, by its own forms, seeks
and expresses as much as it denies it.[201]

The **dialectics** of the Other must become the medium for
ontology.

Adorno rejects the idealist understanding of mediation, not for the sake of any alternatively un-dialectical,
non-mediated confrontation with 'given' reality, but for
the sake of a truly **dialectical** interpretation of mediation.

Mediation of the object means that it must not
be statically, dogmatically hypostatized but can
be known only as it entwines with subjectivity;
mediation of the subject means that without
the moment of objectivity it would be literally
nil.[202]

The anti-idealist polemic "that the object takes precedence even though indirect itself," he concludes, "does
not cut off the subject-object dialectics," for "immediacy
is no more beyond dialectics than is mediation."[203]
Rather "a true preponderance of the particular would not
be attainable except by changing the universal," by challenging ontology itself with a radicalized subjectivity--a
'negative', dialectical mediation.[204]

Adorno is arguing against what he sees to be the
inherently reactionary, anti-theoretical bias of the dominant attempts to resist the absolute 'subjectivity' of
post-Hegelian idealism with an equally absolute turn to
the immediacy of 'objectivity'.

The confidence that from immediacy, from the
solid and downright primary, an unbroken
entirety will spring--this confidence is an
idealistic chimera. To dialectics, immediacy
does not maintain its immediate pose. Instead
of becoming the ground, it becomes a moment.[205]

If, contra idealism, otherness cannot be reduced to the
freedom and spontaneity of constitutive subjectivity, no
less, contra ontology, can thought correct this fault "by
humbly deferring to sheer existence," by abandoning the
"moment of freedom and spontaneity."[206] If "according
to its own concept, the subjective form of traditional
epistemology always exists only as a form of something

objective, never without objectivity," then the object "cannot be without a subject either," for "if the object lacked the moment of subjectivity, its own objectivity would become nonsensical."[207] Yet Adorno saw just such a re-enactment of the pre-Kantian struggle to overcome the 'rationalist' epistemological tactic by means of a pre-critical, typically 'empiricist' a-theoreticism occurring in philosophical approaches as apparently divergent as scientific 'objectivism',[208] positivism,[209] sociology of knowledge,[210] Husserl's phenomenology and Heidegger's fundamental ontology.

Adorno does not see this **'ontological** fallacy' as having occurred merely in reaction to idealism; rather he sees it as having been set on its modern course by the very Kantian 'dialectic of difference' which had figured so strongly in Adorno's argument against idealism. Thus despite his appreciative retrospective of the function of Kant's thing-in-itself in his immanent critique of idealism, Adorno maintained that the anti-theoretical posture of the ontologizing turn to the Other paradoxically had its roots in "the so-called 'Kantian-block', the theory of the bounds of possible positive cognition," which "derives from the form-content dualism" that structures the Critique of Pure Reason.[211] The crux of Adorno's argument is that

the authority of the Kantian concept of truth turned terroristic with the ban on thinking the absolute. Irresistibly, it drifts toward a ban on all thinking. What the Kantian block projects on truth is the self-maiming of reason, the mutilation reason inflicted upon itself as a rite of initiation into its own scientific character. Hence the scantiness of what happens in Kant as cognition, compared with the experience of the living, by which the idealistic systems wished to do right, even though in the wrong fashion.[212]

A negative **dialectics** must challenge this result of the Kantian position at the same time that it affirms Kant's having "disdained the passage to affirmation,"[213] by means of the retention of the function of the thing-in-itself. Kant "forestalled a mythology of the concept,"[214] because "his own position remained open, in a grandiose ambiguity."[215] But he risked absolutizing the openness itself, to the point of risking the absolutization of non-conceptuality.[216]

202

Thus a negative **dialectics** does not revoke the anti-idealist invocation of the consistent non-identity of the object, "the surplus over the subject."[217] It remains opposed to Hegel's contention that "the structure of reality was ultimately identical to rational subjectivity."[218] To the contrary, such resurgent concern with **being** is criticized for having 'succeeded' at this--but at the unacceptable price of **dialectic** itself. If mediation is not, as idealism had supposed, a logic of totality--a logic of **integration**--then neither can it simply be renounced. Rather mediation must be shown, through a sustained, dynamic method of criticism, to entail a dialectic of **disintegration** of totality for the sake of a preponderant and dynamic non-identity.[219] As Buck-Morss has written,

> ...Adorno considered the object simply not rational, although it was rationally understandable. But only a dialectical logic could grasp the inner contradictions of phenomena which reproduced in microcosm the dynamics of the contradictory social whole. ... Even as the subject 'entered into' the object, then, it was not swallowed up but maintained the distance necessary for critical activity.[220]

Mediation for Adorno is a dialectics-of-**otherness**, but a **dialectics** nonetheless. Such a dialectics is "neither a system nor a contradiction,"[221] but a **rational** deconstrual of the idealistic, subjectively perspectival world precisely by means of unlocking the power of the **nonconceptual** itself. "For there could no more be truth without a subject freeing itself from delusions than there could be truth without that which is not the subject, that in which truth has its archetype."[222]

However true it is that "subjectivity, thinking itself, is called explicable not by itself but by facts, especially by social facts," in the case of negative dialectics "the objectivity of cognition in turn is said not to exist without thinking, without subjectivity."[223] Philosophy must not merely exchange the mystifications of absolute subjectivity for those of anti-theoretical postures which bow once more to heteronomous social relations. In the cases of both Zen Buddhism and Heidegger's ontology, Adorno states unequivocally that

> doctrines which heedlessly run off from the subject to the universe, along with the philosophy of Being, are more easily brought into accord with the world's hardened condition and

with the chances of success in it than is the tiniest bit of self-reflection by a subject pondering upon itself and its real captivity.[224]

Thus Adorno's philosophy resists what he understands to be the paradoxical "perennial anti-intellectualism" of post-Enlightenment, bourgeois subjectivity which, fearing "that its consistent pursuit will explode those conditions" of society which allow its freedom, would rather limit itself than exercise its freedom in social criticism.[225] Negative dialectics resists such a sacrifice of "rationality and critique in objective harmony with a society which descends into the darkness of immediate lordship."[226] Rather, following the lead of Hegel, Adorno consistently argues for the revolutionary subjectivity in objectivity, not just the reverse.

In this way Adorno proposes a **non**-idealist ontology, just as Bonhoeffer had called for an ontology which was **genuine**, not **systematic**. Such an 'ontology' would be one in which what Marx had called philosophy's "ennui, the longing for a content,"[227] can not be denied, but, as importantly, cannot merely be affirmed. For as Adorno sharply quipped, "the ontological need can no more guarantee its object than the agony of the starving assures them of food."[228] Thus while "knowledge is not supposed to prepare the phantasm of a whole,"[229] as idealism had thought, it must not merely submit to the nonconceptual, but "strive, by way of the concept, to transcend the concept."[230] "The cognitive utopia," according to Negative Dialectics, "would be to use concepts to unseal the nonconceptual with concepts, without making it their equal"[231]--and without resigning from the challenge.

The immanent critique of the destiny of ontology is thus not an argument against the meaning of **being**, but an argument against any presumed **immediacy** of being which obviates the perpetual need for a genuinely **critical** theory, a theory whose concepts are precisely "the categories in which the particular is understood."[232] Adorno does not shy away from the apparent contradiction, that dialectics "as criticism of the system recalls what would be outside the system; and [that] the force that liberates the dialectical movement in cognition is the very same that rebels against the system."[233] Or as he put it in another context, "the dialectical concept is mediation, not something which exists in itself," however much "this imposes on the dialectical concept the duty of not pretending that there is any truth set apart from the mediated, from the facts." If dialectical critique cannot "reify

204

its concepts," then neither is "unreflected facticity" thinkable for dialectics.[234]

As the title of his book makes plain, "such dialectics," for Adorno, "is negative," refusing to join post-Hegelian idealism in the "coincidence of identity and positivity," the "inclusion of all nonidentical and objective things in a subjectivity expanded and exalted into an absolute spirit...."[235] And yet the limit on the ontological inferences to be drawn from idealist epistemology does not leave us mute before 'given' reality. A **negative** dialectic is of itself inescapably and profoundly conceptual. Negative dialectics can brook no "theoretical resignation before individuality."[236] Rather, it recognizes that

> thought as such, before all particular contents, is an act of negation, of resistance to that which is forced upon it; this is what thought has inherited from its archetype, the relation between labor and material. ... The effort implied in the concept of thought itself, as the counterpart of passive contemplation, is negative already--a revolt against being importuned to bow to every immediate thing.[237]

Philosophy "becomes mythology" not only through its metaphysical pretensions to unlock absolute rationality, but also "at the point where, believing in some ultimate datum"--whether 'objects', 'facts', 'existence', or 'being' --it cuts "reflection short."[238]

The particular is not 'true' by its very givenness, but "by virtue of its mediatedness."[239] According to Adorno, "thought forms tend beyond that which merely exists, is merely 'given',"[240] "the idol of a pure present."[241] Dialectics as **critical** theory obtains to the extent that reason, stripped of its idealistic metaphysical pretensions, can yet oppose, in Marcuse's words, "all ready acceptance of the given state of affairs," the status quo as immediacy.[242] For as Hegel had said, "quite generally, the familiar, just because it is familiar, is not cognitively understood."[243]

As Adorno himself put it, "every concept of dialectic would be null without the moment of subjective reflection," for "what is not reflected in itself does not know contradiction"[244]--the internal conflict to which Hegel had made philosophy aware in asking "that the state-of-affairs should 'demand' a movement of consciousness,"[245] the movement of the mediacy of

205

thought within the apparent immediacy of the given. In the case of negative dialectics, Adorno explains,

> while doing violence to the object of its syntheses, our thinking heeds a potential that waits in the object, and it unconsciously obeys the idea of making amends to the pieces for what it has done. In philosophy, this unconscious tendency becomes conscious.[246]

Otherwise, "what acts as the overcoming of idealism just drives the power of order in domineering thought into irrationality," by which "thought gives up its critical right over what is thought."[247]

Because dialectics for Adorno is **negative**, critical, such dialectics "will not allow itself to be robbed of the distinction between essence and appearance,"[248] the non-identity at the heart of what Bonhoeffer had referred to as the 'genuinely transcendental' epistemological paradigm. Because such negative-ontology is **dialectical**, conceptual, it still "must adhere to Hegel's statement that essence must appear."[249] Thus negative dialectics must locate itself within what Adorno describes as "the tense non-identity of essence and appearance."[250] For Adorno

> essence can no longer be hypostatized as the pure, spiritual being-in-itself. Rather, essence passes into that which lies concealed beneath the facade of immediacy, of the supposed facts, and which makes the facts what they are. ... This essence too must come to appear like Hegel's: swathed in its own contradiction. It can be recognized only by the contradiction between what things are and what they claim to be.[251]

This is the 'critical theoretical' role of the subject in negative dialectics: "...without abandoning it, we can think against our thought, and if it were possible to define dialectics, this would be a definition worth suggesting."[252]

Negative dialectics therefore confronts Nietzsche, who "had ridiculed the **difference** between essence and appearance."[253] To deny "that there is an essence," according to Adorno, "means to side with appearance, with the total ideology which existence has since become."[254] Adorno's dialectics, to the contrary, seeks to give voice to the fact that the essential which appears in the phenomenon is that whereby it became what it is, what was silenced in it and what, in painful stultification, releases that which yet becomes.[255]

He thus remains indebted to what he calls "the most enduring result of Hegelian logic," the methodological dictum that "the individual is not flatly for himself," but "in himself, he is his otherness and linked with others."[256] That is to say, the epistemologically-modeled encounter with otherness--and the social ontology it invites--is itself not unmediated, intuitive, and thus "dispensed from critique,"[257] but the result of a **dialectical mediation** by the subject, however **negative.** "Dialectics," Adorno wrote in Against Epistemology, "is the quest to see the new in the old instead of just the old in the new. As it mediates the new, so it also preserves the old as the mediated."[258]

Ontology is thus challenged to overcome its traditional conflict with dialectics, its claim that, as Nietzsche wrote, "what is does not become; whatever becomes is not,"[259] yet without thereby contributing to any attempt to heal "the concept 'Being' of the wound of its conceptuality, of the split between thoughts and their content."[260] A negative-dialectical social ontology maintains, rather, that "truth is the articulation of this relationship"[261] between being and becoming, between reality and thought, between particular and its concept--each, as Buck-Morss has said, "affirmed only in its **nonidentity** to the other."[262]

Husserl's phenomenology provides a case in point for Adorno of the limits of the attempt by traditional theory to deal with the challenge of nonidentity.[263] It is not the task of the present study to consider phenomenology at length, but to understand the light it sheds on Adorno's attempt to articulate a genuinely negative **dialectical** conception of the preponderance of objectivity, the sociality of the epistemological paradigm. This can be seen in what Buck-Morss has referred to as Husserl's attempt "to hold onto both reason and reality-- "to reach knowledge of the object ... without letting go of the traditional idealist concept of reason as universal and absolute."[264] As Adorno states the matter,

If there were alive in Husserl some authoritarian drives, the desire to vindicate for truth a superhuman objectivity which must merely be recognized, there was also the contrary alive in him, a very critical attitude with an almost exaggerated fear in committing himself to any truth which could not be regarded as eternal and absolutely certain.[265]

Thus, according to Adorno, for the sake of its own theoretical, critical voice in the face of the "concept of the non-deducible given (unableitbaren Gegebenheit), as developed by the positivist schools," phenomenology developed a method which, Negative Dialectics itself declares, "as a whole is a stand against irrationalism,"[266] against the self-mutilation of reason. "It is thus no accident," Adorno wrote, "that phenomenology in Husserl took precisely its starting point from transcendental idealism...."[267] Yet thereby phenomenology tends to risk reverting, according to Adorno, to that very idealism which it desires equally not to embrace.[268]

Thus in order to surmount its own intrinsic tendency towards idealism, Husserl's

> attack was directed not only against positivism and empiricism, but against idealism, and his effect was largely that of an anti-idealist philosopher. It became such an attack by the slogan "Zu den Sachen," "Back to the subject-matter itself," and the motive of his insistence upon notions such as intuition is in fact this anti-idealist desire of getting back to the materials themselves.[269]

In this sense Adorno could write that "Husserl's philosophy was precisely an attempt to destroy idealism from within, an attempt with the means of consciousness to break through the wall of transcendental analysis, while at the same time trying to carry such an analysis as far as possible."[270] Above all, Adorno argued, Husserl yearned "for a philosophy receptive to the objects, a philosophy that would substantialize itself."[271]

But Husserl, Adorno argues, had been able to succeed in this enterprise only to the extent that

> he has renounced the claim of the productive power of mind, the Kantian and Fichtean spontaneity, and resigns himself, as only Kant himself had done, to take possession of the sphere of that which is adequately within his reach.[272]

208

Yet this "self-resignation of Husserlian phenomenolo-gy,"[273] in which "the critique of criticism became pre-critical,"[274] drove it into its own form of the "the ne-cessary contradiction between a positivistic concept of givenness and an idealist concept driven to the extreme of a 'pure' being, free of all empirical admixture...."[275]

Phenomenology's tactic of "stopping with the im-mediately given object"[276] was thus correct in attempting thereby to circumvent the dangers of idealism; but phen-omenology failed in that the 'given' was not objective enough--in that, "freed from everything factual and con-tingent,"[277] it bracketed out precisely the empirical, particular other upon which non-identity depends, and spoke instead of "an 'other in principle'."[278]   And phen-omenology's critical methodology was correct in refusing to submit to the empirical, unreflected status quo; but phenomenology failed in that such subjectivity was not subjective enough--in that it proved unable finally to sustain the radical **social ontology** that the 'given' was intended to guarantee.   "For consciousness is only ab-solute as long as it ceases to tolerate any otherness which is not just proper to consciousness--and thus not otherness at all."[279]

Thus in saying that "phenomenology is something that, in the name of 'research', viz. the description of the state-of-affairs, it passionately disowned till the very end: epistemology," Adorno thus is not to be understood as ignoring the very attempts of phenomenology to sur-mount the aporias of epistemology.[280]   To the contrary, Adorno is arguing for the provocative retrieval of the significance of "phenomenology's **epistemological** inclina-tion to ascertain how knowledge of objecthood is in general possible and how it may be identified in the structure of consciousness."[281]   This is crucial for Ador-no, in order to show the way in which phenomenology attempts to place thought precisely in the lacuna be-tween itself and its other--to think the non-identity which cuts across not only the subject but the object, not only through thought, but through being as well.

That motivates dialectical logic, which raises such a contradiction to being a determination of the thing itself (die Sache selbst), and thus maintains as well as negates the concept of the immediate. This conclusion, however, is forbidden to Husserl by the absolutism of formal logic which he himself proclaims, viz. pure freedom from contradiction. As a compensation his theory models all mediated knowledge on immediacy.[282]

As Buck-Morss summarizes, "Husserl failed, but according to Adorno his failure was precisely his success, for it brought the dilemmas and inner antagonisms of idealist philosophy to their fullest articulation."[283]

If this is the case, then we are now in a position to understand what was at stake in Adorno's undisguised antipathy towards Heidegger.[284] **On the one hand,** Heidegger's fundamental ontology appears to join in Adorno's repudiation of the dialectic-of-identity of idealism. And Adorno does admit that "Heidegger's approach is true insofar as he ... denies traditional metaphysics...."[285] For Heidegger's ontological difference argues against the absorption of otherness, against the denial of the qualitatively other, against the mystifications of immediacy and pure presence, no less than does Adorno's negative dialectics. Heidegger himself might well have written the lines by Adorno, lamenting that

> ever since the fundament of knowledge came to be sought in supposedly immediate subjective data, men have been enthralled by the idol of a pure present. They would endeavor to strip thought of its historic dimension. The fictitious, one-dimensional Now became the cognitive ground of all inner meaning.[286]

Had not Heidegger himself, some four decades previously, argued precisely against the tradition of western metaphysics--for which "entities are grasped in their Being as 'presence'," meaning that "they are understood with regard to a definite mode of time--the **'Present'**"?[287]

But on the other hand, if Heidegger and Adorno seem mutually to support each other on the issues of difference versus presence, mediacy versus immediacy, there is yet a distinction to be made between them-- indeed a distinction which Adorno makes with a vengeance. Heidegger's turn to Being, according to Adorno, makes the difference, the non-identity, of the Other into an **absolute,** and in so doing breaks apart the non-identity of being **and thought.** For Adorno, Heidegger's approach "becomes untrue where--not unlike Hegel--he talks as if the contents we want to rescue were thus directly in our minds."[288] **Heidegger takes ontology out of its context in dialectics.**

210

Transcendence, both beyond thinking and beyond facts, is derived by this ontology from the undialectical expression and hypostasis of dialectical structures--as if these structures were simply to be named.[289]

He is, as Bonhoeffer had also argued, finally a **systematic ontologist** for whom the priority of the Object comes at the expense of the Subject--Being at the expense of thought. Heidegger, says Adorno, risks "regressing to sacred primordiality, behind the reflection of critical thought."[290]

Adorno was by no means unaware of the difficulties involved in the call to counter the 'ontologizing' tendency towards theoretical quietism by dialectically "uttering the unutterable,"[291] by waging a "criticism of the logic of non-contradiction [which] does not suspend the latter but reflects upon it."[292] Indeed, Adorno wrote, "we fail to do justice to the concept of Being," Adorno writes, "until we also grasp the genuine experience that effects its instauration: the philosophical urge to express the inexpressible."[293]

And yet, just as Adorno's immanent critique of **idealism** had to argue for a **negative** form of dialectical mediation which was adequate to "express the **inexpressible**"--versus the presumptive identities of even Hegel's tactical use of mediacy--Adorno's immanent critique of **ontology** argued for a **dialectical** mediation of that negative form which was adequate to "**express** the inexpressible," rather than submit to it. Ontology and dialectics, we may conclude, assist each other in the formulation of a social ontology precisely to the extent that they sustain their very non-identity from one another. But whereas **idealist dialectics** subverted this non-identity in its systematic overcoming of all Otherness, **systematic ontology** subverts non-identity by denying its dialectical context. Adorno would surmount them both by a 'dialectics of otherness', which names the 'mediatedness' of **both** Subject and Object, thought and being, each by and through and for the Other. An adequate social ontology, according to Negative Dialectics, must sustain not only the 'otherness' of dialectics, but also the 'dialectics' of otherness.

3. Negative Dialectics: Otherness and Marginality

In summary, we can say that Adorno's social ontology is premised upon **plurality as the task** of a critical theory. The **challenge of** negative dialectics is to retain both the **plurality** of particular others and to see such diversity as a dialectical **task**, never an immediate given. The **challenge to** negative dialectics is whether such diversity can persist without the marginalization of either thought or being, the one by the domination of the other. That is to say, can the Other of ontology resist the dialectical urge towards totality? And can dialectics provide and sustain the necessary conceptual context for the non-identity of the Other?

We have argued that the de-centering of the sub-jectively perspectival orientation of idealism, through the method of immanent critique, is at the heart of Adorno's Negative Dialectics. And yet the problematic legacy of epistemology, as Adorno summarized, was that

> only the critique of abstract sensation as well as the abstract 'ego cogito' and being in gen-eral makes room for a movement of the con-cept which is as little prejudiced by the thesis of the identity of subject and object as by that of their rigid dualism. But it does not follow that one would automatically break out of idealism as the simple conclusion of cri-tique. Neither can the immediate moment of sensation be isolated from mediation, nor as in the post-Kantian Idealists, can mediation be isolated from the moment of immediacy. Sen-sation is not to be sublimated (verfluechtigen) in 'spirit'. That would be spiritualism and ideology. It should rather be checked by the constraint that if mediation and immediacy are split off from one another, one moment or the other would be absolutized.[294]

Therefore, Adorno contends,

> it is not the purpose of critical thought to place the object on the orphaned throne once occupied by the subject. On that throne the object would be nothing but an idol. The purpose of critical thought is to abolish the hierarchy.[295]

Negative dialectics does not propose to establish a new ground--an 'objective' one--in place of the prior subjec-tive foundations of idealism. For wherever any "doctrine of some absolute 'first' is taught," Adorno is adamant, it is clear that "there will be talk of something inferior to it, of something absolutely heterogeneous to it, as its

212

logical correlate. _Prima philosophia_ and dualism go together."[296] Adorno is not arguing for such a hierarchical dualism, but for a dynamic, non-hierarchical duality--the nonidentity of subject and object, each dynamically mediated by the other. For "if we cancel the subject's claim to be first," Adorno maintains, then "that which the schema of traditional philosophy calls secondary is no longer secondary either."[297]

And yet, Adorno reflects at another point in Negative Dialectics,

> this much should be granted to Hegel: not only particularity but the particular itself is unthinkable without the moment of the universal which differentiates the particular, puts its imprint on it, and in a sense is needed to make a particular of it. ... Of a particular, nothing can be predicated without definition and thus without universality, and yet this does not submerge the moment of something particular, something opaque, which that [predication] refers to and is based upon.[298]

Negative dialectics is just this double moment of reflection that both **differentiates** the opaqueness of the particular from the transparency of reason, and **defends** that opaque particular from then being totally defined by its rational moment. **Idealist dialectics** hypostatizes mediation, the universality of the concept, and thus risks losing the particular; ontology preserves "the moments of immediacy,"[299] but thereby risks removing the particular from the very dialectical context which sustains its particularity. **Negative** dialectics--understood as a 'genuine ontology'--maintains the particular, but only within the context of dialectics. As negative **dialectics**--understood as a 'genuine transcendental philosophy'--it constructs a conceptual context of non-identity, but precisely for the sake of the appearing Other.

Taken seriously, the double-mediatedness of subject and object means that philosophy cannot be reduced to a **general principle** of negative dialectics: conceptuality and particularity reciprocally defined by non-identical mediacy. Otherwise,

> the separation is no sooner established directly, without mediation, than it becomes ideology, ... The mind will then usurp the place of something absolutely independent--what it is not; its claim of independence heralds the

claim of dominance. Once radically parted
from the object, the subject reduces it to its
own measure; the subject swallows the object,
forgetting how much it is an object itself.[300]

Rather negative dialectics is **theory** in a radically **critical**
mode--**as** practice, **as** intervention on behalf of determinate concepts and concrete particulars. In maintaining
negative dialectics' "immanently critical and theoretical"
manner of enacting "the turn to nonidentity,"[301] Adorno
clearly intends to argue that "the recovery of theory's
independence lies in the interest of practice itself."[302]
Indeed a **critical** theory would demonstrate the extent to
which not only "practice itself was an eminently theoretical concept,"[303] but more importantly that theory itself
is pre-eminently practical. As Gillian Rose has explained,

> as long as philosophy or theory raises claims
> apart from any praxis it is bound to be self-
> contradictory; while if philosophy or theory
> understands itself **as** a form of praxis or in-
> tervention, its aims are then partly indirect,
> and the presentation of them as philosophy or
> theory will give rise to contradictory features.
> Adorno subscribed to both of these positions
> and this contributes to the complexity of his
> criticism of philosophy.[304]

Mediation, according to Adorno's immanent critique,
occurs when concepts are made determinate by their
employment for the sake of the nonconceptual particular.
Particulars become concrete when they are brought into
an intelligible context which provides for the concept of
their heterogeneity. In Matthew Lamb's words, such
theory

> does not move away from the concrete, only
> to be returned to it in the form of some sort
> of practical application. Instead, theory is
> continually moving toward the complexity of
> the concrete and, in the measure that it is
> correct in indicating the underlying concrete
> and contradictory tensions in reality, is cap-
> able of guiding the transformation of real-
> ity.[305]

With such an emphasis on **non**-identity, on philosophy's resistance to idealist totality, it comes as something of a surprise that there is a distinct **utopian** vision
to Adorno's project. His statement from <u>Minima Moralia</u>
at first reading sounds untypically 'affirmative':   "The

214

only philosophy which can be responsibly practiced in the face of despair is the attempt to view all things as they would present themselves from the standpoint of redemption."[306] As he explains,

> to define identity as the correspondence of the thing-in-itself to its concept is <u>hubris</u>; but the ideal of identity must not simply be discarded. Living in the rebuke that the thing is not identical with the concept is the concept's longing to become identical with the thing. This is how the sense of nonidentity contains identity. ... **Utopia would be above identity and above contradiction; it would be a togetherness of diversity.**[307]

Beyond the hierarchies which demean, Adorno muses, "the reconciled condition would not be the philosophical imperialism of annexing the alien. Instead, its happiness would lie in the fact that the alien, in the proximity it is granted, remains what is distant and different...."[308] Thus as Rose has written, "'utopia' is another way of naming the thesis that non-dialectical thought is closed thought, because it implies that the object is already captured. To see that the object is **not** captured is to see 'utopia'."[309] Reconciliation is a matter of **diversity**, not **totality**, yet also a matter of **togetherness**, not **dualism**. In the "state of reconciliation,"[310] negative dialectics negates identity by the demonstration that the **difference** to which epistemology's subject-object tension referred is perpetual non-identity, enduring heterogeneity, and that the proper context for maintaining the non-identity of Otherness, without marginalization, is the negative-dialectical practice of conceptual mediation. 'Reconcilement' names a dynamic conception of 'peace': "distinctness without domination, with the distinct participating in each other."[311] If "in the unreconciled condition, nonidentity is experienced as negativity,"[312] reconcilement names the state in which nonidentity is a **positive** phenomenon.

Dialectical reconciliation is neither "what tolerates nothing that is not like itself,"[313] nor is it the mere **resignation** of subject and object to the false security of an illusory 'relationship' of static presence to each other--even by means of "the theological conception of the paradox."[314] To make his point on this matter, Adorno, as had Bonhoeffer, turns back to the tradition of "the Greek argument whether like is known by like or by unlike."[315] If "Parmenides had already taught that what is perceived and what perceives resemble each

215

other, while Heraclitus pleaded that only the unlike and contrasted can recognize the like,"[316] Adorno follows Heraclitus, not the Eleatics. Negative-dialectical reconciliation resists the idealist epistemologist's quasi-Platonic "circle of identification ... drawn by a thinking that tolerates nothing outside it ... that equalizes everything unequal"[317]--its "false conclusion that the object is the subject," that reason knows the unlike by likening it to itself, while in so doing it really knows itself only."[318] Negative Dialectics proposes the obverse, "the idea of a changed philosophy," which would "become aware of likeness by defining it as that which is unlike itself."[319]

Adorno thus uses the term **reconcilement** in as ironic a sense as he uses the term **dialectics,** or **mediation.** Reconcilement is thus not the terminus ad quem of a positive dialectics according to which the 'many' are merely the occasions for the mediation of the 'One'. Thus the significant dividing line, according to Adorno, between his own position and that of Hegel's is finally

> drawn by our intent: whether in our consciousness, theoretically and in the resulting practice, we maintain that identity is the ultimate, that it is absolute, that we want to reinforce it--or whether we feel that identity is the universal coercive mechanism which we, too, finally need to free ourselves from ....[320]

In a philosophy with the latter intent, according to Adorno,

> reconcilement would release the nonidentical, would rid it of coercion, including spiritualized coercion; it would open the road to the multiplicity of different things and strip dialectics of its power over them. Reconcilement would be the thought of the many as no longer inimical, a thought that is anathema to subjective reason.[321]

It is in this sense that Adorno can say that "dialectics serves the end of reconcilement."[322] It does so not by conjuring "the supposedly pure object lacking any admixture of thought."[323] Rather, negative dialectics reconciles subject and object--thought and being--to what they are **precisely as** 'non identical without being marginal to each other'. Negative dialectics breaks the spell of the Enlightenment's conflation of "criticism and power."[324]

C. Ethics and Otherness: the Morality of Thinking

With the themes of **marginality** and **coercion** we encounter a profoundly **ethical** concern intrinsic to Adorno's turn to the preponderance of the Other, no less than was the case with Bonhoeffer.[325] As Rose has likewise argued, for Adorno the issues of "'morality', 'values' and 'norms' do not imply a moral dimension distinct from other dimensions but characterize the construction and imposition of 'reality'."[326] This final section of the present chapter will argue two theses: (1) that Adorno's invectives against identity-philosophy need to be understood as an explication of his ongoing 'moral conversion' towards the predominance of the ethical implications of the category of totality; and (2) that the subject-object theoretical duality remained the paradigm for Adorno's project in large measure because it encouraged a crucial distinction between the social-ontological problem of **diversity**--the destiny of Otherness vis a vis Identity--and the ethical problematic of **domination**--the obliteration of the non-identity of the Other.[327]

1. Coercion and the Ethical Implications of Totality

Adorno increasingly recognized that to interpret totality as "not an affirmative but rather a critical category"[328] also implied a profoundly **ethical** posture towards Otherness.

> Great philosophy was accompanied by a paranoid zeal to tolerate nothing else, and to pursue everything else with all the cunning of reason, while the other kept retreating farther and farther from the pursuit. The slightest remnant of nonidentity sufficed to deny an identity conceived as total.[329]

Thus Adorno argues that "before all social control, before all adjustment to conditions of dominion, the mere form of thoughts, the form of logical stringency, can be convicted of unfreedom"[330]--the exigency towards totality is itself coercive. As we have seen to be the case with idealism, when the other--the individual, the particular--strains the principle of identity of the rational totality, it "will not appear as something different from and indifferent to the principle, but as a violation of logic,"[331] thus non-rational, un-real. In traditional epistemological theory where the rational is the real, according to Adorno, "there is coercion both of what is being

217

thought and of the thinker"--"whatever does not fit a judgment will be choked off,"[332] both in its rationality and its being.

Negative dialectics' emphasis on the 'remnants of non-identity' resists the coercive integration of the unlike into the like, "the archaic barbarism that the longing subject cannot love what is alien and different."[333] But it does not restrict the application of its subversive tactics to the domain of **theoretical** totality. Critical theory must be itself a form of **practice,** an **intervention** into the forms of 'social control' and the 'conditions of dominion' that find their rationale and justification in the totalizing power of reason. Adorno's work thus dares ask whether or not it is true that "deep down the mind feels that its stable dominance is no mental rule at all, that its ultima ratio lies in the physical force at its disposal."[334] His thesis is that, in Matthew Lamb's words, "the horrors of claiming the identity of reason and reality are not some speculative nonsense of concern only to academics...."[335] The sameness, the unity, the rational integration of unlike into like, cannot be separated from its social basis, from the fact that, as Adorno put it,

> genocide is the absolute integration. It is on its way wherever men are leveled off--"polished off," as the German military called it--until one exterminates them literally, as deviations from the concept of their total nullity. Auschwitz confirmed the philosopheme of pure identity as death. Negative dialectics intervenes in the process of totality for the sake of the non-identical particular.[336]

The coercive power of the subject in accomplishing totality, Adorno argues, is a factor of that very tutelage, freedom from which would seem to define the activity of the Enlightenment's very focus on the subject.[337] This leads negative dialectics back again into irony.

> That there must be freedom is the supreme iniuria committed by the lawmaking autonomous subject. The substance of its own freedom--of the identity which has annexed all nonidentity--is as one with the 'must', with the law, with absolute dominion.[338]

The power of thought "exerts that power which philosophy reflected in the concept of necessity."[339]

Negative dialectics must therefore employ the freedom of thought against the freedom of thought. Negative dialectics must free the necessity of thought from its self-coercion. For "the antithesis of freedom and thought is no more removable by thinking that it is removable for thinking; it calls, rather, for self-reflection in thinking."[340] Negative dialectics thinks that "irrationality [which] is the scar which the irremovable nonidentity of subject and object leaves on cognition--whose mere form of predicative judgment postulates identity...."[341] In unlocking the nonconceptual with concepts, negative dialectics finds its "hope of withstanding the omnipotence of the subjective concept,"[342] the hope of exposing and breaking open "the identity of domination and reason."[343]

Thus non-identity thinking challenges the ethics of totality. If for Hegel's philosophy of identity, "order is good a priori," and "does not have to answer to those living under it,"[344] negative dialectics thinks precisely for the sake of "the breaks that belie identity," for the sake of "the everbroken pledges of that otherness" which 'is' as non-identical.[345] Negative Dialectics, as Martin Jay has noted, thus "probed the 'force field', to use an expression of Adorno's, between consciousness and being, subject and object,"[346] as a tactical resistance to the ethics of totality. Non-identity was a decidedly **moral** category, for it hoped that, in Jay's words, "in the spaces created by the irreducible mediations between subject and object ... human freedom might be sustained"[347]--despite its own coercive potential.[348]

2. Diversity and Domination: The Morality of Thinking

Adorno consistently argued that the social-ontological problem of **diversity**--the destiny of Otherness vis a vis Identity--had profound ethical implications. Resistance to the coercive **domination** of the free subject--and to the obliteration of the non-identity of the Other--required philosophy's attention to what Minima Moralia called "the morality of thinking."[349] In the case of the Other, non-identity is the condition of the possibility of its very existence, of its 'being' at all. Non-identity contradicts the claim of totality; it convicts the system of being "the belly turned mind," and resists the "rage [which] is the mark of each and every idealism."[350] Negative dialectics can be described as a call to 'hearken' to the Other, to be obedient to its otherness. It thus bears strong parallels, as had the work of Bonhoeffer, to Eberhard Grisebach, who, as Dallmayr has noted,

219

in contrast to traditional metaphysics and the legacy of subjectivity, ... advocated a radical reversal aiming at the replacement of constitutive human intervention by an attitude of patient **listening** and attentiveness (<u>Hoerigkeit</u>)--notions which do not seem alien to Heidegger's perspective.[351]

Non-identity thinking is beyond coercion; it resists the domination by the subject for the sake of the diversity of objects.[352] It strongly implies a form of ethics of respect, or what Paul Ricoeur has called in another context "an ethics of the desire to be or the effort to exist."[353]

But despite the resonances of Buber in the notion of 'respect', Adorno's position differs on the issue of mediation.[354] For the claim of the Other to 'be' is not the claim of an immediately-encountered Other, but an Other mediated through the very subjectivity with which it is non-identical. Yet such mediation is not Hegel's tactic "mediately to affirm immediacy"[355] through a fraudulent and illusory otherness which is for the sake of totality. As Dallmayr explains,

> to counteract the defects of traditional rationality, <u>Negative Dialectics</u> suggests a type of reflection which, without abandoning the integrity of thought, opens itself to the domain of non-thought, relinquishing the ambition of control. ... This kind of thought would be characterized by an attitude of letting-be or a respect for non-identity.[356]

Negative dialectics obeys the morality of that thinking that is for the sake of non-identity, which resists the ideology of identity.[357] Indeed, Adorno wrote, "whether or not one can talk of ideology depends directly upon when one can distinguish between illusion and essence...."[358]

Immediacy is thus shown to have disastrous **moral** consequences for the subject which "desperately deceives itself about itself as mediation."[359] As Adorno described it,

> A tendency to regression, a hatred of the complicated, is steadily at work in theory of origins, thus guaranteeing its affinity with lordship. ... The enemy, the other, the non-

identical is always also what is distinguished
and differentiated from the subject's universality.[360]

In thinking the non-identical, Negative Dialectics affirms
that "the falsehood of an unleashed rationality running
away from itself, the recoil of enlightenment into mythology, is rationally definable."[361] For "to think means to
think something ... that which is not identical with
thinking. ... The ratio becomes irrational where it forgets
this...."[362] If this irrationality is left unthought, or if it
is itself 'rationalized', the moral consequence for the
Other is obliteration.

Negative dialectics must articulate the moral consequences of the fact that

the human mind is both true and a mirage: it
is true because nothing is exempt from the
dominance which it has brought into pure
form; it is untrue because, interlocked with
dominance, it is anything but the mind it
believes and claims to be. ... The subject is
the late form of the myth, and yet the equal
of its oldest form.[363]

This had been the subject of Adorno's Dialectic of Enlightenment, the turn of Enlightenment freedom into the
domination by thought.

The retreat from enlightenment into mythology
... [is] not to be sought so much in the nationalist, pagan and other modern mythologies
manufactured precisely in order to contrive
such a reversal, but in the Enlightenment
itself....[364]

The ethics of a negative dialectics would employ the
enlightenment ideals of freedom and autonomy against,
"abstraction, the tool of enlightenment" idealism, which
"treats its objects as did fate, the notion which it rejects: it liquidates them."[365] As Negative Dialectics re-
called this previous discussion, the Enlightenment concern
with freedom "goes against the old oppression and pro-
motes the new one, the one that hides in the principle
of rationality itself."[366] Thus, according to the later
Adorno, "if negative dialectics calls for the self-reflection of thinking, the tangible implication is that if
thinking is to be true--if it is to be true today, in any
case--it must be a thinking against itself."[367] It must
critique the outcome of the Enlightenment "**for the sake**

of the Enlightenment and the rationality which it promised."368

The **morality** of thinking must remain, nonetheless,
thinking. The loss of **critical theoretical** thought was
the point of Adorno's ongoing argument both against
positivism and ontology. In the case of the former, "the
interaction of subject and object is spirited away, a
priori, while spontaneity is excluded by the very method."369 In the case of the latter, Heidegger "pursues
dialectics to the point of saying that neither the subject
nor the object are immediate and ultimate; but he deserts
dialectics in reaching for something immediate and primary beyond subject and object."370

The result is that "fundamental ontology remains,
like phenomenology, an involuntary heir to positivism."371
Adorno's reaction against Heidegger can thus be credited
to a fundamentally **moral** argument against what he saw
as Heidegger's tendency towards 'irrationalism'.

> ...The direct insight stipulated by Heidegger as
> the sole title to a philosophy worth of Being
> will not succeed ..., unless by the spontaneity
> of thought which Heidegger disdains. ... That
> the philosophy of Being turns the ... exemption
> from the rational process into a transcendence
> of the reflecting intellect--this is an act of
> violence as desperate as it is prudent.372

Much of the vituperative quality of Adorno's response to
Heidegger may be understood as an expression of Adorno's sense of the latter's complicity, at least to the
extent that ontology had proved to be detached from the
politics of the National Socialist era, in the social enactment of this violence.

Thus in spite of the strong 'ontological' element of
Adorno's own Negative Dialectics, he felt compelled to
resist any implication that "Being, which the mind trans-
mits," can be "ceded to receptive vision," to the immediacy of intuition. For in so doing, "philosophy converges
with a flatly irrationalist view of life."373 In the case
of Heidegger, Jaspers and Buber, Adorno argued, "philosophy becomes mythology at the point where, believing in
some ultimate datum, they cut reflection short."374 In
what he derogatorily called their Jargon of Authenticity,
Adorno saw "subterranean links between existentialist
irrationalism and the cultural crisis that helped prepare
the way for fascism" in the 1930's, in that "it offered a
pseudo-immediacy that ultimately served to perpetuate

222

the social domination of the subject."[375]   "Today as in Kant's time," according to Adorno, "philosophy demands a rational critique of reason, not its banishment or abolition."[376]

Adorno's <u>Negative Dialectics</u> refused, however, to aver to "the primacy called for in the doctrines of Kant and Fichte, that of practical reason over theory," which according to Adorno, is a primacy "actually of reason over reason...."[377] For despite the fact that

> moral conduct is evidently more concrete than a merely theoretical one; yet it becomes more formal than theoretical conduct in consequence of the doctrine that practical reason is independent of anything 'alien' to it, of any object.[378]

Adorno thus argues against what he calls "the specious character of such concreteness--the complete abstraction of subsuming human beings under arbitrary concepts and treating them accordingly...."[379] Rather "true practice, the totality of acts that would satisfy the idea of freedom does indeed require full theoretical consciousness,"[380] whereas "from the primacy of practical reason it was always only a step to hatred of theory."[381]

And yet, clearly "practice also needs something else, something physical which consciousness does not exhaust, something conveyed to reason and qualitatively different from it."[382]   Although Heidegger's argument against presence indeed did seek "to hold on to that which points beyond itself," the ontological difference between Being and entities, he could do so only if he was willing "to leave behind, as rubble, that beyond which it points,"[383] the material entity itself.   Therefore, Adorno argues, Heidegger's anti-theoretical, ontological "immediacy does call a halt to the idolatry of derivation, ..."[384]   But

> it is also something abstracted from the object, a raw material for the subjective process of production that served as a model for epistemology.   What is given in poor and blind form is not objectivity; it is merely the borderline value which the subject, having confiscated the concrete object, cannot fully master in its own domain.[385]

Ironically, by means of the ontological **difference**,

> the **dialectics** of Being and entity--that no
> Being can be conceived without an entity, and
> no entity without transmission--is suppressed
> by Heidegger. ... Though driven out with a
> pitchfork, entity returns: a Being purged of
> entity is a primal phenomenon only so long as
> the excluded entity lies nonetheless within it.
> ... The term 'ontological difference' permits his
> philosophy to lay hands even on the insoluble
> moment of entity.[386]

In making the ontological difference **immediate,** Heidegger
lost both the critical-theoretical subject and the particular object--the one by the other.[387]

Thus his engagement with the tradition of dialectical **materialism**, specifically the Marxian argument a-
gainst the abstractness of exchange value, has for Adorno a decidedly **ethical** function for philosophy--that of
dialectically sustaining the value of the **material,** 'ontical'
Other, its right to 'be' as non-identical, and chronicling
the failure of the history of society to allow it that
right.

> It is when things in Being are read as a text
> of their becoming that idealistic and material-
> istic dialectics touch. But while idealism sees
> in the inner history of immediacy its vindica-
> tion as a stage of the concept, materialism
> makes that inner history the measure, not just
> of the untruth of the **concepts,** but even more
> of the **immediacy in being.**[388]

If "it is by passing to the object's preponderance," and
the moral challenge of maintaining it, "that dialectics is
rendered materialistic,"[389] then that materialism is itself
defined by its response to "the need to lend a voice to
suffering," the suffering of that subjugated "objectivity
that weighs upon the subject," challenging the subject's
domination.[390] Thus, Adorno concludes,

> the course of history forces materialism upon
> metaphysics, traditionally the direct antithesis
> of materialism. What the mind once boasted
> of defining or construing as its like moves in
> the direction of what is unlike the mind, in
> the direction of that which eludes the rule of
> the mind and yet manifests that rule as ab-
> solute evil.[391]

The ethical function of materialism is to sustain the diversity of the particulars, in the face of the pain and suffering of the object under the heel of a dominating subjectivity.[392] Dialectical materialism for Adorno is a demystification of the fact that

> whoever treats objectivity or 'thing'-quality as radically evil and aims to dissolve reality as a whole in pure praxis or self-production, tends to be animated by hostility to the Other or stranger, ... by hostility to that domain of non-identity which would provide freedom not only for 'consciousness' but for a reconciled humanity.[393]

Thus for Adorno, "pain and ... negativity" are "the moving forces of dialectical thinking," for even "the smallest trace of senseless suffering in the empirical world belies all the identitarian philosophy that would talk us out of that suffering."[394] Or as Held has summarized, "if history has any unity, it is that given by suffering."[395] It is the task of **dialectics** not to remystify, but to **give voice to that suffering.**

3. The Melancholy Science: Constructing Constellations

Adorno's negative dialectics is what he called in Minima Moralia a "melancholy science,"[396] written for a "time not for first philosophy but last philosophy."[397] Even its utopian vision appears beneath the pall of a latent apocalypticism, **both** denying totality as a metaphysical theodicy and ironically affirming "the idea of a world that would not only abolish extant suffering but revoke the suffering that is irrevocably past."[398] Thus it must remain forever a fragmentary thinking, intent on the morality of style, a "regard for the object, rather than for communication."[399] Nevertheless, "to be incomplete and at the same time conscious of the fact remains a feature ... particularly of the kind of thought worth dying with."[400] "The task to be accomplished," Adorno wrote in Dialectic of Enlightenment, "is not the conservation of the past, but the redemption of the hopes of the past."[401]

Thus Adorno's is no statement of resignation.

> The current objection ... that a happy spirit is impermissible amidst the growing misery of the exploding populations of poor countries, after

225

the catastrophes that have occurred and in view of those that are impending--this objection has more against it than that it mostly makes a virtue of impotence. ... True, we can really enjoy the spirit any more, because a happiness bound to see through its own nonentity ... would be no happiness. ... But when a man can do nothing that will not threaten to turn out for the worst even if meant for the best, he will be bound to start thinking--and that justifies him as well as the happy spirit. ... Paradoxically, it is the desperate fact that the practice that would matter is barred which grants to thought a breathing spell it would be practically criminal not to utilize.[402]

Thus the melancholia of philosophy is by no means a call for "faith in nothingness;" such nihilism "would be the palliative of a mind proudly content to see through the whole swindle."[403] Negative dialectics must **think** the non-identical through "conceptions, in the particular, of the totality that is inconceivable as such."[404] For all this "grayness could not fill us with despair," Adorno wrote, "if our minds did not harbor the concept of different colors, scattered traces of which are not absent from the negative whole. The traces always come from the past, and our hopes come from their counterpart, from that which was or is doomed...."[405]

Non-identity thinking must, as Martin Jay has commented, "continue thinking what [is] becoming more unthinkable in the modern world."[406] It must speak the "tentative, experimenting word,"[407] **both** foregoing the hubris of denying non-identity in the midst of a finite existence in which subject and object, thought and being, are so painfully separate, **and** affirming the destiny of the particular, its 'material' element, which would sustain its non-identity--even in a reconciled state.[408]

If Adorno's method is un-systematic, indeed anti-systematic, it is not for that matter random. It is, to the contrary, a **constructive** enterprise--but only if we remember that Negative Dialectics is the art of constructing non-identities. "As a corrective to the total rule of method, philosophy contains a playful element which the traditional view of it as a science would like to exorcise."[409] For "the systematic trend lives on in negation alone,"[410] in "the constellation of subject and object in which both penetrate each other" precisely as non-identical and Other.[411]

Despite this playful quality of this method of constructing constellations, it is rigorous precisely in its conceptual attentiveness to the preponderance of the object. Indeed

> cognition of the object in its constellation is cognition of the process stored in the object. As a constellation, theoretical thought circles the concept it would like to unseal, hoping that it may fly open like the lock of a well-guarded safe-deposit box: in response, not to a single key or a single number, but to a combination of numbers.[412]

In constructing a constellation, "by gathering around the object of cognition, the concepts potentially determine the object's interior. They attain, in thinking, what was necessarily excised from thinking."[413]

Thus theoretical thinking comes to serve the object, rending "the veil it is [itself] weaving around the object," becoming "the object's agent, not its constituent."[414] It becomes the 'genuine ontology' for which Bonhoeffer had called, precisely as its constellations reveal the extent to which the object "is objective as sedimented history," which

> is in the individual thing and outside it; it is something encompassing in which the individual has its place. Becoming aware of the constellation in which a things stands is tantamount to deciphering the constellation which, having come to be, it bears within it.[415]

The 'negativity' of the object, its non-identity, its non-conceptuality, finds its context through the contextualization of the process of a negative **dialectics.** A negative dialectics would thus not only deny the totalizing claims of Vernunft, but also it would resist the instrumentalization of rationality into a reductionist Verstand.

Adorno's Negative Dialectics is confirmation writ large of his friend Horkheimer's contention that

> idealist philosophy or metaphysics cannot be 'shaken to its foundation' by mere theoretical rejection. Nor can it be negated simply by 'turning one's back on philosophy and with head averted, mumbling a few angry and banal phrases about it'.[416]

227

As Adorno wrote, "even after breaking with idealism, philosophy cannot do without speculation,"[417] any more than after breaking with Heidegger it can do without any ontology. The future of a genuinely **critical** "metaphysics depends upon whether we can get out of this aporia otherwise than by stealth."[418] For "to negate a negation does not bring about its reversal; it proves, rather, that the negation was not negative enough."[419] To this extent we can agree with Held's summary observation that "Adorno's final position draws closer to aspects of the spirit of Kantian philosophy than to the spirit of many other philosophical positions."[420] A genuinely **negative** dialectics--Bonhoeffer's 'genuine transcendental philosophy'--must turn "even against itself," refusing to "come to rest in itself, as if it were total. This is its form of hope."[421] As a form of **theory** it makes no pretense to "transfigure the **existence** of its elements," but only by means of constructing constellations to "bring them into a configuration in which the elements unite to form a script,"[422] in which "represented in the inmost cell of thought is that which is unlike thought."[423] And yet it proposes to think those "thoughts [that] have to be answered for as though they were deeds."[424] Thinking cannot step outside the transcendental philosophical tradition, because it cannot step outside non-identity; yet to think **for the sake of the Other** requires all the subtlety--and all the risk--that is offered by dialectics. Adorno wagered that such was the task of a <u>Negative Dialectics</u>.

NOTES

[1] Adorno, "The Actuality of Philosophy," p. 120.

[2] Adorno, Against Epistemology, p. 39; see Jay, "The Concept of Totality in Lukacs and Adorno," Telos 32 (Summer 1977), pp. 131-134. Given the frequent use of the word 'totality' in this chapter, a brief note of explanation as to its employment may be in order. Martin Jay has pointed out five ways in which totality is used in Adorno's work: (1) 'longitudinal totality': universal **history** as theodicy; (2) 'latitudinal totality': bourgeois **society** as one-dimensional; (3) 'expressive totality': **epistemology** as a rage against reducible otherness; (4) 'decentered totality': **praxis** as an external adjunct to theory (5) 'normative totality': future **reconciliation** as an affirmative category. Given these distinctions, it is clear that our concern is chiefly with the third, and its relation to the fourth and fifth. This is not to deny the importance of **history** or **society** for Adorno's project; rather it simply represents the limits of the scope of the present project.

[3] Adorno, Negative Dialectics, p. xx.

[4] Ibid., p. xix; see Buck-Morss, The Origin of Negative Dialectics, p. 233, n. 2, which pointed out that as late as Adorno's 1963 foreword to his Drei Studien zu Hegel [(Frankfurt am Main: Suhrkamp, 1969), p. 8], Adorno had referred only generally to his efforts to formulate "an altered concept of the dialectic." This was not directly stated until the Negative Dialectics.

[5] Adorno, Negative Dialectics, p. 406.

[6] Ibid., p. 175.

[7] Ibid., p. 5.

[8] Hegel, Works, vol. 5, p. 16; quoted in Adorno, Negative Dialectics, p. 174-175.

[9] Adorno, Against Epistemology, p. 25. See Raymond Geuss, The Idea of a Critical Theory. Habermas and the Frankfurt School (Cambridge: Cambridge University Press, 1981), pp. 88-95 on epistemology.

[10] Adorno, Negative Dialectics, p. 406. Cf. Gerard Granel, "The Obliteration of the Subject in Contemporary Philosophy," in Humanism and Christianity, Concilium 86

(New York: Herder and Herder, 1973), pp. 64-72, and Charles Winquist, "The Subversion and Transcendence of the Subject," in <u>JAAR</u> 68/1 (March 1980):45-60.

[11]Adorno, <u>Negative Dialectics</u>, p. 406.

[12]Ibid., p. 12.

[13]In an important sense, it is the post-Hegelian 'Hegel' against whom Adorno inveighs throughout <u>Negative Dialectics</u>, not Hegel's work <u>per se</u>.

[14]Buck-Morss, <u>The Origin of Negative Dialectics</u>, p. 63.

[15]T.W. Adorno, <u>Stichworte. Kritische Modelle, 2</u> pp. 39-40; translated by Joan Lockwood and Herbert W. Richardson in <u>Religion and Political Society</u>, ed. J. Moltmann, et al. (New York: Harper and Row, 1974), p. 138.

[16]Adorno, <u>Negative Dialectics</u>, p. 40.

[17]Ibid., p. 140.

[18]Buck-Morss, <u>Origin of Negative Dialectics</u>, p. 63; according to Buck-Morss, p. 233, n. 1, it was actually Horkheimer who first articulated the case against the idealist premise that the real is rational and the rational, real; she notes his <u>Anfaenge der buergerlichen Geschichtsphilosophie</u> (Stuttgart: Hohlhammer, 1930), pp. 185-197. Cf. Adorno, <u>Negative Dialectics</u>, p. 26: "Kant had already held that the emancipated <u>ratio</u>, the <u>progressus ad infinitum</u>, is halted solely by recognizing nonidentities in form, at least."

[19]"Subject and Object," p. 499.

[20]Ibid.

[21]Adorno, <u>Negative Dialectics</u>, p. 170.

[22]"Subject and Object," p. 499.

[23]Adorno, <u>Negative Dialectics</u>, p. 13.

[24]Adorno, <u>Against Epistemology</u>, p. 27.

[25]Ibid.

[26]Adorno, <u>Negative Dialectics</u>, p. 171.

[27]Adorno, Against Epistemology, p. 27.

[28]Adorno, Negative Dialectics, p. 61.

[29]Ibid.

[30]Ibid.

[31]Adorno, "The Actuality of Philosophy," p. 121.

[32]Ibid., p. 122.

[33]Ibid., p. 124.

[34]Ibid., p. 123.

[35]Hegel's Science of Logic, trans. A.V. Miller (New York: Humanities Press, 1969), p. 581; quoted in Against Epistemology, p. 5.

[36]Adorno, Negative Dialectics, p. 61.

[37]Ibid., p. 97.

[38]Ibid., p. xx. See Rose, The Melancholy Science, p. 54: "The 'ontological need' thus amounts to the desire by philosophers of a specific period to break out of traditional philosophy, especially its neo-Kantian revival, but this outbreak did not involve a reinvigorated Hegelian attack on neo-Kantian philosophy nor a Marxian one. It did involve an attack on philosophical subjectivism and on philosophical and psychological relativism, and it did aim to found an objective reality. All these aims were paramount to Adorno. The 'outbreak' resulted, however, in the founding of 'ontology', not dialectical materialism, and Adorno devoted much of his criticism of this philosophy to showing that it relapsed into the very idealism which it was designed to avoid. It was an outbreak 'into the mirror' [Adorno, Negative Dialectics, p. 84], a dramatic pun on the idea of breaking out of the philosophy of reflection."

[39]Adorno, Against Epistemology, p. 134.

[40]Ibid., p. 27.

[41]Adorno, Negative Dialectics, p. 143.

[42]Ibid., p. 66.

[43]Adorno, Against Epistemology, p. 34.

[44]Ibid., p. 7.

[45]Ibid., p. 33. In the critique of immediacy, Adorno appears to have in mind Bergson, more than the usual object of his anti-ontological polemic, Heidegger. Adorno, Negative Dialectics, p. 9: "... Absolutized duration, pure becoming, the pure act--these would recoil into the same timelessness which Bergson chides in metaphysics since Plato and Aristotle."

[46]Adorno, Negative Dialectics, p. 11.

[47]Ibid., p. 90.

[48]Ibid., p. 8.

[49]Ibid., p. 8.

[50]Ibid., p. 156.

[51]Ibid., p. 154. Thus Adorno joins the so-called left-Hegelian tradition in separating Hegel's **method** from his **metaphysics**--this despite the recognition that Hegel himself had intended to resist precisely "the Kantian separation of form and substance." [Adorno, Negative Dialectics, p. 144].

[52]Adorno, Against Epistemology, p. 136.

[53]Ibid., p. 27: "The last thing the critique of epistemology--whose canon is the mediacy of the concept--is supposed to do is proclaim unmediated objectivism. That is the job of contemporary ontologies or the thought bureaucrats of the Eastern bloc."

[54]Rose, The Melancholy Science, p. 22.

[55]Adorno, Negative Dialectics, p. 157; the passage continues: "In Hegel, this meaning won a partial victory over Hegel--although Hegel, of course, could not admit the untruth in the compulsion to achieve identity. As the concept is experienced as nonidentical, as inwardly in motion, it is no longer purely itself; in Hegel's terminology, it leads to its otherness without absorbing that otherness."

[56]Ibid., p. 15.

[57]Hegel, Works, 4.78; quoted in Adorno, Negative Dialectics, p. 7.

[58]Adorno, Negative Dialectics, p. 24.

[59]Ibid., p. 9.

[60]Ibid., p. 156.

[61]Ibid., p. 5.

[62]Ibid., p. 30.

[63]Ibid., p. 51: "The dichotomy of subject and object is not to be voided by a reduction to the human person, not even to the absolutely isolated person."

[64]Ibid., p. 12; also see p. 142 for Adorno's summary of the four meanings of 'identity'; cf. Buck-Morss, The Origin of Negative Dialectics, p. 238, n. 48, where she notes the similarities between Adorno's use of the term 'identity' and the four meanings of the term in Heidegger's "Identity and Difference."

[65]Adorno, "The Actuality of Philosophy," p. 120.

[66]Adorno, Negative Dialectics, p. 184; also see p. 43: "To yield to the object means to do justice to the object's qualitative moments. ... What is **different** is the **qualitative**...." (emphases added).

[67]Ibid., p. 290; cf. p. 406: "Kant...in his doctrine of the transcendent thing-in-itself, beyond the mechanisms of identification...had indeed conceived transcendence as nonidentical...." Also see Adorno, "Subject and Object," p. 507.

[68]Ibid., p. 66.

[69]Ibid., p. 12.

[70]Ibid., p. 13.

[71]Ibid., p. 313.

[72]Ibid., p. 12.

[73]See Buck-Morss's comment to this effect in The Origins of Negative Dialectics, p. 78.

[74]Adorno, Negative Dialectics, p. 406.

75Ibid., p. 329.

76Ibid., p. xx.

77Adorno, "The Actuality of Philosophy," p. 221.

78Adorno, Negative Dialectics, p. 145.

79Ibid., p. 30.

80Cf. Marcuse's similar approach in Reason and Revolution.

81Adorno, Negative Dialectics, p. 145.

82Ibid., p. 292.

83Ibid., p. 389.

84Ibid., p. 174.

85Adorno, "Subject and Object," p. 499.

86Adorno, Negative Dialectics, p. 174.

87Ibid., p. 174.

88Ibid., p. 175.

89Ibid.

90Ibid., p. 136.

91Ibid., p. 174.

92Ibid., p. 40.

93Ibid., p. 139: "But as in truth subject and object do nc solidly confront each other as in the Kantian diagram --as they reciprocally permeate each other, rather --Kant's degrading of the thing to a chaotic abstraction also affects the force that is to give it form. ... To be able to define and articulate what it confronts, so to turn it into a Kantian object, the subject must dilute itself to the point of mere universality. ... It must cut loose from itself as much as from the cognitive object, so that this object will be reduced to its concept, according to plan. The objectifying subject contracts into a point of abstract reason, and finally into logical noncontradictoriness, which in turn means nothing except to a definite object."

94Adorno, Against Epistemology, p. 27.

95Adorno, Negative Dialectics, p. 174.

96Ibid.

97Ibid., p. 385.

98Ibid.

99Ibid., p. 3.

100Adorno, Against Epistemology, p. 26; emphases added.

101Adorno, Negative Dialectics, p. 198; emphases added. Also see Garbis Kortian, Metacritique: The Philosophical Argument of Juergen Habermas, trans. John Raffan (Cambridge: Cambridge University Press, 1980), pp 93-100, "from epistemology to social theory."

102Hegel, Phenomenology of Spirit, pars. 178-196; see Held, Introduction to Critical Theory, p. 203.

103Adorno, "Introduction," to The Positivist Dispute in German Sociology, trans. Glyn Adey and David Frisby. (London: Heinemann, 1977), p. 39.

104Adorno, "Subject and Object," p. 503.

105Adorno, Negative Dialectics, p. 21; cf. p. 20: "According to Nietzsche's critique, systems no longer documented anything but the finickiness of scholars compensating themselves for political impotence by conceptually construing their, so to speak, administrative authority over things in being."

106Adorno, "Introduction," to The Positivist Dispute in German Sociology, p. 38.

107Adorno, Negative Dialectics, p. 10; cf. p. 65 where Adorno makes the parallel argument for the social foundations of ontology.

108Ibid., p. 177; cf. p. 368: "Metaphysical reflections that seek to get rid of their cultural, indirect elements deny the relation of their allegedly pure categories to their social substance. They disregard society, but en-

235

courage its continuation in existing forms, in the forms which in turn block both the cognition of truth and its realization."

109Ibid., p. 5.

110Max Horkheimer and Theodor W. Adorno, Dialectic of Enlightenment, p. 82.

111Adorno, Against Epistemology, p. 29-30.

112"Subject and Object," p. 499. See p. 502, where Adorno continues, saying that "potentially, even if not actually, objectivity can be conceived without a subject; not so subjectivity without an object."

113Adorno, Negative Dialectics, p. 26.

114Ibid., p. 4.

115Adorno, Against Epistemology, p. 29.

116Ibid., p. 28.

117Held, Introduction to Critical Theory, p. 204.

118Adorno, Against Epistemology, p. 29.

119Adorno, Negative Dialectics, p. 64. Also see p. 25, where Adorno says that Hegel's approach "was to let each concept pass into its otherness without regard to an overlay from above; to Hegel, the totality of this movement meant the system."

120Hegel, Phenomenology of Spirit, par. 37.

121Marcuse, Reason and Revolution, p. 6.

122Hegel, Phenomenology of Spirit, par. 80.

123Ibid., par. 59; see Adorno, Negative Dialectics, p. 120: Hegel's "own concept of nonidentity--to him a vehicle for turning it into identity, into equality with itself--inevitably has its opposite for its content; this he brushes aside in a hurry. ... There is truly no identity without something nonidentical--while in his writings identity, as totality, takes ontological precedence, assisted by the promotion of the indirectness of the nonidentical to the rank of its absolute conceptual Being."

124Marcuse, Reason and Revolution, p. 24.

125 Adorno, <u>Negative Dialectics</u>, p. 27; cf. p. 25: "There is contradiction as well as kinship between this concept of system--a concept that concludes, and thus brings to a standstill--and the concept of dynamism, of pure, autarkic, subjective generation, which constitutes all philosophical systematics."

126 Ibid., p. 27.

127 Ibid.

128 Ibid., p. 327.

129 Ibid., p. 27; cf. p. 25: "Hegel could adjust the tension between statics and dynamics only by construing his unitarian principle, the spirit, as a simultaneous being-in-itself and pure becoming, a resumption of the Aristotelian-scholastic actus purus; and that the implausibility of this construction...will prevent the resolution of that tension is also immanent in the system." Also see Adorno, <u>Negative Dialectics</u>, p. 26: "It imitates a central antinomy of bourgeois society. To preserve itself, to remain the same, to 'be', that society too must constantly expand, progress, advance its frontiers, not respect any limit, not remain the same." And Adorno, <u>Negative Dialectics</u>, p. 331 on Hegel's ontologization of time.

130 Ibid., p. 153.

131 Ibid., p. xix.

132 Ibid., p. 5; emphasis added.

133 Ibid., p. 28.

134 Ibid., p. 39.

135 Ibid.

136 Ibid., p. 120; emphasis added.

137 Ibid., p. 157: "Only in the accomplished synthesis, in the union of contradictory moments, will their difference be manifested."

138 Ibid., p. 119.

139 Ibid., p. 120.

140 Ibid., p. 27; cf. p. 157.

[141]Ibid., p. 7.

[142]Ibid., p. 157.

[143]Hegel, Phenomenology of Spirit, par. 20.

[144]See Adorno, Negative Dialectics, p. 158.

[145]Hegel, Works 4, 543, quoted in Adorno, Negative Dialectics, p. 160.

[146]Adorno, Against Epistemology, p. 9.

[147]Adorno, Minima Moralia, p. 50.

[148]Buck-Morss, The Origin of Negative Dialectics, p. 77.

[149]Adorno, Negative Dialectics, p. 402; cf. p. 382: "By its consistency, idealism violated Kant's metaphysical reservation. A thought that is purely consistent will irresistibly turn into an absolute for itself."

[150]Ibid., p. 160.

[151]Ibid., p. 8. Yet see The Origin of Negative Dialectics, p. 72 where Buck-Morss reminds us that "it is important to realize that what was ... at stake was the very possibility of rational understanding. For if reality could not be brought into identity with universal, rational concepts, ... then it threatened to splinter into a profusion of particulars which confronted the subject as opaque and inexplicable."

[152]Adorno, Negative Dialectics, p. 8.

[153]Adorno, "Introduction," to The Positivist Dispute in German Sociology, p. 36.

[154]Adorno, "The Actuality of Philosophy," p. 127.

[155]Adorno, "Introduction," to The Positivist Dispute in German Sociology, p. 12.

[156]Adorno, Against Epistemology, p. 24.

[157]Adorno, Negative Dialectics, p. 119.

[158]Ibid., p. 346; see also p. 116: "As each individual entity is reduced to its concept, to the concept of the

ontical, that which makes it an entity as opposed to the concept will disappear. The formal, generally conceptual structure of all talk of the ontical, and of all equivalents of this talk, takes the place of the substance of that concept, a substance heterogeneous to the conceptuality. What makes this possible is that the concept of entity ... is the concept which encompasses out-and-out nonconceptuality, that which is not exhausted by the concept, yet without ever expressing its difference from the encompassed."

159Ibid., p. 137.

160Ibid., p. 137.

161Ibid.

162Ibid., p. 138; cf. p. 86: "Concepts, instruments of human thought, cannot make sense if sense itself is a negation, if every memory of an objective meaning beyond the mechanisms of concept formation has been expelled from the concepts."

163Ibid., p. 136.

164Adorno, Against Epistemology, p. 185. On the transcendental and empirical subject in Kant see Adorno, Negative Dialectics, p. 241: "That the constituens is to be the transcendental subject and the constitutum the empirical one does not remove the contradiction, for there is no transcendental subject other than one individualized as a unity of consciousness--in other words, as a moment of the empirical subject. The transcendental subject needs the irreducible non-identity which simultaneously delimits the legality." Also see Horkheimer and Adorno, Dialectic of Enlightenment, p. 83.

165Adorno, Negative Dialectics, p. 173.

166Ibid., p. 138.

167Ibid., p. 328; see p. 5; Adorno argues that since Hegel's 'totality' "is structured to accord with logic, ... whose core is the principle of the excluded middle, whatever will not fit this principle, whatever differs in quality, comes to be designated as a contradiction. Contradiction is nonidentity under the aspect of identity...." The Hegelian conflation of particular and particularity is the exemplar of Adorno's repeated, ironic contention that (Adorno, Negative Dialectics, p. 38) "all his statements to the contrary notwithstanding, Hegel left the subject's primacy over the object unchallenged."

168Ibid., p. 334.

169Adorno, Against Epistemology, p. 127.

170Adorno, Negative Dialectics, p. 200.

171Ibid., p. 200.

172Adorno, Against Epistemology, p. 37.

173Adorno, Negative Dialectics, p. 350.

174Ibid., p. 77.

175Ibid. Cf. "Subject and Object," p. 500-501.

176Adorno, Against Epistemology, p. 24.

177Ibid., p. 182; see Hegel, Logic, trans. Wallace, p. 19.

178Ibid., p. 182; see Adorno, Negative Dialectics, p. 33, who says in Marxian tones: "We are not to philosophize about concrete things; we are to philosophize, rather, out of these things."

179Adorno, Negative Dialectics, p. 147.

180See Adorno, Against Epistemology, p. 4: "The Hegelian system must indeed presuppose subject-object identity, and thus the very primacy of spirit which it seeks to prove. But as it unfolds concretely, it confutes the identity which it attributes to the whole. What is antithetically developed, however, is not, as one would no doubt currently have it, the structure of being in itself, but rather antagonistic society." Also see Adorno, Negative Dialectics, p. 318.

181Adorno, Negative Dialectics, p. 141.

182Ibid., p. 223; cf. p. 275: "Spooking in the transcendental subject, in the pure reason that interprets itself as objective, is the supremacy of the object--a moment without which the subject could not perform Kant's objectifying actions either."

183Ibid., p. 183; see p. 189: "Preponderance of the object is a thought of which any pretentious philosophy

will be suspicious. Since Fichte, aversion to it has been
institutionalized." See Dallmayr, Twilight, p. 135.

184Adorno, Negative Dialectics, p. 153.

185Ibid., p. 186.

186Ibid., p. 27.

187Ibid., p. 153.

188Ibid.

189Ibid., p. 179-180; this is developed in a crucial
passage that follows on pp. 183-184: "Due to the ine-
quality inherent in the concept of mediation, the subject
enters into the object altogether differently from the
way the object enters into the subject. An object can
be conceived only by a subject but always remains something other than the subject, whereas a subject by its
very nature is from the outset an object as well. Not
even as an idea can we conceive a subject that is not an
object; but we can conceive an object that is not a
subject. To be an object also is part of the meaning of
subjectivity; but it is not equally part of the meaning of
objectivity to be a subject. ... It is not by chance that
the Latin word subjectum, the underlying, reminds us of
the very thing which the technical language of philosophy has come to call 'objective'. The word 'object', on
the other hand, is not related to subjectivity until we
reflect upon the possibility of its definition."

190Ibid., p. 121. See also p. 177: "The more auto-
cratically the I rises above entity, the greater its imper-
ceptible objectification and ironic retraction of its constitutive role. Not only the pure I is ontically transmitted by the empirical I ... the transcendental principle
itself, the supposed 'first' of philosophy as against entity, is so transmitted."

191Ibid., p. 200.

192Ibid., p. 13.

193Ibid., p. 13.

194Ibid., p. 89.

195Buck-Morss, The Origin of Negative Dialectics, p.
81. See Adorno, "Subject and Object," p. 504, who notes
that "subjectivity--as distinct from primitive materialism,

which really does not permit dialectics--becomes a moment that lasts."

196Adorno, Negative Dialectics, p. 185.

197Ibid., p. 136.

198Ibid., p. 8.

199Ibid., p. 184.

200Ibid., p. 153.

201Ibid., p. 181.

202Ibid., p. 186; emphases added.

203Ibid.

204Ibid., p. 313.

205Ibid., p. 40.

206Adorno, Against Epistemology, p. 24. See Matthew Lamb, "The Challenge of Critical Theory," in Sociology and Human Destiny, ed. Gregory Baum (New York: Seabury Press, 1980), p. 190, who has pointed out that at first, "empirical rationality acted as a champion of non-identity inasmuch as the incipient sociology (e.g., Comte) and psychology (e.g., Freud) raised further relevant questions challenging the status quo of the ancien regime. As long as an empirically oriented psychology and sociology...challenged the hegemony of an 'abstract', authoritarian universality ... they performed important critical roles. [They]... called attention to the plurality of concrete particulars not identifiable with the cultural conceptualism and uniformity of the status quo." Cf. Horkheimer and Adorno, Dialectic of Enlightenment, p. 92-93.

207"Subject and Object," p. 509, which chastises Hume's epistemology for its **denial** of subjectivity, even though itself **directed by** subjectivity.

208Adorno, Negative Dialectics, p. 40: "In sharp contrast to the usual ideal of science, the objectivity of dialectical cognition needs not less subjectivity, but more." Cf. p. 91: "The reduction of the object to pure material, which precedes all subjective synthesis as its necessary condition, sucks the object's own dynamics out of it: it is disqualified, immobilized, and robbed of whatever would allow motion to be predicated at all."

Cf. "Subject and Object," p. 505, on scientific reduction-ism.

209Adorno, Negative Dialectics, p. 314: "The positi-vistic cognitive ideal of inwardly unanimous, noncon-tradictory, logically unimpeachable models is untenable due to the contradiction immanent in what is to become known--due to the antagonisms of the object. They are the antagonisms of the universal and particular in socie-ty, and the method denies them in advance of any con-tent." Cf. Adorno, "The Actuality of Philosophy," p. 125-126; and Rose, Melancholy Science, pp. 77-82, 95-102.

210Adorno, Negative Dialectics, p. 197: "A sociology of knowledge fails before philosophy: for the truth con-tent of philosophy it substitutes its social function and its conditioning interests, while refraining from a critique of that content itself, remaining indifferent toward it." See Rose, Melancholy Science, p. 22; Adorno, Prisms 35-49, "The Sociology of Knowledge and its Conscious-ness;" Jay, "The Frankfurt School's Critique of Mannheim and the Sociology of Knowledge," Telos 20 (Summer 1974).

211Ibid., p. 386.

212Ibid., p. 388. On p. 73, Adorno argues that although in the First Critique "the chapter on amphiboles mocks the brazen desire to know the inside of things," this "is not just the Enlightenment's No to a metaphysics that confuses the concept with its own reality; it is also the obscurantist No to every refusal to capitulate to the facade." Also see Adorno, Negative Dialectics, p. 385.

213Ibid., p. 385.

214Ibid., p. 389.

215Ibid., p. 385.

216It is the lack of attention to Adorno's **own** dialectic that has made commentators like Bubner argue that **either** Adorno did not take seriously enough Hegel's argument against the thing-in-itself, **or** Adorno is to be understood as having **evaded** the issue by a turn to the **aesthetic object.** See Bubner, Modern German Philoso-phy, pp. 180-182; cf. Adorno, Aesthetic Theory (Boston: Routledge & Kegan Paul, 1984), Chapter 9 on "Subject-Object," pp. 234-243. Also see Jay, Marxism and Total-ity, p. 272.

217Adorno, Negative Dialectics, p. 375.

218Buck-Morss, The Origin of Negative Dialectics, p. 86.

219Adorno, Negative Dialectics, p. 145; also see p. 409, omitted in the English translation: "Die Idee einer Logik des Zerfalls ist die aelteste seiner philosophischen Konzeptionen: noch aus seinen Studentenjahren." ["The idea of a logic of disintegration is the oldest of his (the author's) philosophical conceptions: hearkening from his student years."]

220Buck-Morss, The Origin of Negative Dialectics, p. 86.

221Adorno, Negative Dialectics, p. 11.

222Ibid., p. 375.

223Ibid., p. 140.

224Ibid., p. 68.

225Ibid., p. 37.

226Adorno, Against Epistemology, p. 33; cf. Adorno, Negative Dialectics, p. 199-200, 263.

227Karl Marx, "Critique of Hegel's Dialectic," in Karl Marx: Early Writings, trans and ed. T.B. Bottomore (New York: McGraw-Hill Book Company, 1964), p. 216.

228Adorno, Negative Dialectics, p. 65.

229Ibid., p. 14.

230Ibid., p. 15.

231Ibid., p. 9.

232Ibid., p. 28.

233Ibid., p. 31.

234Adorno, "Introduction," to The Positivist Dispute in German Sociology, p. 63.

235Adorno, Negative Dialectics, p. 141.

236Ibid., p. 161.

[237]Ibid., p. 19.

[238]Ibid., p. 126.

[239]Adorno, "Introduction," to The Positivist Dispute in German Sociology, p. 35.

[240]Adorno, Negative Dialectics, p. 19.

[241]Ibid., p. 53.

[242]Marcuse, Reason and Revolution, p. 11.

[243]Hegel, Phenomenology of Spirit, par. 31.

[244]Adorno, Against Epistemology, p. 27.

[245]Ibid., p. 136.

[246]Adorno, Negative Dialectics, p. 19.

[247]Adorno, Against Epistemology, p. 138.

[248]Adorno, "Introduction," to The Positivist Dispute in German Sociology, p. 11; see Adorno, Negative Dialectics, p. 112, which argues that the validity of Heidegger's project lay in its protest against just such a leveling of "the distinction between essence and appearance, the inherent impulse of philosophy as thaumazein, as discontent with the facade." Adorno's argument with Heidegger rests finally on the issue of whether this **difference** between essence and appearance can be established **immediately**, beyond dialectical mediation.

[249]Adorno, "Introduction," to The Positivist Dispute in German Sociology, p. 12.

[250]Ibid., p. 34.

[251]Adorno, Negative Dialectics, p. 167.

[252]Ibid., p. 141.

[253]Ibid., p. 169.

[254]Ibid., p. 169. See George Friedman, The Political Philosophy of the Frankfurt School (Ithaca: Cornell University Press, 1981), pp. 120-121, who states Adorno's point that when positivism "declares the essences to coincide with appearance," thus abolishing essences,

"philosophy loses it critical function." Positivism thereby "forces effective opposition over into abstract metaphysics, thus making criticism appear guilty of irrelevance. Worse, it may actually force the opposition into embracing an affirmative ontology." It is this double bind, between irrelevance and affirmative ontology, that negative dialectics wishes to critique.

255Adorno, "Introduction," to The Positivist Dispute in German Sociology, p. 36.

256Adorno, Negative Dialectics, p. 161.

257Adorno, Against Epistemology, p. 153. Also see Adorno, Negative Dialectics, p. 393.

258Adorno, Against Epistemology, p. 38.

259Friedrich Nietzsche, Twilight of the Idols, in The Portable Nietzsche, ed. and trans. Walter Kaufman (New York: The Viking Press, 1968), p. 480.

260Adorno, Negative Dialectics, p. 70.

261Adorno, "Introduction," to The Positivist Dispute in German Sociology, p. 36.

262Buck-Morss, The Origin of Negative Dialectics, p. 63. Compare the reading of Husserl by Theunissen, The Other, pp. 13-163 and Dallmayr's comment on it in Twilight, p. 54: "According to Der Andere, Husserl's effort to escape the confines of solipsism was ultimately due to the inherent inability of subjectivity to transgress its own boundaries and to make room for genuine interaction."

263Dallmayr, Twilight pp. 54-55.

264Buck-Morss, The Origin of Negative Dialectics, p. 71. Cf. Dallmayr, Twilight 42: "To a considerable extent, Husserl's opus can be viewed as the culmination--and perhaps incipient turning point--of the modern philosophy of subjectivity and of its cognitive-theoretical as well as practical-purposive ambitions." Cf. Buck-Morss, The Origin of Negative Dialectics, p. 71; Jay, Adorno, p. 32.

265Theodor Adorno, "Husserl and the Problem of Idealism," p. 12.

266Adorno, Negative Dialectics, p. 70.

267 Adorno, "The Actuality of Philosophy," p. 121.

268 Ibid., p. 121: The previous quotation concludes: "...and the late products of phenomenology are all the less able to disavow this origin, the more they try to conceal it."

269 Adorno, "Husserl and the Problem of Idealism," pp. 17-18.

270 Ibid., 6; also see p. 17.

271 Adorno, Negative Dialectics, p. 47. Cf. Dallmayr, Twilight, 43: "Throughout his life, Husserl struggled valiantly against the pitfalls of solipsism and intellectual self-enclosure. What was at stake in this endeavor was major--the objectivity of cognition...." Adorno's argument against Husserl parallels, at least on this issue, that of Immanual Levinas in Totality and Infinity: An Essay on Exteriority (Pittsburg: Duquesne University Press, 1969). Derrida explains Levinas's position in Writing and Difference, p. 123: "Husserl allegedly missed the infinite alterity of the other, reducing it to the same. To make the other an alter ego, Levinas says frequently, is to neutralize its absolute alterity."

272 Adorno, "The Actuality of Philosophy," p. 122.

273 Ibid., p. 122.

274 Adorno, Negative Dialectics, p. 62.

275 Adorno, Against Epistemology, p. 160.

276 Buck-Morss, The Origin of Negative Dialectics, p. 73.

277 Adorno, "Husserl and the Problem of Idealism," pp. 18.

278 Adorno, Against Epistemology, p. 163; Also see p. 132 on the "ontologization of the factical" in Husserl; and Adorno, "The Actuality of Philosophy," p. 121: "It is the deepest paradox of all phenomenological intentions that, by means' of the same categories produced by subjective, post-Cartesian thought, they strive to gain just that objectivity which these intentions originally opposed." See Buck-Morss, The Origin of Negative Dialectics, p. 71 on Husserl's search for "a pure logic uncontaminated by empirical heterogeneity," and p. 77 on the distinction between empirical objects and intentional

objects: "What appealed to Husserl, of course, was that
this doctrine could be used to justify his 'bracketing out'
process: if judgments of truth could be made about objects whether or not they actually existed, then phenomenology could avoid resting its case on the shaky, uncer-
tain ground of empirical beings--just those transitory
particulars which Adorno and Benjamin considered crucial."

279Adorno, Against Epistemology, p. 184; see pp.
148-149: "For Husserl the material moment is, even in
the process of cognition of content, not really the sub-
stratum of cognition but rather the sheer function of the
spiritual moment, an accident. ... What the tradition took
to be first, viz, sensation, Kant's 'material', becomes last
for him, a telos cited by the progress of knowledge, the
ultimate 'fulfillment' of intentions." Also see pp. 150-155
on "sensation and perception." Adorno's judgment is
based on his sense of Husserl's failure, as Dallmayr has
also argued in Twilight, p. 45 on Husserl's Formal and
Transcendental Logic and the Fifth of the Cartesian
Meditations, "to show how my own consciousness was
able to constitute another subjectivity, which was simultaneously an ego and different from my ego...."

280See Adorno, Against Epistemology, p. 2: "...I did
not allow myself to be intimidated by Husserl's assurance
that pure phenomenology is not epistemology, and that
the region of pure consciousness has nothing to do with
the concept of the structure of the given in the immanence of consciousness (Bewusstseinsimmanenz) as it
was known to pre-Husserlian criticism."

281Ibid., p. 125.

282Ibid., p. 129.

283Buck-Morss, The Origin of Negative Dialectics, p.
71; cf. Adorno, Against Epistemology, p. 155; and Adorno,
"The Actuality of Philosophy," p. 121-122.

284See Buck-Morss, The Origin of Negative Dialectics, p. 239, n. 56 on Heidegger as the foil for Adorno's
work, from "The Actuality of Philosophy," to Negative
Dialectics.

285Adorno, Negative Dialectics, p. 98; also see p. 67:
Heidegger "zealously set off his version of ontology from
objectivism, and his anti-idealist stand from realism,
whether critical or naive.... Of all the impulses given by
the ontological need the most enduring may have been

the disavowal of idealism." See Heidegger, The Essence of Reasons, trans. Terrence Malick (Evanston: Northwestern University Press, 1969). Cf. Adorno, Negative Dialectics, p. 91. See Dallmayr 57, 61, who emphasizes similarly Heidegger's "effort to move beyond the confines of subjectivity," his "critique of subjectivity."

286Adorno, Negative Dialectics, p. 53.

287Martin Heidegger, Being and Time, trans. John Macquarrie and Edward Robinson (New York: Harper and Row, 1962), p. 25. See Dallmayr, Twilight, pp. 7, 56-71; and Theunissen, The Other, pp. 167-198; and Rose, Melancholy Science, pp. 70-76.

288Adorno, Negative Dialectics, p. 98. Cf. p. 158: "The nonidentical is not to be obtained directly, as something positive on its part...." See Buck-Morss, The Origin of Negative Dialectics, p. 239, n. 50.

289Adorno, Negative Dialectics, p. 108.

290Ibid., p. 71. Also see p. 70: "...He tacitly followed a procedure in which the relation to the discursive concept, an inalienable element of thought, was sacrificed." And Adorno, Negative Dialectics, p. 70: "A self-denying subjectivity recoils into objectivism. ... This Being ends up in a tautology from which the subject has been evicted: 'But Being--what is Being? It is itself.'" (quoting Heidegger's Platons Lehre von der Wahrheit). See Adorno, Negative Dialectics, p. 98: "...Heidegger's Being, all but indistinguishable from its antipode, the mind, is no less repressive than the mind. It is only less transparent than the mind, ... and therefore even less capable of critical self-reflection on the nature of dominion than the philosophies of the mind had ever been." Also see Adorno, The Jargon of Authenticity, trans. Knut Tarnowski and Frederic Will (Evanston: Northwestern University Press, 1973). Cf. Jay, Adorno, p. 63: "Whether it be the young Lukacs's vision of epic wholeness in Homeric Greece, Heidegger's notion of a fulfilled Being now tragically forgotten, or even Benjamin's faith in a prelapsarian, Adamic oneness of name and thing, he remained deeply skeptical of any restoration of pre-reflective unity. With an almost protodeconstructionist contempt for the metaphysics of perfect presence, [Adorno] attacks all regressive yearnings."

291Adorno, Negative Dialectics, p. 9.

292 Adorno, "Introduction," to The Positivist Dispute in German Sociology, p. 66.

293 Adorno, Negative Dialectics, p. 108.

294 Adorno, Against Epistemology, p. 156.

295 Adorno, Negative Dialectics, p. 181.

296 Ibid., p. 138.

297 Ibid., p. 139.

298 Ibid., p. 328.

299 Ibid.

300 Adorno, "Subject and Object," p. 499.

301 Adorno, Negative Dialectics, p. 143.

302 Ibid., p. 143.

303 Ibid., p. 144.

304 Rose, Melancholy Science, p. 53.

305 Lamb, "The Challenge of Critical Theory," p. 203.

306 Adorno, Minima Moralia, p. 247.

307 Adorno, Negative Dialectics, p. 149, emphases added; on the influence of Ernst Bloch on Adorno's notion of utopia, see Buck-Morss, The Origin of Negative Dialectics, p. 76.

308 Adorno, Negative Dialectics, p. 191. See Jay, Adorno, p. 80: Adorno's utopian vision was one in which "the object will once more regain its rightful place alongside the individual and collective subject in a dialectic of mutually supportive non-identity."

309 Rose, The Melancholy Science, p. 48.

310 Adorno, "Subject and Object," p. 499.

311 Ibid., p. 500.

312 Adorno, Negative Dialectics, p. 30.

313 Ibid., p. 142.

314Ibid., p. 375; see also p. 141: "Not by chance has the paradox been the decaying form of dialectics from Kierkegaard on." See Paul Ricoeur, Conflict of Interpretations: Essays in Hermeneutics, ed. Don Ihde (Evanston: Northwestern University Press, 1974), p. 119 on eclecticism as the enemy of dialectics.

315Adorno, Negative Dialectics, p. 150.

316Adorno, Against Epistemology, p. 143, footnote.

317Adorno, Negative Dialectics, p. 172.

318Ibid., p. 150; cf. p. 146: "The barter principle, the reduction of human labor to the abstract universal concept of average working hours, is fundamentally akin to the principle of identification. Barter is the social model of the principle, and without the principle there would be no barter; it is through barter that nonidentical individuals and performances become commensurable and identical. The spread of the principle imposes on the whole world an obligation to become identical, to become total." Cf. also p. 178.

319Ibid., p. 150.

320Ibid., p.147.

321Ibid., p. 6. See Jay, Adorno, p. 68: "Adorno followed Benjamin in stressing the redemptive power of Gedaechtnis, the reverential recollection of an object always prior to the remembering subject. ... The reversal of forgetting that Adorno wanted was thus not the same as the 're-membering' of something dis-membered, the recovery of a perfect wholeness or original plenitude. It meant rather the restoration of difference and non-identity to their proper place in the non-hierarchical constellation of subjective and objective forces he called peace." Also see Adorno, "Subject and Object," p. 499-500.

322Adorno, Negative Dialectics, p. 6.

323Adorno, "Subject and Object," p. 503.

324Peter Gay, The Enlightenment: An Interpretation (New York: Alfred Knopf, 1966), p. xi.

325This is in contrast to the argument of Buck-Morss, for example, who overstates her claim that the question of morality was Horkheimer's, not Adorno's. See Buck-Morss, The Origin of Negative Dialectics, p. 67.

326Rose, Melancholy Science, p. 19.

327See Adorno, Negative Dialectics, p. 35: "In the history of philosophy we repeatedly find epistemological categories turned into moral ones; the most striking instance, although by no means the only one, is Fichte's interpretation of Kant." On the theme of domination, see Trent Schroyer, The Critique of Domination: The Origins and Development of Critical Theory (N.Y.: Braziller, 1974).

328Adorno, Adorno, "Introduction," to The Positivist Dispute in German Sociology, p. 12.

329Adorno, Negative Dialectics, p. 22.

330Ibid., p. 233. See Scott Warren, The Emergence of Dialectical Theory, pp. 144-160 on critical theory as de-politicized Marxism.

331Adorno, Negative Dialectics, p. 48.

332Ibid., p. 233. See Rose, Melancholy Science, pp. 22-23: "Adorno is more concerned with the Nietzschean perspective that to say that two things are identical is to make them identical, than with the Hegelian emphasis that to say that two things are identical is to assume incorrectly that they are independent of each other."

333Adorno, Negative Dialectics, p. 172.

334Ibid., p. 177.

335Lamb, "The Challenge of Critical Theory," p. 189.

336Adorno, Negative Dialectics, p. 362. See Jay, Adorno, p. 20: "The Jew, he now came to understand, was regarded as the most stubborn repository of that otherness, difference and non-identity which twentieth century totalitarianism had sought to liquidate." Also see Arnold Kuenzli, Aufklaerung und Dialektik. Politische Philosophie von Hobbes bis Adorno (Freiburg, 1971).

337See Adorno, Negative Dialectics, p. 305: Hegel's world spirit as enlightenment dialectics--myth secularized deity; cf. 348, 355, 357.

338Ibid., p. 250.

339Ibid., p. 233.

340Ibid.

341Ibid., p. 85.

342Ibid., p. 85. Thus Rose, The Melancholy Science, p. 25, notes that "Adorno is aware of Nietzsche's argument against hope," and recognizes it as "the argument against philosophical idealism." Nevertheless, "Adorno opts for the ungroundable and unjustifiable hope at the risk of relapsing into philosophical idealism."

343Horkheimer and Adorno, Dialectic of Enlightenment, p. 119.

344Adorno, Negative Dialectics, p. 337.

345Ibid., p. 403.

346Jay, The Dialectical Imagination, p. 54.

347Ibid., p. 64.

348See Adorno, Negative Dialectics, p. 263, 264, 265: "If the thesis of free will burdens the dependent individuals with the social injustice they can do nothing about, if it ceaselessly humiliates them with desiderata they cannot fulfill, the thesis of unfreedom, on the other hand, amounts to a metaphysically extended rule of the status quo. ... All that the subject needs to do to be lost is to pose an inescapable alternative: the will is free, or it is unfree. ... In their inmost core, the theses of determinism and of freedom coincide. Both proclaim identity. ... But freedom itself and unfreedom are so entangled that unfreedom is not just an impediment to freedom but a premise of its concept. ... Without the unity and the compulsion of reason, nothing similar to freedom would ever have come to mind, much less into being; this is documented in philosophy."

349Adorno, Minima Moralia, p. 73.

350Adorno, Negative Dialectics, p. 23. In less polemical fashion in Dialectics of Enlightenment, p. 3, Adorno argues that if the Enlightenment "always aimed at liberating men from fear," then the goal of Enlightenment is that state in which "nothing at all may remain outside, because the mere idea of outsideness is the very source of fear" (p. 16).

351Dallmayr, <u>Twilight</u>, p. 309, n. 36; and see Heidegger, <u>Being and Time</u>, pp. 206-207.

352Adorno, Horkheimer and Adorno, <u>Dialectic of Enlightenment</u>, p. 86, <u>vis a vis</u> what "the work of the Marquis de Sade portrays [as] ... the bourgeois individual freed from tutelage."

353Ricoeur, <u>Conflict of Interpretations</u>, p. 452; also see pp. 449-454.

354Martin Buber, <u>Between Man and Man</u> (London: Routledge & Kegan Paul, 1947), pp. 163-181. Also, on the origin of the transcendental formulation of the issue of 'respect' see Kant, <u>Critique of Practical Reason</u>, trans. Lewis White Beck (Indianapolis: Bobbs-Merrill, 1977), pp. 74-110, esp. 88 and 92; cf. Lewis White Beck, <u>A Commentary on Kant's Critique of Practical Reason</u>, pp. 54, 116, 141, 219-221, 223, 227, 236, 243, n. 13, 282. Also see Paul Ricoeur, <u>Husserl. An Analysis of His Phenomenology</u> (Evanston: Northwestern University Press, 1967), pp. 195-201, "The 'Constitution of the Other' and 'Respect'."

355Adorno, <u>Minima Moralia</u> 73.

356Dallmayr, <u>Twilight</u>, p. 135.

357Adorno, <u>Negative Dialectics</u>, p. 148: "Identity is the primal form of ideology. We relish it as adequacy to the thing it suppresses; adequacy has always been subjection to dominant purposes and, in that sense, its own contradiction. ... The ideological side of thinking shows in its permanent failure to make good on the claim that the non-I is finally the I...." Thus Gillian Rose is correct, I believe, in arguing in <u>The Melancholy Science</u>, p. 51, that Adorno's approach "is analogous to the Marxian tradition of criticizing ideology (<u>Ideologiekritik</u>)." Also see Paul Connerton, <u>The Tragedy of Enlightenment. An Essay on the Frankfurt School</u> (Cambridge: Cambridge University Press), pp. 1-26, 42-52, on critical theory as critique of ideology.

358Adorno, <u>Negative Dialectics</u>, p. 2.

359Adorno, <u>Against Epistemology</u>, p. 20.

360Ibid.

361Adorno, <u>Negative Dialectics</u>, p. 34.

362Ibid., p. 34; cf. p. 128, 148-149.

363Ibid., p. 186.

364Horkheimer and Adorno, Dialectic of Enlightenment, p. xiv; and see Christian Lenhardt, "The Wanderings of Enlightenment," in On Critical Theory, ed. John O'Neill (N.Y.: Seabury, 1976), pp. 34-57; Held, Introduction to Critical Theory, pp. 148-174; Jay, Dialectical Imagination, pp. 252-280; Connerton, The Tragedy of Enlightenment, pp. 60-79; Kortian, Metacritique, 126-134; Rose, Melancholy Science, pp. 104-108.

365Horkheimer and Adorno, Dialectic of Enlightenment, p. 13. See The Origin of Negative Dialectics, p. 60-61, where Buck-Morss argues that Dialectic of Enlightenment "demonstrated that what Max Weber had identified as the increasing rationalization and 'disenchantment' of society did not lead progressively to a rational social order, but instead to new structures of domination...."

366Adorno, Negative Dialectics, p. 214.

367Ibid., p. 365; and see Horkheimer and Adorno, Dialectic of Enlightenment, p. x: "It is a critique of philosophy, and therefore refuses to abandon philosophy."

368Buck-Morss, The Origin of Negative Dialectics, p. 61; emphasis mine.

369Adorno, Negative Dialectics, p. 217.

370Ibid., p. 106; cf. pp. 104, 105.

371Ibid., p. 79.

372Ibid., p. 84.

373Ibid., p. 85.

374Ibid., p. 126. See Rose, Melancholy Science, pp. 62-65 on Kierkegaard.

375Jay, Adorno, p. 52.

376Adorno, Negative Dialectics, p. 85.

377Ibid., p. 243; Ricoeur in Conflict of Interpretations, pp. 416-417 suggests one way in which Adorno's point could be pursued in terms of the Critique of Practical Reason, as a critique of Kant's notion of the highest good as the 'totality' or completion of the will; cf. Adorno, Negative Dialectics, p. 385 on Kant's postulate of immortality, and pp. 228ff., 232 on the freedom of the will in Kant.

378Ibid., p. 236.

379Ibid. Also see p. 242: "For the right practice, and for the good itself, there really is no other authority than the most advanced state of theory. When an idea of goodness is supposed to guide the will without fully absorbing the concrete rational definitions, it will unwittingly take orders ... from that which society has approved." Also see Adorno, Negative Dialectics, p., 261, where Adorno points out that since Kant's categorical imperative is not open to rational criticism, "the ratio turns into an irrational authority."

380Ibid., p. 229. Cf. p. 123 where Adorno argues similarly against existentialism, that "the concept of existence impressed many as a philosophical approach because it seemed to combine divergent things: the reflection on the subject--said to constitute every cognition and thus every entity--and the concrete, immediate individuation of each single subject's experience."

381Adorno, Minima Moralia, p. 88. See Kant, Critique of Practical Reason, pp. 124-126 on the primacy of practical reason. Also see Kortian, Metacritique, pp. 74-79 on "the primacy of practical reason in Kant and Fichte."

382Adorno, Negative Dialectics, p. 229.

383Ibid., p. 102.

384Ibid., p. 187.

385Ibid.

386Ibid., p. 115, emphasis added.

387Ibid., p. 200: "The line that consciousness depends on Being was not a metaphysics in reverse; it was pointed at the delusion that the mind is in itself, that it lies beyond the total process in which it finds itself as a moment. Yet the conditions of the mind are not a noumenon either. The term 'Being' means altogether different things to Marx and to Heidegger, and yet there is

256

a common trait: in the ontological doctrine of Being's priority over thought, in the 'transcendence' of Being, the materialist echo reverberates from a vast distance. ... The doctrine of Being turns ideological as it imperceptibly spiritualizes the materialist moment in thought by transposing it into pure functionality beyond all entity-- as it removes by magic whatever critique of a false consciousness resides in the materialist concept of Being. The word that was to name truth against ideology comes to be the most untrue: the denial of ideality becomes the proclamation of an ideal sphere."

388Ibid., p. 52; cf. Jay, Adorno, 59: "A genuine materialism ... had an ethical function; it must register and draw on the sufferings and needs of contingent human subjects rather than explain them away through an historiosophical theodicy." Also see Jay, Jay, Marxism and Totality, , 260 and Held 218-221. Thus Adorno's reading of Marx is an implicit warning not to turn too quickly from the infrastructural, economic issues to the more 'humanistic' superstructural, cultural issues. This contradicts the standard reading of critical theory among theologians, as represented by David Tracy, Blessed Rage for Order: The New Pluralism in Theology (New York: The Seabury Press, 1975), p. 254, n. 28.

389Adorno, Negative Dialectics, p. 192; cf. pp. 193-196.

390Ibid., p. 17; cf. pp. 362-363: "Perennial suffering has as much right to expression as a tortured man has to scream...." Compare Adorno, Negative Dialectics, p., 320: If Hegel "transfigured the totality of historic suffering into the positivity of the self-realizing absolute, the One and All that keeps rolling on to this day--with occasional breathing spells--would teleologically be the absolute of suffering."

391Ibid., p. 365.

392See Ibid., p. 202-203. Cf. p. 244, where Adorno argues that despite the contribution made by materialism to the preponderance of the object, it erred by losing the centrality of **theoretical** reason: "Marx received the thesis of the primacy of practical reason from Kant and the German idealists, and he sharpened it into a challenge to change the world instead of merely interpreting it. He thus underwrote something as arch-bourgeois as the program of an absolute control of nature. What is felt here is the effort to take things unlike the subject and make them like the subject--the real model of the principle of identity, which dialectical materialism disavows as such." This also disagrees with Buck-Morss's thesis in The Origin of Negative Dialectics, p. 78, that Adorno's was a form of "pre-Kantian materialism."

393Adorno, Negative Dialektik, p. 189, using translation by Dallmayr, Twilight, p. 136.

394Adorno, Negative Dialectics, p. 202, 203.

395Held, Introduction to Critical Theory, p. 205. See Jay, Adorno, 88ff. on suffering and Adorno's position on psychology.

396Adorno, Minima Moralia, p. 15.

397Adorno, Against Epistemology, p. 40.

398Adorno, Negative Dialectics, p. 403.

399Adorno, Minima Moralia, p. 101.

400 Horkheimer and Adorno, Dialectic of Enlightenment, p. 244. This sentence may well have been written by Horkheimer, reminiscent as it is of his 1934 Daemmerung, p. 86: "Metaphysicians are usually impressed only to the smallest degree by what men suffer."

401Horkheimer and Adorno, Dialectic of Enlightenment, p. xv.

402Adorno, Negative Dialectics, p. 244.

403Ibid., p. 379.

404Ibid., p. 28.

405Ibid., p. 377.

406Jay, The Dialectical Imagination, p. 80.

407Horkheimer and Adorno, Dialectic of Enlightenment, p. 244.

408See Rose, Melancholy Science, p. 50, who notes: "Adorno chose a hard path between Benjamin's view of history as the corruption of the world, and Lukacs' view of history according to which reconcilement between subject and object can be 'imputed' as the end of history. Adorno's position is encapsulated in his aphorism,

'Universal history must be construed and denied,'" quoting Adorno, Negative Dialectics, p. 320.

409Adorno, Negative Dialectics, p. 14.

410Ibid., p. 28.

411Ibid., p. 127; cf. p. 105: "Every analysis of a judgment takes to a subject and an object, but this fact does not create a region beyond these moments, a region that would be 'in itself'. The analysis results in the constellation of those moments, not in a third that would be superior, or at least more general."

412Ibid., p. 163.

413Ibid., p. 162.

414Adorno, "Subject and Object," p. 506.

415Adorno, Negative Dialectics, p. 163.

416Horkheimer, Critical Theory, p. 178.

417Adorno, Negative Dialectics, p. 15.

418Ibid., p. 406. See Jay, "The Concept of Totality in Lukacs and Adorno," p. 134. Thus, although Adorno surely would have been stung by Jay's contention that "Negative Dialectics ends with a weak plea for an uneasy alliance between a non-absolutist metaphysics and the negation of identity," he would have enjoyed the irony that Jay concluded from this that "the ghost of the Kantian antinomies remained unexorcised."

419Ibid., p. 160.

420Held, Introduction to Critical Theory, p. 221.

421Adorno, Negative Dialectics, p. 406. That stealth is the only way out, even for Adorno, has been argued, for example, by Bubner, pp. 180ff. My argument throughout has been that while it can legitimately be complained that **Bonhoeffer** had to resort to such a decisionist strategy, Adorno has endeavored to demonstrate the **intrinsic** limits to a thoroughgoing dialectics.

422Ibid., p. 407.

423Ibid., p. 408.

[424]Horkheimer and Adorno, _Dialectic of Enlightenment_, p. 244.

CHAPTER FOUR

CONCLUSION: THEOLOGY AND THE DIALECTICS OF OTHERNESS?

Throughout even the subtleties of the immanent critique of the transcendental philosophical tradition, Bonhoeffer's Act and Being--as all of his early writing-- was a decidedly theological venture. Indeed the present study itself has undertaken the extended conversation with the philosophy of Adorno precisely for the sake of entering more deeply **into** the theological context, rather than for the sake of moving **out of** it. Thus, at the end of this study some more explicit summary judgments are in order, concerning not only further avenues for pursuing the method of immanent criticism, but also the potential theological consequences in doing so.

The methodological issue at stake in the present endeavor, as in the works of Bonhoeffer which we have considered, was the potential for Christian **theology** to draw upon and learn from the legacy of the conceptuality of the **dialectics of otherness.** The present study has argued that Bonhoeffer's early work developed a critical, yet highly appreciative, understanding of the fashion in which **epistemology** has served as the dominant paradigm for modern theology's framework for thinking about **sociality** and the **ethics** of social relationships. The result was Bonhoeffer's attempt to state a sort of post-Hegelian Kantian interpretation of the nature and function of dialectical thought. This served him as a radical intrinsic criticism of the fruitfulness of theology's further investment in the transcendental tradition. The present study has wagered **both** that Bonhoeffer's conceptual concerns were given fuller and more nuanced treatment in Adorno's Negative Dialectics, **and** that these concerns remain for contemporary theology central to its ongoing agenda.

Bonhoeffer and Adorno shared a vision of a dynamic, 'enacted', Kantian duality, which moved beyond the formal synchronicity of undialectical 'relational,' or 'paradoxical', conceptions of the vis a vis of subject and object. They each proposed a new form of **dialectic**, whose very movement is the sustenance of difference, the enactment of the **otherness** of thought and being to each other. Such dialectics is the ongoing process of the double-mediation of subject and object, each by the other, which brings about of the **coherence** of the **non-identical.** For both thinkers, the legacy of Kant, even post-Hegel, remains productive because of the very fact that Kant's 'critical dialectic' spurs reflection to continually reinterpret the 'Kantian metaphysical reservation'. It serves not only as an immanent critique of the idealism of Hegel, but also as an immanent critique of that materialism, positivism and ontology which subsequently reacted against Hegel.

First, the Kantian legacy encouraged both Bonhoeffer and Adorno to undertake a non-metaphysical meditation upon **otherness**, upon the sociality or duality of reality, in the face of the presumptive identity-thinking of romanticist or idealist conceptions of totality. They each developed a form of an ethics of respect for the 'conceptual remainder' in any and all thought, a resistance to the domination of otherness in comprehensive, systematic thinking. They each refused to join in the marginalization of the object. As an outgrowth of his engagement with personalist philosophy, Bonhoeffer thus called for a genuine ontology which is capable of retaining the epistemological moment of receptivity, and which thus ennobles the object as a critique of the concept. Adorno deepened this thinking of the preponderance of the object by an anti-Hegelian archaeology of the significance of particularity. His contribution was to uncover the basis of and tactically resist the very ontological urge which threatens to undo it.

Second, the legacy of Kantian criticism encouraged in both Bonhoeffer and Adorno a renewed respect for **dialectic**. They each affirmed the exigency for rationality in the face of the danger of the ir-rationality of either dualisms or reductionist monisms, both of which are closed to the penetration of critical evaluation. Bonhoeffer and Adorno each came to see ethics as requiring **theoretical** thinking, rather that a deference to **practical** reason alone. For such theory enables precisely the moral critique of any practice that is not open to criticism. Indeed, reflection on the social-ethical category of the 'person' had motivated Bonhoeffer's search for a genuine transcendental philosophy. Thus his peculiar form of personalism itself came to emphasize the epistemological moment of activity as a re-enfranchisement of criticism vis a vis the assumed immediacy of any intuitionism. This same resistance to the loss of theoretical subjectivity in systematic ontological approaches, such as Heidegger's, motivated Adorno's adherence to the theoretical desideratum to retain the function of transcendental philosophy's distinction between essence and appearance--as a **task** not a **given** of dialectical thought.

262

Such a reading of Bonhoeffer and Adorno is convincing to the extent that it persuades the reader of the enduring promise of an immanent critique of the transcendental tradition. The present study has succeeded to the extent that it has resulted in a renewed sense of Bonhoeffer's Act and Being as a successful argument for the need for a **moral conversion** in understanding the implications of theology's investment in the epistemological paradigm. And it has accomplished its goal to the extent that it has also resulted in our ability to see Adorno's Negative Dialectics as providing a conceptual context within which to place Bonhoeffer's reflections on the need for an **intellectual conversion** in our understanding of the method of theology.

A. From Immanent to Transcendent Criticism

For all his appreciation of the transcendental tradition, gained from his most rigorous **immanent critique** of its post-Kantian legacy, Bonhoeffer remained a theologian, not just a transcendental philosopher. That is to say, Bonhoeffer's perspective on the philosophical tradition was governed by what Adorno himself had termed a **transcendent critique**, governed by extrinsic theological warrants, rather than by remaining strictly within a purely 'immanent' form of criticism. As Gillian Rose explains, Adorno himself meant by the term 'transcendent' any critique which "brings alternative and external concepts and criteria to bear," which approaches its object of criticism "from a particular standpoint,"[1] which is external to its own presuppositions. "The transcendent method," Adorno wrote, "assumes an as it were Archimedean position,"[2] outside the phenomenon under consideration, by means of which from the outset to criticize not aspects, but the whole, of the object of critique. Thus the issue still needs to be raised, whether such a move towards a 'holistic' **critical** perspective does not invalidate the entire preceding immanent 'criticism' of philosophies of '**the Whole**'--of Totality.

We will turn momentarily to some suggestions concerning the directions in which contemporary theology might pursue the relationship between the immanent critique of idealism and Bonhoeffer's transcendent critique of idealism from a theological perspective. But this 'theological bent' to all of **Bonhoeffer's** writings, even his methodological explorations, should not blind us to the fact that even in **Adorno's** purely philosophical writings there remained an appreciation for the need for a 'transcendent', or extrinsic, form of criticism--even for the philosopher--at least in certain circumstances.

1. Adorno: Method, Theology and Politics

With regard to at least three factors in Adorno's work we see evidence of his own sense of the potential limits of the purely immanent procedure. We need to understand something of his appreciation of the need perceived by others of his generation for a transcendent, or extrinsic, point of leverage against the monolith of idealism and the culture that it had nourished. Although we can do little more here than sketch the outlines of these three concerns, they do help to point out the specific directions which further discussions between theology and Adorno might take.

The first issue was the general methodological problem, as Gillian Rose has described it, that Adorno "believed that he was confronted by the same paradox which beset Nietzsche, namely, how to present or ground a philosophy or point of view when the aim of that philosophy is to criticize reality or society altogether and thus the prevailing norms of philosophical or sociological discourse as well."[3] A radically **critical** theory, which would criticize Hegel's dictum that reason is "the rose in the cross of the present,"[4] finds itself caught in the thorns of its own radicality. For as Juergen Habermas has noted, Adorno's critical theory "must make use of the same critique which it has declared false."[5] Thus one can describe Adorno's position, as does Martin Jay, as one in which not only is

> the concept ... inadequate to the world, but also ... the world as it presently is constituted is inadequate to certain meanings of the concept. It is the interaction of these complimentary inadequacies that gives thought, so Adorno contended, its critical power to transcend the status quo.[6]

Either thought must be conceived to have a certain power really to **transcend** its own immanent place in the status quo despite its own inadequacies, or the status quo itself must be said not to be as 'inadequate to certain meanings of the concept' as supposed. The first would appear to challenge Adorno's consistent maintenance of the **finitude** of thought; the second would appear to deny the radicality of the **brokenness** of society and the thinking which meditates upon and within it.[7]

This was a particularly acute methodological issue for Adorno, as for Bonhoeffer, because it raised the question of the possibility of a critique of a total cultural structure, such as that being consolidated during their early careers by Nazi ideology, if and when that culture ideologically no longer allowed such radical criticism. If, as Adorno wrote in Negative Dialectics, "the means employed in negative dialectics for the penetration of its hardened objects is possibility--the possibility of which their reality has cheated the objects and which is nonetheless visible in each one,"[8] how does one engage in criticism when one's own culture no longer allows such a possibility? What is the task of the thinker if 'possibility' itself has been thoroughly co-opted by the very identity-philosophy against which criticism is directed? Immanent criticism requires that the critic be "someone who is not entirely engulfed" by the system of thought or culture against which the critique is directed. How then, in the face of the claims to total rationality in idealism or to total ideology in Nazism, Adorno asked himself, can there still be "the unideological thought ... which ... strives to help the things themselves to that articulation from which they are otherwise cut off by the prevailing language"?[9]

The question was thus twofold: first, whether 'the unideological thought' could transcend the limits of a totally ideological culture--whether Nazism in particular had collapsed the distance between ideology and reality so completely that immanent critique was no longer possible. And second, if in that case a 'transcendent perspective' was a necessity, on what foundation could such a transcendent criticism be made?[10] According to Adorno, this dual question of the possibility of an immanent criticism at all in the face of an ideologically determined culture--how "the dialectical critic of culture" can be said "both [to] participate in culture and not participate"[11]--could not be answered 'abstractly', that is to say 'transcendentally', but required the attempted practice of criticism itself. From the inaugural lecture forward, Adorno had maintained that

> thinking which aims at relations with the object, and not at validity isolated in itself, is accustomed to prove its right to exist not by refuting the objections which are voiced against it and which consider themselves irrefutable, but by its fruitfulness, in the sense in which Goethe used the term.[12]

In that sense, Adorno's form of immanent criticism moved beyond the Kantian 'transcendental' method, for there was no static a priori structure on the basis of which to affirm the potential for critical theory. The 'truth' of immanent criticism lay in the 'practice of theory' a posteriori.[13] If the social whole were entirely 'untrue', nothing but ideology, immanent criticism would be impossible. But only an analysis of the results of the attempt at such criticism could ascertain whether or not in fact this was so. Evidencing his continued indebtedness to Hegel, Adorno thus concluded that "the productivity of thinking is able to prove itself only dialectically, in historical concreteness,"[14] in its own immanent procedure. Thinking validates itself only by its ability to continue to think the Other.

Thus, despite his appreciation for the limit-situation in which immanent criticism could be perceived to be an impossibility, Adorno himself consistently chose a rigorous and demanding intrinsic approach, despite its agnostic overtones. For as he wrote in Prisms,

> If stubbornly immanent contemplation threatens to revert to idealism, to the illusion of the self-sufficient mind in command of both itself and of reality, transcendent contemplation threatens to forget the effort of conceptualization required and content itself instead with the prescribed label, the petrified invective, most often 'petty bourgeois', the ukase [edict] dispatched from above.[15]

Although immanent criticism must not presume to be 'in command of both itself and of reality', Adorno concluded, neither can it 'forget the effort of conceptualization required' for criticism at all. Philosophy's vocation, therefore, is that of a melancholy science, but a scientia no less.

The result, as David Held has paraphrased Adorno's conviction is that although "clearly, philosophy cannot transform these [social and ethical] conditions ... it can help to create the precondition for their alteration."[16] "Finally," Adorno wrote, "the very opposition between knowledge which penetrates from without and that which bores from within becomes suspect to the dialectical method."[17] In Adorno's words,

> on its own it [immanent criticism] is unable to resolve the contradictions under which it labours. Even the most radical reflection of the

mind on its own failure is limited by the fact that is remains only reflection, without altering the existence to which its failure bears witness. Hence immanent criticism cannot take comfort in its own idea. It can neither be vain enough to believe that it can liberate the mind directly by immersing itself in it, nor naive enough to believe that unflinching immersion in the object will inevitably lead to truth by virtue of the logic of things if only the subjective knowledge of the false whole is kept from intruding from the outside, as it were, in the determination of the object. The less the dialectical method can today presuppose the Hegelian identity of subject and object, the more it is obliged to be mindful of the duality of the moments.[18]

It is crucial to understand, therefore, that immanent criticism **is** for Adorno a form of 'transcendence' of the status quo. A radically **immanent** criticism is, therefore, not opposed to but rather provides a necessary, although not sufficient, condition for the potential of social and ethical change. Further conversation with Adorno must address directly the strengths and limitations of such an understanding of the function and role of dialectical criticism.[19]

Besides this general methodological issue of the possibility of criticism at all, continued conversation between theology and Adorno needs to address more fully a **second issue** which reveals Adorno's own investment in the issue of transcendent criticism--that of the impact on his thought of his Jewish religious heritage.[20] Two issues in particular invite further attention: first, the issue of the relationship between identity thinking and anti-Judaism; and, second, the relationship between Adorno's Negative Dialectics and the tradition of Jewish negative theology.

Both in his collaborative work with his more theologically inclined colleague Horkheimer, and in his own later work, Adorno the survivor of the holocaust remained acutely aware of the fact, as Dialectics of Enlightenment put it, that "from the outset there has always been an intimate link between anti-Semitism and totality."[21] And the "Meditations on Metaphysics" which conclude his Negative Dialectics begin with the unfathomable injury of the realization that

267

after Auschwitz, our feelings resist any claim of the positivity of existence as sanctimonious, as wronging the victims; they balk at squeezing any kind of sense, however bleached, out of the victims' fate. And these feelings do have an objective side after events that make a mockery of the construction of immanence as endowed with a meaning radiated by an affirmatively posited transcendence.[22]

For Adorno, however much still the Hegelian, the liquidation of Other, that "genocide [which] is the absolute integration,"[23] was forever burned into the memory of the survivor.

Thus the Jewish negative theological tradition entailed for Adorno not merely the anti-metaphysical prohibition against naming God.[24] More importantly it forces the moral question of the social prohibition against claiming to have made 'rational' the "absolute negativity ... which defies human imagination as it distills a real hell from human evil."[25] Thus, as Dialectics of Enlightenment had said,

Jewish religion allows no word that would alleviate the despair of all that is mortal. It associates hope only with the prohibition against calling that which is false as God, against invoking the finite as the infinite, lies as truth. The guarantee of salvation lies in the rejection of any belief that would replace it: it is knowledge obtained in the denunciation of illusion.[26]

Thus, although Jewish theology appears in Adorno's work only indirectly, and generally in a 'secularized' form,[27] it remains an element not to be dismissed.

Undoubtedly, the place to begin an exploration of the impact of the Jewish negative tradition upon Adorno, and its significance for theology's conversation with him, is with Adorno's relationship to Walter Benjamin. Indeed, several recent studies have begun just such an inquiry.[28] Of special interest for the issues with which the present study has been concerned is the question of how Adorno responded to Benjamin's attempt, as Buck-Morss has put it, to achieve "insights which paralleled mystical revelation, while adhering to the Kantian anti-metaphysical rule of staying within the data of experience."[29] Adorno's complaint against Benjamin--that the "juxtaposition of contradictory elements made [his] dialectical images merely reflect contradictions instead of developing them through critical argumentation"[30]--bears striking resemblance to his critique of ontology which we have traced in Chapter Three. That is to say, it gives important clues to Adorno's rejection of static **paradoxes**, in favor of **dialectical thinking**, a characteristic of his work from his thesis on Kierkegaard[31] to the Negative Dialectics.

Adorno's connection with Benjamin should also shed important light on the former's understanding of utopia, as the state of diversity without domination. Benjamin's dream of the utopian future was, to be sure, decidedly theological, while Adorno increasingly emphasized the potential for art, not theology, to serve as the refuge for the utopian impulse.[32] Such a line of investigation, therefore, would need to focus attention increasingly upon Adorno's work on history, and the indebtedness there, too, upon Benjamin's "Theses on the Philosophy of History."[33]

Yet, although the Adorno-Benjamin connection has recently gained attention, there are other obvious sources of the influence on Adorno's understanding of the Jewish negative theological tradition which have not yet been widely explored. For example, the precise effect of the theology of his colleague, Horkheimer, still needs to be determined, particularly in light of Horkheimer's own later emphasis on the theological implications of **otherness**,[34] and in favor of the preponderance of particularity.[35]

Finally, the **third issue** which would need to be addressed in order to come to a complete sense of the exigence towards extrinsic criticism in Adorno is that of the nature and significance of the heterodox Marxian thread which is tightly woven into the fabric of Adorno's project. For the sake of our own interests, the present study has intentionally bracketed any development of the Marxian aspect of Adorno's work. This has been done for two reasons: (1) Since Bonhoeffer's own reading of Hegel was unquestionably pre-Marxian, we have endeavored to push that reading as far as it would go as an **immanent** critique of idealism; and thus we have risked making Adorno into too much of a 'Hegelian' precisely for the sake of showing the manner in which the 'materialist' moment in Negative Dialectics was intrinsic to the transcendental tradition, not merely an extrinsic addition from the Marxist perspective. (2) We have implicitly followed a reading of Adorno's own 'Marxism' that understands it not so much in terms of infrastructural,

269

economic and political, concerns, but in terms of super-structural, cultural and moral, motivations. Thus we have interpreted the **practical** side of Adorno's Marxian concern by means of the **theoretical,** the **materialist** by means of its **phenomenological** function for reinterpreting dialectic as a form of **dynamic ascesis:** the purification of thinking in the practice of it.[36] This is, the present study is aware, only a reading of Adorno's Marxian emphases. And a full appreciation of the limits of immanent criticism for Adorno would need to explore in detail the consequences of focusing, alternatively, on the more 'scientific' approach to Marx.[37]

2. Bonhoeffer: Revelation and Epistemology

In "The Theology of Crisis and its Attitude Toward Philosophy and Science," Bonhoeffer succinctly states what is for him the basic **theological** limitation of a purely immanent, or intrinsic, criticism of transcendental philosophy's form of conceptuality.

> ... The deepest antinomy seems to me to be the antinomy between pure act and reflection--as the old dogmatics said, actus directus and reflectus. God is known only in the pure act of referring to God. Theology and philosophy are executed in reflection, into which God does not enter. Philosophy **essentially remains in reflection... Theology at least knows of an act of God, which tears man out of this reflection** in an actus directus toward God.[38]

Thus it should come as no surprise that from Bonhoeffer's inaugural lecture forward, the problem of a 'transcendent criticism' of idealism, from a theological perspective extrinsic to its presuppositions, is at the forefront of his attention. Yet, one of the most striking features of the structure of the inaugural lecture, "Man in Contemporary Philosophy and Theology," was Bonhoeffer's ability naively to affirm both the validity of the enterprise of idealism's investments in **dialectics** and the **theology of otherness** which grounded his clearly **theological** mode of criticism of idealism. The result is the acute, if largely unintentional, antinomy with which Bonhoeffer the theologian struggled: how to remain committed to an immanent criticism of idealism that accepted its legitimate achievement and, at the same time, to interpret those achievements in light of the extrinsic or transcendent criticism afforded by his theological perspective.

270

On the one hand, Bonhoeffer's theological sympathies with Barth's theology of revelation are clear. He is committed to the **historicality** of revelation, by which he means a clearly anti-idealist conception of God's action in time, not merely "as a beginning (potentiality)," but "as at the same time consummation (reality)."[39] The Christian category of revelation thus, according to Bonhoeffer, demands a certain **ontological** interpretation of its 'being in' the finite world, and thus demands as well an emphasis on the structures which **mediate** such 'being'.[40] "Theological concepts of being must have precisely this as their ontological premise, that the Is can in no way be detached from the concrete definition [konkreten Bestimmung]. Any formalistic attempt to fall back on 'something of a more general nature', supposedly discoverable behind the specific conditions of divinity, must serve to obliterate the Christian idea of revelation."

> This is where a **genuine** ontology comes into its own, inasmuch as it defines the 'being in...' in such a way that cognition, finding itself in the world of entity, suspends itself when confronted by the being of the entity and does not force it under its control. ... From here opens the prospect of genuine theological concepts of being.[41]

"...The pure ontology of revelation," Bonhoeffer concludes, must "be thought of as enjoying a mode of being which embraces both entity and non-entity, while at the same time 'suspending' within itself man's intention of it--faith."[42] And one cannot miss the Barthian quality of Bonhoeffer's contention that

> all thought remains in itself so long as existence remains in itself. But revelation, the Word, leads existence out of itself into a state of self-criticism [zur Krisis ueber sich selbst]. Even when existence has been placed in truth, its thinking about itself and God remains within itself, but is repeatedly disturbed by the reality of revelation in a way which distinguishes it from profane thought....[43]

Thus he follows Barth in turning the tables on liberal theology and asserting the priority of the knowledge of **God in revelation** over knowledge of **humanity as receptive** to that revelation. Faith is thus to be thought of as "the genuine transcendental act, [in which] God always remains non-objectively-accomplished, so that the

existential act of thinking-God is completed in consciousness, but is not any longer accessible to the reflection
of consciousness on itself...."[44]

On the other hand, Bonhoeffer wished to assert, as
Carl Michalson has written of Karl Heim, that "the
Christian revelation, ... notwithstanding man's inability to
come upon it by himself, is a 'rational event'--as Barth
himself once called it."[45] The reference to Heim here is
not arbitrary, since Bonhoeffer himself struggled, shortly
after the completion of Act and Being, to differentiate
his own position from Heim's.[46] His difficulty in doing
so, we would argue, was due to the fact that the position which Bonhoeffer attributed to Heim came so very
close to Bonhoeffer's own position in Act and Being.
For, having shown that Heim refused to think of revelation as "the **transcendental** reduction to the thinking
subject" or "the **ontological** reduction to the being of the
entity," Bonhoeffer described Heim's alternative in a
fashion applicable to the genuine transcendental philosophy and the genuine ontology for which Bonhoeffer had
himself argued in Act and Being:

> To these two systematic possibilities of inter-
> preting the 'question of the ultimate', resting
> in themselves, there is added a third, the
> critical-transcendental possibility. The asking
> and thinking I does not let itself be taken up
> into being and does not take being up into
> itself, but it recognizes itself in the act as
> being limited both backwards and forwards,
> touching on the limit without perpetuating the
> encounter.[47]

For, as Bonhoeffer had written in Act and Being, the
problem is not whether or not we can escape the act-
being problematic; rather the challenge for theology is
that of "**adequately** interpreting the idea of revelation
from the standpoint of the act-being problem."[48] "**The
idea of revelation must therefore yield an epistemology
of its own.**"[49]

Thus, **precisely on Barthian theological grounds,**
Bonhoeffer is led to propose what appears to be a most
un-Barthian theological program.

> ...It may be that ... we shall find in genuine
> transcendentalism and ontology ... certain
> contributions to the solution of the act-being
> problem **within** the concept of revelation, if
> only because they have exhaustively fathomed

272

and argued the philosophical dilemma of act and being, or because we shall be able to adopt their polar standpoints of man as pure act 'with reference to', and thought 'suspended' in being, in order to test against revelation, in the sharpest possible antithesis, the merits of explanation in terms of act or being. If that is so, we may be sure that these theories will emerge from their encounter with the idea of revelation in a wholly new guise, **but equally we shall know that the 'with reference to' and the 'suspension' are amenable to theological interpretation, hence, after all, of service in understanding the idea of revelation.**[50]

Bonhoeffer is clearly dissatisfied with the fact that in Barth's theology "no light is shed on how we can envisage the human religious act in conjunction with the divine act of belief, unless we sever them to allot them essentially different spheres, or suppress the 'subjectivity' of God if not, alternatively, the existential impact of revelation."[51] The task of theology, Bonhoeffer wrote, is "to make room for revelation, i.e. to form theological concepts of act and being."[52]

Still, Bonhoeffer cannot be rightly understood to have intended that the immanent criticism of the transcendental tradition is to provide a **religious** a priori. There is no propadeutic to revelation for Bonhoeffer any more than for Barth or Kierkegaard; nothing can prepare for the contingent fact of revelation. "If revelation is essentially an event brought about by the free act of God," Bonhoeffer wrote, "it outbids and supersedes the existential-ontological possibilities of existence."[53] Yet the a priori of all human **thinking** can be sought out, for all thought is the same kind of thought, no matter what its object.

But then the concept of the a priori expresses no more than that for the formal understanding of this Word, certain mental forms are presupposed, in which case, to be sure, the sense of a specifically religious a priori is lost. ... The purely formal understanding of the Word requires no other forms of thinking than those of the a priori of pure thought itself.[54]

Thus, Bonhoeffer notes near the end of Act and Being, that "to object that categories of a generally metaphysical nature have been employed in the foregoing is to overlook the necessity of a certain formal 'pre-comprehension' as a standpoint from which questions--even if wrong ones--can be framed, whose answer is subsequently returned by revelation together with a fundamental correction of the question."[55]

Thus, even in his unwillingness to embrace either Rudolf Bultmann's or Reinhold Seeberg's emphasis on the existential immediacy of revelation--rather than Barth's emphasis on revelation's very mediacy--we can see the immanent critique of the transcendental tradition serving Bonhoeffer as an important heuristic device by which to approach his theological contemporaries. Bonhoeffer's turn from the intrinsic perspective of the immanent critique of idealism to the extrinsic perspective of theology is not to be understood, therefore, as a theologically imperialistic **answer** to the problem of the relationship between immanent and transcendent critique. Rather, it is a pointed reminder of the seriousness of the very **questions** which he intends to raise in dialogue with the intrinsic philosophical perspective.

Such a strategy seems particularly important given the fact that **within** the various transcendent perspectives of his own contemporaries, Bonhoeffer saw operative the same tension that he had shown in the transcendental philosophical tradition: between those who articulate the God-humanity relationship in terms of a dialectic of identity and those who depend on the alternative paradigm of the dialectic of difference.[56] The challenge of theology, according to Bonhoeffer, is to escape the totalizing exigencies of the idealist tradition, and to articulate the 'real limit of revelation' which is at the heart of that which is distinctively 'theological'. Otherwise,

> any limit, so long as man can impose it by thought, is determined by the possibility of going beyond it; i.e. even the man who wishes to understand himself from his limitations in the end understands himself from his possibilities. In the face of this we assert: **The concept of possibility has no place in theology and therefore in theological anthropology.**[57]

And by 'possibility' Bonhoeffer clearly means the possibility of a total adequacy between thought and being, between finite human understanding and the reality of humanity as created, fallen, and redeemed by God. And it was to articulate this tension, this difference, that Bonhoeffer felt theology was justified in drawing upon

274

the formal, epistemological distinction between subject
and object.

Therefore the centrality of the theological category
of revelation does not imply the rejection of the category of understanding for Bonhoeffer; it rather demands
a **distinct sort** of understanding. That is to say,

> if, then, the concept of possibility is to be
> rejected from theology, something positive is
> to be added: man understands himself not in
> reflection on himself, but in the act of refer-
> ence to God.... Here the distinction is to be
> made between actus directus and actus reflex-
> us; only in actus directus is there real self-
> understanding ... Now as theology only pro-
> ceeds in actus reflexus, it cannot itself be a
> genuine self-understanding of man--as philo-
> sophy claims for itself; it can only be a copy.
> In this copy all will depend on reality not
> being once again rationalized by the category
> of possibility.[58]

For theology the epistemological paradigm, and the immanent criticism of that paradigm's pretension for truth,
is no substitute for the truth of revelation. It is but a
'copy' [Nachzeichnen] of the truth of revelation. But its
fruitfulness depends on its providing a form of thinking
adequate to the task of conceiving of the reality of
revelation, as Bonhoeffer put it, such that revelation's
reality is not "once again rationalised by the category of
possibility."[59]

Theology requires a conceptuality which **both** retains receptivity--the actus directus of faith--to the
object of revelation **and** always remains self-critical of
its adequacy for the task. Bonhoeffer's methodology thus
prospects a line of reasoning similar to that later proposed by Gabriel Marcel: "before it is anything else,
consciousness is above all consciousness **of** something
which is other than itself, what we call self-consciousness being on the contrary a derivative act...."[60] That is
to say, theology needs a form of rationality by which to
affirm its "exigence-for-transcendence,"[61] the actus directus of faith. Yet, theology requires a type of reasoning which resists triumphalism, whose very receptivity
remains open to critical self-evaluation. Theology as
actus reflexus must never occur without critique. Or as
Paul Ricoeur has written of the method of phenomenology, it cannot be "reflection without a spiritual discipline (ascese), without a purification of its own see-

ing."[62]   Thus even as "philosophy reaches its boundaries,
and awaits the first glimmers of the fires of revelation,"[63] theology must retain its **philosophical-critical**
posture.   Theology's **receptivity** does not necessarily
imply naivete.   And philosophy's immanently **critical**
method may indeed assist theology in sustaining a faithful telling of the revelation of the available and this-
worldly, but uncoercibly transcendent, God.[64]

B. Evaluations

1. Bonhoeffer and His Interpreters

The present interpretation of Bonhoeffer's Act and
Being is indebted to several previous studies.   In Germany Juergen Moltmann's Herrschaft Christi und soziale
Wirklichkeit nach Dietrich Bonhoeffer[65] was significant
in that it provided one of the first glimpses of the effects of a re-evaluation of Bonhoeffer on the basis not
just of the Letters and the Ethics, but of the early
dissertations.   From the American Protestant perspective,
Clifford Green's work, The Sociality of Christ and Humanity, almost single-handedly placed the early period of
Bonhoeffer's career, particularly the two dissertations,
Sanctorum Communio and Act and Being, into the perspective of the biographical information that had been
provided in Eberhard Bethge's Dietrich Bonhoeffer.[66]
From the Roman Catholic perspective, Ernst Feil's Die
Theologie Dietrich Bonhoeffers[67] provided what is still
the benchmark for any sustained attempt to view the
entire corpus of Bonhoeffer as a coherent systematic-
theological enterprise.   Andre Dumas' Dietrich Bonhoeffer: Theologian of Reality gave some of the first lucid
discussions of the philosophical and methodological issues
that provided the context for Bonhoeffer's own reflections.[68]   And Heinrich Ott's Reality and Faith for the
first time attempted a constructive theological articulation that was more 'in' rather than 'on' the theology of
Bonhoeffer.

And yet in general there still persists a disregard
for the early, as compared to the later, work of Bonhoeffer.[69]   And even in those recent studies of Bonhoeffer which do try to take account of Sanctorum Communio
and Act and Being, their philosophical foundations and
methodological contributions are virtually ignored, often
due to the continued synoptic approach of much of even
the best work on Bonhoeffer.[70]   In other cases it is a
factor of a certain propensity to allow hagiography to
overshadow theology.   And in still other cases it is the

result of a marked hostility to the philosophical emphases in the early writings among those who argue that Bonhoeffer's academic writings are, as Thomas Day has charged, "obtuse and unsuccessful," precisely because of their "residual abstractness" vis a vis the 'concreteness' of the actions of Bonhoeffer the martyr.[71] Thus in a certain sense, Bethge's musing about Bonhoeffer of two decades ago is still ours as well: "Admitting that the life of this man has spoken--can his theology make any impact?"[72] Surely, many of the **writings** of Bonhoeffer have made an impact; yet it is still not clear what Bonhoeffer's "theology" was, or is yet to be.

Thus the present study of the critique of the transcendental philosophical tradition in the early theological writings of Bonhoeffer has risked emphasizing the **methodological** contributions of Bonhoeffer, at the expense of the **constructive theological** contributions that Bonhoeffer was able to make as a result of his struggles with method. We have wagered that such an approach could best bring to light the nature of the 'intellectual conversion' from idealism which was the desideratum from Bonhoeffer's early investment in Barth. And yet, that investment took Bonhoeffer down several not so Barthian paths--at least routes one would not expect the neo-**orthodox** Barth to tread. Still, those transcendental investigations **have** been tread by others like Karl Rahner, who have claimed to have been no less influenced by Barth than was Bonhoeffer.[73] A re-reading of Bonhoeffer, with ears more attuned to the **philosophical** partners with whom he conversed, might lead towards such new **theological** partners for Bonhoefferian theology as well.

2. Adorno and His Interpreters

If Adorno is to continue to provide assistance in such a theological enterprise, then it becomes necessary to more accurately place him within the context of his interpreters, particularly those who would argue that he would lead us astray. Three lingering questions would have to be addressed: (1) Whether Critical Theory in general, and Adorno's in particular, does not lead, as Matthew Lamb has asked, "to a futile substitution of writing for action," or as critics of the early work of Bonhoeffer likewise have charged, 'phraseology' for 'reality'?[74] (2) Whether, even if Critical Theory can be acquitted of this charge, some **other** Critical Theorist, such as Juergen Habermas, might not be a better partner in dialogue for theology? (3) Whether, in any case, phenomenology and ontology have not themselves been misrepresented by Critical Theory, and whether Husserl and Heidegger--Bonhoeffer and Adorno notwithstanding--might not themselves be the legitimate heirs to the transcendental conversation? We can do no more than briefly hint at the direction that might be taken in responding to these three questions by the interpreters of Adorno.[75]

First, one of the most common criticisms of Adorno--and of special concern for the further interpretation of Bonhoeffer, who himself led a decidedly 'engaged' life--is that his negative dialectics is itself actually bound to the status quo, precisely because it provides no **practical** tactic for challenging and changing it. As Paul Piccone asked in his review of Adorno's Against Epistemology, has not "its refusal even to begin to provide concrete alternatives for fear of reinforcing precisely the state of affairs that it is meant to challenge relegated it to an unrelenting critical stance that parasitically fed on the degenerate situation it attacked"?[76] In similar fashion, Ben Agger has charged that "Adorno is unjustified in resigning from the effort to build a socialist society in the actual here and now of everyday politics."[77] Willi Oelmueller has summarily stated the charge against Adorno: "dissociation of reflection and action."[78]

Thus, despite Adorno's contention that "only an essentially undialectical philosophy ... could maintain that the old problems could simply be removed by forgetting them and starting fresh from the beginning,"[79] there are those like Buck-Morss who have wondered aloud whether Adorno's dialectics did not itself, ironically, pose finally as the prima dialectica[80] he abhorred?

> Did the perpetual motion of Adorno's arguments go anywhere? Did they lead out of the bourgeois interieur or simply hang suspended within it like the new art form of mobiles?[81]

Thus the first question that would have to be addressed in future work is that of whether it is to Adorno's credit or detriment that, as Gillian Rose concluded her study of Adorno by saying, "his 'morality' is a praxis of thought not a recipe for social and political action."[82] The present study has clearly wagered on the fruitfulness of a reading of Adorno's theory as itself **radical practice.**

Second, Martin Jay has noted the fact that,

> as a number of critics have noted, the pos-
> sibility of a non-hypostatized intersubjectivity,
> a public realm in which non-coercive, rational
> discourse might take place among equals, was
> absent from his thinking, as it was in Critical
> Theory as a whole until Habermas. ... [Adorno
> evidenced a] hostility to the dialogic, com-
> municative function of language. ... Instead of
> probing the possibility that such a potential
> might still exist, Adorno damned 'the liberal
> fiction of the universal communicability of
> each and every thought' and withdrew increas-
> ingly into a defense of autonomous art as what
> he liked to call the 'Statthalter' [representa-
> tive] of non-identity.[83]

Adorno's fault, according to Jay, was his "overwhelmingly
critical use of the concept of totality, which turned into
a fear of anything collective, communitarian or intersub-
jective," as well as Adorno's "insistence on the utter
'falseness' of the present totality...."[84] Likewise critics
such as Jean Cohen and Seyla Benhabib have argued that
Habermas's approach is superior to that of Adorno precisely because of Habermas's emphasis on the potential to
conceive utopia on the model of intersubjectivity.[85] The
present study has, to the contrary, followed the interpretation of those like Joel Whitebook and Gillian Rose,
who have argued that Adorno's notion of the cunning of
the 'dialectics of enlightenment' is merely **circumvented**,
not bettered, by Habermas's 'ideal speech situation',
which is unable to take seriously enough Adorno's in-
junction against all forms of identity-philosophy.[86]

Third, and the more promising constructive criticism
of Adorno, is the charge that in polemically presenting
his argument against idealism Adorno misrepresented the
positions of both Husserl and Heidegger, primarily by
disregarding the later projects of both thinkers. Ad-
judication of this issue could profitably begin by compar-
ing the actual position of Negative Dialectics to both
Husserl's position in The Crisis of European Sciences and
Transcendental Phenomenology[87] and Heidegger's criticism of metaphysics in The End of Philosophy.[88] Both
Husserl's phenomenology and Heidegger's 'destruction of
metaphysics', as we have already suggested in Chapter
Three above, may themselves finally be of great assistance in furthering Adorno's own supposed critique of
them.

C. Contributions

1. Adorno: Philosophy and Style

Despite the dominant focus of attention upon questions concerning Adorno's **method**, his most enduring contribution to the continuing dialogue between transcendental philosophy and theology may well come, to the contrary, under the rubric of **style.** His stylistic motto might well have been the lines from Max Bense's "Ueber den Essay und seine Prosa," which Adorno quoted appreciatively:

> For whoever seeks to criticize must necessarily experiment. He must create conditions under which an object becomes visible anew ....[89]

From the final pages of the inaugural lecture onward, we find Adorno self-consciously experimenting with the style, the strategy of expression, which would 'create conditions' capable of making 'visible anew' not only the exigencies of his life and times, but also the subject matter about which his thought and writing were concerned. And again we find the paradigm of the epistemological relation of subject and object intruding creatively on these deliberations, as it did on his meditations on method.

While for his Critical Theoretical contemporaries such as Max Horkheimer, "the problem of 'the object' tended to dissolve into (Marxian) sociology, the problem of 'the subject' into (Freudian) psychology, and critical theory attempted to explain their interrelations," Adorno's method of immanent criticism was distinctive because it "discerned a dialectical process **within philosophy itself,**" the explication of which was the goal of his evolving negative dialectics.[90] And for this task, Adorno realized, philosophy required a style as well as a method that would resist the assumptions of idealism, particularly its affirmative ontological faith in the adequacy of reason to the totality of finite reality.

> Philosophy which no longer makes the assumption of autonomy, which no longer believes reality to be grounded in the <u>ratio</u>, but instead assumes always and forever that the law-giving of autonomous reason pierces through a being which is not adequate to it and cannot be laid out rationally as a totality--such a philosophy will not go the entire path to the rational

presuppositions, but instead will stop there
where irreducible reality breaks in upon it.[91]

This resulted for Adorno in a style of thinking and writing whose characteristics apply suggestively to Bonhoeffer's work as well.

We will restrict our concluding remarks here concerning the contribution of Adorno to four characteristics of Adorno's style: (1) It was characterized by an
emphasis on particulars, not universals; (2) it affirmed
the priority of a type of thinking that occurs in the
'spaces' between subject and object, between finite
thought and finite being--among the riddles and traces of
meaning--and issues in deliberately fragmentary and
essayistic communications; (3) it effected a strategy of
trial combinations of images and thoughts that hold onto
the 'difference' inherent in a radically suspended, negative, dialectics--rather than the teleological strategy of
the identity-thinking of systems; (4) it construed philosophy as an enterprise whose coherence was not <u>a priori</u>,
but <u>a posteriori</u>, the creative product of an experimental
and polyphonically-'musical' style of thought, itself conceived as performative practice. We are proposing that
Adorno's conception of philosophical 'style'[92] has been
significant for our work here precisely because it has
'created conditions' in which we may be able to make
'visible anew' in our concluding remarks on Bonhoeffer,
the latter's continuing significance for any theology done
in the wake of idealism.

First, philosophy's search for strategies of style by
which to enact its method, Adorno said all the way back
in the inaugural lecture, must begin by affirming that
"the idea of philosophic interpretation does not shrink
back from that liquidation of philosophy which to me
seems signalled by the collapse of the last philosophic
claims to totality" of idealism.[93]   Rather, a post-idealist
style of thinking, renounces the priority of "the question
of totality," precisely so that it may begin with that
which idealism neglected: the irreducible **particular,** which
in idealism served a merely "symbolic function," in that
it "appeared to represent the general," the totality, of
which it was but a moment.[94]

Philosophy, according to Adorno, requires a style of
thought and expression which begins to "learn to do
without [this] symbolic function; ... it must give up the
great problems, the size of which once hoped to guarantee the totality, whereas today between the wide meshes
of big questions, interpretation slips away."[95]   There was

thus a certain empiricist, or as Adorno was increasingly to claim, materialist, bent to his work from the start which was more anti-Hegelian than affirmatively Marxist in its genesis. Adorno proposed a philosophic style in which "the function which the traditional philosophic inquiry expected from meta-historical, symbolically meaningful ideas," is accomplished through an emphasis upon the particular, the "inner-historically constituted, non-symbolic ones."[96] Adorno's attention was caught by the marginal, the prosaic, the ordinary individual or detail, in which was immortalized not the whole, but its own particular history. These, he argued, must be the foundation of a post-idealist philosophical style.

Thus, **second,** where idealism assumed the possibility of the ultimate identity of subject and object, thought and being, Adorno emphasized that finite, historical reality is broken and fragmentary.

> While our images of perceived reality may very well be <u>Gestalten</u>, the world in which we live is not; it is constituted differently than our of mere images of perception. The text which philosophy has to read is incomplete, contradictory and fragmentary....[97]

Immanent criticism works with the "fleeting, disappearing traces within the riddle figures of that which exists and their astonishing entwinings."[98] Therefore a style of thought is required which allows, even nurtures, the articulation of "the 'breaks' (<u>Brueche</u>) in its logic; the gaps of its systematic unity."[99]

These breaks, fractures, fissures in reality are not philosophy's **intended** result, but are **unintentional,** indeed often <u>a priori</u> 'impossible', products of the historical process. Adorno's search was for a strategic style by means of which to **say** these breaks, to memorialize "the non-identity between ... **intent** and its concrete **objectification,"**--between the intended rational identity of idealism and the historical plurality of the social, cultural world in which we live.[100] In the words of the inaugural lecture,

> construction out of small and unintentional elements thus counts among the basic assumptions of philosophic interpretation ... The historical images (<u>geschichtliche Bilder</u>) would at the same time be themselves ideas, the configuration of which constituted unintentional

truth (intentionlose Wahrheit), rather than that truth appeared in history as intention.[101]

Contrary to the traditions of immanent criticism of Schleiermacher and Dilthey, philosophy in the style of Adorno proposed that "the task of philosophy is not to search for concealed and manifest intentions of reality, but to interpret unintentional reality..."[102] In Martin Jay's words, "the alternative he was presenting ... denied that interpretation meant the recovery or recollection of an intended meaning. Anamnesis was not an Erinnerung of an original subject-object unity. Truth could only be discovered through permitting constellations of existing elements to become illuminations, sudden and momentary revelations of a non-totalized reality."[103]

In this notion of the un-intentional truth of that philosophy which thinks in the conceptual space opened by the disparity between subject and object, thought and being, "one can discover," Adorno pointed out, "what appears as such an astounding and strange affinity existing between interpretive philosophy and that type of thinking which most strongly rejects the concept of the intentional, the meaningful: the thinking of materialism."[104] This demanded of philosophy, Adorno recognized, a style of expression adequate not to totality or identity but to these fragments, traces, and breaks in which truth is to be found. For this reason Adorno's favorite choice of format was the essay, for it "thinks in breaks (in Bruechen) because reality is brittle (bruechig) and finds its unity through the breaks, not by smoothing them over."[105] "The uncompleted and broken form of the essay was far more appropriate," as Adorno's literary legacy makes plain, than "the massive volume of conventional philosophy..."[106] Thus even a 'major' work such as Negative Dialectics is deliberately aphoristic, ironic, and in its very form an embodiment of the negativity which its own dialectical method binds together only with the greatest reluctance.

Yet, third, if "Adorno agreed with Goethe, who cautioned: 'Do not look behind the phenomena; they are themselves the truth'," he also realized, as we have seen above, that "the interpretive process necessitated more than immediate experience of the 'given'; it required the active intervention of the thinking subject."[107] Adorno's subject, compared with that of idealism, was a chastened, finite, but critical organon, yet not one without its own hope. For, as the inaugural lecture put it,

283

with the disintegration of all security within
great philosophy, experiment makes its entry...
The mind (<u>Geist</u>) is indeed not capable of
producing or grasping the totality of the real,
but it may be possible to penetrate the detail,
to explode in miniature the mass of merely
existing reality.[108]

The style of Adorno drove particulars like wedges into
the unintentional fissures of idealist totality. It hoped
to disintegrate the monolithic presumptions of identity
for the sake of the forgotten particular, bound against
its own nature into a whole that 'merely existed', but
could not be confused with reality. "The result," however, in Jay's words, "was not a relativistic chaos of
unrelated factors, but a dialectical model of negations
that simultaneously constructed and deconstructed patterns of a fluid reality."[109]

As David Held's interprets Adorno's approach,"in
order to break the grip of all closed systems of thought
(Hegelian idealism, for example, or orthodox Marxism)
and to prevent an unreflected affirmation of society
typical of bourgeois ideology, Adorno conceived of his
writings as a series of analyses and interventions."[110]
They are exercises of a critical rationality which resisted
the temptation to become syntheses and self-congratula-
tory systems. "The inevitable gap between concept and
object, which he claimed materialism preserved and
idealism denied, meant that Adorno's own concepts were
themselves not to be taken as perfectly true to reality."[111] This required a philosophical style in which "the
contradictions and antinomies of the object were reproduced in the structure of his text,"[112] reproduced
through the service of a critical, and de-constructive
rationality. Such rationality, such 'negative dialectics'
"has to bring its elements... into changing constellations,
... into changing trial combinations," which eschew the
pretension of system building.[113] For this reason, Adorno said in the inaugural lecture, "I speak purposely of
grouping and trial arrangement, of **constellation** and
construction."[114]

Adorno's philosophical style articulates a polemically
suspended, deliberately **non-affirmative**, dialectic--which
is **dialectic** still. It groups and arranges its insights in a
tensive-coherence, not in totalizing systems. It proposes
"models, by means of which the <u>ratio</u>, examining and
testing, approaches a reality which refuses to submit to
laws." It is a process of "exact fantasy," a style "which
rearranges the elements of the question without going

284

beyond the circumference of the elements,"[115] without the conceit of trying to burst the limits of finitude.

> The whole, as a positive entity, cannot be antithetically extracted from an estranged and splintered reality by means of the will and power of the individual; if it is not to degenerate into deception and ideology, it must assume the form of negation.[116]

The negation of 'estranged and splintered reality' required "a dialectics that would resist the positive negation of the negation, the perfect identity of subject and object, celebrated by Hegelianism and Hegelian Marxism."[117] Immanent criticism needed a style that would maintain "an untotalized 'forcefield' of apparently contradictory statements, which both reflects and resists the reality it tries critically to analyze."[118] In Adorno's words of the inaugural lecture,

> the interpretation of given reality and its abolition are connected to each other, not, of course, in the sense that reality is negated in the concept, but that out of the construction of a configuration of reality the demand for its [reality's] real change always follows promptly ... Materialism has named this relationship with a name that is philosophically certified: dialectic. Only dialectically, it seems to me, is philosophic interpretation possible.[119]

Adorno's 'negative dialectics' was therefore not only a method for respectfully approaching the object of its investigation--the method of the "logic of aporias" of immanent criticism--but also a style, in which the final, collected 'constellation' of insights, "not (logical) sequence, produces the idea," which is never triumphant in itself, but only as it illuminates the need for concrete change.[120]

Adorno's prototypical, "properly written texts," he reflected in <u>Minima Moralia</u>, "are like spiders' webs":

> tight, concentric, transparent, well-spun and firm. They draw into themselves all the creatures of the air. Metaphors flitting hastily through them become their nourishing prey. Subject matter comes winging towards them. The soundness of a conception can be judged by whether it causes one quotation to summon another. Where thought has opened up one

cell of reality, it should, without violence by the subject, penetrate the next. It proves its relation to the object as soon as other objects crystallize around it. In the light that it casts on its chosen substance, others begin to glow.[121]

He was careful to clarify that his idea of "interpretation does not mean to suggest a second, a secret world which is to be opened up through an analysis of appearances."[122] Adorno's philosophical stylist is not "someone who wants to find in the riddle the reflection of a being which lies behind it, a being mirrored in the riddle, in which it is contained." Instead, the function of the stylist "is to light up the riddle-<u>Gestalt</u> like lightning and thus negate it (<u>aufzuheben</u>), not to persist behind the riddle and imitate it."[123] Adorno's search for style "sought above everything else to sustain and create the capacities for new and genuine critical thinking."[124]

Fourth, there is a certain 'aesthetic', particularly 'musical', quality to Adorno's style.[125] That is to say, philosophic interpretation of the legacy of western rationality, according to Adorno, should invoke in the reader the sort of participation which he felt was exemplified, for example, in Schoenberg's early music, which "requires the listener spontaneously to compose its inner movement and demands of him not mere contemplation but praxis."[126] The listener is not 'given' a tonal totality, toward which the appropriate stance is that of the spectator. Rather the listener is given an unexpected, experimentally non-tonal riddle, whose 'meaning' cannot be imputed to the 'intention' of the composer. Whereas traditional tonality had assumed the unity of a harmonic totality, Schoenberg's music had de-constructed the holistic tonal constructions, as well as the responses these constructions had intended the listener to have. As Martin Jay has commented, "instead of being complicitous with the growing facade of universalism, the false totality that Adorno and his colleagues saw as dominating contemporary consciousness," Schoenberg's music was "truly progressive" because it acted to "preserve the determinate negations of this illusory, yet pervasive whole," of tonal harmony, just as philosophy must sustain itself precisely in the fragmentary, unintentional clues given it by a broken society.[127]

Here the question of style rejoins the method of immanent criticism. The participatory composition of the 'inner movement' of Schoenberg's music by the listener was, in Adorno's opinion, just that sort of experimentation, or trial interpretation, which could bring to light the **unintentional** meaning of the music. In a like manner, Adorno's style of philosophy wished to evoke the same performative practice in the reader as had the 'a-tonal' music of Schoenberg in the listener. To conceive of thinking as having a musical style meant for Adorno to emphasize the ultimate impossibility of **reducing** reality to transparent conceptuality. Whereas the totality of a philosophical system "is essentially conceptual and thus threatens to dominate the non-identical and heterogeneous particulars subsumed under it," the totality of the musical composition "is non-conceptual and thus less inclined to eliminate otherness." Music is both given to and constituted by the listener as well as the composer. And "the irreducibly mimetic moment in music means it can never be wholly a construction of the dominating subject."[128] Subject and object, thought and reality, totality and particularity, are retained in music such as that of Schoenberg through the riddles, traces, fragments, tonal constellations, and the experimental tensive-coherence of form.[129]

The same is true, we will claim below, in the theology of Bonhoeffer's <u>Act and Being</u> as in Adorno's <u>Negative Dialectics</u>. They were two of those creative individuals in modern society about whom sociologist Leopold von Wiese wrote, who "with a certain melancholy, ... sense themselves to be fragments, which can never achieve a satisfying unity."[130] And the greatness and the grave complexity of their early works lies in the fact that these writings so accurately reflected the fragmented reality in which their thought had to occur. The writings of both are, as Gillian Rose has said of Adorno, "eminently quotable but egregiously misconstruable."[131] The challenge of the present study has been to re-construe their work, turning the eminently quotable back into the riddle, the misconstruable back into the fragment and trace which can still be placed into productive, if not final, trial combinations and constellations.

2. Bonhoeffer: Theology and Style

Such a reading of the contribution of Adorno suggests that we might interpret Bonhoeffer, no less than Adorno, to have proposed not so much a **method** or **system** for theology, but a **style**, which, in the words of his letter to Bethge in 1944, could "move out again into the open air of intellectual discussion with the world, and risk saying controversial things."[132] Bonhoeffer the pastor and Bonhoeffer the prisoner never ceased being

Bonhoeffer the thinker and theologian. Hanfried Mueller was prophetic, we would argue, when two decades ago he wrote that

> if we do not wish to continue Bonhoeffer's struggle, then we will not be able to follow his thinking, or take up his theology and carry it forward. Otherwise we would slide into a Bonhoeffer orthodoxy, an ultimately sterile imitation which tries in vain, by reconstructing and systematizing, to make a dead man speak. Any heritage treated in such a fashion cannot but remain mute.
>
> I believe that the right way to follow Bonhoeffer is to take up his development, his path, his intention and the tendency of his work: to follow him rather than stifle his vigor and vitality with a system. I think that understanding of the **whole** Bonhoeffer will come about not by systematizing everything he thought as though it were all on the same level, and thus relativizing it, but rather by taking up the **movement** of his thought in its entirety as the thing which can lead us further.[133]

The enduring contribution of Bonhoeffer may itself, then, be that **style** of the movement of his thought, rather than merely those things **about which** he wrote--which ironically have all too often fostered the very 'sterile imitation' which would stifle him, not allow him to provide new life for contemporary theology. In conclusion, therefore, let us turn briefly to the question of the style of a theology 'in' not merely 'on' the legacy of Bonhoeffer.

a. Essays and Fragments

With the exception of his two dissertations, Bonhoeffer wrote only one other book-length manuscript, Nachfolge [The Cost of Discipleship], in 1937. The rest of his writings were in the form of letters, sermons, essays, lecture notes and speeches, such as those collected in the Gesammelte Schriften; short, though densely packed, lectures published at the request of students, such as Schoepfung und Fall [Creation and Fall], lectures published posthumously, reconstructed from student notes, such as Bethge's reconstrual of the Christologie lectures [Christ the Center]; and brief, occasional pieces, such as the Gemeinsames Leben [Life Together], written for the

Finkenwalde seminarians. Even those works for which he is best known are but edited fragments: the Ethik [Ethics] is a reconstruction of several discontinuities, unfinished drafts for a book; and Widerstand und Ergebung [Letters and Papers from Prison] is Bethge's edited release of a significant portion, but not all, of the letters Bonhoeffer wrote from prison in the last years of his life.

Altogether his literary legacy is a rich but fragmentary array, of which it is difficult to make a coherent, much less a complete, whole. Yet on the whole, Bonhoeffer scholarship has paid very little notice to the effect this occasional, piecemeal output had on Bonhoeffer's style of thinking theologically, and the connection between this style and the question of his methodology.[134] Thus, as Andre Dumas wrote, "our task in working with Bonhoeffer's fragments is not to use them to draw faulty conclusions from a few ideas, but to incorporate them into systematic research of our own...."[135] Thus the first unfulfilled requirement for a theology in the style of Bonhoeffer is that we make of his fragments more than a pastiche of "eminently quotable but egregiously misconstruable" edifications.[136]

b. Anti-systematic Theology

Thus although Bonhoeffer's theological style precludes **systematic** explication, it is not to be taken as a-systematic--as if only the organizing principle were lacking. Rather, Bonhoeffer's theology is 'systemic', or better, **anti**-systematic. It is best read in the spirit of Nietzsche, who wrote: "I mistrust all systematizers and I avoid them. The will to a system is a lack of integrity."[137]

Theology in the style of Bonhoeffer refuses, as Adorno's philosophy refused to seek foundational principles, to become prima theologia. Rather a tensive constellation of theological loci--christology in Christ the Center, creation in Creation and Fall, sin in Act and Being, and the community of the Church in Sanctorum Communio--provide a nexus of concerns within the coherence of which theology can be said to occur. Theology 'is' neither **one** of the loci, nor the **totality** of them. Theology is the dynamic interaction of their particular themes, each a monad reflecting the others, without which the individual cannot become intelligible. A coherent, yet anti-systematic dogmatics is the second unfulfilled requirement of a theology in the style of Bonhoeffer.

c. Polyphony Out of Silence

As Bonhoeffer suggested in the <u>Letters and Papers</u>, theology may best be described as **polyphonic,**[138] a musical style of thinking.[139] As such it can take up into its movement not only the present but also the past."Theology is the memory of the Church,"[140] the dynamic narrative of the event of revelation.[141] Narratives composed as living, in-complete, thus anti-, texts are the third unfulfilled requirement of a theology in the style of Bonhoeffer.

Such a theology claims that its privileged moment of access is ever beyond direct expression, and that its expressions are themselves indirect, mediated, mystery. Thus it is little wonder that such theology was so quickly identified with the proclamation of the death of God;[142] for it would affirm God, <u>etsi deus non daretur</u>.[143] As Bonhoeffer wrote in 1936 to his friend Ruediger Schleicher,

> if it is I who determines where God is to be I will always find there a God who somehow resembles me, who pleases me, who is akin to my being. But if it is God who determines where he wants to be it will most likely be in a place which is not akin immediately to my being, which does not please me. That place, however, is the cross of Christ.[144]

A dwelling with the silence of the 'between', the patience not to force 'dialogue', is that out of which alone can emerge any theology in the style of Bonhoeffer.

d. Revelation and Non-Identity: Towards a New Theology of Otherness?

Bonhoeffer's conversation with the transcendental tradition's **dialectic of otherness** was for the sake of a changed conceptuality for the **otherness of theology.** Revelation retained a certain precedence over dialectics for Bonhoeffer. Yet the transcendental legacy of dialectics provided Bonhoeffer with a new way to conceive of the 'critical', even subversive, nature of receptivity-to-the-Other as responsibility-to-the-other. Theology in the style of Bonhoeffer, above all, would be a theology of the non-identity of God hidden-revealed, of Creator-creature, of sin-grace, of community-individual. It is memory and hope, thought and faith; "the past is 'suspended' in the future, reflexion in intentionality."[145] Theology would think the unthinkable, fathom the unfathomable:

> the new [humanity] of the future, who no longer looks back on [itself] but only away from [itself] to the revelation of God, to Christ; the [humanity] who is born out of the narrowness of the world into the breadth of heaven, who becomes what [it] was or, it may be, never was: a creature of God--a child.[146]

Theology in the style of Bonhoeffer must come to terms with the fact that "thought, even theological thought, will always be 'systematic' by nature and can therefore never comprehend the living person of Christ...."[147] And it must be capable of affirming as well that "action comes not from thought, but from a readiness for responsibility."[148] And yet theology's most profound knowledge may most properly come from the knowledge of its own readiness for responsibility, the knowledge that "yet there is obedient and there is disobedient thinking."[149] Theology in the style of Bonhoeffer, played out of the silence of theology's present improbability, can be only the dialectics of obedience and responsibility to the Other.

NOTES

[1]Gillian Rose, The Melancholy Science, p. 151.

[2]Theodor Adorno, Prisms, p. 31.

[3]Rose, The Melancholy Science, p. 18.

[4]G. W. F. Hegel, The Philosophy of Right and Law, in The Philosophy of Hegel, ed. Carl Friedrich (N.Y., 1954), p. 226.

[5]Juergen Habermas, "The Entwinement of Myth and Enlightenment," New German Critique 26 (Spring-Summer 1982), p. 22.

[6]Jay, Adorno, p. 61.

[7]See Rose, The Melancholy Science, p. 48: "To say that consciousness is 'completely reified' is to say that it is capable only of knowing the appearance of society, of describing institutions and behaviour as if their current mode of functioning were an inherent and invariant characteristic or property, as if they, as objects, 'fulfill their concepts'. Therefore, to say that consciousness of society is completely reified implies that no critical consciousness or theory is possible."

[8]Adorno, Negative Dialectics, p. 52.

[9]Adorno, Prisms, p. 29.

[10]See Jay, Adorno, p. 117.

[11]Adorno, Prisms, p. 33.

[12]Adorno, "The Actuality of Philosophy," p. 132.

[13]Ibid., p. 132: "I will not decide whether a particular conception of man and being lies at the base of my theory, but I do deny the necessity of resorting to this conception. It is an idealist demand, that of an absolute beginning, as only pure thought by itself can accomplish."

[14]Ibid., p. 132.

[15]Adorno, Prisms, p. 33.

[16]Held, Introduction to Critical Theory, p. 204.

[17] Adorno, Prisms, p. 33.

[18] Ibid., pp. 32-33.

[19] See Buck-Morss, The Origin of Negative Dialectics, pp. 82-95, "The Logic of Disintegration: The Role of the Subject," and pp. 24-42, "Marx Minus the Proletariat: Theory as Praxis;" Dallmayr, The Twilight of Subjectivity, pp. 270-293; Jay, The Dialectical Imagination, pp. 41-71 on Horkheimer and Adorno; Jacoby, Social Amnesia, pp. 19-45, "Revisionism: The Repression of a Theory."

[20] See Jay, Adorno, 19-20, 107; Jay, Dialectical Imagination, 41-85; Tracy, The Analogical Imagination. Christian Theology and the Culture of Pluralism (New York: Crossroad, 1981), pp. 356, 368, n. 54; Buck-Morss, pp. 5-6, 48-49; Rudolf Siebert, "Adorno's Critical Theory of Religion: Toward a Negative Theology," AAR. Philosophy of Religion and Theology. Proceedings, 1976, 115-117; Douglas C. Bowman, "Bonhoeffer and the Possibility of Judaizing Christianity," in A Bonhoeffer Legacy, pp. 76-86.

[21] Horkheimer and Adorno, Dialectic of Enlightenment, p. 172; pp. 168-208, "Elements of Anti-Semitism: Limits of Enlightenment." Also see Richard L. Rubenstein, The Cunning of History. The Holocaust and the American Future (New York: Harper and Row, 1975); Hillel Levine, "On the Debanalization of Evil," in Sociology and Human Destiny. Essays on Sociology, Religion and Society, ed. Gregory Baum (New York: Crossroad, 1980), pp. 1-26; Martin Jay, "The Jews and the Frankfurt School: Critical Theory's Analysis of Anti-Semitism," New German Critique 19 (Winter 1980).

[22] Adorno, Negative Dialectics, p. 361.

[23] Ibid., p. 362.

[24] Cf. Dietrich Bonhoeffer, Letters and Papers from Prison, The Enlarged Edition, ed. Eberhard Bethge (New York: Macmillan, 1978), letter of 21.11.43, p. 135.

[25] Adorno, Negative Dialectics, p. 361.

[26] Horkheimer and Adorno, Dialectic of Enlightenment, p. 23; see Lamb, "The Challenge of Critical Theory," in Sociology and Human Destiny, p. 190: "The nonidentity of God and the world was emphasized by the Jewish negative theology: there can be no images of God

and his name cannot be uttered. Christianity emphasized how the transcendent God was immanent in the world through Christ. But it too preserved negative theology: in Christ God was identified with the powerless and the poor, with those nonidentified with 'the world' and called to a mysterious Kingdom of God."

27See Buck-Morss, The Origin of Negative Dialectics, p. 141.

28See Richard Wolin, Walter Benjamin: An Aesthetic of Redemption (New York: Columbia University Press, 1982), especially Chapter Six, "The Adorno-Benjamin Dispute," pp. 163ff.; Susan Buck-Morss, The Origin of Negative Dialectics, pp. 136-184; Eugene Lunn, Marxism and Modernism: An Historical Study of Lukacs, Brecht, Benjamin and Adorno (Berkeley: University of California Press, 1982); Jay, Marxism and Totality, pp. 246ff.

29Buck-Morss, The Origin of Negative Dialectics, p. 6.

30Ibid., p. 144.

31Theodor Adorno, Kierkegaard Konstruktion des Aesthetischen (Tuebingen: J.C.B. Moehr, 1933).

32E.g., see Theodor Adorno, Aesthetic Theory, pp. 366-367: "Art and the primacy of the object."

33Theodor Adorno, "Die Idee der Naturgeschichte," in Gesammelte Schriften, I (Frankfurt am Main: Suhrkamp Verlag, 1973); Dialectic of Enlightenment; also see Russell Jacoby, "Towards a Critique of Automatic Marxism: The Politics of Philosophy from Lukacs to the Frankfurt School," Telos 10 (1971):119-146; Held, Introduction to Critical Theory, pp. 148-174; Buck-Morss, The Origin of Negative Dialectics, pp. 168ff. See Walter Benjamin, "Theses on the Philosophy of History," in Illuminations, trans. Harry Zohn (N.Y.: Shocken Books, 1978), pp. 253-264. For an excellent summary of the rootedness of the transcendental tradition's problem of history in the work of Kant himself, see Jay, Marxism and Totality, pp. 45-48 on Kant's Critique of Judgment, "What is Enlightenment?," and "Idea for a Universal History from a Cosmopolitan Point of View."

34See Max Horkheimer, Die Sehnsucht nach dem ganz Anderen (Hamburg: Furche-Verlag, 1970). And little, too, is known of the effect of works such as Franz Rosenzweig's The Star of Redemption, which Adorno had read, and which itself spoke out strongly against idealism's concept of totality; e.g. see Star of Redemption, p. 13: "Reason is entitled to a home in the world, but the world is just that: a home; it is not totality."

35See Buck-Morss, The Origin of Negative Dialectics, p. 5: "Among the books by writers who, like Bloch, reintroduced religious elements into philosophy in its present crisis, Franz Rosenzweig's Der Stern der Erloesung (The Star of Redemption), published in 1920, was significant, not because it influenced Adorno directly (although he was surely acquainted with both the book and the man), but because it returned to specifically Jewish religious thought in an attempt to redeem philosophy from its current atrophy. ... In place of Hegel's totalistic view, Rosenzweig insisted that reality was fragmentary, composed of a 'plenitude' of individual, distinct phenomena: 'Whence they are coming or whither going has not been inscribed in their foreheads: They simply exist. But in existing they are individual, each one against all other, "particular," "not-otherwise".' (quoting Star, p. 238.)"

36See Dallmayr, "Phenomenology and Critical Theory: Adorno," pp. 367-405.

37This study has been indebted in particular to Buck-Morss, The Origin of Negative Dialectics, pp. 24-42, "Marx Minus the Proletariat: Theory as Praxis;" Bubner, Modern German Philosophy, pp. 166-169 on "The Impact of Lukacs," and 169-173 on "Neo-Marxists"; and Russell Jacoby, "Marxism and the Critical School," Theory and Society, I (1974), pp. 231-238 and Dialectic of Defeat: Contours of Western Marxism (Cambridge: Cambridge University Press, 1981), who places Adorno squarely within the traditon of critical, rather than scientific, Marxism.

38Bonhoeffer, "The Theology of Crisis," p. 124.

39Bonhoeffer, Sanctorum Communio, p. 104; on Bonhoeffer's stringent rejection of the concept of 'possibility', see his six points in defense of the thesis that "the concept of possibility has no place in theology and therefore in theological anthropology," in "Man in Contemporary Philosophy and Theology," pp. 59-61. This theme is still with Bonhoeffer even in his letters to Bethge from prison; see Bonhoeffer, Letters and Papers from Prison, letter of 30.4.44, p. 282: "The transcendence of epistemological theory has nothing to do with the

transcendence of God. God is beyond in the midst of
our lives."

40Bonhoeffer, Act and Being, pp. 115-116.

41Ibid., p. 68.

42Ibid., p. 113.

43Ibid., p. 89.

44Ibid., p. 38, which continues: "But while the process of genuine transcendental thought has perpetual
reference to transcendence and is therefore (in principle)
open and inconclusive, the philosophizing of idealism
already implies the system--God himself is within it. In
this way idealist thought is exposed as an illusion of
movement within a self-contained repose." Thus as Bonhoeffer later said in Act and Being, p. 84: "All Barth's
theological propositions are rooted in the necessity of
saying **not-God** when I speak of God (because I speak of
him), and **not-I** when I speak of the believing I; thus due
regard is paid to the idea that genuinely theological
concepts do not fit into an undialectical system--if it
were otherwise, concepts of an act-character would have
petrified, within the system, into fixed ontological ab-
stractions, and the concept of contingency would be
excluded: the 'coming' changed to the 'existing' God.
Revelation would have sunk to rest in the theological
system. This is countered by the critical reservation."
Also see Act and Being, pp. 84-85, n.4.

45Carl Michalson, "Karl Heim," in A Handbook of
Christian Theologians, ed. Dean G. Peerman and Martin
E. Marty (New York: World Publishing Co., 1965), p. 283.

46Bonhoeffer, "An Assessment of Karl Heim," in No
Rusty Swords (London: Collins, 1965), pp. 347-359.

47Ibid., pp. 348-349.

48Bonhoeffer, Act and Being, p. 72; emphasis added.

49Ibid., p. 15; emphases added.

50Ibid., p. 70; emphases added.

51Ibid., p. 94.

52Ibid., p. 69. On Bonhoeffer's concept of revelation, see Dumas, Dietrich Bonhoeffer: Theologian of

Reality, pp. 6-15; Ott, Reality and Faith, pp. 226-238; Geffrey B. Kelly, "Bonhoeffer's Theology of History and Revelation," in A Bonhoeffer Legacy, pp. 89-130, and "Revelation in Christ. A Study of Bonhoeffer's Theology of Revelation," Ephemerides Theologicae Louvanienses 50/1 (May 1974):39-74; James Patrick Kelley. Revelation and the Secular in the Theology of Dietrich Bonhoeffer. Ph.D. dissertation, unpublished; Yale University, 1980; Hopper, A Dissent on Bonhoeffer, pp. 83-84; Day, Dietrich Bonhoeffer on Christian Community and Common Sense, pp. 42-46. Thus, it should come as no surprise that Bonhoeffer's most damning criticism of Karl Heim was not that he employed a critical-transcendental approach, but that it was not critical **enough**. See Bonhoeffer, "An Assessment of Karl Heim," pp. 357-358: "Because an uncritical ontology underlies the whole of Heim's sketch, an ontology which provides the basis for speaking about man and his relationship to God, what is said about man in revelation must come to grief. That there is no general determination of being for man which would not alone be defined by the definition of being a sinner or being under grace, and that God 'is' as the Creator, the Holy One and the merciful one, that a true ontology would have to begin here, can only seen from the point of revelation."

53Bonhoeffer, Act and Being, p. 75.

54Bonhoeffer, Akt und Sein, p. 36; trans. mine.

55Bonhoeffer, Act and Being, p. 174.

56Bonhoeffer, "Man in Contemporary Philosophy and Theology," p. 57.

57Ibid., pp. 59-60.

58Ibid., p. 61.

59Ibid.

60Gabriel Marcel, The Mystery of Being, I, trans. G. S. Fraser (South Bend, Ind.: Gateway Editions, 1950), pp. 51-52.

61Marcel, The Mystery of Being, I, p. 39.

62Ricoeur, Husserl, p. 232.

63Marcel, The Mystery of Being, II, trans. Rene

Hague (South Bend, Ind.: Regnery/Gateway Inc., 1951), p. viii.

[64]See Ronald Gregor Smith, "This-Worldly Transcendence," in The Whole Man. Studies in Christian Anthropology (Philadelphia: Westminster Press, 1969), pp. 97-111.

[65](Munich: Chr. Kaiser Verlag, 1959), "The Lordship of Christ and Human Society," trans. Reginald H. Fuller and Ilse Fuller, in Juergen Moltmann and Juergen Weissbach, Two Studies in the Theology of Bonhoeffer (New York: Charles Scribner's Sons, 1967), pp. 21-93.

[66]See Green, The Sociality of Christ and Humanity, pp. 105-144 on Act and Being and pp. 1-51 on other interpretations of Bonhoeffer; cf. "Appendix D. Notes on Akt und Sein," pp. 552-566 of the original unpublished dissertation by the same title, Th.D. dissertation, Union Theological Seminary, 1971.

[67]Ernst Feil, Die Theologie Dietrich Bonhoeffers. Hermeneutik. Christologie. Weltverstaendnis (Munich: Chr. Kaiser, 1971). An excellent translation of Feil's book was published too late to be used in the research for the present study. See The Theology of Dietrich Bonhoeffer. Translated by H. Martin Rumscheidt. Philadelphia: Fortress Press, 1984.

[68]See Dumas, Dietrich Bonhoeffer. Theologian of Reality, pp. 97-117 on Act and Being, and pp. 236-280 on other interpretations of Bonhoeffer in general.

[69]See, for example, Tiemo Rainer Peters, Die Praesenz des Politischen in der Theologie Dietrich Bonhoeffers, who virtually ignores Act and Being.

[70]For example Geffrey B. Kelly, Liberating Faith. Bonhoeffer's Message for Today (Minneapolis: Augsburg Publishing House, 1984); John W. de Gruchy, Bonhoeffer and South Africa. Theology in Dialogue; Thomas I. Day, Dietrich Bonhoeffer on Christian Community and Common Sense. In many, if not most, cases this is due to the continued dominance of interest in Bonhoeffer's biography, rather than his theology. The benchmark for almost all biographical information on Bonhoeffer remains Eberhard Bethge, Dietrich Bonhoeffer. Theologe. Christ. Zeitgenosse [Dietrich Bonhoeffer. Man of Vision. Man of Courage].

[71]Day, Dietrich Bonhoeffer on Christian Community and Common Sense, pp. xi, xii.

[72]Eberhard Bethge, "The Challenge of Dietrich Bonhoeffer's Life and Theology," in World Come of Age, p. 25.

[73]See Karl Rahner, Theological Investigations, Vol. VI: Concerning Vatican Council II (New York: Seabury Press, 1974), pp. 71-81 on "Philosophy and Theology," and Theological Investigations, Vol. IX: Writings of 1965-1967, 1 (New York: Seabury Press, 1973), pp. 46-63 on "Philosophy and Philosophising in Theology," and Sacramentum Mundi, Vol. V (New York: Herder and Herder, 1970), pp. 20-24 on "Philosophy and Theology."

[74]Matthew Lamb, "The Challenge to Critical Theory," in Solidarity With Victims. Toward a Theology of Social Transformation (New York: Crossroad, 1982), p. 45. See Clifford Green, "Interpreting Bonhoeffer: Reality or Phraseology?" Journal of Religion 55 (1975):270-275.

[75]On recent interpretations of Adorno in general, see Martin Jay, "Adorno in America," New German Critique 31 (Winter 1984): 157-182.

[76]Paul Piccone, "Review of Against Epistemology," Telos 56 (Summer 1983), p. 229; also see Buck-Morss, The Origin of Negative Dialectics, p. 189: "Hence, in the name of revolution, thought could never acknowledge a revolutionary situation; in the name of utopia, it could never work for utopia's realization."

[77]Ben Agger, "On Happiness and the Damaged Life," in On Critical Theory, ed. John O'Neill (New York: Seabury Press, 1976), pp. 12-33, n.b. p. 15.

[78]Willi Oelmueller, "The Limitations of Social Theories," in Religion and Political Society, ed. Juergen Moltmann (New York: Harper and Row, 1974), p. 139.

[79]Adorno, "The Actuality of Philosophy," p. 130.

[80]Adorno, Negative Dialectics, p. 154.

[81]Buck-Morss, The Origin of Negative Dialectics, p. 190.

[82]Rose, The Melancholy Science, p. 148.

83Jay, <u>Marxism and Totality</u>, p. 272, referring to Adorno, <u>Minima Moralis</u>, p. 80; also see Albrecht Wellmer, "Communications and Emancipation: Reflections on the Linguistic Turn in Critical Theory," in <u>On Critical Theory</u>, pp. 231-263. The best introduction to the issues involved in the relation between Adorno and Habermas is Axel Honneth, "Adorno and Habermas," <u>Telos</u> 39 (Spring 1979): 45-61.

84Jay, <u>Marxism and Totality</u>, p. 274.

85Jean Cohen, "Why More Political Theory?," <u>Telos</u> 40 (Summer 1979): 70-94 and Seyla Benhabib, "Modernity and the Aporias of Critical Theory," <u>Telos</u> 49 (Fall 1981): 39-59.

86See Joel Whitebook, "Saving the Subject: Modernity and the Problem of the Autonomous Individual," <u>Telos</u> 50 (Winter 1981-1982) and Rose, <u>The Melancholy Science</u>, pp. 146f., and <u>Hegel Contra Sociology</u> (London: Athlone, 1981), pp. 33f., who argues that Hegel is finally superior to both Habermas and Adorno, since the latter reverted to an insufficient neo-Kantianism. Also see Dallmayr, <u>Twilight of Subjectivity</u>, pp. 179-223.

87See Paul Piccone, "Review of Theodor W Adorno, <u>Against Epistemology</u>," pp. 229-235, and "Beyond Identity Theory," in O'Neill, <u>On Critical Theory</u>, pp. 129-144; and Fred R. Dallmayr, "Phenomenology and Critical Theory: Adorno," pp. 379ff., and <u>Twilight of Subjectivity</u>, pp. 42-56.

88Dallmayr, "Phenomenology and Critical Theory: Adorno," pp. 385ff., and <u>Twilight of Subjectivity</u>, pp. 56-71; and Hermann Moerchen, <u>Adorno und Heidegger--Untersuchung einer philosophischen Kommunikationsverweige</u> (Stuttgart: Klett-Cotta, 1981).

89Quoted in Rose, <u>Melancholy Science</u>, p. 14.

90Benjamin Snow (Susan Buck-Morss), "Introduction to Adorno's 'The Actuality of Philosophy'," p. 114.

91Adorno, "The Actuality of Philosophy," p. 132. See Jay, <u>Adorno</u>, 23: "To reveal as best we can the unique phenomenon that was Adorno, we must therefore conceptualize him in a manner which will be as true to the unresolved tensions in his thought as possible, rather than seek to find some putative coherence underlying them." Also see Jay, "Adorno in America," p. 161: "...What made Adorno so remarkable a figure was the fact that the negative dialectics he so steadfastly defended, with its valorization of non-identity and heterogeneity, was concretely exemplified in his own intellectual composition, which never produced any harmoniously totalized worldview."

[92]On the influence of Benjamin on Adorno's method, see Held's summary in Introduction to Critical Theory, pp. 206ff., and Buck-Morss, "The Dialectic of T. W. Adorno," Telos, No. 14 (Winter 1972). The themes of (1) a critique of identity theory, (2) the grasp of the universal through the particular, (3) truth as unintentional [intentionslose], or subjectively unintended, and (4) constellations are each seen in Benjamin's Origin of German Tragic Drama, trans. John Osborne (New Left Books, 1977). On the influence of Nietzsche on Adorno's style, see Held, Introduction to Critical Theory, pp. 208ff. and Rose, The Melancholy Science, Ch. 2, n.b. the themes of the critique of identity theory and rejection of idealism as implying "the inferiority of the 'not-I'." Also see Richard Wolin, Walter Benjamin: An Aesthetic of Redemption, pp. 84-90 on the essay, pp. 90-106 on constellation, and pp. 162-212 on the Adorno-Benjamin Dispute.

[93]Adorno, "The Actuality of Philosophy," p. 129.

[94]Ibid., p. 127.

[95]Ibid., p. 128.

[96]Ibid.

[97]Ibid., p. 126.

[98]Ibid.

[99]Buck-Morss, The Origin of Negative Dialectics, p. 80.

[100]Ibid.

[101]Adorno, "The Actuality of Philosophy," p. 128.

[102]Ibid., p. 127.

[103]Jay, Marxism and Totality, p. 256.

[104]Adorno, "The Actuality of Philosophy," p. 127.

[105]"Der Essay als Form," in Noten zur Literatur, Vol. 1 (Frankfurt, 1958), p. 25.

106 Jay, Marxism and Totality, p. 259.

107 Buck-Morss, The Origin of Negative Dialectics, pp. 80-81; see Adorno, Negative Dialectics, p. 40.

108 Adorno, "The Actuality of Philosophy," p. 133.

109 Jay, Adorno, p. 15.

110 Held, Introduction to Critical Theory, p. 211.

111 Jay, Marxism and Totality, p. 265.

112 Held, Introduction to Critical Theory, p. 211.

113 Adorno, "The Actuality of Philosophy," p. 127.

114 Ibid., p. 131. On the origin of the notion of 'constellations' see Walter Benjamin, The Origin of German Tragic Drama, p. 35.

115 Ibid., p. 131.

116 Adorno, Prisms, p. 164.

117 Jay, Marxism and Totality, p. 261.

118 Ibid., p. 266.

119 Adorno, "The Actuality of Philosophy," p. 129.

120 Adorno, Gesammelte Schriften, VII (Frankfurt: Suhrkamp, 1970), p. 541. On constellation, see Adorno, Negative Dialectics, pp. 162-166. See Buck-Morss, The Origin of Negative Dialectics, pp. 96-110, "The Method in Action: Constructing Constellations." Cf. Jay, Adorno, p. 15, who describes the constellation as "a juxtaposed rather than integrated cluster of changing elements that resists reduction to a common denominator, essential core, or generative first principle. ... The result was not a relativistic chaos of unrelated factors, but a dialectical model of negations that simultaneously constructed and deconstructed patterns of a fluid reality."

121 Adorno, Minima Moralia, p. 87.

122 Adorno, "The Actuality of Philosophy," p. 126.

123 Ibid., p. 127.

[124]See Gillian Rose, The Melancholy Science, pp. 11-26, "The Search for Style."

[125]See Adorno, Aesthetic theory, pp. 293-296, "On the concept of style." See Buck-Morss, The Origin of Negative Dialectics, pp. 122-135, "Theory and Art: In Search of a Model;" and Bubner, Modern German Philosophy, pp. 179-182 on "Adorno's shift to aesthetics."

[126]Adorno, Prisms, pp. 149-150. See Jay, Marxism and Totality, pp. 252ff. As Jay points out, Adorno was attracted to the pre-1925 'free atonality' of Schoenberg's so-called expressionist phase, prior to the serial compositions using the 12-tone row, which Adorno saw as the ultimate triumph of 'system' even in Schoenberg. Cf. Buck-Morss, The Origin of Negative Dialectics, p. 15: "It seems clear that Schoenberg's revolution in music provided the inspiration for Adorno's own efforts in philosophy, the model for his major work on Husserl during the thirties. For just as Schoenberg had overthrown tonality, the decaying form of bourgeois music, so Adorno's Husserl study attempted to overthrow idealism, the decaying form of bourgeois philosophy."

[127]Jay, Marxism and Totality, p. 254.

[128]Jay, Adorno, p. 142.

[129]On the persistence of the symphonic analogy in German academic thought in the late-nineteenth and early twentieth centuries, see Ringer, The Decline of the German Mandarins, pp. 108, 117, and 397: "The symphonic analogy, like the concept of wholeness, certainly did not originate in the 1920's. One might almost say that it was always implied in the German intellectual tradition. But it acquired a new popularity--and the status of a habit--during the crisis of learning. It almost always came into play when a German academic of this period discussed the relationship between an individual and the group to which he belonged."

[130]Quoted in Ringer, The Decline of the German Mandarins, p. 262.

[131]See Rose, The Melancholy Science, pp. 11-26 on "The Search for Style." Such an understanding of Adorno's search for style strongly suggests a comparison with the work of Jacques Derrida, e.g., "Violence and Metaphysics," in Writing and Difference, pp. 79-153, and "On an Apocalyptic Tone Recently Adopted in Philosophy" Semeia 23 (1982):63-97. On the relationship between

Adorno and Derrida, see Terry Eagleton, <u>Walter Benjamin:</u> <u>Or Towards a Revolutionary Criticism</u> (London: Verso, 1981); Michael Ryan, <u>Marxism and Deconstruction: A</u> <u>Critical Articulation</u> (Baltimore: Johns Hopkins University Press, 1982), pp. 73- 81 [Yet Ryan doesn't seem to appreciate the extent to which Adorno does not attack reason <u>per se</u>, but specifically **identity**-thinking!]; Mark Taylor, <u>Erring.</u> A Postmodern A/theology (Chicago: University of Chicago Press, 1984), who nods respectfully towards Adorno on pp. 28, 33, 137, 146; Dallmayr, <u>Twilight of Subjectivity</u>, pp. 107-115, 167-173; Jay, <u>Adorno,</u> p. 5; Peter Puetz, "Nietzsche and Critical Theory," <u>Telos</u> 50 (Winter 1981-82).

132Bonhoeffer, <u>Letters and Papers from Prison,</u> letter of 3.8.44, p. 378.

133Hanfried Mueller, "Concerning the Reception and Interpretation of Dietrich Bonhoeffer," trans. Antony Phillips and Ronald Gregor Smith, in <u>World Come of Age,</u> pp. 183-184.

134See Dumas, <u>Dietrich Bonhoeffer: Theologian of</u> <u>Reality</u>, pp. 163-174, 293-295.

135Ibid., 280, speaking of Reist's <u>The Promise of</u> <u>Bonhoeffer</u> (pp. 116-121). The present study is indebted especially to Heinrich Ott's <u>Reality and Faith.</u> The <u>Theological Legacy of Dietrich Bonhoeffer,</u> which is the only study of Bonhoeffer to make a determined effort at relating style and method in interpreting his work.

136Rose, <u>The Melancholy Science</u>, pp. ix-x.

137Friedrich Nietzsche, "Twilight of the Idols," in <u>The Portable Nietzsche</u>, p. 470.

138Bonhoeffer, <u>Letters and Papers from Prison</u>, pp. 303, 305.

139See Stephen Crites, "The Narrative Quality of Experience" <u>JAAR</u> 39 (Summer 1971), pp. 292-311 on music as a meta-style.

140Bonhoeffer, <u>Act and Being</u>, p. 143.

141On narrative as a non-systematic method for theology, see Julian Hartt, <u>Theological Method and Imagination</u> (New York: Crossroad Books, 1977), pp. 219-254 on "Story as the Art of Historical Truth." See Jay, <u>Adorno</u>, p. 74 on narrative. Cf. Johann Baptist Metz,

Faith in History and Society. Toward a Practical Fundamental Theology, trans. David Smith (New York: Seabury, 1980), pp. 154-168, "A transcendental and idealistic or a narrative and practical Christianity?" and pp. 205-218, "Narrative;" and pp. 70-83, 88-118, and 184-204 on history, memory and apocalyptic.

142See John A. T. Robinson, Honest to God (Philadelphia: Westminster, 1963), which has probably contributed as much as anything to the identification of Bonhoeffer with the radical theologians. See Alasdair Heron, "Theologies Secular, Radical and Political," in A Century of Protestant Theology, pp. 152-168.

143Bonhoeffer, Letters and Papers from Prison, letter of 16.7.44, p. 360.

144Bonhoeffer, Letter of 8.4.36, in Gesammelte Schriften, III, pp. 27-28.

145Bonhoeffer, Act and Being, p. 16.

146Ibid., p. 184.

147Ibid., p. 146.

148Bonhoeffer, Letters and Papers from Prison, p. 298.

149Bonhoeffer, Act and Being, p. 146.

WORKS CONSULTED

Adorno, Gretel and Rolf Tiedemann. "Editorisches Nachwort." In T.W. Adorno, Gesammelte Schriften, Band 7, Aesthetische Theorie. Frankfurt am Main: Suhrkamp Verlag, 1970.

Adorno, T. W. "The Actuality of Philosophy," Telos 31 (Spring 1977): 120-133. ["Die Aktualitaet der Philosophie," Gesammelte Schriften, Band 1. Frankfurt am Main: Suhrkamp Verlag, 1973.]

_____. Aesthetic Theory. Boston, MA: Routledge & Kegan Paul, 1984. [Aesthetisches Theorie. Gesammelte Schriften, VII. Frankfurt: Suhrkamp, 1970.]

_____. Against Epistemology: A Metacritique. Studies in Husserl and Phenomenological Antinomies. Translated by Willis Domingo. Cambridge, MA: The MIT Press, 1983. [Zur Metakritik der Erkenntnistheorie. Studien ueber Husserl und die phaenomenologischen Antinomien. Stuttgart: W. Kohlhammer, 1956.]

_____. Drei Studien zu Hegel. Frankfurt am Main: Suhrkamp Verlag, 1969.

_____. "Der Essay als Form," in Noten zur Literatur, Vol. I. Frankfurt am Main: Suhrkamp Verlag, 1958.

_____. "Husserl and the Problem of Idealism." The Journal of Philosophy 37/1 (January 4, 1940): 5-18.

_____. "Introduction." To The Positivist Dispute in German Sociology, pp. 1-67. Translated by Glyn Adey and David Frisby. London: Heinemann Educational Books, Ltd., 1977.

_____. The Jargon of Authenticity. Translated by Knot Tarnowski and Frederic Will. Evanston: Northwestern University Press, 1973. [Jargon der Eigentlichkeit. Zur deutschen Ideologie. Frankfurt am Main: Suhrkamp Verlag, 1977.]

_____. Kierkegaard: Konstruktion des Aesthetischen. Tuebingen: J. C. B. Mohr Verlag, 1933 [1962, 1966].

_____. "Metacritique of Epistemology." Telos 38 (Winter 1978-1979): 77-103.

_____. Minima Moralia. Reflections from Damaged Life. Translated by E. F. N. Jephcott. London: Verso, 1974. [Minima Moralia. Reflexionen aus dem beschaedigten Leben. Gesammelte Schriften Band 4. Frankfurt am Main: Suhrkamp Verlag, 1980.]

_____.Negative Dialectics. Translated by E. B. Ashton. New York.: The Seabury Press, 1973. [Negative Dialektik, in Gesammelte Schriften, Band 6. Frankfurt am Main: Suhrkamp Verlag, 1973.]

_____.Philosophische Fruehschriften. Gesammelte Schriften, vol. 1. Edited by Rolf Tiedemann. Frankfurt am Main: Suhrkamp, 1973.

_____. Prisms. Translated by Samuel and Shierry Weber. Cambridge, MA: The MIT Press, 1982. [Prismen. In Gesammelte Schriften, Band 10/1. Frankfurt am Main: Suhrkamp Verlag, 1977.]

_____. Stichworte. Kritische Modelle, 2. Frankfurt: Suhrkamp Verlag, 1969.

_____. "Subject and Object." In The Essential Frankfurt School Reader, pp. 497-511. Edited and with introductions by Andrew Arato and Eike Gebhardt. New York: Urizen Books, 1978. ["Zu Subjekt und Objekt." In Stichworte. Kritische Modelle 2. Frankfurt am Main: Suhrkamp, 1969.]

Agger, Ben. "On Happiness and the Damaged Life." In On Critical Theory, pp. 12-33. Edited by John O'Neill. New York: Seabury Press, 1976.

Allison, Henri E. "Things in Themselves, Noumena, and the Transcendental Object." Dialectica, 32/1 (1978): 41-76.

Barth, Karl. Church Dogmatics, II/1. Edited by G. W. Bromiley and T. F. Torrance. Edinburgh: T & T Clark, 1957.

_____. "Evangelical Theology in the 19th Century." In The Humanity of God, pp. 11-33. Richmond, VA: John Knox Press, 1972.

_____. "From a Letter to Superintendent Herrenbrueck." In World Come of Age, pp. 89-92. Edited by Ronald Gregor Smith. Philadelphia: Fortress Press, 1967.

_____. Protestant Theology in the Nineteenth Cen-
tury. Valley Forge: Judson Press, 1976.

_____. The Word of God and the Word of Man.
Translated by Douglas Horton. New York: Harper
and Brothers, 1957.

Baum, Gregory, ed. Sociology and Human Destiny. Essays on Sociology, Religion and Society. Minneapolis: The Winston-Seabury Press, 1980.

Beck, Lewis White. A Commentary on Kant's 'Critique of
Practical Reason'. Chicago: University of Chicago
Press, 1960.

_____. "Neo-Kantianism." In The Encyclopedia of
Philosophy, Vol. 5, pp. 468-473. Edited by Paul
Edwards. New York: Macmillan Publishing Co.,
1967.

Benhabib, Seyla. "Modernity and the Aporias of Critical
Theory." Telos 49 (Fall 1981): 39-59.

Benjamin, Walter. "Theses on the Philosophy of History."
In Illuminations, pp. 253-264. Translated by Harry
Zohn. New York: Schocken Books, 1978.

_____. Origin of German Tragic Drama. Translated
by John Osborne. London: New Left Books, 1977.

Bethge, Eberhard. "The Challenge of Dietrich Bonhoeffer's Life and Theology." In World Come of Age,
pp. 22-88. London: Collins, 1967.

_____. Dietrich Bonhoeffer. Man of Vision. Man
of Courage. Translated by Eric Mosbacher, Peter
and Betty Ross, Frank Clarke, William Glen-Doepel.
New York: Harper and Row, 1977. [Dietrich Bonhoeffer. Theologe. Christ. Zeitgenosse. Muenchen: Chr. Kaiser Verlag, 1967.]

Bettis, Joseph. "Theology and Critical Theory in Marcuse
and Barth." Studies in Religion 7/2 (1978): 193-205.

Bochenski, I. M. Contemporary European Philosophy.
Berkeley: University of California Press, 1956.

Bonhoeffer, Dietrich. Act and Being. Translated by
Bernard Noble. Introduction by Ernst Wolf. New
York: Harper and Brothers, 1961. [Akt und Sein.

Transzendental-philosophie und Ontologie in der systematischen Theologie. 2nd Edition. Munich: Christian Kaiser Verlag, 1956.]

_____. "An Assessment of Karl Heim." In No Rusty Swords, pp. 347-359. London: Collins, 1965.

_____. Christ the Center. Translated by Edwin H. Robertson. San Francisco: Harper and Row, 1978. [Christologie. Gesammelte Schriften, Band III, pp. 166-242. Edited by Eberhard Bethge. Munich: Christian Kaiser Verlag, 1960.]

_____. "Concerning the Christian Idea of God." In Gesammelte Schriften, Band III, pp. 100-109. Edited by Eberhard Bethge. Munich: Christian Kaiser Verlag, 1966.

_____. The Cost of Discipleship. Translated by R. H. Fuller, with some revisions by Irmgaard Booth. New York: Macmillan Publishing Co., Inc., 1977. [Nachfolge. Munich: Christian Kaiser Verlag, 1937.]

_____. Creation and Fall. Temptation. Two Biblical Studies. Translated by John C. Fletcher. New York: Macmillan Publishing Col, Inc., 1976. [Schoepfung und Fall. Munich: Christian Kaiser Verlag, 1937.]

_____. Ethics. Translated by Neville Horton Smith. New York: The Macmillan Company, 1965. [Ethik. Munich: Christian Kaiser Verlag, 1949.]

_____. Gesammelte Schriften. Edited by Eberhard Bethge. Munich: Chr. Kaiser Verlag, v. 1: 1965; v. 2: 1965; v. 3: 1966; v. 4: 1965; v. 5: 1972; v. 6: 1974.

_____. Letters and Papers From Prison. The Enlarged Edition. Translated by Reginal Fuller, Frank Clark, John Bowden, et al. New York: Macmillan Publishing Co., 1978. [Widerstand und ERgebung: Briefe und Aufzeichnungen aus der Haft. Munich: Christian Kaiser Verlag, 1970.]

_____. "Man in Contemporary Philosophy and Theology." In No Rusty Swords, pp. 46-65. Translated by Edwin H. Robertson. London: William Collins Sons & Co., Ltd., 1965; New York: Harper and Row, 1971. ["Die Frage nach dem Menschen in der gegenwaertigen Philosophie und Theologie." In Gesammelte Schriften, Band III, pp. 62-84. Edited by Eberhard Bethge. Munich: Christian Kaiser Verlag, 1966.]

_____. No Rusty Swords. London: William Collins Sons & Co., Ltd, 1965; New York: Harper and Row, 1971.

_____. Sanctorum Communio. A Dogmatic Inquiry into the Sociology of the Church. London: Collins, 1963. [Sanctorum Communio. 4th edition. Munich: Christian Kaiser Verlag, 1969. Also Sanctorum Communio. Edited by Joachim von Soosten. Band I, Dietrich Bonhoeffer Werke (Munich: Christian Kaiser Verlag, 1986).]

_____. "The Theology of Crisis and its Attitude Toward Philosophy and Science." In Gesammelte Schriften, Band III, pp. 110-126. Edited by Eberhard Bethge. Munich: Christian Kaiser Verlag, 1966.

Bottomore, T.B., editor. Karl Marx: Early Writings. New York: McGraw Hill, 1964.

Bowman, Douglas C. "Bonhoeffer and the Possibility of Judaizing Christianity." In A Bonhoeffer Legacy, pp. 76-86. Edited by A. J. Klassen. Grand Rapids, MI: William B. Eerdmans, 1981.

Brazill, William J. The Young Hegelians. New Haven: Yale University Press, 1970.

Brown, James. Kierkegaard, Heidegger, Buber and Barth. A Study of Subjectivity and Objectivity in Existentialist Thought. New York: Collier Books, 1971. [Originally published as Subject and Object in Modern Theology. London: SCM Press, 1955.]

Buber, Martin. Between Man and Man. London: Routledge & Kegan Paul, 1947.

_____. I and Thou. Translated by Walter Kaufman. New York: Charles Scribner's Sons, 1970.

Bubner, Ruediger. Modern German Philosophy. Translated by Eric Matthews. Cambridge: Cambridge University Press, 1981.

Buck-Morss, Susan. "The Dialectic of T. W. Adorno." Telos 14 (Winter 1972): 137-144.

_____. The Origin of Negative Dialectics. New York: The Free Press, 1977.

Burtness, James H. "Reading Bonhoeffer: A Map to the Literature." Word and World. II/3 (Summer, 1982): 277-284.

_____. Shaping the Future. The Ethics of Dietrich Bonhoeffer. Philadelphia: Fortress Press, 1985.

Butler, Clark. G. W. F. Hegel. Boston: Twayne Publishers, 1977.

Butler, E. M. The Saint-Simonian Religion in Germany: A Study of the Young German Movement. Cambridge: Cambridge University Press, 1926.

Cohen, H. Religion der Vernunft aus den Quellen des Judentums. Frankfurt am Main, 1929.

Cohen, Jean. "Why More Political Theory?" Telos 40 (Summer 1979): 70-94.

Connerton, Paul. The Tragedy of Enlightenment. An Essay on the Frankfurt School. Cambridge: Cambridge University Press, 1980.

Copleston, Frederich. A History of Philosophy. Vol. 7, Pt. II. New York: Doubleday, 1965.

Cox, Harvey. "Using and Misusing Bonhoeffer." Christianity and Crisis 24 (1964): 199-201.

Crites, Stephen. "The Narrative Quality of Experience," Journal of the American Academy of Religion 39 (September 1971): 291-311.

Dallmayr, "Phenomenology and Critical Theory: Adorno." Cultural Hermeneutics 3/4 (July 1976): 367-405.

_____. Twilight of Subjectivity. Contributions to a Post-Individualist Theory of Politics. Amherst: University of Massachusetts Press, 1981.

Davis, Charles. Theology and Political Society. Cambridge: Cambridge University Press, 1980.

_____. "Toward a Critical Theology." In AAR. Philosophy of Religion and Theology. Proceedings, pp. 213-229. 1975.

Day, Thomas I. Dietrich Bonhoeffer on Christian Community and Common Sense. Toronto Studies in Theology, Vol. II; Bonhoeffer Series, no. 2. New York: The Edwin Mellen Press, 1982.

de Gruchy, John W. Bonhoeffer and South Africa. Theology in Dialogue. Grand Rapids, MI: Wm B. Eerdmans, 1984.

Derrida, Jacques. Margins of Philosophy. Chicago: University of Chicago Press, 1982.

_____. "The Ends of Man." Philosophy and Phenomenology and Phenomenological Research, Vol. 30 (1969): 31-57.

_____. "On an Apocalyptic Tone Recently Adopted in Philosophy," Semeia 23 (1982): 63-97.

_____. Writing and Difference. Translated by Alan Bass. Chicago: University of Chicago Press, 1978.

Deschner, John. "Bonhoeffer Studies in English." Perkins School of Theology Journal. 22/23 (Spring, 1969): 60- 68.

Descombes, Vincent. Modern French Philosophy. Translated by L. Scott Fox and J. M. Harding. Cambridge: Cambridge University Press, 1980.

Dumas, Andre. Dietrich Bonhoeffer: Theologian of Reality. Translated by Robert McAfee Brown. New York: The Macmillan Company, 1971.

Dupre, Louis. The Philosophical Foundations of Marxism. New York: Harcourt, Brace & World, Inc., 1966.

Eagleton, Terry. Walter Benjamin: Or Towards a Revolutionary Criticism. London: Verso, 1981.

Ebner, Ferdinand. Das Wort Und Die Geistigen Realitaeten. Pneumatologischen Fragmente. Reginsburg, 1921.

Emmet, Dorothy and Alasdair MacIntyre, eds. Sociological Theory and Philosophical Analysis. New York: The Macmillan Company, 1970.

Esthimer, Steve. Max Scheler's Concept of the Person. Ann Arbor: University Microfilms, 1983.

Fabro, Cornelio. "Death-of-God Theology and the End of
Religion (Bonhoeffer)." In God in Exile. Modern
Atheism. A Study of the Internal Dynamic of Mo-
dern Atheism, From Its Roots in the Cartesian
Cogito to the Present Day, pp. 1014-1033. Trans-
lated by Arthur Gibson. Westminster, Md.: Newman
Press, 1968.

Farley, Edward. Ecclesial Man. A Social Phenomenology
of Faith and Reality. Philadelphia: Fortress Press,
1975.

Feil, Ernst. The Theology of Dietrich Bonhoeffer. Translated by H. Martin Rumscheidt. Philadelphia: Fortress Press, 1984. [Die Theologie Dietrich Bonhoeffers. Hermeneutik. Christologie. Weltverstaendnis.
Muenchen, Mainz: Chr. Kaiser Verlag, Matthias-
Gruenewald Verlag, 1971.]

_____. "Standpunkte der Bonhoeffer-Interpretation.
Versuch einer kritischen Zusammenfassung." Theo-
logisches Rundschau 64 (1968): 1-14.

Feyerabend, Paul. "Against Method." In Minnesota Studies in the Philosophy of Science, Vol. 4, pp. 17-130.
Edited by M. Radnor and S. Winokur. Minneapolis:
1970.

Fiorenza, Francis S. "Fundamental Theology and the
Enlightenment." The Journal of Religion. 62/3
(July 1982): 289-298.

Friedman, George. The Political Philosophy of the Frankfurt School. Ithaca: Cornell University Press, 1981.

Frings, Manfred S. Max Scheler. A Concise Introduction
into the World of a Great Thinker. Pittsburg, PA:
Duquesne University Press, 1965.

Gadamer, Hans-Georg. Hegel's Dialectic. Translated by
Christopher Smith. New Haven: Yale University
Press, 1976.

_____. "The Philosophical Foundations of the Twen-
tieth Century." In Philosophical Hermeneutics, pp.
107-129. Berkeley: University of California Press,
1977.

Gardner, E. Clinton. Christocentrism in Christian Social
Ethics. A Depth Study of Eight Modern Protest-

ants. Washington, D. C.: University Press of America, Inc., 1983.

Gay, Peter. The Enlightenment: An Interpretation. New York: Alfred Knopf, 1966.

George, Rolf. "Transcendental Object and Thing In Itself: The Distinction and It's Antecedents." In Akten des 4 Internationalen Kant-Kongresses, pp. 186-195. Edited by Gerhard Funke. Berlin: Walter de Gruyter, 1974.

Geuss, Raymond. The Idea of A Critical Theory. Habermas & the Frankfurt School. Cambridge: Cambridge University Press, 1981.

Gilkey Langdon. "The New Watershed in Theology." Soundings 67/2 (Summer 1981): 118-131.

Gill, Robin. The Social Context of Theology. London and Oxford: Mowbrays, 1975.

Gloege, G. "Person, Personalismus." In Evangelisches Kirchenlexikon, cols. 129ff. Goettingen: Vandenhoeck und Ruprecht, 1959.

Godsey, John D. and Geffrey B. Kelly, editors. Ethical Responsibility: Bonhoeffer's Legacy to the Churches. Toronto Studies in Theology. Vol 6. New York and Toronto: The Edwin Mellen Press, 1981.

_____. "Reading Bonhoeffer in English Translation: Some Difficulties." Union Seminary Quarterly Review. 23/1 (Fall 1967): 79-90.

Gotterbarn, Donald. "Objectivity Without Objects, A Non-Reductionist Interpretation of the Transcendental Object." In Akten des 4. Internationalen Kant- Kongresses, pp. 196-203. Edited by Gerhard Funke. Berlin: Walter de Gruyter, 1974.

Gould, Carol. Marx's Social Ontology. Cambridge, MA: MIT Press, 1980.

Grabau, Richard F. "Kant's Concept of the Thing Itself: An Interpretation." Review of Metaphysics 16 (1962-63): 770-79.

Granel, Gerard. "The Obliteration of the Subject in Contemporary Philosophy." In Humanism and

Christianity, pp. 64-73. Concilium 86. New York: Herder & Herder, 1973.

Green, Clifford J. "Interpreting Bonhoeffer: Reality or Phraseology." Journal of Religion. 55 (April 1975): 270-275.

_____. The Sociality of Christ and Humanity. Dietrich Bonhoeffer's Early Theology. 1927-1933. Missoula, MT: Scholars Press, 1975.

_____. "A Theology of Sociality: Bonhoeffer's Sanctorum Communio." In The Context of Contemporary Theology. Essays in Honor of Paul Lehmann, pp. 65-84. Edited by Alexander J. McKelway and E. David Willis. Atlanta: John Knox Press, 1974.

Grisebach, Eberhard. Gegenwart. Ein kritische Ethik. Halle: M. Niemeyer, 1928.

Habermas, Juergen. "The Entwinement of Myth and Enlightenment." New German Critique 26 (Spring-Summer 1982): 3-12.

Hartt, Julian N. Theological Method and Imagination. New York: Crossroad Book, 1977.

Heer, Friedrich. The Intellectual History of Europe. Translated by Jonathan Steinberg. London: Weidenfeld and Nicolson, 1966.

Hegel, G. W. F. The Christian Religion. Edited and translated by Peter C. Hodgson. Missoula, MT: Scholars Press, 1979.

_____. Hegel's Science of Logic. Translated by A. V. Miller. New York: New Humanities Press, 1969.

_____. "Introduction," to Hegel's Lectures on the History of Philosophy. In On Art, Religion, Philosophy, pp. 207-317. Edited by J. Glenn Gray. New York: Harper Torchbooks, 1970.

_____. The Logic of Hegel. Translated by William Wallace. Oxford: Clarendon Press, 1892.

_____. Phenomenology of Spirit. Translated by A. V. Miller. Oxford: Oxford University Press, 1979.

316

_____. The Philosophy of Right and Law. In The Philosophy of Hegel. Edited by Carl Friedrich. New York, 1954.

_____. Science of Logic. Translated by W. H. Johnston and L. G. Struthers. London: George Allen and Unwin, 1929.

Heidegger, Martin. Being and Time. Translated by John Macquarrie and Edward Robinson. New York: Harper and Row, 1962. [Sein und Zeit. Tuebingen: Max Niemeyer Verlag, 1979.]

_____. The End of Philosophy. Translated by Joan Stambaugh. New York: Harper and Row, 1973.

_____. The Essence of Reasons. Translated by Terrence Malick. Evanston: Northwestern University Press, 1969.

_____. Kant and the Problem of Metaphysics. Translated by James S. Churchill. Bloomington: Indiana University Press, 1975.

Heim, Karl. "Reply." In God Transcendent. Foundation for a Christian Metaphysic, pp. 235-239. New York: Charles Scribner's Sons, 1936. [Glaube und Denken: Philosophische Grundlegung einer christlichen Lebensanschauung. Berlin, 1934.]

Held, David. Introduction to Critical Theory. Horkheimer to Habermas. Berkeley: University of California Press, 1980.

Heron, Alasdair. A Century of Protestant Theology. Philadelphia: Westminster, 1980.

Honneth, Axel. "Adorno and Habermas." Telos 39 (Spring 1979): 45-61.

Hopper, David H. A Dissent on Bonhoeffer. Philadelphia: The Westminster Press, 1975.

Horkheimer, Max and Theodor Adorno. Dialectic of Enlightenment. Translated by John Cumming. New York: The Seabury Press, 1972. [Dialektik der Aufklaerung. Philosophische Fragmente. Amsterdam: Querido, 1947; also in Gesammelte Schriften, Band III. Frankfurt am Main: Suhrkamp Verlag, 1981.]

Horkheimer, Max. Anfaenge der buergerlichen Gesch-
ichtsphilosophie. Stuttgart: Hohlhammer, 1930.

_____. Critical Theory. Translated by Matthew J.
O'Connel & others. New York: Herder and Herder,
1972.

_____. Die Sehnsucht nach dem ganz Anderen.
Hamburg: Furche Verlag, 1970.

Husserl, Edmund. Cartesian Meditations. An Introduction to Phenomenology. Translated by Dorian
Cairns. The Hague: Martinus Nijhoff, 1977.

_____. The Crisis of European Sciences and Trans-
cendental Phenomenology. An Introduction to Phenomenological Philosophy. Translated by David Carr.
Evanston: Northwestern University Press, 1970.

Hyppolite, Jean. Genesis and Structure of Hegel's Phenomenology of Spirit. Translated by Samuel Cherniak
and John Heckman. Evanston: Northwestern University Press, 1974.

Jacoby, Russell. Dialectic of Defeat: Contours of Western
Marxism. Cambridge: Cambridge University Press,
1981.

_____. "Marxism and the Critical School." Theory
and Society I (1974): 231-238.

_____. Social Amnesia: A Critique of Conformist
Psychology from Adler to Laing. Boston: Beacon
Press, 1975.

_____. "Towards a Critique of Automatic Marxism:
The Politics of Philosophy from lukacs to the
Frankfurt School." Telos 10 (1971): 119-146.

Janik, Allan and Stephen Toulmin. Wittgenstein's Vienna.
New York: Simon and Schuster, 1973.

Jay, Martin. Adorno. Cambridge: Harvard University
Press, 1984.

_____. "Adorno and Kracauer: Notes on a Troubled
Friendship." Salmagundi 40 (Winter, 1978): 42-66.

_____. "Adorno in America." New German Critique
31 (Winter 1984): 157-182.

_____. "The Concept of Totality in Lukacs and Adorno." _Telos_ 32 (Summer 1977): 117-137.

_____. _The Dialectical Imagination. A History of the Frankfurt School and the Institute for Social Research, 1923-1950._ London: Heinemann, 1973.

_____. "The Frankfurt School's Critique of Mannheim and the Sociology of Knowledge." _Telos_ 20 (Summer 1974): 72-89.

_____. "The Jews and the Frankfurt School: Critical Theory's Analysis of Anti-Semitism." _New German Critique_ 19 (Winter 1980): 137-149.

_____. _Marxism and Totality: The Adventures of a Concept from Lukacs to Habermas._ Berkeley: University of California Press, 1984.

_____. "The Metapolitics of Utopianism." _Dissent_ (July-August, 1970): 342-350.

Johnson, Roger A. and Ernest Wallwork. _Critical Issues in Modern Religion._ Englewood Cliffs, NJ: Prentice-Hall, Inc., 1973.

Kant, Immanuel. _The Critique of Judgment._ Translated by James Creed Meredith. Oxford: Clarendon Press, 1978.

_____. _Critique of Practical Reason._ Translated by Lewis White Beck. Indianapolis: Bobbs-Merrill, 1977.

_____. _Critique of Pure Reason._ Translated by Norman Kemp Smith. New York: St. Martin's Press, 1965.

_____. "Idea for a Universal History from a Cosmopolitan Point of View." In _On History_, pp. 11-26. Translated and edited by Lewis White Beck. Indianapolis: Bobbs-Merrill, 1963.

_____. _Prolegomena to Any Future Metaphysics._ Indianapolis: Bobbs-Merrill, 1977.

_____. _Religion Within the Limits of Reason Alone._ Translated by Theodore M. Greene and Hoyt H. Hudson. New York: Harper and Row, 1960.

_____. "What is Enlightenment?" In On History, pp. 3-10. Translated and edited by Lewis White Beck. Indianapolis: Bobbs-Merrill, 1963.

Kelley, James Patrick. Revelation and the Secular in the Theology of Dietrich Bonhoeffer. Ph.D. dissertation, unpublished. Yale University, 1980.

Kelly, Geffrey B. "Bonhoeffer's Theology of History and Revelation." In A Bonhoeffer Legacy, pp. 89-130. Edited by A. J. Klassen. Grand Rapids, MI: William B. Eerdmans Publishing Co., 1981.

_____. Liberating Faith. Bonhoeffer's Message For Today. Minneapolis: Augsburg Publishing House, 1984.

_____. "Marxist Interpretations of Bonhoeffer." Dialog 10/3 (Summer, 1971): 207-220.

_____. "Revelation in Christ. A Study of Bonhoeffer's Theology of Revelation." Ephemerides Theologicae Louvanienses 50/1 (May, 1974): 39-74.

Kierkegaard, Soren. Concluding Unscientific Postscript. Translated by David F. Swenson and Walter Lowrie. Princeton: Princeton University Press, 1968.

_____. Works of Love. Translated by Howard and Edna Hong. New York: Harper Torchbooks, 1962.

Klassen, A.J., editor. A Bonhoeffer Legacy. Essays in Understanding. Grand Rapids, MI: William B. Eerdmans Publishing Company, 1981.

Kortian, Garbis. Metacritique: The Philosophical Argument of Juergen Habermas. Translated by John Raffan. Cambridge: Cambridge University Press, 1980.

Kuenzli, Arnold. Aufklaerung und Dialektik. Politische Philosophie von Hobbes bis Adorno. Freiburg, 1971.

Kuhns, William. In Pursuit of Dietrich Bonhoeffer. London: Burns and Oates, 1967.

Kuske, Martin. Das Alte Testament als Buch von Christus. Dietrich Bonhoeffers Wertung und Auslegung des Alten Testaments. Goettingen: Vandenhoeck & Ruprecht, 1971.

Lamb, Matthew. "The Challenge of Critical Theory." In Sociology and Human Destiny, pp. 183-213. Edited by Gregory Baum. New York: Seabury Press, 1980.

_____. Solidarity with Victims: Toward a Theology of Social Transformation. New York: Crossroad, 1982.

Langan, Thomas. The Meaning of Heidegger. New York: Columbia University Press, 1961.

Lash, Nicholas. A Matter of Hope. A Theologian's Reflections on the Thought of Karl Marx. Notre Dame, Indiana: University of Notre Dame Press, 1982.

Lauer, Quentin. Essays in Hegelian Dialectic. New York: Fordham University Press, 1977.

_____. Hegel's Concept of God. Albany: State University of New York Press, 1982.

_____. A Reading of Hegel's Phenomenology of Spirit. New York: Fordham University Press, 1976.

Lawrence, P.A. Georg Simmel: Sociologist and European. Sunbury-on-Thames, Middlesex: Thomas Nelson and Sons Ltd., 1976.

Lehmann, Paul. "Bonhoeffer: Real and Counterfeit." Union Seminary Quarterly Review 31/3 (March 1966): 364-369.

Lenhardt, Christian. "The Wanderings of Enlightenment." In On Critical Theory, pp. 34-57. Edited by John O'Neill. New York: Seabury, 1976.

Levinas, Emmanuel. Totality and Infinity: An Essay on Exteriority. Pittsburg: Duquesne University Press, 1969.

Levine, Hillel. "On the Debanalization of Evil." In Sociology and Human Destiny. Essays on Sociology, Religion, and Society, pp. 1-26. Edited by Gregory Baum. New York: Crossroad, 1980.

Lieber, Hans-Joachim. Kulturkritik und Lebensphilosophie. Darmstadt: Wissenschaftliche Buchgesellschaft, 1974.

Lindsay, A. D. <u>Kant</u>. London: Ernest Benn Limited, 1934.

Livingston, James C. <u>Modern Christian thought From the Enlightenment to Vatican II</u>. New York: Macmillan Publishing Co., Inc., 1971.

Loemker, L. E. "Spranger (Franz Ernst) Eduard." In <u>The Encyclopedia of Philosophy</u>, Vol. 8, pp. 1-2. New York: Macmillan, 1967.

Loewith, Karl. <u>From Hegel to Nietzsche</u>. Translated by D. E. Green. Garden City: Anchor Doubleday, 1967.

Lonergan, Bernard. <u>Method in Theology</u>. New York: Seabury Press, 1972.

Lovin, Robin. <u>Christian Faith and Public Choices. The Social Ethics of Barth, Brunner, and Bonhoeffer</u>. Philadelphia: Fortress Press, 1984.

Lowe, Walter. "Christ and Salvation." In <u>Christian Theology: An Introduction to Its Traditions and Tasks</u>, pp. 196-222. Edited by Peter C. Hodgson and Robert H. King. Philadelphia: Fortress Press, 1982.

_____. "The Issue of Presence in Modern Theology." A paper presented before the Southeastern Region of the American Academy of Religion, March 1984.

_____. "The Critique of Philosophy in Bonhoeffer's <u>Act and Being</u>." An unpublished manuscript, 1966.

Lunn, Eugene. <u>Marxism and Modernism. An Historical Study of Lukacs, Brecht, Benjamin and Adorno</u>. Berkeley: University of California Press, 1982.

Macomber, W.B. <u>The Anatomy of Disillusion</u>. Evanston: Northwestern University Press, 1967.

Marcel, Gabriel. <u>The Mystery of Being</u>. Vol. I: Translated by G. S. Fraser. South Bend, IN: Gateway Editions, 1950; Vol. II: Translated by Rene Hague. South Bend, IN: Regnery/Gateway, Inc., 1951.

Marcuse, Herbert. <u>Reason and Revolution. Hegel and the Rise of Social Theory</u>. Boston: Beacon Press, 1960.

Marle, Rene. Bonhoeffer. The Man and His Work.
Translated by Rosemary Sheed. New York: Newman
Press, 1968.

Martin, David, ed. Sociology and Theology. Alliance and
Conflict. Brighton, Sussex: The Harvester Press
Limited, 1980.

Marty, Martin E. The Place of Bonhoeffer: Problems and
Possibilities in His Thought. New York: Association
Press, 1962.

Marx, Karl. "Critique of Hegel's Dialectic." In Karl Marx:
Early Writings, pp. 195-219. Translated and edited
by T. B. Bottomore. New York: McGraw-Hill Book
Company, 1964.

_____. "Theses on Feuerbach." In Karl Marx: Sel-
ected Writings, pp. 156-158. Edited by David Mc-
Lellan. Oxford: Oxford University Press, 1977.

Marx, Werner. Hegel's Phenomenology of Spirit. Translated by Peter Heath. New York: Harper and Row,
1975.

Mayer, Rainer. Christuswirklichkeit. Grundlagen, Entwicklung und Konsequenzen der Theologie Dietrich
Bonhoeffers. Stuttgart: Calwer Verlag, 1969.

Metz, Johann Baptist, Juergen Moltmann, and Willi Oelmueller. Kirche im Prozess der Aufklaerung. As-
pekte einer neuen 'politischen Theologie'. Muench-
en, Mainz: Chr. Kaiser Verlag, Matthias-Gruenewa-
ld-Verlag, 1970.

Metz, Johann Baptist. Faith in History and Society.
Toward a Practical Fundamental Theology. Translated by David Smith. New York: Seabury, 1980.

Michalson, Carl. "Karl Heim." In A Handbook of Christ-
ian Theologians, pp. 273-294. Edited by Dean G.
Peerman and Martin E. Marty. New York: World
Publishing Co., 1965.

_____. Worldly Theology. The Hermeneutical Focus
of an Historical Faith. New York: Charles Scribner's Sons, 1967.

Mitzman, Arthur. Sociology and Estrangement. Three
Sociologists of Imperial Germany. New York: Alfred
A. Knopf, 1973.

323

Moerchen, Hermann. <u>Adorno und Heidegger--Untersuchung einer philosophischen Kommunikationsverweige</u>. Stuttgart: Klett-Cotta, 1981.

Moltmann, Juergen. "The Lordship of Christ and Human Society." In <u>Two Studies in the Theology of Bonhoeffer</u>, pp. 21-94. Translated by Reginald H. Fuller and Ilse Fuller and edited by Juergen Moltmann and Juergen Weissbach. New York: Charles Scribner's Sons, 1967. [<u>Herrschaft Christi und soziale Wirklichkeit nach Dietrich Bonhoeffer</u> (Munich: Christian Kaiser Verlag, 1959.]

_____. <u>Theology of Hope. On the Ground and the Implications of a Christian Eschatology</u>. New York: Harper and Row, 1967.

Moltmann, Juergen, editor. <u>Religion and Political Society</u>. New York: Harper and Row, 1974.

Montefiore, Alan, ed. <u>Philosophy in France Today</u>. Cambridge: Cambridge University Press, 1983.

Mosse, George L. <u>The Crisis of German Ideology: Intellectual Origins of the Third Reich</u>. New York: Universal Library, 1964.

_____. <u>The Culture of Western Europe. The Nineteenth and Twentieth Centuries</u>. Chicago: Rand McNally & Company, 1961.

Mueller, Hanfried. "Concerning the Reception and Interpretation of Dietrich Bonhoeffer." In <u>World Come of Age</u>, pp. 182-214. Edited by Ronald Gregor Smith. Philadelphia: Fortress Press, 1967.

_____. <u>Von der Kirche zur Welt. Ein Beitrag zur der Beziehung des Wortes Gottes auf die Societas in Dietrich Bonhoeffers theologischer Entwicklung</u>. Hamburg-Bergstedt: Herbert Reich Evangelische Verlag, 1961.

McLellan, David, editor. <u>Karl Marx: Selected Writings</u>. Oxford: Oxford University Press, 1977.

Nicholls, William, ed. <u>Conflicting Images of Man</u>. New York: The Seabury Press, 1966.

Nietzsche, Friedrich. <u>Twilight of the Idols</u>. In <u>The Portable Nietzsche</u>, pp. 465-563. Edited and translated by Walter Kaufman. New York: The Viking Press, 1968.

Oelmueller, Willi. "The Limitations of Social Theories." In Religion and Political Society, pp. 127-169. Edited by Juergen Moltmann. New York: Harper and Row, 1974.

Ogilvy, James. Many Dimensional Man. Decentralizing Self, Society, and the Sacred. New York: Oxford University Press, 1977.

Oliver, Harold H. Relatedness. Essays in Metaphysics and Theology. The Hague: Martinus Nijhoff, 1981. [Macon, Ga.: The Mercer University Press, 1984.]

O'Neill, John, ed. On Critical Theory. New York: The Seabury Press, 1976.

Ott, Heinrich. Reality and Faith. The Theological Legacy of Dietrich Bonhoeffer. Translated by Alex A. Morrison. Philadelphia: Fortress Press, 1972. [Wirklichkeit und Glaube. Erster Band: Zum theologischen Erbe Dietrich Bonhoeffers. Zurich: Vandenhoeck & Ruprecht, 1966.]

Peters, Tiemo Rainer. Die Praesenz des Politischen in der Theologie Dietrich Bonhoeffers. Eine historische Untersuchung in systematischer Absicht. Muenchen, Mainz: Chr. Kaiser Verlag, Matthias-Gruenewald- Verlag, 1976.

Pfeifer, Hans. Genf '76. Ein Bonhoeffer-Symposion. Muenchen: Chr. Kaiser Verlag, 1976.

Phillips, John A. Christ for us in the Theology of Dietrich Bonhoeffer. New York: Harper and Row, 1967.

Piccone, Paul. "Beyond Identity Theory." In On Critical Theory, pp. 129-144. Edited by John O'Neill. New York: Seabury, 1976.

_____. "Review of Against Epistemology." Telos 56 (Summer 1983): 229-235.

Pinson, Koppel. Modern Germany. New York: The Macmillan Co., 1954.

_____. Pietism as a Factor in the Rise of German Nationalism. New York: Octagon Books, Inc., 1968.

Puetz, Peter. "Nietzsche and Critical Theory." _Telos_ 50 (Winter 1981-1982): 105-114.

Rahner, Karl. _Hearers of the Word._ New York: Seabury Press, 1969.

_____. _Sacramentum Mundi: An Encyclopedia of Theology._ Vol. V. New York: Herder and Herder, 1970.

_____. "Philosophy and Theology." In _Theological Investigations._ Vol. VI, _Concerning Vatican Council II,_ pp. 71-81. New York: Seabury Press, 1974.

_____. "Philosophizing in Theology." In _Theological Investigations._ Vol. IX, _Writings of 1965-1967,_ pp. 46-63. New York: Seabury Press, 1973.

Reardon, B. M. G. _Religious Thought in the Nineteenth Century, Illustrated from Writers of the Period._ Cambridge: Cambridge University Press, 1966.

Reist, Benjamin A. _The Promise of Bonhoeffer._ Philadelphia and New York: J. B. Lippincott Company, 1969.

Richardson, William J. _Heidegger: Through Phenomenology to Thought._ The Hague: Martinus Nijhoff, 1974.

Ricoeur, Paul. "The Antinomy of Human Reality and the Problem of Philosophical Anthropology." In _Readings in Existential Phenomenology,_ pp. 390-402. Edited by Nathaniel Lawrence and Daniel O'Connor. Englewood Cliffs, N.J.: Prentice Hall, 1967.

_____. _The Conflict of Interpretations: Essays in Hermeneutics._ Edited by Don Ihde. Evanston: Northwestern University Press, 1974.

_____. _Husserl. An Analysis of His Phenomenology._ Evanston: Northwestern University Press, 1967.

_____. "L'Interpretation non religieuse du Christianisme chez Bonhoeffer." _Cahiers du Centre protestant de l'Ouest_ (1966): 3-20.

Ring, Nancy Carolyn. "Doctrine within the Dialectic of Subject and Object: A Critical Study of the Positions of Paul Tillich and Bernard Lonergan." Ph.D. dissertation, Marquette University, 1980.

Ringer, Fritz K.   The Decline of the German Mandarins. The German Academic Community 1890-1933.   Cambridge, MA: Harvard University Press, 1969.

Rintelen, Fritz-Joachim von.   Contemporary German Philosophy and Its Background.   Bonn: H. Bouvier u. Co. Verlag, 1970.

Robinson, John A. T.   Honest to God.   Philadelphia: Westminster, 1963.

Rose, Gillian.   Dialectic of Nihilism.   Post-Structuralism and Law.   N. Y.: Basil Blackwell, 1984.

_____.   Hegel Contra Sociology.   London: Athlone, 1981.

_____.   The Melancholy Science.   An Introduction to the Thought of Theodor W. Adorno.   New York: Columbia University Press, 1978.

_____.   "Review of Negative Dialectics."   American Political Science Review 70 (1976): 598-599.

Rosenzweig, Franz.   The Star of Redemption.   Translated by William W. Hallo.   New York: Holt, Rinehart and Winston, 1970.

Rubenstein, Richard L.   The Cunning of History.   The Holocaust and the American Future.   New York: Harper and Row, 1975.

Rumscheidt, Martin, ed.   Footnotes to a Theology.   The Karl Barth Colloquium of 1972.   Waterloo, Ontario: Wilfrid Laurier University Press, 1974.

Ryan, Michael.   Marxism and Deconstruction: A Critical Articulation.   Baltimore, Maryland: The Johns Hopkins University Press, 1982.

Santmire, H. Paul.   "Ernst Troeltsch: Modern Historical Thought and the Challenges to Individual Religions."   In Critical Issues in Modern Religion, pp. 365-399. Englewood Cliffs, N. J.: Prentice-Hall, Inc., 1973.

Schacht, Richard.   "Husserlian and Heideggerian Phenomenology."   In Hegel and After.   Studies in Continental Philosophy Between Kant and Sartre, pp. 207-227.   Pittsburg: University of Pittsburg Press, 1975.

327

Schaper, Eva. "The Kantian Thing-in-itself as a Philosophical Fiction." Philosophical Quarterly 16 (1966): 233-243.

Scharlemann, Robert. The Being of God. Theology and the Experience of Truth. New York: Seabury Press, 1981.

Scheler, Max. Formalism in Ethics and Non-Formal Ethics of Values. A New Attempt toward the Foundation of an Ethical Personalism. Translated by Manfred S. Frings and Roger L. Funk. Evanston: Northwestern University Press, 1973. [Der Formalismus in der Ethik und die materiale Wertethik. Halle, 1913-1916.

_____. On the Eternal in Man. Translated by Bernard Noble. New York: Harper & Brothers Publishers, 1960. [Vom Ewigen im Menschen. Leipzig: 1921.]

_____. The Nature of Sympathy. Translated by Peter Heath. London: Routledge & Kegan Paul Ltd., 1954. [Zur Phaenomenologie und Theorie der Sympathiegefuehle und vom Liebe und Hass. 1913]

Schrader, George. "The Philosophy of Existence." In The Philosophy of Kant and Our Modern World, pp. 27-61. Edited by Charles W. Hendel. New York: The Liberal Arts Press, 1957.

_____. "The Thing in itself in Kantian Philosophy." In Kant: A Collection of Critical Essays, pp. 172-188. Edited by Robert Paul Wolff. New York: Anchor Books, 1967.

Schroyer, Trent. The Critique of Domination: The Origins and Development of Critical Theory. New York: Braziller, 1974.

Schuetz, Alfred. "Max Scheler's Epistemology and Ethics." Review of Metaphysics 11 (1957): 304-314; 12 (1957): 486-501.

Siebert, Rudolf J. "Adorno's Critical Theory of Religion." AAR. Philosophy of Religion and Theology Proceedings, pp. 115-117. 1976.

Simmel, Georg. Sociology of Religion. Translated by Curt Rosenthal. New York: Arno Press, 1979. [Die Religion.]

_____. The Conflict in Modern Culture and Other Essays. Translated by K. Peter Etzkorn. New York: Teachers College Press, 1968.

Simon, Walter. European Positivism in the Nineteenth Century. Ithaca: Cornell University Press, 1963.

Smith, Norman Kemp. A Commentary to Kant's 'Critique of Pure Reason'. Atlantic Highlands, N. J.: Humanities Press, 1962.

Smith, P. Christopher. "Heidegger, Hegel, and the Problem of das Nichts." International Philosophical Quarterly 8 (1968): 379-405.

_____. "Heidegger's Critique of Absolute Knowledge." New Scholasticism 45 (Winter 1971): 56-86.

Smith, Ronald Gregor, ed. World Come of Age. Philadelphia: Fortress Press, 1967.

Smith, Ronald Gregor. "This-Worldly Transcendence." In The Whole Man. Studies in Christian Anthropology, pp. 97-111. Philadelphia: The Westminster Press, 1969.

Smith, Steven G. The Argument to the Other. Reason Beyond Reason in the Thought of Karl Barth and Emmanuel Levinas. Chico, CA: Scholars Press, 1983.

Snow, Benjamin [Susan Buck-Morss]. "Introduction to Adorno's 'The Actuality of Philosophy'." Telos 31 (Spring 1977): 113-119.

Solomon, Robert C. From Rationalism to Existentialism. The Existentialists and their Nineteenth-Century Backgrounds. Atlantic Highlands, N. J.: Humanities Press, 1972.

Spiegelberg, Herbert. The Phenomenological Movement. A Historical Introduction. The Hague: Martinus Nijhoff, 1976.

Spykman, Nicholas J. The Social Theory of Georg Simmel. New York: Russell & Russell, Inc., 1964.

Stackelberg, Roderick. Idealism Debased. From Voelkisch Ideology to National Socialism. Kent, Ohio: The Kent State University Press, 1981.

329

Stenius, Erik. "On Kant's Distinction between Phenomena and Noumena." In <u>Philosophical Essays Dedicated to Gunnar Aspelin</u>, pp. 230-246. Lund, 1963.

Stern, Fritz. <u>The Failure of Illiberalism</u>. New York: Alfred Knopf, 1972.

_____. <u>The Politics of Cultural Despair. A Study in the Rise of the Germanic Ideology</u>. Berkeley: University of California Press, 1961.

Taminiaux, Jacques. "Finitude and the Absolute: Remarks on Hegel and Heidegger." In <u>Heidegger. The Man and the Thinker</u>, pp. 187-208. Edited by Thomas Sheehan. Chicago: Precedent Publishing, 1981.

Tar, Zoltan. <u>The Frankfurt School. The Critical Theories of Max Horkheimer and Theodor W. Adorno</u>. New York: Wiley, 1977.

Taylor, Mark C. <u>Erring. A Postmodern A/theology</u>. Chicago: The University of Chicago Press, 1984.

Theunissen, Michael. <u>Der Andere: Studien zur Sozialontologie der Gegenwart</u>. Berlin: Walter de Gruyter, 1977. [See <u>The Other</u>.]

_____. "<u>Bubers negative Ontologie des Zwischen</u>." <u>Philosophisches Jahrbuch</u> 71 (1964).

_____. <u>Gesellschaft und Geschichte: Zur Kritik der Kritischen Theorie</u>. Berlin: Walter de Gruyter, 1970.

_____. <u>Hegels Lehre vom absoluten Geist als theologisch-politischer Traktat</u>. Berlin: Walter de Gruyter & Co., 1970.

_____. <u>The Other. Studies in the Social Ontology of Husserl, Heidegger, Sartre, and Buber</u>. Translated by Christopher Macann. Cambridge, MA: the MIT Press, 1984.

_____. <u>Sein und Schein: Die Kritische Funktion der Hegelschen Logik</u>. Frankfurt am Main: Suhrkamp Verlag, 1978.

Thevenaz, Pierre. <u>What is Phenomenology?</u> Translated by James M. Edie, Charles Courtney, and Paul Brockelman. Chicago: Quadrangle Books, 1962.

Tillich, Paul. Mysticism and Guilt-Consciousness in Sch-
    ellings' Philosophical Development. Translated by
    Victor Nuovo. Lewisburg: Bucknell University Press,
    1974.

_____. Systematic Theology. Vol. I: Chicago: Uni-
    versity of Chicago Press, 1951; Vol. III: Chicago:
    University of Chicago Press, 1963.

Toennies, Ferdinand J. Community and Society. Trans-
    lated and edited by Charles P. Loomis. East Lans-
    ing: The Michigan State University Press, 1957.
    [Gemeinschaft und Gesellschaft. Grundbegriffe der
    reinen Soziologie. Berlin: Verlag Karl Curtius,
    1926.]

Tracy, David. Blessed Rage for Order: The New Plural-
    ism in Theology. New York: The Seabury Press,
    1975.

_____. The Analogical Imagination: Christian Theol-
    ogy and the Culture of Pluralism. New York: Cros-
    sroad, 1981.

VanderMarck, William. "Fundamental Theology: A Biblio-
    graphical and Critical Survey." Religious Studies
    Review 8/3 (July 1982): 244-253.

Vidler, Alec R. "Christianity, Liberalism, and Liberality."
    In Essays in Liberality, pp. 9-28. London: SCM
    Press, 1957.

Warren, Scott. The Emergence of Dialectical Theory.
    Philosophy and Political Inquiry. Chicago: Univ. of
    Chicago Press, 1984.

Wedemeyer, Karl Heinz. The Social Philosophy of Diet-
    rich Bonhoeffer. Ph.D. dissertation, Boston Univ-
    ersity Graduate School, 1969.

Weingartner, Rudolph H. Experience and Culture. The
    Philosophy of Georg Simmel. Middletown, Conn-
    ecticut: Wesleyan University Press, 1960.

Welch, Claude. Protestant Thought in the Nineteenth
    Century. New Haven: Yale University Press, 1972.

Wellmer, Albrecht. "Communications and Emancipation:
    Reflections on the Linguistic Turn in Critical Theo-
    ry." In On Critical Theory, pp. 231-263. Edited by
    John O'Neill. New York: Seabury Press, 1976.

331

Whitebook, Joel. "Saving the Subject: Modernity and the Problem of the Autonomous Individual." _Telos_ 50 (Winter 1981-82): 79-102.

Willey, Thomas E. _Back to Kant. The Revival of Kantianism in German Social and Historical Thought, 1860-1914._ Detroit: Wayne State University Press, 1978.

Williams, John R. _Martin Heidegger's Philosophy of Religion._ Waterloo, Ontario: Wilfrid Laurier University Press, 1977.

Winquist, Charles. "The Epistemology of Darkness: Preliminary Reflections." _Journal of the American Academy of Religion_ 49/1 (March 1981): 23-34.

_____. "The Subversion and Transcendence of the Subject." _Journal of the American Academy of Religion_ 48/1 (March 1980): 45-60.

Woelfel, James W. _Bonhoeffer's Theology. Classical and Revolutionary._ Nashville: Abingdon Press, 1970.

Wolff, Kurt H. _The Sociology of Georg Simmel._ New York: The Free Press, 1950.

Wolff, Kurt H., ed. _Georg Simmel, 1858-1918. A Collection of Essays, with Translations and a Bibliography._ Columbus: The Ohio State University Press, 1959.

Wolin, Richard. _Walter Benjamin: An Aesthetic of Redemption._ New York: Columbia University Press, 1982.

Zahrnt, Heinz. _The Question of God. Protestant Theology in the Twentieth Century._ Translated by R.A. Wilson. New York: Harcourt, Brace & World, Inc., 1969.

Zaner, Richard M. _The Way of Phenomenology. Criticism as a Philosophical Discipline._ Indianapolis: Bobbs-Merrill, Inc., 1970.

INDEX